The Dynamics of Big Business

Throughout the twentieth century, big business has been a basic institution. Large corporations have provided a fundamental contribution to the wealth of nations and, at the same time, have had a remarkable impact on the political and social systems within which they have operated. It is difficult to understand the development of the most advanced economies if we do not consider the specific evolution of big business in every national case. On the other hand, it is not possible to explain the shape and behavior of big business without considering its development as part of the history of the country in which they operate. The largest US, German, British and French firms were key actors in favoring their nations' development and, even at the end of the twentieth century, made a very important contribution to their growth. In many countries, a stable core of large corporations developed only relatively lately, or did not develop at all, and under these circumstances, big business was not able to significantly participate in the economic growth of such countries. Scholars who dealt with the economic history of Italy and Spain are generally unanimous in tagging these nations as industrial latecomers, ineffective in promoting big autochthonous private and state-owned firms, dominated by family companies, and characterized by a strong competitive advantage on the part of small and medium-sized enterprises. At the same time, Spanish and Italian business and economic historians have tended to say little about the role and features of big business.

This book fills a significant gap in the work on the development of Southern European capitalism and its large corporations by analyzing the Italian and Spanish cases and comparing them with each other and with what has occurred in the United States and in the largest European nations. Examining both the macro dynamics (national but also supra national) and the micro level, utilizing samples of big corporations and going deeply into some company cases, this volume identifies some important protagonists of the Italian and Spanish economies (such as the state, families and foreign investors) and investigates a wider panorama which includes the political, economic and social relationships of the corporations, providing insights into the form of capitalism that exists in these countries.

Veronica Binda conducts business history research at Bocconi University, Milan, and is a visiting professor at Pompeu Fabra University, Barcelona. She has published articles in *Business History, Business History Review, European Journal of International Management, Revista de Historia Industrial, Información Comercial Española* and *Imprese e Storia*.

Routledge International Studies in Business History

Series editors: Ray Stokes and Matthias Kipping

The Dynamics of Big Business
Structure, Strategy and Impact in Italy and Spain

Veronica Binda

Routledge
Taylor & Francis Group

NEW YORK AND LONDON

First published 2013
by Routledge
711 Third Avenue, New York, NY 10017

Simultaneously published in the UK
by Routledge
2 Park Square, Milton Park, Abingdon, Oxon OX14 4RN

First issued in paperback 2018

*Routledge is an imprint of the Taylor & Francis Group,
an informa business*

Library of Congress Cataloging in Publication Data

Binda, Veronica.
The dynamics of big business : structure, strategy, and impact in Italy
    and Spain / by Veronica Binda.
        p. cm. — (Routledge international studies in business history ; 22)
    Includes bibliographical references and index.
    1. Big business—Italy.   2. Big business—Spain.   3. Corporations—
Italy.   4. Corporations—Spain.   I. Title.
    HD2356.I8B56 2013
    338.6'440945—dc23
    2012042458

ISBN 13: 978-1-138-34016-9 (pbk)
ISBN 13: 978-0-415-89614-6 (hbk)

Typeset in Sabon
by Apex CoVantage, LLC

To my grandmas and grandpas.

Contents

PART IV
Summing Up

List of Figures

List of Tables

Acknowledgments

This book would not have been possible without the support of the many people who have sustained my work both in Italy and Spain throughout the years.

First of all, I wish to thank Franco Amatori, who since the very beginning has enthusiastically supported this research, and provided untiring guidance as part of a rich path of personal and professional learning, of which this book represents only one of the major achievements. His valuable suggestions, his trust and his daily encouragement have been indispensable in allowing me to take my first steps toward completing this work with confidence and to face up to the small and big obstacles that presented themselves during the research.

I am also grateful to Albert Carreras, whose fundamental recommendations and limitless availability were crucial to my research in Spain as well as my professional training during these years. His suggestions and constant encouragement made sure I never tired of broadening my interest in and contact with new perspectives.

The Institute of Economic History at Bocconi University, the environment in which this book was conceived, was essential in providing the opportunities and motivation to bring this research to a successful conclusion. Andrea Colli and Francesca Polese in particular have been instrumental to the realization of my project, not only by directly providing advice but also by organizing useful meetings and debates. The outcomes of this research owe a lot to the vivacity and initiative shown by Andrea and Francesca in creating several opportunities for discussion among doctoral students, and to the comments of the scholars and students who participated enthusiastically. A special thanks in this sense also goes to my "travelling companions" and PhD colleagues, who were always ready to help me with small and big suggestions, in particular to Guido Alfani, Michela Barbot, Francesco Boldizzoni, Andrea Caracausi, Matteo Di Tullio, Alan Mantoan, Claudio Marsilio, Marina Nicoli, Mario Perugini, and Daniele Pozzi.

In conducting this work, I have also been able to rely on the help of colleagues who contributed to this research by reading and annotating the manuscript in part or in its entirety. A very special thanks goes to Matthias Kipping, who was committed to following my progress throughout the research. The long talks with him constantly helped to improve the work and encouraged me to deal in depth with new themes and perspectives. My wholehearted gratitude is moreover for Bernardo Batiz-Lazo, Youssef Cassis, Jordi Catalan, Álvaro Ferreira da Silva, Giovanni Federico, Paloma Fernández, Patrick Fridenson, Walter Friedman, Fernando Guirao, Martin Iversen, Abe de Jong, Nuria Puig, Harm Schröeter, Luciano Segreto, Ray Stokes, Carles Sudrià, Xavier Tafunell, Pierangelo Toninelli, Eugenio Torres, John Wilson and Richard Whittington, who commented on my preliminary work at different stages during workshops and conferences, and gave constructive feedback and suggestions. I am very grateful also to Adoración Álvaro, Héctor García, Francisco Medina and Javier Vicente, who have helped me to understand Spanish history and culture. The contribution of Eline Van de Wiele was fundamental in working at editing my English as well as the generous help provided by the Department of Policy Analysis and Public Management at Bocconi University in funding the language editing of this work.

The biggest debt of gratitude is nevertheless the one that I owe all those who have trusted in me and stood by me throughout these years. I would have achieved little or nothing without the love and the unreserved support of my family, whose presence and unconditional support never failed. A wholehearted thanks finally goes to all my friends in Italy, who were my first supporters, and in Spain, in particular to Marta, Fede and Rafa, who were always present to share joys and sorrows with me, and made my stay in Barcelona a wonderful experience every day.

1 Introduction

1.1 BIG BUSINESS, STATE OF THE ART AND CONTROVERSIES

Throughout the twentieth century, big business has been a basic institution in the Western world. Large corporations have provided a fundamental contribution to the wealth of nations and, at the same time, have had a remarkable impact on the political and social systems within which they have operated. It is difficult to understand how the most advanced economies developed unless we consider the specific evolution of big business in every national case. At the same time, however, it is impossible to explain the shape and behavior of big business without considering its development as part of the history of the country in which it operates.

The largest US, German, British and French firms were key actors in furthering their nations' development and, even at the end of the twentieth century, made a very important contribution to the growth (Shutt and Whittington 1987; Chandler, Amatori and Hikino 1997; Davies et al. 1999). In any case, there were large variations across the world. In many countries, a stable core of large corporations developed only at a relatively late stage, or did not develop at all. Under these circumstances, big business was not able to contribute significantly to the economic growth of the country.

The aim of this book is to provide an in-depth analysis of big business' role and behavior in Italy and Spain since the end of World War II up to the present day. Even though, at the middle of the twentieth century, the Italian and Spanish economies were still quite backward when compared to those of the United States and the largest European nations, in a few decades, Italy and Spain had been able to catch up with the rest of the advanced world. But what role did big business play in this growth path, and how did it behave? The existing literature does not allow us to exhaustively answer these questions because there is still a substantial lack of information in both countries about the role and the features of a relevant number of large corporations and their transformation over time. If the role of big business might have been overestimated for the largest European economies and the United States as some scholars suggested (e.g., Piore and Sabel 1984; Sabel and Zeitlin 1997; Scranton 1997), it could have been underestimated for the Italian and Spanish cases. The main purpose of this book is to complement the traditional view of the historical development of big business in these nations by providing new information and significant insights into the behavior and into the economic, political and social impacts of the large corporations in Italy and Spain in a comparative perspective.

In this sense, this works fills in some substantial gaps in the literature and complements similar studies on big businesses worldwide (Chandler 1962; Scott 1970; Wrigley 1970; Channon 1973; Dyas and Thanheiser 1976; Cassis 1997; Whittington and Mayer 2000), providing a wide panorama of their features and their transformation in a quite neglected area such as Southern Europe. At the same time, the book combines a micro perspective with a macro one, investigating both specific company cases and vast populations of firms with the aim to contribute to several debates that arose around the topic of big business during the last decades, such as, for instance, its actual role in contributing to the wealth of a nation in comparison with small and medium-sized enterprises, and the hypothetical convergence of large corporations' behavior throughout the world during the second half of the twentieth century.

Many investigations into the impact and behavior of large companies within the world's leading economies have been conducted, and big business has been variously defined over the last decades (e.g., Cassis 2008). Peter Drucker's book *The Concept of the Corporation*, published in 1946, probably represents the starting point of the research done in this field. The first systematic study on the emergence of large corporations, titled *Strategy and Structure*, was published by Alfred Chandler in 1962 and focused on one of the nations in which big business succeeded at a very early stage: the United States. Based on an empirical reconstruction of the administrative activities of the largest US companies in the first part of the twentieth century as well as on a more detailed study of the history of four companies (Du Pont, General Motors, Standard Oil and Sears), this investigation represents not only the first organic empirical analysis of big business from a historical perspective, but it is also the first description and interpretation of the success achieved by the large US corporations during the last century.

According to the results of Chandler's analysis, the big companies that emerged in the United States at the turn of the twentieth century basically shared two common features that enabled them to succeed and become major protagonists of the US and global economies.

The first feature is that they were all active within a small number of sectors. These sectors belonged to the Second Industrial Revolution technological paradigm and were characterized as being capital and energy intensive and by a fast and continuous productive process.

Secondly, according to Chandler, the largest corporations in the United States followed a common growth path. Their first step was to accumulate resources while the economy was growing and industrializing quickly, approximately from the end of the Civil War up to World War I. In those years, the companies that operated within those sectors affected by the Second Industrial Revolution were able to achieve large economies of scale, thus becoming large corporations. The second step taken by these firms was to rationalize the use of their resources. For the first time, they adopted a "functional" organizational form in order to manage their increasingly extended activities. As competition grew and the markets became increasingly saturated, several companies took a third step: they started to use the surplus generated by their core activity to enter new geographical markets and new product areas. The existence of potential economies of scope in the Second Industrial Revolution sectors made this process easier and more convenient; a single operating unit was able to produce and/or distribute several different products at lower per-unit costs. The increased size and complexity of their activities finally pushed the corporations to complete a fourth step: the adoption of a new organizational form. The need to separate the general strategic planning of large and diversified companies from their day-to-day management and to give to each geographic or product area the careful attention it required lead to the diffusion of a "multidivisional" structure during the interwar period.

In the period after World War II, the economic advantage of the United States within those parts of the world that had embraced the model of market capitalism started to draw attention. Its large corporations appeared to be the main protagonists of the United States' success, since at the time they were the world's biggest enterprises, generating a vast proportion of their country's wealth. The impressive achievements of this nation and its companies made the existence of a real "American challenge" evident in Europe (Servan-Schreiber 1967), and focused attention on the dynamics and behavior of US companies. *Strategy and Structure*, which identified the diversification strategy and the multidivisional structure as the real key to success for the American corporations, quickly became a best seller within this context.

Chandler's work made a significant impact during the 1960s and 1970s, both in terms of its academic influence and in the managerial practices it described. Advisors at the US management consultancy McKinsey brought copies of *Strategy and Structure* to their customers both in the United States and in Europe (McCraw 1988), and Chandler's ideas started to dominate the field also in the academic world. "Chandlerism" was becoming a "new orthodoxy" (Alford 1994; John 1997).

During the 1970s, *Strategy and Structure* inspired both another Chandlerian work on the origin and early dynamics of the largest companies in the United States in several sectors—*The Visible Hand* (Chandler 1977)—and a number of pieces of research on big business in the most advanced European nations, which were conducted at the Harvard Business School (Scott 1970; Channon 1973; Rumelt 1974; Dyas and Thanheiser 1976). The main purpose of these investigations, collectively known as the "Harvard Program," was to check the diffusion of the strategies and structures of US big business in the Old Continent.

The findings of these investigations showed an increasing strategic and organizational convergence among the largest European corporations. In the United Kingdom, Germany and France, the number of large diversified companies increased markedly between 1950 and the early 1970s, as did the number of multidivisional companies. Big businesses in the world's largest economies seemed destined to become increasingly similar in terms of their strategies and structures, and the "made in the USA" diversification strategy and multidivisional structure appeared to be the most efficient also in the European context. According to these Chandlerian-inspired investigations, despite the peculiarities of each nation, industrial societies were destined to converge, and were actually converging, toward the most efficient kind of business behavior.

However, it was precisely during the 1970s that something happened that at least partially stopped this trend. Big companies in the United States increasingly moved away from the related diversification strategy and started to enter sectors in which they had no capabilities (Jacobi 1985; Chandler 1994). The economic crisis hit large manufacturing corporations in the West hard, while a new technological paradigm was starting to spread (Malerba and Orsenigo 1996; Freeman and Louçã 2001: Louçã and Mendonça 2002). Japanese companies were gaining on the large US corporations and even surpassing them, despite the fact that they adopted completely different strategies and structures (Ito 1992; Morikawa 1992, 2001). At McKinsey, "the phone stopped ringing" (McKenna 1997, 230), and in the academic world, Chandlerian work started to come under attack.

During the 1980s, the role of big business within national economies was also reconsidered. New dynamics and mechanisms of economic growth were studied, and the attention of scholars shifted from large corporations to small and medium-sized companies (Piore and Sabel 1984; Becattini 1987; Sabel and Zeitlin 1997).

However, the disputes on big business did not come to an end. On the contrary, the publication of *Scale and Scope* in 1990, in which Chandler compared the 200 largest corporations in the United States, Germany and the United Kingdom during the first half of the twentieth century, has revitalized the debate on big business (Chandler 1990). It not only attracted a series of criticisms (e.g., Supple 1991; Hannah 1995), but also inspired a process of revision and extension of the Chandlerian and the Chandlerian-inspired works (Friedman 2010).

During the 1990s, the belief in the absolute supremacy of the large corporations in contributing to the wealth of nations declined, the idea of the existence of universal principles of efficiency was abandoned, and the presumed superiority of those strategies and structures promulgated by the Harvard Program was questioned. Scholars from different disciplines and nationalities increasingly stressed the role of the historical and institutional context in shaping capitalism within a nation and in determining the success of corporate strategies and structures. The Chandlerian arguments were accused of being "without geography" (Kogut 1992) and "timeless" (Teece 1993).

Moreover, scholars argued that the Third Industrial Revolution deeply affected the strategies and structures of large corporations all over the world. New technologies in transport and communications shrunk space (Vernon 1977) and favored the diffusion of new business behaviors. Huge managerial hierarchies and large, integrated companies were declining to the advantage of a renewed entrepreneurial vitality and new organizational forms. It seemed that the "visible hand" (Chandler 1977) of management was progressively "vanishing" (Langlois 2003).

The criticisms directed at the traditional paradigm as well as the new context that was spreading represented real challenges for scholars, and further investigations were carried out (Jones and Zeitlin 2008). US scholars reconsidered the dynamics of the large US corporations under different perspectives (e.g., Fligstein 1990; Lazonick 1991; Markides 1995; Roy 1997; Galambos 2000), while an increasing and renewed interest started to surround big business in the rest of the world. Japan and its business groups (*keiretsus*) were studied more and more frequently (McCraw 1986; Fruin 1992; Dore 2000), as were other East Asian nations such as the Asian Tigers (Singapore, Hong Kong, Taiwan and South Korea; e.g., Amsden 1989; Clark and Kim 1995) and, later on, China and India (Lai 2003; Tripathi 2004). Latin America also started to draw the attention of scholars, in particular Argentina and Brazil (Barbero 2003). The debate on the large corporations outside the United States now involves a much greater number of countries, as is reflected by the recent publications of several books on comparative business history and business history around the world in the first years of the new millennium (e.g., Amatori and Jones 2003).

In most cases, international comparative studies on business organization have supported the position of the "contextualist" versus the "universalist" scholars, arguing that most corporations across the world are very different from those in the US, since they have emerged and grown within a very different context (Whittington and Mayer 2000, chap. 2). *Divergent Capitalisms* (1999) is a book by one of the most prominent contextualist scholar in this field, Richard Whitley, and it compares East Asian (South Korea and Taiwan) and East European (Hungary and Slovenia) countries. Stephan Haggard (1990) compared the industrialization processes and the entrepreneurial strategies adopted in Korea, Taiwan, Singapore, Hong Kong, Mexico and Brazil, whereas in *The Limits of Convergence. Globalization and Organizational Change in Argentina, South Korea, and Spain*, Mauro Guillén (2001) argued that convergence in the organizational behavior of the companies in newly industrialized countries was not happening.

In the ideal struggle between universalist and contextualist positions, Europe is, and was, probably the harshest battlefield. The economic relevance and the behavior of large corporations in the Old Continent, which is characterized by several national facets but at the same time by some features shared by every country (Whitley and Kristensen 1996; Amatori 1999; Weimer and Pape 1999; Whittington and Mayer 2000; Barca and Becht 2001, Schröter

2007), remains a real dilemma. In 2000, two management scholars, Richard Whittington and Michael Mayer, checked the findings of the Harvard Program using the same methodology. Their efforts resulted in a very unique book, of which the first part stresses the persistence of relevant differences in the ownership and managerial culture of the largest European corporations compared to the US ones. Then, surprisingly, the second part confirms that on the eve of the new millennium, despite all their national idiosyncrasies, the predominant form of big business in the United Kingdom, Germany and France was the diversified and multidivisional company described by Alfred Chandler in the United States fifty years ago (Whittington and Mayer 2000).

1.2 RESEARCH QUESTIONS AND CONTRIBUTIONS TO THE FIELD

In spite of all the efforts made so far, the results of several decades of research on big business are thus still ambivalent, and our understanding of this topic is largely incomplete.

On one hand, many investigations have been undertaken and some relevant similarities among the big businesses of the most advanced Western nations have emerged. At the beginning of the new millennium, big business still represented an important part of the wealth of the United States, Germany, the United Kingdom and France, and the strategies and structures adopted by the large corporations in these countries appeared to be quite similar. Even though the variety in ownership and governance structures remained quite large, almost all the major European and US companies had adopted a product-diversification strategy and a multidivisional structure (Whittington and Mayer 2000).

On the other hand, even though some national cases started to be analyzed, much still remains to be studied with regard to the economic relevance and the historical behavior of the large corporations in the rest of the world. Moreover, big business—as well as ideas about business history—has changed a lot since Chandler wrote his books. Major questions in this field remain unanswered. Taking the criticisms of Chandler's findings and conceptualizations into account, this work suggests that the use of his methodology might help us to deal with these questions. This book provides information and discusses facts relating to the history of big business in Italy and Spain, with the aim of moving forward in two main directions.

First of all, it will contribute to the field by assessing the relevance of big business in the economic, political and social systems of these two Southern European nations through an investigation of their dynamics from an international comparative perspective. We know that, despite their delay, the Italian and Spanish economies were able to catch up with the rest of the advanced world after World War II. But how did big business behave in this journey, and what role did it play?

The existing literature does not allow us to answer these questions in great detail, because there is still a substantial lack of information in both countries about the role and the defining features of a significant number of large corporations and their transformation over time. Scholars who have dealt with the economic history of Italy and Spain are generally unanimous in tagging these nations as industrial latecomers (e.g., Nadal 1975; Zamagni 1990), ineffective in promoting big autochthonous private and state-owned firms (e.g., Carreras and Tafunell 1997; Gallino 2003), dominated by family-run companies (e.g., Colli 2002c; Colli, Fernández Pérez and Rose 2003) and characterized by a competitive advantage on the part of small and medium-sized enterprises (e.g., Fuá and Zacchia 1983; Becattini 1987; Giner and Santa María 2002; Boix Domenech and Galletto 2004; Catalan, Miranda Encarnación and Ramón Muñoz 2011). At the same time, Spanish and Italian business and economic historians have not tended to say very much about the role and features of big business as a whole.

Very few works have been written on the behavior and the impact of the largest corporations on the wealth of the Southern European countries (Amatori 1997b; Carreras and Tafunell 1997; Vasta 2006), and almost no one has dealt with the historical transformation of their strategies, ownership and organizational structures based on a large amount of empirical evidence. Business historians have been particularly concerned with producing company monographs and sectoral studies, while devoting very little attention to syntheses of the big business panorama based on large amounts of empirical evidence (Amatori and Bigatti 2003; Carreras, Tafunell and Torres 2003).

Apart from a pioneering investigation carried out during the 1990s by Albert Carreras and Xavier Tafunell (1994) on the largest Spanish companies, almost nothing has been written in Spain about the relevance and behavior of a large population of big business in the country. We have more information in this area on Italy. Nevertheless, after a first investigation conducted at the beginning of the 1970s and following on from the Harvard Program (Pavan 1976), until recently no one had dealt with large populations of big business and tried to assess their behavior and contribution. In this area, it is important to stress the contribution made by Giovanni Federico and Pier Angelo Toninelli (2003a) on the transformation of the strategies and structures of the Italian companies up to the early 1970s, as well as a more extensive analysis of the evolution of big business in Italy included in the first section of a recent book on the different forms of enterprises in the country, edited by Andrea Colli and Michelangelo Vasta (2010a). These investigations suggest that the impact of big business in Italy and Spain was more significant than scholars had previously thought. Moreover, they confirmed the traditional view of the importance of actors such as the state and some important families to the development of large corporations in these Southern European nations, but at the same time, they stressed the relevance of actors such as the foreign multinationals.

Bearing in mind the fact that the impact of large corporations could have been underestimated in these countries and that much remains to be studied on its dynamics, this book thus moves forward by adding empirical evidence on the transformation over time of the relevance of large corporations, and by providing significant new insights into the identity of the large firms in these nations, their main protagonists, and the relationships among the state, the private entrepreneurs and the foreign investors. Moreover, a comparison of two Southern European nations allows us to identify several features that issues on big business have in common and that according to the literature are also more widespread in other Mediterranean countries. At the same time, this comparison enables us to clearly distinguish what has been characteristic of each of these two countries in terms of the development of large corporations.

The second aim of this book is to use the empirical evidence gathered in Italy and Spain in order to contribute to the international debate on the types of big business behavior around the world in terms of corporate governance, strategies and structures, adding new empirical evidence on and interpretations of two nations belonging to an area that up to now has been largely neglected. What can the history of the dynamics of large corporations in two countries such as Italy and Spain tell us about the presumed existence of a more efficient way to manage big business? Specifically, this book aims to move forward in three areas.

First, in line with some recent investigations that strove for a greater emphasis on context, and in particular on the role of the state and the political economy on business behavior (e.g., John 2006), this work argues that the strategic and organizational choices made by companies do not depend exclusively on technology and are not based solely on the aim of reducing costs. They are deeply influenced by the political and social framework in which they develop. Many of the choices made by Italian and Spanish large companies could be considered as irrational. However, as this work demonstrates, they were clearly very rational, because they allowed these firms not only to survive but also to grow successfully within their specific context.

Furthermore, several studies have shown that rules, institutions, markets and cultures have led to a significant country-based heterogeneity in the predominant forms of ownership as well as corporate control and governance practice, finance methods and, to some extent, sector specializations (e.g., Haggard 1990; Albert 1991; Whitley and Kristensen 1996; La Porta, López-de-Silanes and Shleifer 1999; Whitley 1999; Barca and Becht 2001; Guillén 2001). Investigations into business organization revealed the existence of a variety of structures. However, some common features, quite different from the ones registered in the United States and most advanced European nations, seem to emerge among the companies that developed in the latecomer nations. Alternative organizational structures that were not examined in Chandler's time, such as highly diversified business groups, are now attracting the attention of many scholars because of their high diffusion rate around the world (Colpan, Hikino and Lincoln 2010). Because both Italy and Spain were industrial latecomers, strongly influenced by the very relevant direct and indirect role of the state in their economies, and dominated by family companies and foreign multinationals, these countries are more typical in an international context than the few nations in which big business originally emerged. Nevertheless, the Southern European area has, to a large extent, been left out of the debate on strategies and structures. With few exceptions (e.g., Pavan 1976; Federico and Toninelli 2003; Binda and Iversen 2007; Galán and Sánchez-Bueno 2009b; Binda and Colli 2011; Binda 2012), the diffusion of the Chandlerian diversified and multidivisional large corporation has not been verified, and even recent literature on business groups does not pay sufficient attention to these nations. The second aim of this book is, therefore, to fill this gap.

Third, the work argues that, in order to understand big business and its behavior both outside the United States and throughout a longer period, it is necessary to reconsider the definition of big business and to take the relevant transformations that affected the identity of large corporations during the last few decades into account. Chandler (1990, chap. 1) argued that large firms, typical of the Second Industrial Revolution, only developed in those sectors that could exploit vast scale and scope economies and that had high barriers to entry. However, nowadays it is not sufficient to study domestically owned big corporations that belong to the manufacturing sector. Even though these companies were considered the pillars of wealth in the United States during the 1960s and 1970s, they are becoming less representative because of the increasing importance of new technologies and of the services sector in the big business panorama. Moreover, especially in the latecomer nations, domestically owned firms had to deal with competition from foreign multinationals almost from the very beginning. This book suggests that it is necessary to study the big business of every nationality and in every sector in order really to understand its nature, role and behavior in a country, as a study of the Italian and Spanish cases shows.

1.3 METHODOLOGY, DEFINITIONS AND SOURCES

This section aims to describe in detail the methodology adopted to perform the analysis, to provide definitions of the categories of ownership, strategy and structure, and to discuss the sources on which the research was based.

To obtain data that can be compared to the findings on the United States and Europe, the research was based on the Chandler-inspired methodology adopted from the 1970s onward by the team of scholars who studied the behavior of large corporations in Europe—the so-called Harvard Program—and that was most recently taken up again by Richard Whittington and Michael Mayer (2000; Scott 1970; Wrigley 1970; Dyas 1972; Thanheiser 1972; Channon 1973; Dyas and Thanheiser 1976; Pavan 1976;

Whittington and Mayer 2000). Even though they contained minor differences, all the investigations that followed the Harvard Program adopted a very similar methodology. Richard Rumelt, Derek Channon, Gareth Dyas and Heinz Thanheiser selected populations composed of the 100 largest manufacturing companies based on turnover in 1970 in the United States, United Kingdom, France and Germany, respectively. Then, focusing only on domestically owned enterprises, they investigated the transformations in the diversification strategy and organization of these firms, going back to 1950 by using a standard scheme for the classification of strategies and structures. Later on, Richard Whittington and Michael Mayer adopted the same methodology in order to study the largest corporations in France, Germany and the United Kingdom from the 1970s to the early 1990s. Thanks to the adoption of a shared methodology, it has thus been possible to compare the strategies and structures of the British, German and French big business from 1950 to 1993.

The adoption of the Harvard Program approach allows us to compare data on Southern Europe with that on other nations. Nevertheless, in order to consider both the important transformations that have occurred in the last few decades (such as the new dynamics resulting from European integration and the globalization process, the revolution in financial systems, the new role of the state and the growth and consolidation of the service sector) and the idiosyncrasies of the Italian and Spanish context, important amendments to the Harvard methodology were necessary.

The main divergence from the Harvard methodology concerns the composition of the populations in terms of the inclusion criteria of the companies. This should be taken into account when studying the result of the comparisons. Although previous investigations have dealt only with domestically owned manufacturing corporations, in this book, services and foreign enterprises have also been included in the Italian and Spanish populations. This adjustment was made necessary, on one hand, by the relevance of foreign firms, which brought technology, capital and knowledge to these industrial latecomer countries and maintained a very consistent presence (e.g., Muñoz, Roldán and Serrano 1978; Gallino 2003; Binda 2005a; Colli 2013), and, on the other hand, by the increasingly important role that nonmanufacturing sectors have played for several decades (Nohria, Dyer and Dalzell 2002). Excluding foreign and services companies from the populations would have meant neglecting very large corporations and only observing very small businesses compared to those in the United States (Binda 2005a). Moreover, compared to the Harvard Program studies, the present investigation added internationalization (defined as the percentage of exports and foreign affiliate sales to firms' total sales) to diversification as a major growth strategy.

Four benchmark years were selected on which to base the empirical analysis: 1950, 1973, 1988 and 2002. Studying 1950 makes it possible to observe the consequences of the reconstruction years in both countries. An analysis of 1973 allows us to consider the large corporations which developed during the golden age, before they were affected by the oil crisis. Examining 1988 makes it possible to observe the behavior adopted by large corporations in response to the 1970s crisis, as well as the emergence of new technologies and international dynamics. Finally, 2002 demonstrates the impact of the restructuring and the phenomena of European and international integration in transforming the identity and behavior of big business. For each benchmark year and in both countries, a population composed of the 100 largest nonfinancial corporations in terms of their sales in 1973, 1988 and 2002 and their assets in 1950, was selected.

Once the populations were determined, extensive basic information on each of the firms was collated. A concerted effort was made to identify which of these companies belonged to a formal or informal business group with a common main shareholder and a single strategy and/or structure. Both in Italy and Spain, in fact, large corporations very often have not consolidated their activities on a single balance sheet. Instead, they have operated throughout a more or less huge galaxy of controlled, participated and/ or linked corporations that formed formal or informal business groups, whose borders were not always clear and had changed over time. Before starting the investigation on the corporate strategies and structure of the 100 largest companies selected for the population, it has thus been necessary to gain an understanding of which of the companies were really free to define with proper autonomy their strategies and structure and, on the other hand, which ones shaped their behavior according to the directions of a formal or informal parent company or holding even though they had their own legal status and were able to formally draw up autonomous annual reports.

The original populations of the 100 largest "individual" companies were thus redefined and the companies that belonged to the same group were gathered into a single "decision unit." The criteria used to include a company within a decision unit were necessarily dictated in part by official information and in part by subjective interpretation. It was almost always obvious that a company should be included as part of a group when its share capital composition or official declarations confirmed its status of a nonautonomous company that belongs to the group in question. However, in several cases, it was not as easy to find information on cross-shareholdings, interlocking directorates or loan dependence. In order to clarify whether a company was autonomous or not, it has been necessary to use secondary sources and/or unofficial information on that company. The adoption of such criteria meant the introduction of a certain level of arbitrariness in the identification of the decision units became unavoidable, but it would not have been possible to consider separately the strategies and structures of companies that belonged to an ampler group and that were thus not able to decide them. Several examples explain this point throughout the book. The only case in which companies controlled by other firms were considered as individual, even though they could not autonomously determine their strategies and structures, was that of the foreign multinational subsidiary.

Here it was in fact more interesting to study the behavior that the subsidiary displayed in Italy or in Spain during a specific period than the strategies and structure of its parent company at home.

Once the decision units had been identified, the populations of the "individual units" were completed with basic information on the firms, such as their main budget items, the number of employees, their ownership and the sector to which they belonged. Then, the population of decision units was studied, and the ownership, strategies and structures of the decision units in Italy and Spain in all the four benchmark years investigated.

The ownership structure and the control mechanisms, which are often considered as fundamental in the interpretation of company behavior, were the first elements to be considered. The aim of the investigation was to understand which kind of ownership was predominant among the largest companies in the two countries and if and how things changed over time. The analysis conducted by Chandler of the largest corporations in the United States argued that families very often had neither sufficient funds available to acquire and maintain large and expensive plants in those sectors typical of the Second Industrial Revolution nor the technical and organizational capabilities needed to coordinate activities that were becoming more extensive and more complicated. During the twentieth century, the share capital owned by the largest corporations had to be dispersed among more and more owners and a separation between corporate ownership and control occurred especially in the listed companies (Berle and Means 1932; Cheffins and Bank 2009). The diffusion of corporate ownership was less common in Europe as well as in other national contexts, which are still currently characterized by concentrated ownership structures and where the stock exchange played a minor role (e.g., La Porta, López-de-Silanes and Shleifer 1999). In order to investigate which ownership categories were more common among the largest corporations in Italy and Spain over time, and to see whether a separation between ownership and control occurred, the same definitions used by Whittington and Mayer (2000) have been adopted. Ownership is broadly divided into two categories: dispersed and concentrated. Following the usual practice in the agency and corporate governance literature, the threshold level for dispersed ownership was set at that where no shareholder has 5% or more of the voting stock (Whittington and Mayer 2000; Shleifer and Vishny 1996). Thereafter, concentrated ownership was divided into six subcategories in which corporations are cataloged according to their single largest shareholder: personal, bank-financial, state, firm, foreign, cooperative and foundational. It has to be stressed that also in this case an attempt was made to ensure substance prevails over form. In several cases, the real owners tended to hinder the real ownership of their companies also by using quite sophisticated mechanisms and *escamotages*. Therefore, companies owned by financial holdings that were in turn completely controlled by one entrepreneur or family have been considered as personal and not as companies owned by another firm. The same criterion have been adopted for state-owned holdings or, in the Spanish case, for those companies controlled by banks that were in turn used by families as holdings. These companies have also been considered as personal.

The next step was to analyze the strategies adopted by the corporations. According to Chandler (1962, 1990), related diversification provided crucial help in ensuring the continued production of new products, cutting costs and increasing the efficiency of the large corporations in the United States and within the industries characterized by the Second Industrial Revolution technologies. The largest US corporations started to adopt a strategy of related-product diversification on a massive scale during the first half of the twentieth century, and the path toward an even stronger diversification continued in the post-postwar period (Markides 1995). A strategic convergence toward the US diversification trend began in the 1950s and was already evident among the largest British, German and French companies in the 1970s (Channon 1973; Dyas and Thanheiser 1976). Thirty years later, Whittington and Mayer (2000, 145) found this course to have been completed, and could thus claim that diversification in Europe had progressed in the direction predicted by the Harvard Program team. Single business activity, the most common strategy in the postwar years, declined in Germany, France and the United Kingdom. On the other hand, at the end of the century, related diversification had been adopted by at least half of the population. In order to investigate the predominant strategic choices of the Italian and Spanish big business and how this changed over time in accordance with the Harvard methodology, every decision unit was also studied and cataloged in one of four product diversification categories: single business (if at least 95% of the revenue was aggregated from one business area), dominant business (if one business area generated at least 70% but less than 95% of the revenue), related business (if no business area generated more than 70% of the revenue but there was a market or a technological correspondence between the business areas) and unrelated business (if no business area generated more than 70% of the revenue and there was no or only limited market or technological correspondence between the different business areas).

In traditional studies, the analysis of an individual firm's strategic behavior is limited to its product diversification strategy. In this research, however, another kind of strategy was also considered: the diversification of the geographical market—that is to say internationalization—originally present in Chandler's conceptualizations but neglected in subsequent investigations. In fact, it is interesting to consider whether enterprises have been able to exploit growth opportunities by expanding not in new product areas but in new geographical markets during the last few decades, which have been underpinned by new technological opportunities in terms of communication and transport and by an increasing integration of European and international economies. It was therefore worthwhile to check if, how and when the internationalization strategy was adopted by the major firms in Italy and Spain and whether product diversification and internationalization were alternative or concomitant strategies. The level of internationalization has been defined using the same principles as for that used to define diversification. Every firm was thus classified as belonging to one of four internationalization strategy categories: home-oriented (if less than 10% of revenue was aggregated from international activities), partly home-oriented (if between 10% and 50% of revenue was aggregated from international activities), partly internationally oriented (if between 50% and 90% of revenue was aggregated from international activities) and internationally oriented (if at least 90% of revenue was aggregated from international activities). Because many companies did not provide exact information on their own international activities, covering both exports and revenue generated by production abroad, it was necessary to also use indirect information in order to obtain a more realistic and informed estimate of their behavior.

The final step was to analyze the organizational behavior of the decision units, in order to understand by which organizational forms companies had decided to manage their activities and strategies. In *Strategy and Structure*, Chandler stressed the central role played by the organizational forms in determining the performance of a company, leading to the classic formulation of this issue: "unless structure follows strategy, inefficiency results" (1962, 314). Yet, the structure adopted by companies quite often adapted more easily to other elements than it did to strategy. During the last century, factors such as the attitude to delegating important decisions, the fiscal policies, the financial framework and other kinds of incentives joined with strategic needs in pushing companies to adopt one kind of organizational form or another.

According to Chandler (1962), the first organizational achievement of large corporations in the United States during the first stages of their growth was to adopt a functional structure. This organizational form then became inadequate when the product diversification of firms began to increase. During the 1920s, a new kind of organizational form emerged: the multidivisional form (M-form). As it allowed companies to coordinate and to manage the increasing degrees of diversification and internationalization effectively, the multidivisional structure dominated the big business panorama in the United States. From the 1950s, the M-form also started to spread gradually throughout most advanced European nations. During the 1970s, an investigation by Channon, Dyas and Thanheiser already showed the diffusion of this structure in the United Kingdom, Germany and France (Channon 1973; Dyas and Thanheiser 1976). By 1993, the M-form had become the most widely adopted organizational structure of European big businesses (Whittington and Mayer 2000).

In order to investigate the predominant organizational forms adopted by the Italian and Spanish large corporations and to verify the eventual diffusion of the multidivisional form, the Harvard Program categories were used once more, and the decision units were categorized as four "ideal" kinds of organizational structure: functional (if a firm was centralized around key functions such as manufacturing and marketing), functional/holding (if a company had a functionally centralized core and a small periphery of other businesses), holding (if a firm was highly decentralized, lacking central administrative control over its activities) and multidivisional (if a company decentralized its operations into clearly defined divisions, while keeping central headquarters control over strategy and investments through systematic accounting and planning mechanisms). As can be observed from the definitions themselves, the attribution of a firm to one kind of structure or another involves a degree of arbitrariness. Moreover, these kinds of structures are ideal, and it is very unlikely that a company fully fits in with one of these definitions. In many cases firms were thus attributed to the structure to which they were most similar. Other problems emerged because several corporations had adopted "hybrid" structures that covered more than one definition. In addition, although companies almost always wrote about their strategies, they rarely provided information on their organizational structure. This is even truer for their past structures, which have thus been more difficult to reconstruct.

National yearbooks on company data were used to compile the rankings. The Italian 1950 ranking was built based on the information in the yearbook *Società Italiane per Azioni: Notizie Statistiche* (Associazione fra le Società Italiane per Azioni 1953), while the 1973, 1988 and 2002 benchmark years are based on the yearbook *Le Principali Società Italiane* (Mediobanca 1974, 1989, 2003). For Spain, the information used to compile the first ranking comes from the *Anuario Financiero que Comprende el Historial de Valores Públicos y de Sociedades Anónimas en España*, while the other three benchmark years were obtained on the basis of the *Fomento de la Producción – Las Mayores Empresas Españolas* rankings (*Anuario Financiero que Comprende el Historial de Valores Públicos y de Sociedades Anónimas de España* 1951–1952; Fomento de la producción 1974, 1989, 2003).

With regard to information on the numbers, the ownership and the strategies and structures of the companies, an attempt was at first made to use annual reports and some national company and stock exchange yearbooks as the main sources (Mediobanca various years; Credito Italiano, various years; Banco de Bilbao various years; Bolsa de Barcelona various years; Bolsa de Madrid various years). However, given what is available, it was not possible to gather all the information needed, especially for the first benchmark year. A serious lack of information emerged from these sources, particularly for family and nonlisted companies and for the subsidiaries of foreign firms. This lack of data made it necessary to look for indirect information, such as economic press releases, business histories and case studies, and the biographies of entrepreneurs and managers, in order to obtain a more realistic and informed estimate of their behavior. Moreover, because scant information is available on turnover for 1950, the population was compiled by taking into consideration the 100 largest corporations in both Italy and Spain based on their assets rather than their sales.

1.4 STRUCTURE OF THE BOOK

This introduction has included a literature review on the issues associated with big business, a statement on which research questions will be addressed and what contributions will be made to field, and a description of the methodology, definitions and sources used to conduct the empirical investigations. The main body of the book is structured in terms of four sections, a conclusion and finally an appendix.

The first section investigates the history of Italy and Spain from the 1940s up to the present day and assesses the economic, political and social frameworks in which big business operated in these countries in the long term. The transformation of Italy and Spain is analyzed, respectively, in Chapters 2 and 3, mainly by considering the changes that took place in terms of the role and behavior of four actors: the state, the families, the financial system and foreign companies. There are four well-defined periods: the wars and the reconstruction years (1939–1950), the Italian and Spanish economic miracles (1950–1973), the crisis and the economic restructuring (1973–1988) and the recent developments (1988–2002). Italy and Spain are considered separately in two different chapters, but similarities and differences between them are emphasized.

Section II is devoted to an analysis of the long-term evolution of big business in Italy and Spain. In this section, Chapter 4 compares the economic impact of the 100 largest companies on the GDP of Italy, Spain and the most advanced economies worldwide between 1950 and 2002, proving that big business played a decisive role in contributing to the economic growth of Italy and Spain, even though these countries had, and still have, a competitive advantage in terms of small and medium-sized companies. Moreover, by looking at several case studies, this chapter studies the social and political role of large corporations, stressing that they were very important in furthering Italian and Spanish social development, not only through their business welfare plans but also by playing a large part in shaping the process of urbanization and modernization in these countries. Chapter 5 deals with the transformation of the sectors to which the 100 largest companies in Italy and Spain belong, showing the decline of some sectors and the rise of other activities and emphasizing the similarities and differences between these two nations. The owners of the 100 major corporations in Italy and Spain in 1950, 1973, 1988 and 2002 and the extent of the power of their management during these times are described in Chapter 6. By examining empirical evidence and using data on the history of several companies, this part of the book argues that dispersed ownership, which broadly characterized the Anglo-Saxon system, was largely absent in these Mediterranean nations. At the same time, even though there are significant differences between them, both in Italy and in Spain, certain business owners such as the state, families, banks and multinational companies were particularly important.

Following on almost fifty years after the publication of *Strategy and Structure* by Alfred Chandler, the third section of this book is completely devoted to the analysis of the transformations in the strategies and structures of big business in Italy and Spain between 1950 and 2002. The aims of Chapters 7, 8 and 9 are, first of all, to examine the spread of the diversification strategy and of the multidivisional structure in these two Southern European nations and, second, to investigate the adoption of another kind of strategy: the internationalization of business activity. Short case studies serve to provide examples of what has occurred in both countries in terms of the adoption of one kind of strategy and structure or another, and how this changed over time. Chapters 7 and 8 focus on the diffusion, respectively, of the product diversification strategy and of the geographic market diversification strategy within the largest corporations in Italy and Spain. They show that the diffusion of the related diversification strategy in these nations was late and only partial when compared to the great success it had in the United States and in other European nations, and that an extensive diffusion of alternative strategies in Italy and Spain as the single business and the unrelated business strategies took place. They also demonstrate that many companies decided to sell or produce abroad from the 1970s onward, despite this behavior having been very rare in the 1950s and 1960s. Although Italian and Spanish companies adopted this behavior with varying intensity and timings, the overall trend led to the emergence of Italian and Spanish multinationals that were able to become quite competitive within Europe and America.

The final part of the third section, namely, Chapter 9, is devoted to the study of the organizational behaviors of the largest companies in Italy and Spain from 1950 to the present day. With regard to their organizational choices, the empirical evidence shows that big business in Italy and Spain followed the predominant model of multidivisional companies only in part and only belatedly. Although there are differences between them, it is clear that if during first years of industrial growth of these nations the functional form was the most widely adopted, in the long term, the main alternative to the multidivisional was the holding structure.

The last section of the book is devoted to interpret the characteristics of capitalism in Italy and Spain as well as the trends that governed the dynamics of big business from a wider comparative perspective. Chapter 10 focuses on Italy and Spain by investigating the similarities and differences between these two countries and stressing the continuities and discontinuities that characterized big business ownership structures, strategies and organizational forms. Whereas the first part of the chapter underlines how much Italy and Spain have differed from each other, the second part claims that their forms of capitalism have several characteristics in common and that in both cases very similar alternative forms of big business spread: these two nations were similar in the way they developed different kinds of big business from the US-inspired models. Chapter 11 then explains why were these kinds of alternative strategies and structures developed in Italy and Spain. The first part of the explanation considers the importance of factors that were inherent to company life, such as the industry to which a firm belonged, its ownership structures and its managerial culture, in shaping big business forms. An analysis of the external factors that affected companies' strategic behavior and organizational structures, such as economic policies as well as the Europeanization and the globalization of capital and product markets, then follows. Conclusions are presented at the end of this section.

Part I

Historical Features of Italian and Spanish Capitalism

It has been written that, if a citizen of the Roman Empire could be transported some eighteen centuries forward in time, he would have found himself in a society he could have learned to comprehend without great difficulty. "Horace would have felt himself reasonably at home as a guest of Horace Walpole and Catullus would soon have learned his way among the sedan chairs, the patched-up beauties and the flaring torches of London streets at night" (Waddington 1960, 277). The First Industrial Revolution disrupted this continuity during the last decades of the eighteenth century. However, it was only from the beginning of the twentieth century, and particularly from its second half onward, that Southern European economies as well as people's lives in this area were transformed beyond recognition.

The glory and wealth that characterized Italy and Spain during the modern era gradually vanished as more dynamic economies, such as those of the Netherlands and Great Britain, affirmed their supremacy. Although there were significant differences at a national level, Southern Europe as a whole became a relatively poor and quite underdeveloped area. However, even though the Italian and Spanish economies were still quite backward when compared to those of the United States and the largest European nations in the middle of the twentieth century, within a few decades, they were able to catch up with the rest of the advanced world.

As will be shown, large corporations were among the main protagonists of this growth. At the same time, they both affected and were greatly affected by the general political, social and economic transformations that took place during this era and that completely changed the rules of the game. They were also influenced by the dynamics of the markets, the available technologies, entrepreneurial opportunities and, finally, the cultural and political attitude toward business, in general, and big business, in particular (Prados de la Escosura and Zamagni 1992).

Within a few decades, both Italy and Spain went from being agricultural and relatively poor to rich and industrialized countries, from dictatorship to democracy, from autarky to economic international and European full integration.

Nevertheless, finding a common periodization that allows us to compare important Italian and Spanish facts and trends is not an easy task, because the level of development, size of economy and growth rate of the two nations have until recently been substantially different.

The Italian economy was the first of the two to develop in any kind of meaningful and robust manner. Even though it did so much later than other advanced countries across the world, Italy was the first nation in Southern Europe to embark on a robust and large-scale process of industrialization during the final years of the nineteenth century. Between 1896 and 1914, the country was provided with the necessary prerequisites to really take off during the Fascist period and, even more so, at the end of World War II (Amatori 1995; Ciocca and Toniolo 2003). As described so succinctly by the Italian economic historian Vera Zamagni (1990), within a few decades Italy moved "from periphery to center" and became one of the most advanced nations in the world. Big business was greatly impacted by the new context and at the same time acted as one of the most important pieces of the Italian growth puzzle. It was only in the final decade of the previous millennium that signs of a relative decline began to appear (Toniolo and Visco 2004, 189).

The history of the Spanish economy is quite different, as throughout the last century it was more backward than the Italian economy. According to the distinguished economic historian Jordi Nadal (1975), the First Industrial Revolution as well as the first stages of the Second Industrial Revolution largely failed to have an impact in Spain during the nineteenth century, whereas Italy was experimenting with the beginnings of its industrial take-off. Although new technologies were adopted quite quickly and new large corporations were established in the most advanced sectors, some features of the Spanish economy in addition to unfavorable international circumstances prevented an effective industrialization process from taking place. According to Albert Carreras's estimates, agricultural backwardness, an inadequate level of integration into the international economy of the time, and a succession of political events that negatively impacted on the country (such as the war in Cuba and the emergence of the Francoist autarky), meant that the process of industrialization in Spain lasted a significantly longer time period than in the rest of Europe (Carreras 1993). Despite this, the growth of Spain during the last decade of the dictatorship was impressive. Over the last few decades, Spanish gross domestic product (GDP) has quickly reached a par with those of the richest nations.

Even though the national dynamics of the two countries remained quite peculiar throughout each period, in order to gain an understanding of the behavior of big business, the time frame of this research can be roughly divided into four eras that share some features that were appeared in Italy and Spain and to a certain extent also in many other nations in Europe. Each one of these eras ends with a benchmark year and is characterized by a specific context, which is analyzed based on the transformation in the attitudes and behavior of four actors in particular: governments, financial systems, private entrepreneurs and foreign companies.

The first period roughly coincides with the end of the wars—World War II in Italy and the Civil War in Spain—and the years of reconstruction (1939–1950), which represent an important watershed in their process of industrialization and modernization. Even though important continuities can be identified, it is clear that the shape of big business in Italy and Spain throughout the second part of the twentieth century was greatly influenced by a number of events and political decisions that took place during the 1940s. The Spanish Civil War (1936–1939) and World War II (1939–1945)—in which Spain remained indirectly belligerent—respectively, transformed the Spanish and Italian political, economic and social framework, changing some of the basic features of the context in which companies used to exist and operate.

The second period is the so-called golden age: a period of spectacular economic growth that took place in both nations during the 1950s and 1960s (1950–1973). The 1950s and 1960s witnessed the dawn of a golden age almost all over the world and were characterized by intense economic growth, increasing social development and a strengthening of the process of integration of the European and world economies even though these were still at a seminal stage. In terms of the "numbers" of this growth, in Italy and Spain, real per-capita GDP had one of the most impressive growth during this era. If per-capita GDP between 1950 and 1973 grew at a rate of 2.5% in the United Kingdom and at 4% in France, the Italian and Spanish rate of growth during this same period was 5% and 5.8%, respectively (Eichengreen 2007). The return of peace formed the basis of real "economic miracles" in these nations, although their respective growth involved different "timings." Although the Italian economic miracle began to take shape during the 1950s, in Spain, a real growth spurt took place only ten years later, during the 1960s. Both countries became wealthy and modernized, and by the beginning of the 1970s, they had reached a stable level of industrialization despite the fact that in both cases, the way to the development took place with some distortions and a number of structural weaknesses remained.

The third era is characterized by the economic crisis of the 1970s and its aftermath (1973–1988). Following the golden age, the Italian and Spanish economies had largely caught up with the rest of the advanced world. However, whereas the economic miracles during the 1950s and 1960s particularly highlighted the positive aspects of the path of development that these countries embarked on, the impact of the crisis of the 1970s brought the weaknesses of the economic systems that had developed to the fore in just a few years. The collapse of the Bretton Woods system, the first oil shock in 1973 and the energy crisis that lasted for the rest of the decade represent a very important watershed in Italian and Spanish history as well as in the rest of the world. The cost of energy increased wildly, while big business, which had been growing for at least two decades, had to face a dramatic slowdown of the markets and increasing competition, causing a sudden drop in profits. To make matters worse, economic recession was accompanied by high inflation. It was an age of "changing fortunes" (Nohria, Dyer and Dalzell 2002): old policies seemed no longer to be effective, the big manufacturing businesses accumulated losses, and new technologies were spreading throughout the world in old and new sectors. Old formal and informal rules in the labor, financial and product markets were replaced by new ones, while the space, to borrow a famous expression used by Raymond Vernon, started to shrink. Italy and Spain dealt with the crisis from different perspectives and implemented different measures to an extent, because they were influenced by their own specific social, political and economic situation and by the changes that were occurring in a climate of increasing economic and international integration.

Finally, the last period (1988–2002) shows how these two economies recovered from the effects of the 1970s recession and how their dynamics changed in response to new trends in international and European economic integration. In Italy and in Spain, as in most of the world, the end of the 1980s and the two decades around the turn of the millennium brought the end of an old status quo and the dawn of almost completely new perspectives. Since the early 1980s, the transformation of the world economy has been enormous. The changes that modern capitalist economies have gone through are indeed substantial enough to make economic historians such as Chris Freeman and Francisco Louçã talk about a "new kind of capitalism," or even a new "techno-economic paradigm" (Freeman and Louçã 2001). New sectors replaced some of the old ones; services became steadily stronger than manufacturing; the equilibrium among big, medium and small companies was shaken; and new kinds of owners, strategies and structures emerged throughout the world while globalization challenged the traditional rules of the capital, labor and final product markets.

The 1990s and the beginning of the 2000s saw some significant transformations in Italian and Spanish big business, representing a period in which the overall competitiveness of large national firms was seriously challenged both by aggressive companies in emerging markets, and by the fact that, after the Treaty of Maastricht, governments had to abandon their consolidated policy of directly and indirectly protecting their "national champions." Privatization and liberalization were accompanied by a program of reforms in both these nations, which led to the creation of a new institutional framework that was meant to respond more effectively to the new trends in technology and the international economy.

In 2009, the Italian and Spanish GDPs were respectively the seventh and ninth highest in the world (World Bank 2010). Yet, their long-term weaknesses remain strongly rooted and represent potential threats for their future.

In order to understand the relevance and the dynamics of big business in these two nations, the rest of this section is devoted to an assessment of the political and economic frameworks in which big business operated during the four periods previously described and to a description of the role played during each one of these periods by the state, private entrepreneurs, the financial systems and foreign investors in influencing the behavior of large corporations.

2 Italy
Toward a Democratization of Big Business?

2.1 "HOW TO LOSE THE WAR AND WIN THE PEACE" (1939–1950)

On the eve of World War II, Italy had already found its way to industrialization. In addition, despite the defeat suffered in World War I, the efforts made to participate in the military conflict favored further developments in the postwar period, as the challenging book edited by Vera Zamagni *Come Perdere la Guerra e Vincere la Pace* (*How to Lose the War and Win the Peace*; 1997) suggests. The obstacles to this process were many, as are the number of interpretations of the causes, features, size, and timing of the "big spurt" in Italy (e.g., Sereni 1947; Romeo 1959; Gerschenkron 1962; Caracciolo 1969; Bonelli 1978; Luzzatto 1980; Cafagna 1989; Zamagni 1990; Cohen and Federico 2001; Fenoaltea 2003). Nevertheless, almost everyone today agrees on the fact that Italy could already be considered an industrial country by the start of World War I and that, despite the outbreak of economic crises and wars, it was able to carry on with the industrialization process during the Fascist era (Gualerni 1976; Sarti 1977; Sapelli 1978; Toniolo 1980). It did so mainly through the consolidation and strengthening of the large corporations, which had been founded around the turn of the twentieth century in those sectors typical of the Second Industrial Revolution. Statistical information on Italian industrial production and on its added value during the 1920s and 1930s, as well as on the number of employees involved in manufacturing, demonstrate that modern industrial sectors had an increasing impact on the country, despite the fact that there were significant differences in growth between these sectors (Federico 2003; Carreras and Felice 2010). Italy's industrial structure was definitively consolidated during this period, even though its GDP remained, at the end of the 1930s, significantly lower than that of the more developed industrial powers such as Germany, the United Kingdom and Japan (Castronovo 1980; Zamagni 1990; Maddison 1995; Amatori and Colli 1999).

World War II greatly affected the industrial productive structure of the country, as well as several areas of its infrastructure. Nevertheless, the damage wrought was relatively moderate. The postwar years, in part thanks to the new opportunities provided under the Marshall Plan, witnessed a relatively fast recovery and marked the beginning of a new and prosperous era for Italy.

The history of Italian economic affairs during the postwar period and of the economic boom that followed it, as well as interpretations thereof, was eloquently discussed by several respected scholars. They stressed in particular the importance of the dynamics during these years to the general and long-term development of the country (Mori 1977; Bonelli 1978; Castronovo 1980; Zamagni 1990, 1997; Amatori and Colli 1999; Amatori et al. 1999). In order to understand the relevance of big business and the shape it started to take in this period, it is crucial to stress two important choices that were made by the Italian government of the time.

The first is the decision to maintain and strengthen the system of state-owned companies that had been created before World War II (Romeo 1988). The history of the "State Entrepreneur" in Italy dates back to the 1930s, when the state-owned holding Istituto di Ricostruzione Industriale (IRI) was established in 1933 in order to take over the industrial stakes held by the major universal banks of the country (Banca Commerciale Italiana, Credito Italiano and Banco di Roma). These banks had demonstrated themselves to be unable to manage their close ties with big industry, especially following the economic crisis of 1929 (Cianci 1977). On the eve of the war, IRI already controlled vast amounts of the Italian industrial production: 80% in shipbuilding, 45% in steel, 39% in the electromechanical industry, and 23% in the mechanical sector (Cianci 1977, 43–58; Castronovo 2011).

When the fascist regime collapsed and World War II came to an end, Italian entrepreneurs called IRI into serious question. They criticized both the poor economic performance shown by the holding up to that point, as well as the mere fact that an economic institution that "finds money when it wants it and at the prices it prefers" (Ministero per la Costituente 1947, 339) continued to exist and compete at the same level as the private companies that did not have such privileges. Nevertheless, the need to sustain the economic recovery after the war, the absence of private buyers for IRI's companies and the political influence of some lobbies that considered direct ownership of the country's largest companies by the state to be fundamental to the pursuit of specific economic, political and social aims not only allowed the "State Entrepreneur" to survive, but also favored his strengthening and expansion (Amatori 2000). The direct ownership of a very significant percentage of the largest Italian companies and strong state intervention in the national economy had a large and long-term impact not only on the strategic behavior of state-owned enterprises but also on the strategies and structures adopted by private entrepreneurs and managers.

A second choice that would turn out to be definitive for Italy's development and for the strategies and structures adopted by the country's big businesses during the following decades was the decision to further Italian integration into the international economy, and thus to accept the constraints and opportunities resulting from an increased interaction with the other economic powers of the Western world.

The first important step made in this direction is represented by the prompt reply given by some Italian politicians and entrepreneurs to the hand outstretched by the United States through the Marshall Plan. Any doubts about whether Italy was a country where big business could flourish were pushed aside (Ministero per la Costituente 1947; Castronovo 1980; Sapelli 1987). Thanks to the European Recovery Program, Italy was able to take advantage of US aid and foster cutting-edge companies, thereby restructuring its industrial plants according to the modern and efficient models of large-scale production that had emerged in the United States in previous years (e.g., Amatori 1997b; Bairati 1983; Osti and Ranieri 1993).

The next step toward integration was the signing of the Treaty of Rome in 1957, through which France, Western Germany, Italy, Belgium, the Netherlands and Luxembourg established the European Economic Community (EEC). Despite some very influential lobbies claiming that it was necessary to maintain a strictly protectionist policy for the weak Italian manufacturing sectors, the benefits of the "European choice" in the medium as well as in the long term were tremendous. Increased integration in Europe presented new opportunities and gave rise to new attempts to make companies more competitive. Some of the enterprises that were able to take advantage of this new situation became real national leaders and serious competitors abroad during the following decades (Amatori and Colli 1999; Zamagni 1990; Fauri 2006).

During this period, large corporations achieved an increasingly important position within the Italian economy and adopted some of the characteristics that would go on to define them for the rest of the twentieth century. With very few exceptions, the largest enterprises that nowadays dominate the big business panorama in Italy already existed by the middle of the century (Amatori 1997b). The morphogenesis of the Italian industrial system did not differ greatly from that of other advanced nations, thanks in part to the existence of large companies in industries typical of Second Industrial Revolutions, such as electricity (Edison, SADE and SME), chemicals (Montecatini and SNIA Viscosa), steel (Finsider and Falck), automobiles (FIAT and Alfa Romeo), rubber (Pirelli), heavy machinery (Ansaldo), office machinery (Olivetti), department stores (La Rinascente) and the newly founded petrochemical group Ente Nazionale Idrocarburi.

It could be claimed that by the middle of the twentieth century, big business had already emerged in Italy, that it operated in the same sectors as in the most advanced nations in the world and that it was on its way to playing a major part in the economic growth of the country. Looking at the role played by the government, families and foreign investors as well as the development of the financial markets in those years is indispensable to gaining an understanding of the strategic and organizational choices made by the large corporations and the impact these had on their performance.

The fact that the state exercised direct control over the country's largest companies through its holding IRI is of crucial importance. However, state intervention also influenced the characteristics and attitudes of large private corporations. The government had fostered large private corporations since the Unification of the country, promoting their creation, financing them, supporting them by placing orders and rescuing them when they performed badly (Bonelli 1978). Two adjectives used by Italian scholars are particularly effective in explaining the nature of Italian capitalism at the end of World War II.

The first is "political". Large private companies were well aware that the government would have done everything in its power to help big businesses in "strategic sectors" and would not have let them go bankrupt. Most of the largest enterprises thus shaped their growth strategy based not on economic reasons but on "strategic reasons," such as getting into a better position to bargain with the country's political powers (Amatori 1997a). Terni, a steel company that became the most important producer of electric power in central Italy during the 1920s and that expanded into the electrochemical sector, represents the most typical example of this attitude. The company continued to produce steel for military purposes even during periods of peace, but asked the state for advantageous conditions as well as protection for the development of the company's new activities (Bonelli 1975).

The second adjective that aptly defines the Italian capitalist system of the mid-twentieth century is "concentrated". A few companies, in some cases a few men, were at the center of large groups that were built on cross-shareholdings, collusive agreements and pyramids that in turn controlled sizeable "slices" of the national economy (Amatori and Bezza 1990; Battilossi 1992; Segreto 1993; Amatori and Brioschi 1997; Barca et al. 1997). In the words of Ettore Conti, a famous Italian industrialist and businessman who was active during the first part of the twentieth century, "Agnelli, Cini, Volpi, Pirelli, Donegani, Falck, and very few others literally dominate all the industrial fields" (1986, 432). Even though non-family-run business groups did exist in Italy during this period, in particular those in the electricity and chemical sectors, almost all the private largest corporations in the country, belonged to families and dynasties that played a crucial part in Italy's process of industrialization. These also include FIAT in automobiles, Pirelli in rubber and Olivetti in office machinery.

Foreign capital also played a significant role in the country's industrialization. An important feature of Italian capitalism during the first decades of the twentieth century is the large presence of foreign firms (Nitti 1915). However, also in this case, state intervention was fundamental to the acceptance of foreign firms, and later on to putting partial constraints on imports of foreign capital and technologies. Before World War I, the presence of foreign capital was pervasive in particular in the capital and technology-intensive sectors (Zamagni 1978), but in the interwar period, a process of "Italianization" of foreign firms occurred. In part due to political reasons during the Fascist era, a number of important companies in utilities, metallurgy and mechanics came under full Italian control, although foreign investments still dominated many areas of manufacturing (Colli 2010). In the postwar years, the amount and importance of foreign investment in the country still reflected past dynamics. At the same time, however, foreign investment and aid coming in particular from the Marshall Plan in terms of capital, know-how and technology, were fundamental to providing Italian private and state-owned firms with the material and immaterial resources they needed to develop.

When it comes to the characteristics of the financial system, it has to be stressed that the lack of transparency and of regulation of the stock market contributed to making the banks a major economic force in the financing of business during the reconstruction era. Nevertheless, state intervention also had a great impact on the financial sector and its contribution to the development of the national economy. Even though the so-called German model of universal bank was predominant in Italy during the first stage of its industrialization, banks were unable to act as shareholders of companies after 1936, when, following the economic crisis that involved the banks as well as the enterprises they had invested in, a bill made the separation between banking and industry almost compulsory (Colajanni 1995). During the 1930s, Italy abandoned a financial system based on universal banks. At the same time, however, it did not strengthen the role that the stock exchange could play, distancing itself from both the "Rhenan" and the "Anglo-Saxon" systems (Albert 1991).

2.2 THE GOLDEN AGE (1950–1973)

In Italy, the 1950s were characterized by very significant growth. In the period between 1956 and 1963, income increased at an annual rate of almost 6%, while the growth rate of investment, industry, construction and exports was between 9% and 11% (Zamagni 1990; Amatori and Colli 1999). Worldwide, only Japan experienced higher rates of growth. The Italian per-capita GDP grew from 37% to 64% of that of the US between 1950 and 1973 (Eichengreen 2007, 18). Meanwhile, the fundamental nature of Italian economy was changing irreversibly: a country that had until recently been agricultural became an industrial and services-based nation (Pellegrini 2003, 201).

The economic expansion and the development of the advanced technology sector were initially led by an unprecedented growth in domestic demand. This was particularly the case for durable goods (goods spanning a wide area, from houses to automobiles, to household electrical appliances), which could be bought by workers whose salary had actually increased. Mass production and new kinds of retail stores were becoming more common in Italy, as were mass consumption and a US style of behavior (Djelic 1998; Berta 1998; Galimberti and Paolazzi 1998; Scarpellini 2001).

From 1958 onward, exports also started to play an important role. Italy became increasingly integrated into the international and in particular the European economy (Fauri 2006). As a result, sales of more sophisticated and higher added-value end products abroad increased, and the total number of worldwide Italian exports grew between 1950 and 1970 (Zamagni 1990, 465). The distance that separated Italy from the most advanced European nations, such as the United Kingdom, Germany and France, was gradually narrowing, and Italy could finally be considered as an advanced nation within the world economy, thanks to the excellent results of some of its sectors and companies and to the general positive performance of its economic system on the whole.

Such rapid growth was quite surprising to the world's most advanced nations and to the Italian people, who used to think that Italy could rely on its beautiful landscape and agricultural wealth but not on any industrial capabilities or resources. Nevertheless, the Americanization and the enrichment of the country during this so-called economic miracle were evident to everybody. At the end of the 1950s, an Italian entrepreneur told to a journalist a nice short story about the "theory on hornets." According to this theory, all the scholars of natural sciences studying the anatomy of the hornet unanimously agreed on the fact that this insect should not be able to fly. It is too heavy, and its wings are too small and weak. Nevertheless, contradicting all these international scholars, the hornet flies. The same, according to the entrepreneur, was happening with Italian capitalism (Galimberti and Paolazzi 1998, 1).

In spite of this, the Italian economic miracle was not without its weaknesses and distortions. In 1963, the rate of growth plateaued for the first time. In addition, during the 1960s, something that would go on to characterize the economic development of the country for a long time started to emerge: severe tensions between capital and work. The autumn of 1969 went down in history as the Autunno Caldo (Hot Autumn) owing to a series of massive strikes in the factories of Northern Italy. A strengthening of the unions, which emerged out of the continuous strikes and boycotts of the production lines, allowed workers to reach important achievements, such as the endorsement of the Workers' Statute in 1970. This movement seriously compromised one of the main strengths of Italy's companies, namely, their cheap labor. In spite of this, the unions were not able to ease the social tension that culminated in extreme outbursts of violence as terrorist organizations spread in the following decade (Colajanni 1990; Accornero 1992; Turone 1992).

In addition, Italy's economic growth did not solve the problem of the gap between the north and the south of the country. The government implemented a series of measures in an attempt to address this issue. In a wide-ranging plan for the development of the Mezzogiorno region (the southern part of Italy), which was mainly based on private initiatives, the state established a specific financial state-owned institution (Cassa per il Mezzogiorno), subsidized companies with free grants and allowed tax breaks. Even though this area did develop further, these measures together with other economic policies, revealed themselves not to be particularly effective even in the short term. On one hand, several large factories were built in an area that was not ready for them yet, given their lack of infrastructure. Their size and isolation made these plants similar to real "cathedrals in the desert." On the other hand, instead of furthering development and creating employment opportunities, over investment in the area brought about an excess of productive capacity while demand experienced a slowdown, in a context of rising inflation and, following the oil crisis of 1973, increases in the prices of energy and raw materials.

Large corporations were fundamental protagonists of economic growth and social development while, at the same time, their behavior was strongly influenced by the new environment created by the economic miracle.

For the first time, big business was really brought to the fore. Even though some attempts at implementing mass production systems had been made earlier (Berta 1998), it was only during this period that large US-inspired plants became effective and that the domestic market became able to deal with this kind and quantity of goods. The idea that, in order to grow, it was necessary to "do like it in the USA" was evident in behavior of the country's largest companies. The money coming from the Marshall Plan was used to build modern and large-scale plants that made it possible to significantly reduce per-unit costs and to reach the local market. Private and state-owned companies grew together in this context. In a country whose people were increasing their purchasing power and starting to buy motor vehicles, state-owned companies produced cheap steel (Finsider), built highways (Autostrade) and dealt with oil production and distribution (ENI), while private companies produced tires (Pirelli) and cars and motorcycles affordable for the local market (FIAT and Piaggio).

Looking at how the state, the financial system, private entrepreneurs and foreign investors influenced the behavior of big business, it is possible to identify some discontinuities in the roles played by the latter two, while the government and the banks did not change their attitude to a great extent. The years of industrial growth were characterized by a quite concentrated kind of capitalism. As in the past, strong state intervention meant that only a very small number of parties controlled the most advanced industries and the largest parts of big business. Nevertheless, in an era of enrichment and new opportunities, the "cake" was becoming bigger and bigger. It was thus possible for new actors to enter the scene and get a slice of this larger cake. New participants, such as foreign multinationals and relatively young entrepreneurs, found their place within national capitalism and in the big business panorama.

State interventionism was one of the most characteristic elements of Western regimes after World War II and represents a common backdrop to the economic miracles that were happening all over Europe. During the golden age, state intervention did not diminish in Italy. On the contrary, the number of state-owned companies increased and the government's aim to control the economy persisted and in some cases even strengthened. In 1953, a state-owned holding in the oil and energy sector—ENI—was established. The government also created a holding in mining (EGAM) in 1958, and a few years later, in 1962, another financial holding (EFIM), which diversified from its core sector of heavy machinery into aluminum, glass and food. In the same year, the energy sector was nationalized and ENEL, a new state-owned company, was born. The Ministry of State Shareholdings was established in 1956. A precise chain of command was established: political parties controlled the public holdings, which in turn controlled the majority percentage of shares of their sector subholdings, which in turn controlled the operating companies. Political parties started to heavily influence the strategies adopted by companies, providing them with an endowment fund but at the same time obliging them to operate on criteria based on social rather than economic criteria (Amatori 2000; Toninelli and Vasta 2010). One famous example of this behavior is the enactment of laws that compelled public bodies and state-owned companies to allocate 60% of their investment budget to Southern Italy.

The direct power that the state could exert over such important companies was dangerous given the quite peculiar Italian political context. Even though the country had a stable democratic regime, there was no possibility of changes in power occurring because the major opposition force to the dominant Italian party—the Christian Democrats—was the Communist Party. Due to the escalation of the cold war and given the strategic position of Italy, communists could not be allowed to govern the country.

In terms of continuities, it should also be stressed that no strong disruptions to the financial system with which large corporations had to deal can be detected. The stock exchange continued to be a mysterious place where savers generally did not like to buy industrial shares. There are several reasons for this. The monetary policies of those years directed savers to the massive underwriting of state bonds (Cotula 1989; Conte and Piluso 2010), while those who decided to invest in industrial company shares very often had incurred serious losses, because of a lack of transparency and because the strategic decisions made by the top management of the largest companies almost always went against the interests of their minority shareholders (Amatori and Brioschi 1997). The companies themselves very often adopted relatively sophisticated tools to raise capital without losing control of their firms, such as pyramid structures. At the same time, the whole market was relatively static and the low levels of regulation of the Italian stock market contributed to discouraging listing, mainly at a fiscal level (Pagano, Panetta and Zingales 1996; Siciliano 2001). In 1970, the economist Enrico Filippi (1970, 17) observed that

> In Italy shares are not considered as a normal and fundamental tool to finance the company, but mainly (or better, uniquely) as a tool of control. Due to this fact, they must not circulate, and their number must not increase.

The system remained predominantly bank-oriented, and the Italian financial system was quite peculiar, considering that the three major banks—Banca

Commerciale Italiana, Credito Italiano and Banco di Roma—were state-owned financial institutions that were devoted only to short-term loans and were prevented by law from owning large numbers of shares in companies. The only bank that was starting to intervene in corporate activity was Mediobanca, an institution that was founded in 1946 and that, together with the three previously mentioned banks, was destined to become very influential in particular during the 1970s (Piluso 2005).

The golden age represents a period of great opportunity, which made it possible for new families to emerge and conquer the higher levels of capitalism. Mass consumption was gradually spreading and the variety of goods that were affordable for families increased every year. The emergence of business opportunities in new products, or in existing products that were affordable for the majority of the population for the first time, allowed a number of brilliant entrepreneurs to find very profitable business areas, and to establish new companies that would be counted among the country's largest within a few years. During the economic miracle new big family-owned businesses emerged, or grew in size for the first time. This was the case for instance for Industrie Zanussi, Merloni, Indesit and Zoppas in the electrical appliances; for API, SARAS and Erg in the oil sector; of Galbani, Barilla, Industrie Buitoni Perugina, Ferrero, Carapelli and Locatelli in foodstuffs; Arnoldo Mondadori Editore and Rizzoli Editore in publishing; Supermercati Pam and Esselunga in supermarkets; Gruppo Finanziario Tessile and Manifattura Lane Marzotto in clothing; and Italcementi in cement and construction materials.

New opportunities also attracted foreign investors, who could simultaneously complement and compete with the local large corporations and who partly changed the dynamics of competition for Italian big business. In 1956, new laws were enacted with the aim of making it easier for foreign investors to invest as well as to disinvest in the country (Colli 2010, 102). In particular, from the 1960s onward, direct foreign investment was moreover considered as a fundamental source of support for the development of the country and as an important tool for balancing the discrepancy between the north and south of the peninsula. The general climate was favorable for foreign investors, and an explicit legislative effort was made in order to stimulate the inflow of foreign capital. The efforts made to change fiscal legislation represent perhaps one of the most obvious examples of this (Del Buttero 1946; Colli 2010).

2.3 THE FAILED LANDING (1973–1988)

Despite the impressive achievements of the economic miracle era, some structural weaknesses of the Italian economy that had not been addressed made it more difficult for companies and in particular for large corporations, to adequately respond to the oil shocks and the economic crisis that spread across the world during the 1970s. The collapse of the Bretton Woods system, the first oil shock in 1973 and the subsequent recession that lasted for the rest of the decade represent a very important watershed in Italian as well as worldwide history. The cost of energy increased wildly, while big business, which had been growing for at least two decades in tandem with the development of the national economy and of domestic demand, saw a dramatic slowdown of the market and an increase in competition, causing their profits to suddenly drop. To make matters worse, economic recession was accompanied by high levels of inflation. Political unrest began to spread across Italy, marking the beginning of a period of domestic terrorism, which in part affected the already severe industrial tension (Berta 1998).

This period was a tough one for Italy in several ways. The state-owned shareholding system was the first victim. The expansion of productive capacity, which had been carried out with little regard for market conditions, as well as the dislocation of the most advanced plants in the southern part of the nation, made the financial situation of IRI more and more difficult in an increasing number of industries. Against a backdrop of a continuous and exponential rise in the cost of energy, growing rigidity in the labor market, worsening of social unrest, and the persistent weakness of the financial markets, companies were no longer able to sustain the increasingly expensive social investment obligations imposed on them by the up to that point. In 1977, the deficit of the state-owned companies, subventions excepted, was more than 6 trillion Italian lire (Castronovo 1980, 317).

Private companies fared no better. The increasing price of energy and the slowdown of demand in a market that had become more and more mature made it very difficult for large corporations to survive and remain competitive. To make matters worse, this turmoil occurred while a new generation of entrepreneurs and managers were coming to power. They were the sons of the protagonists of the Italian economic miracle, but very often they had not inherited the necessary experience, and in some cases, the same capabilities, from their fathers. Nevertheless, they still had to operate in an environment that had become much more difficult and hostile than that of the 1950s and the 1960s.

As the large corporations found themselves in deep crisis and the big industrial sectors typical of the Second Industrial Revolution matured, two new and important developments took place. The first one was the reconsideration of small and medium-sized companies as a potential way for the country to gain a competitive advantage over others. The second was a wave of restructuring of the Italian state-owned and big privately owned groups, which coincided with the creation of new rules and a new institutional context for the economy.

Small companies, either on their own or grouped together in local systems of production or industrial districts, are an enduring feature of the Italian economy and represent a "Carsic river" in the history of the country, which was able to spread capabilities in different sectors (Colli 2002a, 2002b; Carnevali 2005). Industrial districts based on small enterprises could be found in almost every region of the country throughout the twentieth century. These businesses had an initial strong link with agricultural production, which diminished over time (Perugini and Romei 2010). The economic miracle of the country was led mainly by big manufacturing corporations that operated in capital and scale-intensive sectors that were not suitable for small and medium-sized enterprises. Very few people have underlined the existence and the importance of this kind of company up to the 1970s, when the crisis experienced by big business made the role of small and medium-sized enterprises increasingly decisive.

It was in this period that small firms and industrial districts became more apparent, and the more extensively investigated. The findings published by Giacomo Becattini and other respected Italian scholars on industrial districts in Italy reached all corners of the world, inspiring similar studies (Becattini 1989, 1998, 2000) during the 1980s and 1990s. The business scholar Michael Porter argued that the competitive advantage of Italy clearly lay in its small companies (Porter 1990). Small enterprises as well as those medium-sized companies typical of the "Made in Italy" movement gradually became the new heroes of the country, even more so when compared to the large corporations that appeared unwieldy and obsolete (Bagnasco 1977; Fuà and Zacchia 1983; Porter 1990; Brusco and Paba 1997; Bellandi 1999). Companies with few employees formed the backbone of Italy during the crisis of the 1970s. Between 1971 and 1981, the percentage of the total Italian workforce employed in companies with more than 500 workers dropped from 31% to 23%, whereas the percentage of the Italian workforce employed in companies with fewer than 100 workers increased to 60% (Amatori and Colli 1999, 316).

The turmoil caused by the oil crisis also forced several big businesses to change their strategies and structures. The restructuring of the largest public and private groups over the second part of the 1970s and the early 1980s was quite a complex process, and it was characterized in particular by a partial refocusing strategy of some of the largest groups based on sell-offs (e.g. Fornengo and Silva 1993).

The need to rescue the large corporations which until that moment had been the pillars of the national economy, the international spread of an increasingly liberal point of view and, a few years later, the strengthening of the process of European integration, represented fundamental incentives for renewing the Italian economic system and to formulate new rules. In 1983, a new law on common funds was enacted with the aim of modernizing national capitalism and introducing new aspects such as pension funds. The new legislation on institutional investors favored, during the 1980s, a considerable effervescence of the stock market. However, many laws on antitrust, corporate governance and protection for minority shareholders had not been enacted yet. Neither during the golden age nor throughout the crisis period was the government particularly concerned with creating a legal framework in which big business could prosper in a sensible manner.

Many business groups thus benefited from these favorable conditions in the financial market, simply extending their leverage through a multiple listing of former divisions or business areas (Brioschi, Buzzacchi and Colombo 1990). The result of this process was an increase in the overall number of listed companies but also in the use of control-enhancing mechanisms through which owners exerted their control, such as pyramid structures, cross-shareholdings, voting agreements and nonvoting privileged shares. As a consequence, the control structure of the largest companies remained virtually intact (Amatori and Brioschi 1997).

Scholars argued about a "failed landing" of the Italian economy (Pirani 1991), meaning that if more stable political and institutional conditions had been provided, Italy would have been able to get a front-row position in international competition. But something went wrong and, during this era, many factors contributed to the country's failure to achieve this goal. High-tech projects in electronics and nuclear energy failed. The state as an entrepreneur degenerated. Mature sectors such as the chemical industry were not able to exploit their resources and wasted enormous amounts of money. The historical "big families" of Italian capitalism were able to manage neither the hand-over from one generation to the next nor the upheavals of the market while the battle between industrialists and workers became increasingly fervent (Soria 1979; De Biase and Borsa 1992; Salvati 2000; Gallino 2003; Amatori 2008).

By the beginning of the 1980s, the effects of the economic crisis seemed to have definitively shaped the destiny of big business in Italy. Nevertheless, against a backdrop of modernizing financial systems, the government, private entrepreneurs and foreign companies lay the basis for a metamorphosis, rather than simply a decline, of large corporations.

As has been mentioned earlier, state-owned companies were facing their darkest hour. The social contributions that politicians from the Ministry of State Shareholdings had asked the state holdings to make had severely affected their performance. Moreover, the energy and market crises of the 1970s had a negative impact on precisely those industries where national, public companies were stronger and more present. One interesting example is found in the state-owned holding Finsider, a steel company that acted as one of the main protagonists of the Italian economic miracles. During the second half of the 1950s, Finsider's top management decided to construct a big steel plant in Taranto, in the south of the country. It would have been possible to respond to the increasing demand for steel in Italy by simply increasing the size of existing plants. Yet, in order to support the policy of development for the Mezzogiorno area, Finsider chose Taranto as its industrial location. The need to provide more employment opportunities, and consequently reach a political consensus, brought about an enormous expansion of the production capacity of this plant. However, when the demand for steel dropped during the 1970s, this excess capacity became evident, resulting in a disastrous economic situation (Osti and Ranieri 1993;

Pini 2000). The goal of reaching a political consensus had prevailed over market results in many other state-owned enterprises.

Large private companies were facing very difficult industrial relations and a general drop in demand. Moreover, as has been mentioned, most of them were family-run businesses that were experiencing the difficult shift from one generation to the next exactly during the 1970s. Very often, the old generation was not able to adapt to the new, unfavorable climate after decades of golden age. At the same time, their successors were often lacking in the managerial capabilities that should had allowed them to help their companies survive (Cingolani 1990). Only a relatively small number of big businesses were able to emerge from this period unscathed and achieve success, as will be discussed below (Colli 2002a, chap. 2).

The precarious position in which large private businesses found themselves also changed the relationship between companies and the financial system. Difficulties in obtaining enough money to self-finance their growth, as had been possible during the economic miracle, made private firms more dependent on the banks. Mediobanca, the investment bank founded after World War II, started to extend its influence and intervene more in the most important decisions made by the largest private companies, which had significant consequences for Italian capitalism. The head of the bank, Enrico Cuccia, strongly believed in the role of families as owners and managers of companies (Colajanni 1990). He thus tended to "freeze" large quotas of a firm's shares and to organize syndicates of control in a period when recession and globalization called for the mobilization of the maximum amount of resources available. It was only during the 1980s that new rules started to be enacted and the stock exchange could improve its role, even though investors continued to be penalized while these rules were in the process of being drawn up.

Finally, the combination of negative events during this period affected the morphogenesis and features of large corporations in Italy, because it had a large impact on the flow of direct foreign investment. A period of violent political unrest that started during the 1970s, added to the poor industrial relations in the plants and the general economic crisis, made it very difficult for foreign companies to operate in the country and discouraged foreigners from entering, causing a real reduction in the total amount of direct foreign investment in Italy with further negative effects (Scalfari 2008, 83–85).

2.4 EVERYTHING MUST CHANGE IN ORDER TO REMAIN THE SAME? (1988–2002)

As was the case in almost all over the world, the end of the 1980s and the two decades around the turn of the millennium witnessed the end of the old equilibrium and the emergence of an almost completely new perspective in Italy.

The last two decades were particularly eventful and turbulent for the Italian economy. The political forces that had dominated since the end of World

War II were dismantled in the wake of several big scandals. Crucial reforms have been implemented, and at present, new rules seem to regulate business activity. In spite of this, the Italian economy is losing ground from a historical perspective, and the feeling is that old habits die hard in this country. The circumstances in which large corporations had until recently operated could therefore only be "new" on a superficial level. The common opinion in the country is summed up succinctly by a phrase used by the protagonist of the famous Italian historical novel *Il Gattopardo* by Giuseppe Tomasi di Lampedusa: "everything must change in order to remain the same." Despite the seemingly new features of Italian capitalism, protagonists and habits may not be too different from those of the past.

In terms of both domestic and international events, 1992 represents a very important year. This was the year when the Mafia asserted its power over the Italian state by murdering Giovanni Falcone and Paolo Borsellino, two magistrates who had been trying to break its stranglehold on Sicily. However, 1992 was also the year when a new era in Italian economic and political life started, following the judicial inquiry known as Mani Pulite (Clean Hands). It brought to light what would be called Tangentopoli (Bribesville): a system of bribery, corruption and illegal financing of political parties at the highest levels of the Italian financial and political spheres (e.g., Di Pietro and Valentini 2001). Ministers, former prime ministers, members of parliament and entrepreneurs were involved. Mani Pulite transformed the Italian political scene. The party that had governed Italy since the postwar era, the Christian Democrat Party (Democrazia Cristiana), and other major political forces, such as the Italian Socialist Party (Partito Socialista Italiano), the Italian Social Democratic Party (Partito Socialista Democratico Italiano) and the Italian Liberal Party (Partito Liberale Italiano) disappeared or were completely downsized and reorganized.

Despite the fact that the beginning of a "Second Republic" was claimed, continuities with the old political system also remained strong (Martinelli and Chiesi 2002). The elections in 1994 were won by a new party established by the entrepreneur Silvio Berlusconi, Forza Italia (Go Italy!) (Molteni 1998; Fiori 2006). However, severe tensions with the Northern League (Lega Nord), a recently founded federalist and regional political party and Forza Italia's main ally, brought about new elections in 1996 that were won by the center-left coalition L'Ulivo (The Olive Tree), headed by the politician, economist and former IRI president Romano Prodi. Democratic Italy underwent real changes in power for the first time since the end of World War II: center-left coalitions remained in power between 1996 and 2001 and between 2006 and 2008, whereas center-right coalitions governed between 2001 and 2006 and between 2008 and 2011. Nevertheless, the Italian political system has remained quite weak and unstable if compared to other European democracies. The anger at and the lack of confidence in Italian politics were and still is very high among the country's citizens. Against this backdrop of domestic turbulence, 1992 finally represents a watershed also in terms of Italian involvement in European integration dynamics, as the Treaty of Maastricht was finally signed that year.

The performance of the Italian economy was not that bad during the 1980s and its GDP had grown. However, unemployment increased, there was a significant foreign trade imbalance, and the public deficit reached unsustainable levels. The ratio between public debt and gross national product reached 1.11 in 1992 (Graziani 1998) and in 1993 the gross national product rate of growth was negative (Balcet 1997, 85–86). Compliance with the Maastricht standards already had positive effects in the medium term. The state had to recover its debts and to reduce its direct economic intervention, and, at the same time, to create a new legal and institutional framework that would have been potentially more conducive to the growth of companies and big business in a market economy. However, adapting to the Maastricht parameters was a very tough task for Italy, which faced one of the most serious financial crises in its history at the beginning of the 1990s.

Moreover, during this period the problems experienced by the state-owned enterprises system reached their peak. In 1993, the losses incurred by IRI reached about 30 billion euros, which caused a large shift in public opinion against the state shareholdings. These came to be associated with inefficiency and waste and were largely held responsible for the country's financial crisis (Cavazzuti 1996; Barca and Trento 1997; Amatori 2000).

An intense privatization process, which lasted almost the whole decade and dismantled most of the previously pervasive system of state ownership, took place (Affinito, De Cecco and Dringoli 2000). In fewer than ten years, the Italian Treasury sold assets worth over a 100,000 billion Italian lire in public utilities, manufacturing and banks and insurance.

Both in response to the new European context, and to make the process of privatization that was considered fundamental at the end of the 1980s possible, a large-scale transformation of the architecture of the financial markets was necessary, as was the introduction of a better regulation of the stock exchange. All of this implied an improvement in the corporate governance standards of large companies. Created in 1974, the stock exchange regulatory agency Consob started to be effective from the mid-1980s. At the beginning of 1998, another legal milestone, the new legislative decree known as Legge Draghi (Draghi Laws), was enacted. It represents a real reform of Italian corporate law and was motivated by the need to expand the national stock market by creating new regulations and increasing the transparency both for institutional and individual investors. The aim of the bill was to increase the protection of minority shareholders by generally improving disclosure, by means of a restrictive regulation of shareholder agreements and of takeover bids (Associazione Disiano Preite 1997; Belvedere et al. 2000).

New rules as well as the privatization, and restructuring of large corporations were transforming the big business panorama, while many small companies grew. According to Giuseppe Turani, a "fourth capitalism" started to spread in the country. Following a first capitalism, which had characterized Italy at the beginning of its industrialization and mainly involved big private companies; a second capitalism characterized by the "State Entrepreneur" from the 1930s onward; and a third capitalism involving small companies and industrial districts during the 1960s and 1970s, the fourth capitalism has spread in Italy since the 1980s and includes the companies that are currently more successful. They are medium-sized and strongly internationalized firms, most of which are family-run and that emerged in industrial districts in quite traditional sectors (Turani 1996; Colli 2002a). "Small is beautiful" argued Ernest F. Schumacher in his famous book from 1973. According to two Italian economic journalists who wrote at the end of the 1990s, in Italy "small, but also big is beautiful" (Galimberti and Paolazzi 1998).

However, these achievements have been continuously undermined both by a number of structural social and economic weaknesses of Italy itself (Altan 2000) and by the strengthening of international integration. Notwithstanding the emergence of several new national champions and their positive economic performance, on balance the results of the 1990s and the first few years of the twenty-first century were not that good for Italy, and the economic performance of the whole nation from an international perspective has been declining slightly since then. The country's competitiveness in many capital-intensive industries declined, whereas the process of globalization and heightened competition from the newly industrializing countries seriously affected that area of the Italian economy that was based on small firms in labor-intensive and specialized industries (Faini 2003; Gallino 2003; Toniolo and Visco 2004; Berta 2007).

Focusing on the impact of this turbulent period on the dynamics of big business, it should be stressed that increased European integration, together with the new rules on competition, the transformation of product and financial markets and the impressively large-scale process of privatization, affected the characteristics and behavior of large corporations.

The role of the state, which gradually lost its central position in relation to the ownership and aims of big business represents a major change during these years. The government lost its control over trade protection, over the decisions relating the competitive structure of some strategic sectors and over other policies that influenced the behavior of enterprises, all of which have been transferred to an increasing degree to common central institutions as part of the process of European integration. This factor significantly affected the strategic choices not only of the state-owned firms, but also of the private enterprises that had often based their economic decisions mainly on state support and protection. In the infrastructure industries, such as telecommunications, energy and transportation, the business structure changed from one of dominance by state monopolies toward competition between large, often multinational, listed corporations. In those years, *privatization* and *liberalization* were the key words in Italy as well as across Europe and most of the rest of the world.

Between 1985 and 2008, the amount of proceeds generated by the Italian process of privatization exceeded 152 billion euros, corresponding to more than 114 operations (Privatization Barometer 2005). The extent of the privatization process in Italy significantly changed the panorama of big business in the country (Macchiati 1999; Siniscalco et al. 1999; De Nardis 2000; Mediobanca Ricerche e Studi 2001; Goldstein 2006; Barucci and Pierobon 2007, 2010). State ownership disappeared in many sectors and was markedly reduced in many other ones. Nevertheless, it has to be stressed that during the privatization process the government very often showed a reluctant attitude toward selling companies, and maintained its control over corporate activities through direct ownership or in indirect ways for a long time to come (Bortolotti and Faccio 2004). In many cases, the state retained control through golden shares, privileged shares, voting caps, or through measures taken by regulatory institutions, or in other indirect or informal ways (Nardozzi 2011). In 2002 the state still directly owned and controlled some of the most important and largest companies in Italy, such as ENI in the oil sector, ENEL in electricity and Finmeccanica in aeronautics and defense. Even though the government's direct intervention and ownership vanished from many sectors and was significantly reduced in several others, the state in Italy continues to remain an important entrepreneur.

Another important contextual factor that affected the dynamics of big business was the relatively fast transition from a system based on financing by banks toward a system where the stock exchange played a more dominant role in financing business expansion. The previously mentioned new laws that regulated it, the restructuring process of many large corporations that began during the 1980s and the privatization through IPOs of several of the largest companies gave the stock exchange a brand-new effervescence and made its role increasingly central. The trend of new listings on the Milan Stock Exchange grew considerably from 1994 onward (Perrini 1999, 127). However, the banks did not lose their importance and remained central actors within the Italian system. At the same time, many rules were still not in force by the beginning of the new millennium, while the privatization process of the public sector seems to have failed in its intent to create public companies.

Finally, increased economic integration, particularly after the breakthrough achieved with the creation of the European Single Market in the early 1990s, had important consequences in terms of the pattern and size of international trade and investment in Italy (Fligstein and Merand 2002; Carli 2008), and thus also for entrepreneurial behavior and for the big business dynamics in this country.

These new circumstances offered great opportunities for the old protagonists of the Italian economy. The restructuring process of large corporations, the privatization of state-owned companies, the new international dynamics and the changes in the role of the financial system could have made this nation's capitalism less concentrated and more "democratic" also at the big business level. However, the number of completely "new" companies has been relatively small. Most of the companies that currently dominate Italian capitalism are relatively "old" companies that have gone through one or more phases of restructuring, merging and acquisition and that in some cases have changed their ownership structure, passing from state to private ownership. In this context, it should also be stressed that the process of democratization of the ownership of big business did not take off. Very few firms succeeded in becoming public companies, and most of the former state-owned companies in Italy are actually owned by a small number of important block-holders who are not new at all to the Italian system of high capitalism. Families such as the Rivas, who took ownership of the state-owned steel giant Finsider, or the Benettons, who diversified from clothing into controlling the previously state-owned companies in motorways and restaurants (Favero 2005; Tattara and Crestanello 2008), greatly benefited from the privatization process.

3 Changing Fortunes for Spanish Big Business?

3.1 FRANCO'S DICTATORSHIP AMONG OLD AND NEW PROBLEMS (1939–1950)

While Italy during the mid-twentieth century was moving from Benito Mussolini's dictatorship to a democratic regime, the outcomes of the Civil War transformed the Spanish *República* into a dictatorship. From 1939 onward, the new leader Francisco Franco, also known as Generalísimo or Caudillo de España, adopted new economic policies that greatly affected the management and behavior of big business. His main aim was to further the development of a country that was facing at least three very serious problems.

The first is that, at the time, Spain was one of the most backward economies in Europe. During the late nineteenth and early twentieth centuries, a certain push toward consolidating the industrialization process took place and big companies were established (Carreras and Tafunell 1994). Nevertheless, the industrial activity of the country remained small scale and strongly localized in a few regions, such as Catalonia and the Basque Country (Nadal, Carreras and Carmona Badía 1990; García Ruiz and Manera Erbina 2006). The loss of the American colonies at the end of the nineteenth century and severe political turbulence (republican regimes, monarchies and dictatorships rotated several times within a few decades) formed the background to a relatively slow process of industrial growth that never resulted in a real consolidation of industry as the driving force of the national economy (Nadal 1975). In 1940, only 21.03% of GDP came from industry and only 16.97% of the total working population was employed in manufacturing activities (Carreras 2005, 360).

The second, very serious problem relates to the extensive human and physical capital losses caused by the three-year-long civil war. Taking into account the number of people who died during the war itself and the retaliations that followed, as well as the number of political prisoners and forced expatriations under Franco, the Civil War and its aftermath destroyed or damaged huge swathes of the country's infrastructure and industrial resources (Malefakis 1987; Fusi and Palafox 1997, 327–332).

Last but not least, Franco came to power in a country that had been allied with the Axis powers during World War II. Even though Spain had not officially taken part in the conflict, in 1946, the United Nations approved a measure of diplomatic isolation against it. The country was not completely isolated during the 1940s (Guirao 1998), but it was only from the early 1950s, due to the intensifying of the cold war, that Spain started to gradually be reintegrated into the international community. It was no longer seen as an enemy of a past war, but as a potential ally in the current conflict against the USSR.

The period between the end of the Civil War and 1949, generally known in the literature as the first decade of Autarquía, was characterized by an almost complete closure to foreign trade and by the attempt made by the Francoist government to further the country's development and industrialization on its own. The aims of the policies implemented during this first phase were to catch up with the other industrialized nations and to get out of grinding poverty without importing aid, material goods, raw materials or knowledge from abroad (Ballestero 1993).

According to the Francoist economic policies, the recipe for the growth consisted basically of a large-scale process of public investment in the industrial sector, the active promotion of private initiatives through fiscal incentives, strict regulation of labor relations and the proliferation of controls on prices and currency, together with a significant overevaluation of the exchange rate.

In 1941, in an explicit imitation of the Italian model of the "State Entrepreneur," the Instituto Nacional de Industria (INI) was founded (Gómez Mendoza 2000). Just like the Italian IRI, INI was a holding that directly owned large corporations in sectors typical of big business. Nevertheless, unlike IRI, in its first years, INI started to directly establish companies. Since its inception, INI aimed to play a very active role in promoting the growth, development and industrialization process of the nation by acting in "strategic" sectors, as per its founding law:

> The imperatives of national defense demand . . . the creation of new companies and the multiplications of the ones which already exist . . . It is thus necessary to create an organism which, having its own legal status and economic capability, could give shape and accomplishment to the big programs of industrial resurgence of our country. . . . This will make possible for the State to collect and canalize savings, making them real contributions to the country's economy according to the political principles of our *Movimiento*. (Boyer 1975, 97)

Historians are almost unanimous in claiming that, in spite of the state's "good intentions," the results of the policies of this period were unsatisfactory from an economic perspective. Autarkic regulations brought about serious production imbalances, the black market flourished in several industries, the mechanism for resources allocation was seriously flawed and the technological level of the nation, which was already completely inadequate, further regressed (Barciela López 2003).

By 1950, Spain had not only failed to lift itself out of severe poverty, but it had also worsened its circumstances by adding more delay to its already significant backwardness compared to the most advanced European nations (Carreras 1993; Miranda Encarnación 2003).

In this context, Spanish big businesses adopted some of the features that would go on to define them in the long term. Despite the delay in the process of industrialization, a number of large corporations did already exist on the eve of the Civil War. Most of them were created in the mid-nineteenth century (e.g., Río Tinto in mining), or around the turn of the twentieth century (e.g., Sevillana de Electricidad, Iberduero and Hidroeléctrica Española in electricity, Unión Española de Explosivos and Cros in chemicals and Altos Hornos de Vizcaya and Duro Felguera in metals). However, it was only during the 1940s that the big business panorama in Spain was close to being fully formed and that new companies in modern industries were founded. The new regime thought that the creation of large enterprises in strategic sectors would allow Spain to catch up with the most advanced nations in the world. It therefore directly established large, state-owned companies such as Empresa Nacional Calvo Sotelo in the oil sector, Empresa Nacional del Aluminio and Empresa Nacional Siderúrgica Sociedad Anónima in metals and steel, Empresa Nacional de Electricidad Sociedad Anónima and Empresa Nacional Hidroeléctrica del Ribagorzana in electricity and Empresa Nacional de Autocamiones and Sociedad Española de Automóviles de Turismo (SEAT) in the automotive and trucking sector (Carreras and Tafunell 1997).

When looking at the big business panorama in 1950, it is clear that a number of corporations that belonged to the same sectors as in the most advanced economies were already present in Spain. However, as was the case in Italy, the Spanish corporate system was substantially different from that of the United States, Germany, Britain and France, above all due to the role played by the state. If direct state intervention in the economy had remained relatively marginal during the late nineteenth and early twentieth centuries, things completely changed after Franco's rise to power. The conviction that market dynamics and private initiatives were not adequate on their own to meet the needs of the country led the Francoist government to consistently intervene in the economy, both through direct ownership and by enacting laws that regulated or influenced the behavior of privately owned big business. In 1939, new laws were approved, namely, the Ley de Protección de las Nuevas Industrias de Interés Nacional and Ley de Ordenación y Defensa de la Industria.

The former was aimed at providing incentives for private companies in industries that were considered strategic or that could help in avoiding imports. Companies active in these sectors received fiscal incentives and were subject to lower duties on imports of machinery from abroad. The purpose of the second law was indeed to directly control and regulate economic activity in the country, stating that an authorization from the Ministry of Industry was required to start a new company or to remove or expand an old one (Miranda 2003). It also discouraged foreign investment in the country, with the purpose of helping and protecting national industry. According to the new rules, foreigners could not own more than 25% of the share capital of a company in Spain, and any major decisions had to be made by Spanish investors. The state nationalized many foreign companies, or pushed for their naturalization, or made life impossible for them. As a result, foreign companies, together with their money, technology and know-how, significantly reduced their presence in the country (Álvaro Moya 2010).

In the mid-twentieth century, the Spanish economy was thus developing on the basis of a "state-driven" capitalism. The government founded and owned the major companies, helped and protected national companies by expelling foreign competitors, set the rules of the game and strictly regulated and controlled private capitalism.

Large private corporations did exist in Spain during this period. However, in contrast to Italy, Spanish private capitalism did not essentially coincide with family-run business. Despite the existence and longevity of some very important family-run business groups such those of the Ybarra, Aznar, Marqueses de Comillas and Gil families (Rodrigo Alharilla 2000, 2010; Díaz Morlán 2002; Valdaliso Gago 2006), the significance of the role of banks as shareholders of the largest firms in the country cannot be neglected. Whereas the role of the stock exchange was relatively marginal, the banks followed the German universal model and were simultaneously an important source of funding for private companies as well as one of their largest shareholders. The ownership of the banks has been an important factor since the beginning of the Spanish process of industrialization. Nevertheless, during this period, state intervention was once again key to determining the economic balance of the country. In 1941, the nationalization of railways, which were predominantly bank owned, resulted in a vast amount of money being paid to financial institutions as compensations. Banks quite suddenly obtained very high liquidity and started to buy large amounts of industrial shares (Carreras 2003). Due to a shortage in investment opportunities, the biggest banks of the country focused their attention on a relatively small number of large companies, creating a very concentrated kind of capitalism (Muñoz 1969). Perhaps even more than that of Italy, the Spanish capitalist system was thus "political" and "concentrated"; the state, together with a very small number of banks and families, owned and controlled the largest companies in the country and directed big business behavior in a strictly regulated context, while being almost complete free from foreign competition.

3.2 FROM AUTARKY TO THE BIG SPURT OF THE SPANISH ECONOMY (1950–1973)

Even though the pace of growth was slow and unsteady until the autarkic period came to an end in the late 1950s, the golden age represents a period of sharp growth for the Spanish economy and its large corporations.

The first noteworthy event took place as early as 1950, when the intensifying cold war made it necessary for the United States and the other European countries to turn Spain into an ally. Spain's past as a former friend of the Axis powers was set aside, and a process of integration of the country into the international community within the Western Bloc slowly began. The isolation of Spain officially ended in 1953, when US president Dwight D. Eisenhower went to Spain and signed the Pact of Madrid with Francisco Franco. According to this agreement, the Generalísimo allowed the installation of US air and naval military bases on Spanish territory. The United States, in turn, committed to providing Spain with financial aid. Thanks to this money and to the new, more relaxed climate, advanced and effective foreign technologies and knowledge gradually started to come back to the country (Catalan 2003).

At the same time, it was becoming evident that the autarkic policies had weakened the population and that the state's policies were very far from having satisfactory results. Some fundamental material and immaterial requirements for industrialization were partly or completely missing, and there was no way of obtaining them without having some kind of exchange with other countries. Franco had to abandon the idea of furthering the Spanish industrialization process in a rigid and totally autarkic environment. He therefore started a phase of import substitution policies that were more permissive and flexible in terms of the import of capital goods than previously (Carreras and Tafunell 2003).

The opportunity to access supplies of raw materials, energy sources, and above all technologies from abroad helped kick-start growth after the long stagnation of the 1940s. Between 1950 and 1960, the annual rate of growth of Spanish industrial production was of 6.7% whereas in the rest of Western Europe, it was 5.9% on average (Carreras 1993).

Nevertheless, the path to growth was not always smooth. First of all, the persisting autarkic framework prevented Spain from taking advantage of the opportunities resulting from increased European integration in the same way as other countries were able to during this period (Carreras 1993). Secondly, the lack of competitiveness of the Spanish corporations made it impossible for them to reach a level of exports that would have allowed them to compensate for the amount of foreign capital goods needed in order to further the industrialization process. As a result, Spain's trade imbalance was consistently high.

The need to avoid the imminent risk of bankruptcy pushed the country toward the development and approval of a new development plan in 1959. The Plan de Estabilización was conceived by a team of men belonging to a new managerial class, most of whom belonged to Opus Dei and were known as the "tecnócratas" (Equipo Mundo 1970; Martín Aceña 2000). The plan represented the first significant opening to outside influence after two autarkic decades.

At the same time, the series of measures adopted through the plan represented a way for Spain to swiftly recover its trade balance, and was a very useful tool for promoting a gradual liberalization that in the long term, was fundamental to its economic development. The plan in fact advocated a partial trade opening of the country, which moved from restricting imports to a trade policy based on duties (which nevertheless remained very high particularly in the first few years). This process resulted in an increased integration into European trade channels, reaching its peak in 1970 with the signing of a preferential agreement between Spain and the countries of the EEC.

The Plan de Estabilización also called for the financial opening of the country, which had remained stubbornly closed during the autarky. Before 1959, the amount of foreign capital could not exceed 25% of the share capital of a company, and it was in any case dependent on governmental authorization (Tascón Fernández 2003). Thanks to the new laws, from 1959, foreign investors could own up to 50% of the share capital of a firm without needing any authorization, and could achieve 100% of the ownership of a corporation if they obtained the state's permission. With the exception of some sectors that remained excluded by this legislation, such as defense, oil refining, media and publishing, air transport, banking and electricity, almost all other industries experienced a strong boom in foreign investment over the following years. This affected the behavior of big business and at the same time had a very positive impact on the adoption of new technologies and for the industrial and economic growth of the country. It was mainly thanks to this opening that a real "economic miracle" could begin also in Spain, based on the sum of domestic savings, remittances coming from Spanish emigrants (Román 1972), and foreign investments. The flow of foreign capital did not stop throughout this period, in part because of the country's attractively low cost of labor, the still strong presence of protectionism and the continuously growing domestic market in which the purchasing power of local population was significantly and constantly growing (e.g., Fusi and Palafox 1997) and whose industries were fostering each other's production.

The economic miracle of the 1960s made Spain increasingly similar to the rest of Europe and allowed it to catch up with them, thus significantly narrowing the wealth gap. However, as was the case also in Italy, Spain's growth was neither limitless nor perfect, and some of the elements that initially helped it would eventually cease to exist and in some cases damage the national economy in the long term.

During this period, large corporations became central protagonists of Spain's economic growth. Mass production and mass consumption gradually started to spread in the 1960s. Domestic demand, in its widest meaning, provided the engine for the industrialization process. The adoption of foreign and more effective technologies made the achievement of significant scale economies possible, while intermediate as well as final products could count on a growing market involving both other companies and families.

Looking at the influence exerted during this period by the state, the financial system, private entrepreneurs and foreign investors on big business, it should be stressed that, as in the Italian case, it is possible to identify some discontinuities in the behavior of private local and foreign entrepreneurs, while the government and the banks did not change their attitude to any great extent.

If during the years of the construction of its industrial system Spain was characterized by a quite concentrated kind of capitalism, the new circumstances of the golden age favored a slightly larger number of economic participants. Most of the previous protagonists, like the state, a few families, and a number of banks retained a significant presence. Nevertheless, in an era of enrichment and new opportunities, new participants, such as foreign multinationals and relatively young entrepreneurs found their place within national capitalism and the big business panorama.

The role of government did not decrease, and in some cases grew, in Spain as well as in most other Western nations. On one hand, the number of state-owned companies increased during the golden age. State-owned companies formed the largest businesses and occupied the positions that usually were taken by the private firms. In 1960, based on assets, nine out of the top fifteen corporations were state-owned. They dominated important sectors such as railways, steel, telecommunications, oil, shipbuilding and electricity (Carreras and Tafunell 1997). On the other side, the Francoist government also maintained a strong level of direct intervention in the Spanish economic system during this period of strong growth, as it was convinced it would be able to effectively manage and sustain it. Similar to what happened in Italy, the state chose to invest in specific regions in order to promote the development of those areas, and helped specific companies belonging to strategic sectors by giving them fiscal immunity and subsidies, and by allowing them to operate under preferential financing systems (Carreras and Tafunell 2003). This inevitably influenced their strategic behavior and created significant distortions in the country's economic growth. Maybe even more so than in Italy, the lack of any democratic debate allowed ministers and other authorities in some periods and industries to take aberrant decisions and to keep them up despite economic failures (e.g., San Román and Sudrià 2003). Within a few years, it became evident that such policies were having a bad impact on the performance of some very big companies and sectors and negatively affecting the national economy.

In terms of the financial system, clear discontinuities with the previous period cannot be detected. The lack of transparency and sensible working method of the stock exchange made it possible for the banks to maintain their centrality in financing, and also in gaining ownership of, the major companies of the country. A state-owned system of banks did also exist in Spain, although to a lesser extent than in Italy. However, more importantly, the government also directly regulated the activity of the largest financial institutions of the country, which were private. In terms of the direct ownership of industrial shares, it should be stressed that banks continued to own several of the biggest private companies in Spain, and were able to create huge business groups around them throughout this period (Aguilera 1998; Pueyo Sánchez 2006a, 2006b). On the other hand, in analyzing the role of the private banks in the financial system, it should be stressed that they had to obey to certain political orders. The government wanted to control the system and to direct private savings to a number of specific targets. Banks thus had to direct a substantial part of their resources to investment opportunities determined by the state. The law defined specific percentages of banks' resources—the *coeficiente de caja* and the *coeficiente de inversión obligatoria*—and compelled the banks to direct them to the destination it wanted. The *coeficiente de caja* indicated what percentage of their liabilities (deposits in current accounts and saving accounts) banks had to invest in state bonds, while the *coeficiente de inversión obligatoria* was the amount of their liabilities that the financial institutions had to use for granting loans and credit to those companies that the state thought should receive "preferential treatment." The profitability or the actual future prospects of these companies could not be taken into account by the banks, since everything was basically decided by the state (Carreras and Tafunell 2003, 362–363).

Even though Spanish capitalism remained highly concentrated, new families were able to enter this "Olympus," in some cases challenging established companies and in other cases entering different sectors. Major new opportunities came from the constructions sector. Companies like Entrecanales y Tavora, Huarte y Compañía, Fomento de Obras y Construcciones and Cubiertas y Tejados became very large during this period. Family-run businesses also found fertile ground to grow in department stores (such as El Corte Inglés and Galerías Preciados), food and beverages (like Rumasa, Compañía de Industrias Agrícolas, Centrales Lecheras Españolas, González Byass), steel and mechanics (such as Grupo Comercial Laminados, Echevarría), electrical appliances (Orbaiceta), tourism (such as Meliá) and media (e.g., Victor Sagi Publicidad).

The picture of big business during these golden years should finally include a consideration of the entry of another kind of actor, whose role had remained relatively marginal during the 1930s, 1940s, and 1950s: foreign investors.

The completely hostile attitude toward foreign multinationals during the autarkic era gradually started to change from 1959, when the Plan de Estabilización provided a new and more favorable framework for their entry. Multinationals were not free to operate as they chose. They needed authorization to achieve outright ownership of a company and frequently coordinated their activities with a local partner. Moreover, they were often not accepted socially, making it difficult for them to operate in the Spanish framework. Nevertheless, direct foreign investment and the number of foreign multinationals, particularly from the United States, significantly increased during this period in several industries, with significant consequences for the spread of new technologies and products (Guillén 2001, chap. 5; Tascón Fernández 2002; Álvaro Moya 2010).

3.3 THE SPANISH ECONOMY FROM THE ENERGY CRISIS TO A NEW BOOM (1973–1988)

Life for large corporations changed completely in the 1970s, a decade that represented as much of a watershed in few other counties as it did in Spain. During the 1970s, the country and its companies had to face not only the international and domestic economic crisis but also a complex and very delicate political transition from dictatorship to democracy, which began with Francisco Franco's death in 1975 (Pérez Díaz 1999).

The energy and economic crisis involved more than a simple slowing down of the growth process, as it stressed in particular the gaps and the mistakes of the Francoist economic policies. When comparing the macroeconomic information of Spain to the data from the other international and European countries, it becomes clear that Spain suffered significantly more during this period. The economic collapse particularly affected most of the industries that the Spanish state had considered as strategic and that it had therefore promoted and protected in order to create its own national champions, such as the steel and metal sector and shipbuilding.

Throughout the period of 1975–1985, Spanish GDP grew at an annual rate of 2% while per-capita GDP growth rate was 1.2% (Carreras and Tafunell 2005). At the same time, however, domestic demand dropped, the inflation rate was 15.7% on average, and the unemployment rate grew from less than 3% in 1974 to more than 20% in 1985 (Carreras and Tafunell 2005).

Against a background of political transition at the end of the 1970s, politicians took decisions that had a negative impact on the future of the country's large corporations, such as the choice to force the state-owned firms to rescue many enterprises that were not able to sustain themselves.

Only when a firm and democratic legal and institutional framework had been established, and once the new Spanish Constitution, approved in 1978, recognized "business freedom with respect to the model of the market economy" (art. 38), could a robust project of long-term development and a concrete restructuring of the national economy start. The first political force to win an election in democratic Spain was the Unión de Centro Democrático (Union of the Democratic Center), a center-right party that remained in charge between 1977 and 1982. The next elections were won by the Partido Socialista Obrero Español (Spanish Socialist Workers' Party). The Partido Socialista Obrero Español, led by Felipe González, represented a "new left-wing" political force that found its origins mainly in the opposition movement to Franco that had grown in the universities. Its members belonged to the Spanish middle class and were very young. They remained in power until the victory of the right-wing party Partido Popular (People's Party), led by José María Aznar, in 1996 (Fusi and Palafox 1997; Pérez Díaz 1999).

The post-Franco administration inherited a dire economic situation, in part due to the effects of the 1970s recession. It had to deal with very high inflation, substantial national and international debt, and a number of large corporations already or imminently bankrupt. Moreover, entrepreneurs had to operate amid high political tension and uncertainty, particularly during the first years of democracy. An attempted coup d'état by the Lieutenant Colonel Antonio Tejero took place in 1981, while several regions campaigned for autonomy. The armed Basque nationalist and separatist organization ETA murdered 179 people between 1982 and 1986 (Fusi and Palafox 1997, 391).

According to the Spanish economic historian Gabriel Tortella, Spain paid two times over for Francoism: first when it began, during the postwar period, and, again, when it ended, due to its legacy of a highly regulated and rigid economy. This had a large impact on the behavior of its participants in a situation that asked for high levels of flexibility in order to overcome the problems of the 1970s (Tortella Casares 1994). During the 1980s, economists debated and repeatedly wondered in journals whether there was at least one sector in the whole Spanish economy where economic activity developed following the basic rules of the market economy (e.g., De Pablo Torrente 1983, 1986).

The common line of the economic reforms carried out by the new Spanish government involved a general liberalization and deregulation of the economy. These policies were accompanied by an important reform of the system of industrial relations and by the dismantling and gradual privatization of the state-owned holding INI. During the Francoist decades and the early democratic era, it had become enormous but unsustainable from a financial perspective.

One of the most important achievements of the new democratic Spanish governments was the integration of the country into the European Economic Community. Spain had tried to become part of the EEC since it came into being. Spain officially negotiated for inclusion, but because of its political regime, it only could achieve a preferential agreement. European integration was a priority for democratic Spain. There was a widespread belief that the acceptance of Spain into the EEC would not only have very positive effects on the national economy, but it would also help to strengthen and consolidate its young and still potentially weak democratic regime. A few weeks after the first democratic political elections, in 1977, the new government sent an official request for the full integration of Spain into the EEC to Brussels. Due to the second oil shock, the process took many years and only in 1983 did the improving economic situation for most of Europe make it possible for the EEC to accept Spain request. The agreement was signed in 1985 and from 1986 Spain was officially a member of the EEC (Garmendia Ibáñez 2004).

Integration into the European economy marked the beginning of a difficult period for Spain and its large corporations, since the protection of national companies that had characterized the country's policies for decades had to be abandoned. However, a period of intense economic growth began in 1986, mainly thanks to the new economic policies and to the renewed influx of foreign capital and technologies. Between 1986 and 1990, the first results were evident to everyone: GDP grew at an average of 4.5% every year, direct foreign investment continued to flow uninterruptedly into the country, the network of roads and motorways was expanded by at least three times and Spain was experimenting with a process of modernization of urban structures and investment on a level that was probably unparalleled in Europe (Botti 2000).

Moreover, integration into the EEC required important reforms of the financial system and the creation of new institutions conducive to the development of a new and more modern kind of capitalism. The *coeficiente de caja* and the *coeficiente de inversión obligatoria* were abandoned and the Spanish banking system was partly deregulated. With regard to the stock exchange, a new law in 1988, Ley de Mercado de Valores, regulated and modernized the structure and the working method of the financial markets, creating an integrated system of transactions and establishing a regulator (Comisión Nacional de Mercado de Valores), increasing the level of information that companies had to provide to their investors, and giving a legal basis to institutional investors (Carreras and Tafunell 2003, 428–429). The economy started to grow again, unemployment dropped, and in 1991, Spain became the eighth-largest market economy in the world.

Big business, of course, experienced major changes during this period. By the end of the 1970s, the crisis seemed to have definitively compromised the future of the large corporations in Spain. However, as in Italy, it was precisely under these circumstances that the basis of a metamorphosis, and not just a decline, of big firms was laid by the government, private entrepreneurs and foreign companies on a background of modernizing financial systems.

State-owned big businesses, the great protagonists of the national economy created by the Francoist regime, were experiencing enormous troubles. During the later 1970s and the early 1980s, even though it had been seriously affected by the oil shocks and the economic crisis itself, INI became an active rescuer of private loss-making industrial firms (Martín Aceña and Comín Comín 1991; Carreras, Tafunell and Torres 2000). It reached its maximum size in terms of the number of companies it directly owned, the industries where it was present, and in terms of the losses it incurred. The socialist-run governments began to reform many state-owned companies with the aim of securing their future in a more competitive environment. From 1984, Spanish Socialist Workers' Party started gradually, and almost in secret, to carry out a policy of privatization of INI's companies. During the following years, this process would gather pace.

The economic crisis also seriously affected private companies in Spain, both family and bank owned. It further worsened some of the structural troubles of big family businesses. They had to deal with competition from rivals such as the state-owned firms that, even though they were not very competitive, were much larger in size. Moreover, the data underline how, up to the end of the 1980s, Spanish firms had the lowest rate of self-financing among the countries of the Organisation for Economic Co-operation and

Development (OECD; Pérez 1997) Since it was difficult for them to gain access to resources offered by a small and inefficient stock exchange they almost totally depended on bank loans. Even this route was not without its challenges, because banks often granted credit to their own enterprises or to clients protected by the state and would not risk their own capital on smaller, unprotected firms whose future was more uncertain. Due to the behavior of the banks, private firms that were unable to obtain government support experienced great difficulty in obtaining credit. They were also subject to high interest rates on loans, causing their external debts to increase. Between 1970 and the beginning of the 1990s, the financial costs of the nonfinancial enterprises exceed the rate of return on investment by relatively large amounts on (Maroto Acín 1990). In this context, it should be added that the strong protectionism that lasted until the integration to the EEC had not encouraged private Spanish companies to grow, to look for competitive strategies and structures or to adopt the more efficient technologies. Although the period following 1983 was one of change and opportunity, by the beginning of the 1980s, the delicate process of full transition to democracy had not yet created an environment that was economically and politically stable enough to allow entrepreneurs to operate. The financial burden placed on enterprises rose: at the end of the 1970s, their energy costs increased because of the oil crises, as did the cost of borrowing due to the restrictive monetary policy. Labor costs also surged: the renewed strength of the labor unions, forced into silence during the Francoist period, made it more difficult for the entrepreneurs to bear the cost of labor and to manage the changes that the crisis had caused.

The situation further worsened because the Spanish firms that had survived stabilized their performance and begun to attract the attention of foreign investors. Within a few years, they purchased most of the largest private enterprises (Binda 2005a). Very few big manufacturing enterprises survived this wave of foreign investment, and it was only in the second part of the 1980s that private Spanish entrepreneurs started to recover some of these manufacturing enterprises and, more importantly, to develop new companies through a process of restructuring, merging and acquisitions in nonmanufacturing sectors that would become one of the major strengths of the country (Binda and Iversen 2007).

Amid the decline and restructuring of private and state-owned companies as well as the spread of foreign multinationals, the country's financial markets experienced some very significant changes. First, as has already been stressed, new rules were applied to the banks and to the stock exchange, which made it easier and safer both for investors and companies to use the latter. A second major change that affected the banks was the fact that they experienced major difficulties at the end of the 1970s and during the 1980s (Muñoz, Roldán and Serrano 1978; Cuervo García 1988). A report received by the governor of the Central Bank, José Ramón Álvarez Rendueles, when he assumed the post indicated that the main reason for this was "the unrestrained use of their credit concession to the advantage of companies which were linked to the bank itself and/or the bank's managers" (Cabrera and Del Rey 2002, 52). On one hand, this crisis forced the banks into selling most of their industrial stakes, that is, most of the largest companies of the country, to foreign investors. A process of restructuring of the banking sector and its industrial participation also took place. In a few years, a wave of mergers and acquisitions radically changed the physiognomy of several industries where banks used to play a key role, and new giants were created and prepared to compete on the national and international market (Binda 2005a).

3.4 CONSOLIDATION AND REFORMS (1988–2002)

From the mid-1980s to the first few years of the new century, Spain experienced a real boom that was slowed down only by an economic crisis in 1993. Governments were not afraid of implementing important reforms and breaking completely with the past, something that would probably have been almost impossible without significant political discontinuity and the transition from dictatorship to democracy.

The new political class had to face many economic, political and social problems but in most cases was able to lay the foundations and set up the rules for a new period of economic growth and development. Both left- and right-wring governments acted by consolidating the democratic framework and the institutions that operated within it, although this process was not without problems, tensions and mistakes, all of which greatly affected the behavior of large corporations.

The Spanish Socialist Workers' Party, led by Felipe González, remained in power for fourteen years, from 1982 to 1996. Thanks to this continuity in government, important reforms of the banking system, the stock exchange, the labor market, the fiscal policies of the state and the restructuring of the national debt could be approved (Carreras and Tafunell 2003). At the same time, a process of restructuring and of reorganization of big business took place. Even though political ideologies prevented the socialist governments from carrying out a far-reaching plan of privatization of state-owned companies in this initial period, practical needs pushed them to start the privatization of the major companies in the country (Ariño Ortiz 2004; Cuervo García 1997).

A new golden era seemed to have started, and a climate favorable to a growth in wealth started to spread throughout the country. Problems still remained: industrial relations were very tense and the public debt as well as the tax burdens were substantial. Many services were still not adequate for a modern country. Despite these issues, bankers, financiers, entrepreneurs and managers became new protagonists, in some cases new heroes, and jostled for space on the front pages of all the national newspapers (e.g., García Abadillo and Fidalgo 1989; Navas and Nadal 1990).

In this context, the level of Spanish integration into the European and international community became ever greater. Many achievements characterized Spanish policies in these years and provided new opportunities and challenges for corporations in general and big business in particular. After being accepted as a member of the EEC in 1985, Spain also increased its level of integration into other international institutions and organizations. It had been a member of OTAN since 1982, and participated in the Gulf War of 1990. Moreover, in 1992, the country was chosen as a nonpermanent member of the United Nations Security Council. The international recognition of Spain made it the center of many cultural and sport events at the end of the 1980s and the beginning of the 1990s, which had important repercussions for the construction of facilities and infrastructure and for the economic growth of the country. In 1992, while Italy faced all the problems listed in the previous chapter, Spain was celebrating the Olympic Games in Barcelona and the World Exposition in Seville.

Later on, this second golden age seemed to come to a temporary halt. A relatively deep recession affected the economy in 1992–1993. A series of political scandals also came to light in 1994. This greatly diminished the image and confidence that people had in the socialist party, and in 1996 the election was won by the People's Party led by José María Aznar (Pérez Díaz 1999). The country that the Spanish Socialist Workers' Party passed on to the new right-wing government was very different from the one that they had themselves inherited more than ten years before. It was a stable democracy and a modern country well integrated into Europe, with a dynamic and increasingly rich internal market and system of enterprises.

Economic growth continued under the People's Party–led governments from 1996 to 2004. During this period the unemployment rate significantly declined, public accounts recovered to an impressive extent and the GDP maintained rates of growth that were quite exceptional in the European context. Moreover, around the turn of the millennium, new national champions emerged in big business after processes of mergers and acquisitions, and the process of privatization of the country's largest companies gathered pace. The total turnover generated by this process of privatization during the period 1996–2002 was 29.7 billion euros. Of this turnover, 92% came from IPOs (Ariño Ortiz 2004), which was made possible in part by the reforms of the stock exchange and of financial market legislation during the previous decade.

When the Socialist Party, led by José Luis Rodríguez Zapatero, came back to power in 2004, Spain had already come to be considered an advanced European economy. "Spain Rocks!" was the title of a special report published by *Time* on March 8, 2004, in which a summary read, "Meet the new *conquistadores*; Spaniards leading a national surge in global business and politics, culture and the arts" (*Time* 2004). In terms of purchasing power parity, Spanish per-capita GDP had increased at impressive rates from 1995 to 2004, and in 2005, it had almost reached that of Italy and France (World

Bank 2007). In contrast to Italy, the Spanish economy maintained high rates of growth during the first years of the new millennium, and big business, on the eve of the present economic crisis, seemed to be stronger than ever. Euphoria and twists have characterized the largest corporations in Spain since the end of the 1980s, and the restructuring that occurred as a result of the economic crisis of the 1970s seemed to have made a new period of growth possible up to the current economic crisis.

The strengthening of the process of European integration, new rules for competition, product and financial market, and an impressive process of privatization affected the role and dynamics of the government, private entrepreneurs, foreign companies and financial institutions and consequently corporate behavior.

The role of the state, which gradually lost its dominant role in determining the ownership and aims of big business, represents a major change during this period. *Privatization* and *liberalization* characterized the Spanish economy in those years. The privatization process was completed to the greatest extent in Spain, where direct state ownership of big business almost completely disappeared (Cuervo 1997; Gámir Casares 1999; Bel and Costas 2001; Clifton, Comín and Díaz Fuentes 2003; Ariño Ortiz 2004; Trigo Portela 2004; Binda 2011). The impact of privatization and the income generated by this process has been very high. A realistic estimate of the period 1986–2007 evaluates it to be around 52 billion dollars (Privatization Barometer 2008). The process of privatization has also been very important from a qualitative perspective: the state almost completely ceased to play a decisive role in every industry. For most of the companies, privatization was a lengthy process, which in some cases had been prepared for many years and which occurred very gradually and in different stages. In many cases, the privatization process was carried out by using both one or more IPOs and private bids in the same company. By the beginning of the twenty-first century, despite the fears about the loss of public (and national to an even greater extent) control that have been voiced by some politicians, businessmen and trade unionist, the government had mostly completed the privatization of almost all firms in public hands.

Another important contextual factor that affected big business opportunities and challenges during this era was the relatively swift transition from a system based on bank-led financing toward a system where the stock exchange played a more dominant role in financing business expansion. The new laws that regulated the stock market to protect shareholders, the restructuring process of many large corporations and the IPO-led privatization of several of the largest companies have given the Spanish stock exchange a brand-new effervescence and a central role since the mid-1980s. At the same time, Spanish banks were facing a very serious crisis. However, they did not lose their importance. The financial sector was completely reorganized, and during the 1990s, several mergers and acquisitions among the largest banks in the country took place (e.g., Molina and Martín Aceña

2011). The result was the emergence of very big and competitive financial institutions, such as Banco de Bilbao Vizcaya Argentaria (BBVA) y Banco Santander Central Hispano (BSCH), which became competitive on the international market and, at the same time, started to buy shares in the largest manufacturing and services companies of the country once again.

Putting Spain in the international framework of these years, it should also be stressed that increased economic integration, particularly after the breakthrough achieved with the creation of the European Single Market in the early 1990s, had several consequences in terms of the pattern and size of international trade and investment (Figstein and Merand 2002), and thus also for entrepreneurial behavior. The level of direct foreign investments as well as the number of foreign-owned businesses in Spain remained very high throughout this period, even more so than in Italy (Carli 2008), and affected the strategies and structures of both local and foreign large corporations (Binda and Colli 2012).

As with the previous economic miracle, it should finally be stressed that the new context offered great opportunities both to the old protagonists of the Spanish economy and for entrants to the big business "Olympus." The new dynamics in the role of state-owned companies, the financial system and international investment and trade provided an opportunity to make Spanish capitalism more democratic. The spread of new technologies and sectors allowed private entrepreneurs to start activities that achieved success in a short time frame. At the same time, the corporate restructuring that had taken place during the 1980s as well as the process of privatization allowed relatively new private companies to expand and/or set up new businesses. Yet, there are also clear continuities with the past. With a few important exceptions, many of the companies that currently dominate Spanish capitalism are "old" companies that have gone through one or more phases of restructuring, merging and acquisitions. In some cases, they changed ownership in a context where important blockholders, who were not new at all to Spanish high capitalism, namely, families and banks, remained important.

Part II

The Evolution of Big Business in Italy and Spain

The role played by large corporations and the sectors in which they typically operated in furthering the economic growth of a country was one of the most debated and controversial issues during the twentieth century.

"What is good for the country is good for General Motors, and vice versa" argued the American businessman and politician Charles Erwin Wilson in 1953 when, after a long career within this car company, he became the United States Secretary of Defense. For a long time, large corporations have been considered to be the main economic participants (Chandler and Hikino 1997), and their relevance and characteristics were the subject of studies and debates until the final three decades of the last century, when things began to change.

The importance of the role played by small and medium-sized companies became more evident all over the world from the 1970s and started to draw the attention of academia. By that time, many studies had already been carried out on large corporations, and the analysis of the dynamics of big business was, relatively speaking, pushed into the background while articles and books everywhere focused on small companies as source of innovation, employment and economic success. These studies asserted that the impact of big business on economic growth could have been overestimated (Piore and Sabel 1984; Becattini 1987; Sabel and Zeitlin 1997).

However, around the turn of the new century, big business regained its importance (e.g., Harrison 1990, 1994). Large corporations appeared or consolidated their relevance in the new information technology (IT) and services sectors. Moreover, after a process of restructuring, and in some cases of privatization, they also continued to be very important in the manufacturing industry of many countries.

Neither Italy nor Spain is usually considered as a "country of large corporations," where big business has found fertile ground to grow or where it has been able to gain a significant competitive advantage. Italian and Spanish scholars have often claimed that these two nations developed their large corporations in a context of delayed industrialization, that their fate has been largely determined by political choices and that the economic success of these nations during the last few decades has rested much more on the development of small and medium-sized competitive companies than on the long-term success of big "national champions."

During the postwar years, Italy and Spain were not comparable to the most industrialized nations in terms of their wealth. Compared to the United States, but also to the main European economies, Southern Europe had clearly fallen behind. The Italian per-capita GDP in 1950 did not reach even half of that of the United States and was nowhere near the British, French and German GDP. The situation in Spain was even worse. Spanish per-capita GDP was less than a third of that of the United States, less than half of that of the main European nations, and much lower than Italy's per-capita GDP (Maddison 2007). However, even though Mediterranean Europe remained at the periphery of the most advanced nations in 2000, the economic development of both nations during the second half of the last century has significantly changed the preceding picture. As has been shown in the previous section, within a few decades both Italy and Spain were able to catch up with the rest of the advanced world (Maddison 2007).

What role did big business play in this growth process? Although many scholars have claimed that the relevance of big business might have been overestimated when it comes to the process of growth and development of the largest European economies and of the United States (Piore and Sabel 1984; Sabel and Zeitlin 1997; Scranton 1997), the main purpose of the next chapters is to investigate whether it could have been underestimated for the Italian and Spanish case.

This second section of the book thus aims to investigate the long-term economic, political and social role played by the large corporations in Italy and Spain. Moreover, it tries to assess the real size of the Italian and Spanish companies from an international perspective. It then provides an analysis of the identity of big business in these nations, describing to which sectors the main companies belonged and who their owners were during the second half of the twentieth century.

4 No Country for Large Corporations?
The Role and Impact of Big Business in Italy and Spain

4.1 BIG BUSINESS AND THE WEALTH OF NATIONS: AN ANALYSIS BASED ON GROSS DOMESTIC PRODUCT

How much can big business contribute to the economic growth of a country? What role are large corporations able play in the social development and modernization process of newly industrializing areas? How big can big business be in latecomer nations? Analyzing the importance of large corporations in countries like Italy and Spain during the second part of the twentieth century is not an easy task, and unfortunately, there is no indicator that allows us to calculate how much big business has furthered the wealth and development of these countries. A number cannot provide an exhaustive measurement of the contribution that an enterprise is able to make to the growth of the country in which it operates, and the effects of the emergence of large corporations in a nation cannot be described only in terms of the economic impact they had based, for instance, on their turnover.

When big businesses started to become important protagonists within the most advanced national economies, a series of mechanisms for spreading wealth in fact emerged. "Large corporation" could, for instance, also refer to the establishment of other small, medium-sized, or large corporations that operated in a related sector, or as suppliers or as customers. Moreover, the diffusion of large corporations in many cases favored the pursuit of scale economies and cost reductions, making a substantial increase in the salaries of workers possible. The growth in workers' purchasing power in turn allowed them to buy more than just essential goods, and spurred further growth of other industries, mainly in manufacturing and later on in nondurable goods and services.

Summarizing all of this in a formula or in a few pages would be impossible. However, to provide an idea of what big business has represented in these nations from an economic perspective, the impact of large corporations in Italy and Spain has been analyzed by adopting an indicator commonly used by various scholars in studies of other countries: the turnover of the 100 largest enterprises in terms of Product percentage.

Thanks to the information provided by Leslie Hannah on some of the most advanced nations in the world, it can be claimed that the 100 largest manufacturing and nonmanufacturing companies have had a quite different impact across different periods and in different countries. The 100 largest corporations in the United States, Japan, Germany and the United Kingdom represented, respectively, 23%, 28%, 20% and 22% of the 100 net product in ca. 1947; 33%, 22%, 30% and 40% in ca. 1970; and finally 33%, 21%, 23% and 36% in ca. 1990 (Hannah 1995). Apart from Japan, where the impact of big business on national product has continuously declined since 1947, the largest corporations in the most advanced nations experienced their golden age in earnest around 1970, when they represented a percentage of between 30% and 40% of the national product. This figure declined slightly during the following decades up to 1990, at which point Hannah's work ends.

Following this methodology, the economic role of big business in Italy and Spain has been analyzed using a comparison of the impact of assets (in the 1950 population) and sales (in the 1973, 1988 and 2002 populations) of their 100 largest corporations on current-price GDP during these four benchmark years. This ratio is obviously not infallible, and it is only approximate. Moreover, caution is required when comparing these findings to Hannah's results because multinational companies are not included in his sample, and the net product has been considered for different benchmark years. Even so, using this indicator provides a reasonable way of measuring and comparing the importance of the largest corporations in Italy and Spain to what happened in the world's most advanced nations. In order to complete the analysis, the investigations carried out by other scholars on the impact of the assets of the 200 largest corporations on the Italian and Spanish GDP during the same period has also been considered (Carreras and Tafunell 1997; Giannetti and Vasta 2010).

The information collected in Table 4.1 allows us to stress at least three relevant factors concerning the transformation of the economic weight of the top 100 and 200 enterprises in Italy and Spain based on their impact on GDP.

The first is that the contribution of the largest companies to the GDP in these Southern European nations is very similar to the ratio measured in other European countries as well as in the United States and Japan. Based on this indicator, big business was no less important to the Italian and Spanish economies than it was in Germany, France, the United Kingdom, the United States or Japan in the same period. An important caveat that should be taken into account is that the definition of big business as per this ratio also includes the subsidiaries of foreign multinationals that were established in these latecomer nations and that became a fundamental piece in the puzzle of Italian and Spanish capitalism during the second half of the century.

Secondly, throughout the second half of the twentieth century, the impact of big business on GDP was larger in the poorer country, that is, Spain. This

Table 4.1 The economic impact of big business on Italian and Spanish GDP

Total assets (1950) / turnover (1973, 1988, 2002) of the 100 largest companies based on GDP

%	1950	1973	1988	2002
Italy	23.32	24.68	17.16	31.57
Spain	33.92	29.59	29	44.5

Total assets of the 200 largest companies based on GDP

%	c. 1950	1960	c. 1973	c. 1990
Italy	42.6	54.7	62.3	49.1
Spain	53	65	87	63

Source: Author's elaboration on information from 1950, 1973, 1988, and 2002 populations; Rossi, Sorgato, and Toniolo (1993); Carreras and Tafunell (1997, 281); Giannetti and Vasta (2010, 29); Carreras, Prados de la Escosura, and Rosés (2005); www.istat.it; and www.ine.es.

holds true if we consider both the 100 and the 200 largest corporations, and it is confirmed by the data gathered in this book and by the information provided respectively by Renato Giannetti and Michelangelo Vasta for Italy as well as by Albert Carreras and Xavier Tafunell for Spain.

Finally, it should be stressed that the impact of large corporations on the wealth of these nations followed the same trend both in Italy and Spain, and in the most advanced nations with the notable exception of Japan. When looking at the 200 largest companies, it is clear that the importance of big business grew constantly from 1950 to 1960 and again until 1973. In 1973, large corporations reached their peak in both nations. The figure from Spain is particularly impressive and shows how much the national economy relied on large corporations: 200 companies alone were able to generate 87% of Spanish GDP. Following the energy crisis of the 1970s, the role of big business declined in Italy as well as in Spain. Despite this, around 1990 the 200 largest companies generated almost half and more than half of Italian and Spanish GDP, respectively. When focusing on the 100 largest corporations, it is also clear that the impact of big business remained strong from 1950 to 1973 and declined from 1973 to 1988. Nevertheless, large corporations did not become marginal in either Italy or Spain and regained substantial power during the following decades in both countries. The contribution of the 100 top firms to GDP of the Italian as well as the Spanish economy was greater in 2002 than in 1973.

When analyzing the trends that governed the 100 largest corporations at the end of the reconstruction period in more detail, the industrial backwardness of Italy and Spain during the first half of the last century might lead one to think that big business and its role in these countries was quite small in 1950 and that it then eventually grew in importance during the following decades.

However, the information gathered on this topic provides a quite different and, to some extent, unexpected picture. In fact, the empirical evidence shows not only that in 1950, the role of the 100 largest companies was more than marginal both in Italy and in Spain. It also shows that, while the contribution of Italian big business to national wealth was very similar to that in the most advanced nations, the contribution of big business in Spain was even greater. According to Leslie Hannah (1995), the impact of the 100 largest companies on the product in the United States, Japan, Germany and the United Kingdom was lower than 28% while in Spain the figure stands at 33.92%.

The information gathered for 1973 substantially confirms the importance of the role of big business within the Italian and Spanish economic systems, even though it experienced a slight increase in Italy and a decrease in Spain. Looking at sector-based dynamics, the role played by large corporations was perhaps even more significant. In 1973, the largest companies, in particular the state-owned ones, were the real drivers of the growth of some sectors that were very important for the industrial development of these two nations. IRI's firms in 1969 represented 95% of the national productive capacity of cast-iron, 60% in steel, 80% in shipbuilding and 63% in the merchant and passengers fleet sector (IRI Annual Report 1969, 21). Meanwhile, INI's companies controlled 48.6% of the added value in the oil and petrochemical industry, 51.4% in electricity, 64.6% in iron and steel metallurgy, 35.4% in mining, 39.7% in shipbuilding, 52.4% in car manufacturing, 9.5% in aeronautics, 82.9% in air transport and 67.3% in chemicals (INI Annual Report 1973, 118–119).

Even though large corporations acted as the main protagonists of economic growth, small and medium-sized enterprises were not absent in this era. Their importance is particularly evident when looking at information on national employment. In Italy, due in part to a process of downsizing that characterized the large corporations after World War II, the percentage of workers employed in productive units with fewer than 500 workers grew from 75% to 78% between 1951 and 1961 and represented 77% of the working population in 1971. Finally, by 1981, 83% of the workers in Italy worked in productive units with fewer than 500 employees (Bolchini 2002). The situation was broadly similar in Spain. When the country joined the EEC in the 1980s, its entrepreneurial structure was still characterized by an overwhelming predominance of small and medium-sized firms. Small and medium-sized companies employed 92% of the working population in Spain, much more than in other European countries including those where small and medium-sized firms played a very important role, such as Italy (83%) and Portugal (81%; Tafunell 2005, 721).

The energy crisis of the 1970s severely affected big business and its economic importance, which declined considerably during the following decade in particular.

If 1973 witnessed a peak in the contribution that the largest corporations would make to GDP, the 1980s saw many of these companies fail or undergo a process of restructuring and in some cases refocusing of their activities. By

1988, the importance of large firms had been significantly reduced in Italy, where their contribution dropped from 24.68% to 17.16% of GDP. The decline in Spain was much smaller: from 29.59% to 29%. The percentage of the economy influenced by big business thus remained high, although their contribution to GDP decreased during this period. At the same time, the presence of small and medium-sized companies remained strong and even increased in these nations. The importance of their contribution to the economic success and competitive advantage of these nations became increasingly evident during the 1980s and 1990s. Consider, for instance, the success of the enterprises that characterized the "Made in Italy" trend, as well as the emergence of a capitalism based on small and medium-sized enterprises in both nations (Colli 2002a; Guillén 2005).

Nevertheless, contradicting all forecasts, the contribution of the 100 largest corporations to Italian and Spanish GDP in 2002 returned to its previously large level, and even increased beyond it. At the beginning of the new millennium, the 100 largest companies represented almost 32% of GDP in Italy, much more than they had done during the economic miracle (Berta 2004, 2006). The Spanish figures are even more impressive: the 100 largest companies alone made up almost half of the gross national product (Guillén 2005).

Even though Italy and Spain are countries with a competitive advantage in terms of small and medium-sized enterprises, the information gathered on the economic impact of their large corporations during the last sixty years allows us to claim that the importance of big business in these countries has been very similar to what has occurred in nations where big business has traditionally represented a fundamental part of national wealth—as is the case in the United States, the United Kingdom, Germany, France and Japan. Italian and Spanish large enterprises were at least as important in sustaining the wealth of their country as in most advanced nations, and during the second half of the twentieth century Spain has, on average, been even more dependent on the results of its big business than other advanced nations.

4.2 HOW BIG WAS BIG BUSINESS IN ITALY AND SPAIN?

The fact that big businesses in the Italian and Spanish economies has not been less important than in other developed nations should not obscure the fact that large corporations in these countries were generally smaller in terms of turnover and assets than their homologous national champions fostered by other Western powers.

When compared to other countries, the size of the large companies that grew in Italy and Spain seems significantly smaller, even more so when we look at the first benchmark year. It is also worth noting that Italian companies were larger than their Spanish counterparts immediately after World War II and during the second half of the twentieth century.

In Spain, in 1948, the largest company on the basis of assets fell below those of the company ranked 200th in the manufacturing sector in the United States and of the company ranked 50th in the United Kingdom. According to the Spanish scholars Albert Carreras and Xavier Tafunell (1994), it was precisely during the first years of the Francoist regime that Spanish companies lost ground in comparison to the largest companies in the world, reaching their smallest size around 1960. Also, in Italy, many reasons, such as the small size of the domestic market, fiscal policies, the scare and a fear of nationalization did not incentivize companies to grow in size immediately after World War II even though some exceptions do exist.

In 1959, only 3 Italian companies were included among the 200 largest in the world: FIAT, which ranked 74th; Montecatini, which was 103rd; and Pirelli, which came in at 173rd (Amatori 1997b, 267). In 1962, out of the world's 500 largest companies by turnover, 298 were American, 55 British, 36 German and 27 French, whereas only 7 were Italian and none of them Spanish (Chandler and Hikino 1997, 53).

During the 1960s, both Italian and Spanish companies not only became bigger but also increased their relative size. However, at an international level, they remained "ants." In 1973, of the largest 300 manufacturing companies by turnover outside the United States, 9 companies were Italian (Montedison, FIAT, ENI, Dunlop-Pirelli Union, Finsider, Olivetti, SNIA Viscosa, Alfa Romeo and Zanussi), whereas the Spanish economic miracle had made it possible for 6 Spanish companies to make an appearance (CAMPSA, ENSIDESA, SEAT, Unión Explosivos Río Tinto, CEPSA and Altos Hornos de Vizcaya) ("The 300 Largest Industrial Companies Outside the U.S." 1974, 176–185). In the same year, however, while 3 Italian companies appeared in the prestigious ranking of the top fifty manufacturing companies in the world (Montedison, FIAT and ENI), no Spanish enterprises were able to make an appearance ("The 300 Largest Industrial Companies Outside the U.S." 1974, 185).

The situation had not significantly improved by the end of the 1980s, when only 7 Italian companies ranked among the world's 200 largest corporations, and the 200th industrial firm in the United States would have ranked 12th in Spain (Carreras and Tafunell 1994, 32; Amatori 1997b, 267). No clear improvements can be detected even in the last benchmark year, 2002, when out of the 500 largest companies by turnover, 192 were American, 88 Japanese, 40 French, 35 German, 34 British, 14 Canadian, 13 Korean, 11 Chinese, 11 Dutch and 11 Swiss, while only 9 and 5 were, respectively, Italian and Spanish firms (*Fortune* Global 500 2003, 1–42). In the 2009, *Fortune* Global 500 ranking only 10 Italian and 12 Spanish companies were included compared to 140 American, 68 Japanese, 40 French, 39 German, 26 British and 37 Chinese.

As has been pointed out by other business historians, the relatively small size of the largest corporations is not rare at all within European capitalism (Schröter 2007). Even so, large corporations in Italy and Spain were, and still are, smaller than their British, German and French counterparts. If they were categorized using the criteria of turnover classification adopted at an international level, many of the companies that are labeled as "big" businesses in this book would probably still be considered medium-sized companies nowadays.

In Italy, a large part of the enterprises considered as medium-sized companies by the business historian Andrea Colli in his investigation of the so-called fourth capitalism (Colli 2002a, 98–113) are in fact included in the 2002 data as some of the 100 largest companies of the country. It is moreover interesting to observe that, if one of Italy's main strength actually lies in its medium-sized companies, there is no real contradiction with the argumentation that says that the largest companies of a nation have at the same time been the main protagonists of its growth. It can be claimed that in most of cases in Italy, local "big business" roughly coincides, or has significant overlaps, with medium-sized companies. At least a fifth of the 100 largest companies in Italy were "medium-sized companies" in 2002. If we exclude foreign multinationals from the population of top firms, almost half of the largest enterprises are medium-sized firms. The situation in Spain is broadly similar if we adopt the same criteria and take into account the fact that the size of the Spanish companies in the sample was smaller than that of their Italian counterparts across the ranking.

4.3 THE SOCIAL AND POLITICAL ROLE OF LARGE CORPORATIONS IN TWO MODERNIZING COUNTRIES

As was the case wherever large corporations spread, when big business started to become an important participant in Spain and Italy's economies, it generated new mechanisms that allowed further important increases in wealth but also strongly affected social and political dynamics. Although they modernized at a different pace, both were industrial latecomers, and the spread of big business (both local and foreign) inevitably went hand in hand with a consolidation of the process of industrialization and urbanization, and gave rise to new social and family dynamics.

Creating adequate urban facilities, infrastructures for services and transportation, as well as a new institutional context, for instance, in terms of industrial relations, had to become a priority both in Italy and in Spain from the years of their economic miracles onward. Big businesses were a part of this process, and, as part of a strong relationship with the governments, were generally committed—voluntarily or not—to this role. At the same time, some of the large corporations were also deeply involved in the personal life of their employees, while others were crucial to implementing their governments' policies for creating employment opportunities, particularly in rural and underdeveloped areas. These dynamics meant that the connection between large corporations and the government was a very close one both in Italy and in Spain. On one hand, large corporations, both private and state-owned, were committed to furthering the general development of their country. On the other hand, they created important lobbies to gain privileges in exchange for their economic, political and social role (Amatori and Colli 1999; Sánchez Recio 2003).

The greater contribution of large corporations to the society in which they operated is even more difficult to define and to measure than their economic impact. Many factors should be simultaneously taken into account, and a general interpretation on the social impact of large enterprises in these countries has to consider both the positive and negative effects of their activities, their achievements as well as their failures, and their transformation over time.

During the golden age, large corporations were very important in supporting Italian and Spanish social development, not only through carrying out plans relating to business welfare but also by playing a big part in shaping their process of urbanization and modernization.

In general, large corporations have had an important part to play in promoting the takeoff of sectors such as energy, steel and infrastructure, which were strategically vital to preparing these countries for real industrial development and for a substantial increase in national growth. In the Italy of the economic miracle, businesspeople like Oscar Sinigaglia at the steel giant Finsider, Vittorio Valletta at the car producer FIAT and Enrico Mattei at the petrochemical company ENI, thought that they could provide their country with a new opportunity through the enterprises they were managing (Amatori 2011). They were motivated by the idea of helping Italy reach the highest level of international capitalism and constantly tried to convince the public and the politicians of the importance of their companies' work in creating the infrastructure and growth stimuli that the country needed. The ideas of the most important businesspeople—in particular those with public profiles—and politicians of autarkic Spain were broadly similar. They considered the creation and growth of large companies to be fundamental to laying the foundations for national recovery and growth at an international level.

Moreover, big business itself contributed to the transformation of demographic and labor dynamics in these countries, and caused new and large-scale migrations toward urban centers that local and central authorities were very often unable to manage. Although to different extents, some of the largest firms in both Italy and Spain had to face direct social pressures brought about by economic and social change and dealt with them by constructing suitable infrastructures and housing. The various social interventions carried out by both state-owned organizations and large private companies had far-reaching consequences, completely transforming the social, institutional and geographical environment around their factories as well as the lives of the people that worked in them (e.g., Falck Annual Report 1950, 10–11; FIAT Annual Report 1950, 12–13).

One of the largest Italian multinationals, Olivetti, is a well-known and extensively studied example of a firm that was able to offer a unique view of economic efficiency and social consciousness in this period. Its CEO, Adriano Olivetti, conceived the factory as "[a] place dominated by progress, led by justice, inspired by beauty" (Piol 2004, 19). At the same time, he was able to develop pioneering products in electronics, become a leader in the production of typewriters and buy out one it his major rivals, the US firm Underwood (Soria 1979; Berta 1980).

Olivetti's commitment to integrating the company in its surrounding environment clearly represents an exceptional case. Nevertheless, all the major firms in Italy were involved more or less directly and efficiently in helping with the construction of the institutions and infrastructures that were still lacking in the country, to cope with its new economic and social dynamics. The annual reports of the largest corporations, at least up to the 1970s, never mentioned of the contributions they thought to make to the country's industrial production, technological progress, employment opportunities, social development and urban organization.

> The social and welfare activities undertaken by our Company during the year 1950 for retired employees and their families deserve to be mentioned in these pages

states the 1950 annual report by the Italian steel company Falck.

> We are pleased to inform you that we have completed the first building phase of the "Ina-Casa" Plan. . . . Concerning the "Retirement Plan" . . . we are able to say that since its establishment (1947), 19 former employees have benefited from it . . . We have achieved great results with the summer camps for the sons and daughters of our workers. . . . Furthermore, the whole of our social and worker-assistance operation is going to be enriched by a new and truly precious project, which is desperately needed in one of the most populated employee residential centers in Sesto San Giovanni (an area that was recently expanded with the construction of another group of buildings). We are talking about a new kindergarten, which will be managed according the educational criteria set out by Maria Montessori . . . (Falck Annual Report 1950, 10–11)

In the same year, the Italian automobile company FIAT (Annual Report, 1950, 12–13) claimed that its workers were

> among the most well-assisted in Italy. . . . The facilities and the social services provided by the Company . . . constitute one of the largest systems of company welfare of our Country. We think that it is worthwhile to provide you with a broad picture of our welfare activities at FIAT: Company Health Service FIAT Workers, . . . Assistance in the Factories and Service Departments, . . .; nurseries, . . .; rest house . . .; professional training, . . . recreation, sport and culture, . . .; housing.

Spain's large corporations also had a significant impact on the modernization process of the country and very often included the results of their *obra social* (social work) in their annual reports. The Francoist regime did not only entrust big business with the economic and social development of the country, but also believed that big business should take care of the physical education and religious needs of workers and their families. Finally, big business was seen as a useful tool for the consolidation of those values on which the dictatorship was founded during the golden age (e.g., INI Annual Report 1951). In this context, the impact of the largest state-owned companies seems to have been particularly important.

INI's oil company Empresa Nacional Calvo Sotelo, for instance, wrote in 1950,

> adequately with its modern and important installations, the company is involved in social changes. Our ample social contribution has been made in the shape of modern and important facilities, providing workers and employees with answers to all the needs modern life brings with it in terms of housing, as well as professional, religious and physical education. In Puertollano we have a wonderful small town with the most hygienic and modern services. The urban facilities have all been completed already: road design; asphalting; lighting; a sewer system with its sewage farm; housing for engineers, employees and workers; a main square with a movie theater; schools; medical facilities for any operation. (INI Annual Report 1951, 33)

In addition to the traditional social and cultural activities, and to the construction of houses for workers, to conform with the doctrine of the Francoist regime, the shipbuilding company Empresa Nacional Bazán de Construcciones Navales Militares

> has continued to pay constant and increasing attention to the physical education of workers, holding many exercise sessions and athletic competitions. . . . With regard to religion, the regular activities undertaken in the Company during the past year are in compliance with the established rules. Among these, it is worth mentioning the religious education provided by the '*Hermanos de la Doctrina Cristiana*', . . . which involved lessons on Religion and Spiritual Training for apprentices and workers; Lenten seminars for all the employees and factory workers, and the provision of grants to those workers or their sons who wish to undertake theological studies. (INI Annual Report 1951, 61)

In a national context in which the education system was not oriented toward the industrial technologies and was not aimed at the creation of new and competent managers, it has to be stressed that both in Italy and in Spain the largest companies also played a certain role in human capital development, at all its hierarchical levels.

The electrical company Edison (Edison Annual Report 1950, 19–20) stressed in its annual report that

> the initiatives that Edison is undertaking in terms of the training of its workers deserve a particular mention. They include a 'graduate-training course', . . . ; a training course for young diploma-holders; a number of specialized corporate schools for workers, . . .; a company course for the employees of the commercial units of the company. . . . an exchange program with foreign companies for technicians, which in 1950 was held in collaboration with Electricité de France, and in 1951 it is expected to be held in collaboration with the British Electricity Authority as well.

Spanish companies were also strongly committed to the education of their personnel and trained managers, employees and workers. La Maquinista Terrestre y Marítima represents a good example of this more general trend. In its annual report of 1950, the company claimed,

> we've already mentioned our School of Apprenticeship. Today we are very proud to announce that the work done by the School is much appreciated and that among our staff we already have eighteen wonderful workers and technicians who completed their studies last October. Given the kind of courses we teach, two groups of students will complete their professional education each year. In this way, within a few years, we will be able to count on a selection of workers who will have been adequately prepared and be forever grateful to our Company. (La Maquinista Terrestre y Marítima Annual Report 1950, 12)

Due to their own practical requirements in countries that were still in the process of creating new industrial infrastructures, institutions and welfare systems, and owing to the responsibilities vested in them by their governments, the social intervention of large companies was high both in Italy and in Spain (e.g., Sierra Álvarez 1990; Ciuffetti 2004). At the same time, however, a modern and efficient system for managing industrial relations failed to form, and the gap was instead filled by a paternalistic model that had long been in existence.

Large corporations faced serious difficulties in managing the changes that accompanied Spain's and Italy's economic miracles. Behind the facade of harmony shown in their annual reports, a social context that was far removed from the ideals dreamed of during the golden age very often involved harsh working conditions and a repression of workers' rights.

Italy's growth during the 1950s strongly relied on low salaries and was characterized by an absence of modern industrial relations. The welfare plans, the housing and the infrastructures provided by the state and by companies were not sufficient to manage the great change that was affecting society. Workers experienced acute shortages in terms of housing, transport and health and welfare services. Moreover, despite their apparent commitment to improving their relationship with their workers, when put to the test several large corporations were in fact quite insular and ineffective in managing social conflict, and discipline on the factory floors often turned into a repression of dissent or political divergence (Colajanni 1990b; Berta 1998).

The tension between workers and big businesses became more pronounced from the 1960s onwards in particular, and came to a head in Italy in 1969. FIAT, one of the symbols of the Italian economic miracle who at the same time exploited its workforce ruthlessly (Berta 1998), became one of the main stages of the so-called Hot Autumn: a period of conflict between companies and workers that triggered a decade of severe tension. Big businesses were increasingly seen as greedy exploiters just when the economy was starting to slow down. Sections of corporate annual reports that had previously been dedicated to optimistic accounts of social responsibility often gave way to descriptions of the number of hours lost due to strikes and of the demands made by the unions. By 1973, almost no one still made mention of "minor activities," such as the summer camps held for employees' children. Very few, mainly state-owned companies, still provided information on major initiatives for workers' welfare, such as the creation of welfare services systems, the provision of assistance, the efforts made to ensure workers' safety (precisely the problems that emerged as being the most important during the Hot Autumn; e.g., ENI Annual Report 1973; ENEL Annual Report 1973, Nuovo Pignone, Annual Report 1973) or on the measures taken to stimulate the economic and social development of the Southern part of the country (e.g., Italcementi Annual Report 1973, 7–9).

After a decade of tense conflict that did not lead to any kind of constructive cooperation between corporations and the unions, public mistrust of large corporations due to their failure to achieve these long-term goals probably reached its peak in Italy during the 1980s. Many books were published criticizing the big corporations and businesspeople who had been involved in the economic crashes of the 1970s and 1980s in particular (e.g., De Biase and Borsa 1992). It became clear to the public that many of the large Italian corporations had prioritized the interests of their owners, top managers or a number of politicians, but almost never those of their workers, nor of their society or country as a whole. Although most companies had referred to themselves as "the Company" with a capital letter up to the 1970s, this idea of what a firm constituted was disappearing fast. They were no longer considered a tool for implementing social aims, and companies began to refer to themselves using only lowercase letters.

Even more so than in Italy, the social work of large Spanish corporations was very often only carried out for the sake of keeping up appearances. The harmony and progress described in their annual reports frequently hid severe tensions between workers and management, as well as a mismatch between the declared aims of corporate modernization and the real life of their employees. Under the Francoist dictatorship, the labor market and labor conditions were determined exclusively by the state. The Fuero de

Trabajo was the law that, even though it was amended slightly over time, remained in force during the whole Francoist era. Its main points were

> 1) a harmonic idea of the relationship between capital and labor, with a strong spiritualist and religious background; 2) the exaltation of work; 3) the transformation of labor conditions through direct intervention of state; 4) the marginalization of married women from the workplace; 5) employment security; 6) the improvement of social welfare and of social insurance; and 7) the restriction of the freedom of the unions, and the creation of a Union which serves the state and in which both workers and entrepreneurs co-participate. (Soto Carmona 2003, 220)

Protected from demands and protests, big businesses in Spain continued to stress their contribution to the realization of the political and social development aims of the country in their *Infomes Anuales* (annual reports) up to the end of the 1970s. Even though, owing in part to the tense political environment of the time, the wording they used was more discreet than that used in the 1950s, and they no longer dedicated numerous pages to underlining things like the religious activities or the fitness facilities found in their factories, large corporations continued to claim that they played an important role in ensuring the economic and social development of the country (e.g., Corporación Industrial Bancobao Annual Report 1974, 7).

However, labor conditions were appalling and companies had almost complete control over their workers. Any harmony on the factory floor lasted only as long as its workers did not raise any objections or remained uninvolved in the political opposition movement (Molinero and Ysas 2003). The impoverishment of the working class, in particular during the first decade of Francoism, is demonstrated by the decrease in real wages (Carreras and Tafunell 2005) as well as by the fact that big business was not able to solve the social problems concerning housing, the health system and so on. In the 1970s, several large companies, in particular state-owned firms, still declared their persistence in promoting the building of houses for their workers, in lending them money at privileged rates to buy apartments and houses and in paying for their professional and technical education (Guillén 1994).

The Spanish subsidiaries of foreign multinationals also adopted this approach of emphasizing social commitment in an atmosphere of supposed harmony. Chrysler (Chrysler Annual Report 1973, 12–13), for instance, in addition to providing training for employees at all levels, declared that

> in accordance with the direction followed by the Company for many years, efforts to improve industrial relations have been intensified. Among other things, the provision of medical services, . . ., salary advances to workers, . . ., collective life insurance, . . ., bonuses and social aid, professional development, . . . and grants should be stressed.

While the Italian subsidiary reports during the same period counted the number of hours lost because of strikes, Chrysler (Chrysler Annual Report 1973, 13) in Spain officially thanked its workers:

> once again, we are happy to close this report by publicly recognizing the efficient work delivered by workers and employees of the Company, whose cooperation has been a very positive and determinant factor in achieving the positive results of the year that we consider here.

However, also in this case the point of view of the workers was quite different from the perspective described by the company. If, on one hand, Chrysler officially thanked it workers, on the other hand, clandestine labor unions accused the company of being "more Francoist than Franco himself" because of how strikers in its Madrid factory were treated in January 1969 (Guillén 2001).

When the dictatorship came to an end, labor conflicts also came to a head in Spain, and it seemed that big business needed help, more than it was able to give the country in such a difficult context itself. Severely hit by the economic crisis, companies were almost completely powerless. During the 1980s, however, as the country's wealth grew, big business seemed to be given a second chance by public opinion. Businesspeople and CEOs of large corporations featured on the front page of newspapers and magazines almost every day, and more and more people started to look at them as new heroes. Later on however, at the beginning of the 1990s, a series of scandals involving big industrial groups had a very negative impact on the reputation of big business and the help it could eventually offer society (Cabrera and Del Rey 2002).

The fact that large corporations changed the society in that they were active and shaped the social transformation of both Italy and Spain appears to be unquestioned. Yet, the shape and size of their contribution is very difficult to assess, in part because their social performance was and still is at the center of economic and political debates. The dynamics of the relationship between large corporations and their environment in Italy and Spain seems nevertheless to show that, in the long term, big business did not succeed in creating a constructive and stable material and institutional framework during the years of the economic growth and that the social legitimation of the large corporations was called into question over time in both nations.

4.4 SUMMARY

The aim of this chapter has been to challenge the traditional view of Italy and Spain as countries that were characterized by small and medium-sized companies, and in which big business ultimately played a minor part.

The industrial backwardness of Italy and Spain during the first half of the twentieth century could lead us to think that big business and the role it played in these countries was relatively insignificant after World War II. However, the contrary is true; a comparison of the contribution of the largest 100 companies to the GDP of Italy and Spain and to the GDP of the world's more advanced economies reveals a quite different and to some extent unexpected picture. Even though some of the large corporations in the population were not manufacturing companies, and in some cases were subsidiaries of foreign multinationals, it is still possible to claim that the contribution of big business to the GDP of both Italy and Spain has been very similar to that measured in the most advanced nations throughout the second part of the century. Despite the fact that Italy and Spain are countries with a competitive advantage when it comes to small and medium-sized enterprises, the importance of big business has been very similar to what has been observed in those nations where big business has traditionally represented a fundamental part of national wealth, including the United States, the United Kingdom, Germany, France and Japan. The data moreover demonstrate that big business was of even greater importance in the most backward country, namely, Spain. Looking at the international rankings of those years, it is clear that big businesses in Italy and Spain were smaller in size than were the large companies that operated in the world's most advanced economies. Nevertheless, relative to the smaller size of Italy's and Spain's economies, large corporations were able to make a significant contribution to the national wealth.

In addition to playing a comparable role to that of their counterparts in the most advanced nations, large corporations in Italy and Spain also followed the same trends. Namely, they experienced constant growth from 1950 to the 1970s, declined during the following decades and returned to better economic health at the turn of the century.

Last but not least, the relative importance of large corporations in Southern Europe can also be seen in the fact that they played a significant political as well as social role. This is because, in these latecomer nations, industrialization and modernization went hand in hand. Big businesses were called on to complete or to substitute the actions of the state in a context where growth was fast but several material and immaterial infrastructures were lacking. For example, these companies were responsible for implementing transport and housing facilities for their workers in the growing cities, creating the welfare systems that did not yet exist at a national level, setting up schools, institutions to properly train their employees and so on. Whether their efforts had a positive impact is nevertheless debatable since, with few exceptions, the relationships between large corporations and their workers deteriorated as early as the economic miracle years, and social unrest as well as poor industrial relations became long-term features of these nations' economic systems.

5 Sector-Based Analysis of Large Corporations in Italy and Spain

5.1 SECTORAL DYNAMICS IN THE LONG RUN

The variety in the activities engaged in by corporations underwent significant transformations during the twentieth century. The spread of the Second Industrial Revolution and, later on, of the Third Industrial Revolution technological paradigm throughout the world increased not only the quantity of produced goods but also the number and variety of products and sectors in which corporations and big businesses operated.

Several studies have stressed the correlation between the wealth of the richest nations in the world and the development of large corporations in the manufacturing sectors typical of the Second Industrial Revolution in those countries (Chandler 1977, 1990; Chandler, Amatori and Hikino 1997). However, relatively recently, some scholars have also pointed out the importance of nonmanufacturing sectors in generating large corporations and in stimulating economic growth as early as at the beginning of the big business era (e.g., Wardley 1991). Later on, particularly since the onset of the 1970s crisis in those manufacturing sectors where big business typically operated, the emergence of new manufacturing technologies as well as the rise of new services corporations made the sector-based distribution of the largest corporations all over the world and in the most advanced nations more complicated and varied (e.g., Nohria, Dyer and Dalzell 2002).

As has been shown in previous chapters, large corporations played an important role within the Italian and Spanish economies during the second half of the twentieth century. However, they were established relatively late in comparison to the United States and the most advanced European nations. This is particularly true in Spain, with all the consequences that this can have in terms of international competition dynamics and the need to develop internal capabilities in a hurry. It was not an obvious matter that big businesses in these countries were able to develop and succeed in the same industries in which large, effective foreign companies already existed at world level. At the same time, the circumstances in which the economic booms of Italy and Spain occurred, and the dynamics in the development of their large corporations, was very different from the framework in which big business originated in the United States or in the most advanced European nations. This is true from several points of view. Sectors that drove the economic development of the richest countries might have fared differently in these nations, while alternative industries might have found them to provide fertile ground for growth.

Based on the empirical evidence in the "individual units" populations, this chapter deals with the transformation of the sectors in which the 100 largest companies in Italy and Spain were active during the period 1950 to 2002. It shows the decline of some industries and the rise of others, and stresses the similarities and differences between these two nations in this respect. The first aim is to observe that sectors characterized the large corporations in these two economies both immediately after World War II and during the most intense period of economic growth up to the energy crisis. The second is to see whether the emergence of new sectors and technologies has also affected these two nations during the last few decades and, if so, to what extent.

5.2 INDUSTRY DISTRIBUTION OF THE LARGEST COMPANIES IN ITALY

Looking at the industry distribution of the 100 largest companies in Italy throughout the period under consideration, the main transformation detectable at first glance is the passage from the absolute predominance of one sector to an increasing "democratization" of the panorama, with the largest companies in the country being distributed across an increased number of sectors.

Whereas in 1950, a single sector, namely, electricity, dominated the population, during the 1950s and 1960s, other sectors were also able to foster a reasonable number of large corporations, as reflected by the 1973 and, later on, the 1988 and 2002 populations (see Table 5.1).

By 1973, the electricity sector had lost its predominant position in terms of the number of major companies that belonged to it, giving way to the petroleum, chemical, electrical equipment, food, mechanical, and wholesale and retail trade industries. While the chemical, mechanical, petroleum and wholesales and retail trade sectors retained a strong presence in big business presence during the 1970s and 1980s, the 1988 population reflects a relative decline of industries such as electrical equipment and food in favor of areas such as transportation equipment production and the recreational activities sector. The last benchmark year basically confirms the importance of some sectors for big business in Italy, such as the mechanical, petroleum, transportation equipment and wholesale and retail trade industries, while, following the privatization and liberalization process, the electricity sector regained a strong position in terms of the number of companies present in the population. As can be seen in Table 5.1, industry dynamics were of course quite different during the second

Table 5.1 Industry distribution of the 100 largest companies in Italy

	1950	1973	1988	2002
Brick, pottery, glass and cement	2	1	0	2
Chemicals and pharmaceuticals	9	10	13	4
Computer and related activities	0	1	1	2
Construction	0	5	4	3
Electrical and instrument engineering	3	11	6	4
Electricity, gas and water supply	29	3	3	12
Food, drink, and tobacco	4	13	7	7
Hotels and restaurants	0	0	0	0
Mechanical engineering and metals	14	11	16	9
Mining and extraction	4	0	0	0
Other business activities	0	0	2	1
Other manufacturing activities	1	0	0	1
Other	0	0	0	1
Petroleum	7	14	12	10
Post and telecommunications	1	1	2	4
Publishing, printing and reproduction	2	3	3	4
Real estate activities	0	0	0	0
Recreational, cultural and sporting activities	0	1	4	3
Rubber and plastics	2	2	1	3
Shipbuilding	4	1	1	1
Textiles and clothing	10	5	3	3
Transport	0	1	2	2
Transportation equipment	8	6	7	10
Wholesale and retail trade	0	11	13	14

Source: Appendix Tables 1a, 2a, 3a, 4a.

half of the twentieth century. Some sectors remained active participants in the big business panorama more or less throughout the examined period, while others increased their importance temporarily or permanently, and others still followed an opposite trend (see Table 5.1 and 5.3).

Electricity, gas and water supply is probably the sector that has had the most dramatic drop in relative size in terms of the number of corporations included in the population. It was the real protagonist of big business panorama during the postwar period, but during the following period, its presence declined remarkably. Almost a third of the companies in the Italian population in 1950 belonged to this sector, and it was a central sector for the Italian economy throughout the first half of the twentieth century. Following the nationalization of railways in 1905, the large-scale private investment that had gone into the railway boom was redirected into the electricity sector. In the mid-twentieth century, it was very concentrated: the twenty-nine electricity companies in the population belonged to a few big groups that produced almost all the electric energy of the country (Castronovo 1994, 70; Amatori and Colli 1999, 201). Through the holdings SIP and SME, the Italian state directly controlled 10% of assets in the electricity sector. The private firms Edison, SADE and La Centrale owned, respectively, 14%, 5% and 3% of assets in this industry. The number of companies belonging to the electricity sector dramatically dropped in the 1973 population, mainly due to the nationalization of its private corporations and the foundation of a single state-owned company, Ente Nazionale per l'Energia Elettrica (ENEL), in 1962 (Bolchini et al. 1989; Zanetti 1994; Bruno and Segreto 1996). Also in relative terms, electricity lost its position as the most important source of energy during the 1960s and 1970s to petroleum. The large private companies that had, as part of large groups, represented the real "giants" in the 1950 population disappeared in 1973 and did not reappear in 1988. Only in 2002, following a process of liberalization of this industry, did electricity regain a prominent position among Italy's large corporations. But its sector-based dynamics were quite different from the past, with a single company almost completely dominating the industry—the former monopolist ENEL—and a group of smaller private companies following the leader.

The other sector that experienced a relative down-sizing during this era, although to a lesser extent, is textiles. In 1950, the textile sector was the third largest in Italy in terms of the number of large corporations included among the country's top 100 firms. Companies such as De Angeli Frua, G. Marzotto e Figli, Linificio Canapificio Nazionale, Châtillon, Manifatture Cotoniere Meridionali, Lanificio Rossi, Cotonificio Vittorio Olcese, Cucirini Cantoni Coats, Cotonificio Valle di Susa and Manifattura Lane Borgosesia were both historical participants in the first stages of Italy's industrialization as well as local "giants" (Castronovo 1965; Avagliano 1970; Romano 1975; Ramella 1984). Nevertheless, they numbered relatively few in the population when compared to the companies belonging to the more modern and capital-intensive sectors of the Second Industrial Revolution both in terms of assets and number of employees. During the following benchmark years, the number of textile corporations in the population dropped from ten in 1950 to five in 1973 and to three in 1988 and 2002.

Some of the predominant sectors in Italy were very typical of big business distribution all over the world. The mechanical sector as well as metallurgy, petroleum and transportation equipment have increased their relative importance since the 1950s and remained as protagonists of the Italian big business panorama up to 2002.

The mechanical and metals industries ranked second and third, respectively, in the 1950 and 1973 populations and came in first in 1988. Metallurgy and mechanical companies were very often clustered at the top of the ranking, and in 1950, half of the enterprises that belonged to these sectors, such as Terni, Ilva, Ansaldo, Finmeccanica, Finsider, Falck and Cogne, were among the thirty largest firms in Italy. In contrast to the electricity sector, which was predominantly privately owned for a long time, in the middle of the twentieth century, these industries were almost completely dominated by state-owned companies, whose total assets, through IRI's subholdings Finmeccanica and Finsider and Nazionale Cogne, represented 86% of the population's assets in this sector. The only important private firm during this period was Falck, which ranked twenty-seventh in the population and which in turn controlled an important mechanical company: Franco Tosi. Other relatively minor mechanical companies such as SISMA, Nebiolo, Pignone and Tecnomasio Italiano followed at a considerable distance. Most of them were not autonomous companies, but were controlled by a number of other large companies. Edison owned SISMA, SNIA Viscosa controlled Pignone and Brown Boveri was the major shareholder of Tecnomasio Italiano. Although the situation remained largely unchanged until 1973, with the largest state-owned companies clearly positioned ahead of a small number of private competitors, the energy crisis of the 1970s deeply affected this industry and upset a long-term status quo. The financial situation of the state-owned metallurgy firms was so bad that IRI put its metallurgic subholding Finsider into voluntary liquidation in 1988. In 1987, its losses amounted to 1,462 billion lire (Balconi 1991, 433; Osti and Ranieri 1993; Pini 2000).

Other sectors that expanded during this period and remained long-lasting participants in the big business panorama throughout the second half of the twentieth century were the petroleum and the transportation equipment industries. The former grew between 1950 and 1973 in particular. It was also dominated by one large state-owned holding, ENI, which was founded by Enrico Mattei in 1953 based on its state-owned predecessor AGIP (Colitti 1979, 2008; Briatico 2004; Pozzi 2009). A few private companies also existed and appeared in particular in the 1973 population. They were smaller than the state-owned corporation, and most were family-owned companies, such as Anonima Petroli Italia API, SARAS Raffinerie Sarde, Garrone and SAROM Raffinazione. However, ENI's major competitors were the subsidiaries of large multinationals that appeared at the top of the rankings in 1973, 1988 and 2002. These include Esso Italiana, Shell Italiana, BP Italiana, Total, Mobil Oil Italiana, Chevron Oil Italiana, Fina Italiana, Gulf Italiana and Amoco Italia (later on, Tamoil).

The transportation equipment industry also experienced major growth during the years of the Italian economic miracle, but it was consistently present at the top of the rankings throughout the period 1950–2002. In 1950, the sector was highly concentrated: FIAT owned 9% of the total assets of the population and 81.81% of this sector's total assets. Almost all automobiles in Italy were produced by FIAT; the company's production in this period exceeded 80% of the Italian total (Amatori and Colli 1999, 201) even though other companies such as the state-owned companies Alfa Romeo and the family-owned firms Lancia, Piaggio and Innocenti also existed (Amatori 1996; Castronovo 1999). The growth of the turnover generated by companies belonging to this sector has been very slight but relatively constant roughly throughout the period considered. The main companies in this industry have also remained the same for more than fifty years and, interestingly, in contrast to the oil sector almost all of the main companies have been Italian. Foreign firms traditionally only got involved in distribution and most enterprises that engaged in production did so in collaboration with a local partner, which was usually FIAT. The polarization in this sector has further increased, and very few companies apart from FIAT have been able to maintain ownership and control of firms that were not efficient. At the end of the period, in 2002, FIAT's turnover made up almost the total turnover of this sector among the 100 largest companies in the country.

Around these relatively stable core sectors, the industry distribution of the largest corporations fluctuated. A first wave of changes has been ascribed to the economic growth of the country and to the diffusion of new consumer goods after World War II, while a second has more to do with business dynamics since the end of the 1970s. In the first wave, some of the industries that had grown most during the golden age period lost their prominent position in the Italian big business panorama, such as chemicals, food, construction and electrical equipment and appliances.

The Italian chemical sector had spawned some large and important companies such as Montecatini and, later on, Edison and ENI. However, they failed to make the most of important opportunities during this period, causing the whole sector fall into serious and irreversible difficulty from the 1970s (Scalfari and Turani 1974; Pizzorni 2006). The contribution made by the chemical companies to the total turnover generated by the 100 largest companies in the country dropped from 9% to 2% between 1973 and 2002. The growing domestic and international markets also suited companies in the food sectors (Barciela López and Di Vittorio 2003) and in the electrical appliances industry. During the 1950s and 1960s, Italy was able to foster very large firms in these industries. During the following decades, however, the contribution made by these firms to the national wealth decreased (e.g., Ori 1973; Balloni 1978). In most cases, the relative decline of the Italian firms in these industries was also related to the difficult generational handover that most of them had to face during the 1970s and 1980s and that in some cases even brought about the end of the company (Cingolani 1990).

During the 1980s and 1990s, other sectors started to gain an increasing importance in the country, and another group of companies in nonmanufacturing sectors, such as telecommunications, publishing, advertising and recreational activities, began to grow. Based on the number of companies included among the 100 largest in the country, between 1973 and 2002, the telecommunications sector grew from 1% to 4%, and the recreational activities sector from 1% to 3%. Data concerning the percentage of total turnover represented by these sectors within the population is even more impressive. However, the most impressive growth in the long run has probably been that of the wholesale and retail trade sector between 1950 and 2002. Completely absent from the 1950 population, 11% of the largest corporations in the country belonged to this nonmanufacturing industry in 1973, rising to 13% in 1988 and 14% in 2002. The increasing number of commercial subsidiaries of foreign multinationals helps explain this rise. The growing popularity of supermarkets and department stores in particular after World War II, together with the growth in wealth of the population during the economic miracle, should also be mentioned as contributing factors (Amatori 1989; Scarpellini 2001; Papadia 2005).

5.3 INDUSTRY DISTRIBUTION OF THE LARGEST COMPANIES IN SPAIN

The dynamics of the sector-based distribution of the 100 largest corporations in Spain seem broadly similar to the Italian experience. However, some specific trends emerged in Spain, setting it apart from the Italian example. As Table 5.2 shows, also in Spain the population of the first benchmark year was almost completely dominated by a single sector, namely, electricity, which then progressively lost ground to other industries such as the petroleum sector, producers of transportation equipment, the mechanical and metallurgic industries and the wholesale and retail trade. However, the transformations in the relative weight of certain sectors seems to have been more dramatic in Spain than in Italy, whereas in the 2002 population, there is a sector that seems to have replaced electricity: the wholesale and retail trade industry activity.

In 1950, the situation in Spain was only partly different from that of Italy. Under the dominance of the electricity sector to which more than thirty firms out of the total population belonged, several sector such as chemicals, food, metallurgy and mechanics, transport and transportation equipment each represented about 7% to 10% of the whole population. Some of these sectors further developed during the following years, while others became relatively marginal in comparison to other industries. The main difference between the two nations rests in the role of the transport companies that, while largely absent in Italy, represented almost 10% of the population by number and 27% of the assets of the whole population that year in Spain. This information reflects the substantial economic power that the railway sector still had in Spain in that period. Red Nacional de Ferrocarriles Españoles (RENFE), which had unified and nationalized the previously private railway companies after a long negotiation process with their owners (Carreras 2003, 56), represented on its own almost 23% of the assets of the population of 100 largest companies in the middle of the century. However, also other, nonrailway transport companies occupied important positions in this ranking, in particular in sea transport (Compañía Trasmediterránea, Naviera Aznar and Compañía Trasatlántica), in

Table 5.2 Industry distribution of the 100 largest companies in Spain

	1950	1973	1988	2002
Brick, pottery, glass and cement	0	3	2	1
Chemicals and pharmaceuticals	9	7	7	2
Computer and related activities	0	1	1	2
Construction	3	6	9	8
Electrical and instrument engineering	2	8	5	5
Electricity, gas and water supply	31	8	11	8
Food, drink and tobacco	9	13	6	3
Hotels and restaurants	0	2	2	3
Mechanical engineering and metals	9	9	7	5
Mining and extraction	3	1	1	1
Other business activities	0	1	3	0
Other manufacturing activities	0	0	0	0
Other	0	2	0	2
Petroleum	4	8	9	5
Post and telecommunications	1	1	1	9
Publishing, printing and reproduction	2	3	3	0
Real estate activities	4	0	0	0
Recreational, cultural and sporting activities	0	0	0	1
Rubber and plastics	0	3	2	1
Shipbuilding	4	3	1	1
Textiles and clothing	3	1	0	1
Transport	9	3	3	5
Transportation equipment	7	7	11	9
Wholesale and retail trade	0	10	16	28

Source: Appendix Tables 5a, 6a, 7a, 8a.

air transport (such as Compañía Mercantil Anónima Iberia, which had been recently acquired by a German company; Vidal Olivares 2008) and Aviación y Comercio—AVIACO) as well as in urban and local transport (such as Tranvías de Barcelona and Ferrocarril Metropolitano de Barcelona). The role of the transport sector diminished significantly in the following benchmark year, leaving space for a more democratic, sector-based distribution also in Spain, at least up to the new millennium. Companies such as RENFE and Iberia remained important within the Spanish big business panorama throughout the second part of the twentieth century, but the relative size in particular of railways in the national economy diminished, together with the contribution of the transport sector to the big business panorama.

A similar fate befell the electricity sector. It came first in the ranking based on the number of large companies that belonged to it in 1950, and as in Italy, it was a relatively concentrated sector. Most of the thirty-one companies belonging to this sector had the same owners, namely, the major banks of the country that had moved their money from the transport to the electricity sector following the nationalization of the railways in 1941 (Carreras 2003). With the important exception of Empresa Nacional de Electricidad (ENDESA), which was state-owned, almost all the other companies were part of the business groups led by the main national banks of the country (Antolín 1999). These include for instance Banco de Vizcaya (which owned Iberduero, Sevillana de Electricidad and Electra de Viesgo) and Banco Hispano Americano and Urquijo (Energías e Industrias Aragonesas, Riegos de Levante, Unión Eléctrica Madrileña, Saltos del Alberche, Eléctrica del Langreo and Hidroeléctrica del Cantábrico). Others still formed part of organizations such as the Sociedad Hidroeléctrica Española (Luz y Fuerza de Levante and Compañía Electra Madrid) or belonged to that run by the entrepreneur Juan March. The latter had, after years of fighting, been able to snatch ownership of the companies Riegos y Fuerzas del Ebro and Compañía Barcelonesa de Electricidad from the Canadian-run Barcelona Traction, Light and Power Co., and to create the electricity company Fuerzas Eléctricas de Cataluña (FECSA) (Torres Villanueva 2000).

A few years later, in 1973, other sectors had diminished the importance of these companies to some extent. In contrast to the Italian case, the Spanish electricity companies did not disappear under a new, big, state-owned holding. They and their owners remained the same, but simply became smaller within the national economy and in the big business panorama. Only during the 1980s and in the 1990s did the sector substantially change. Following a process of mergers and acquisitions as well as diversification in the energy sector, new multinational giants such as ENDESA, Gas Natural and Iberdrola were able to emerge. As shown by Table 5.3, the relative decline of the electricity companies in Spain is smaller if we consider their contribution to the turnover of the whole population rather than their absolute number.

Throughout the decades under consideration, and particularly starting from the 1960s, the petroleum and the transportation equipment sectors have maintained their importance. Concerning oil, the absolute number of companies belonging to this sector was smaller than in Italy. This industry included between 4% to 9% of the population throughout the period under consideration, even though oil companies always ranked in the top in all the benchmark years. Unlike in Italy, the main protagonists of this sector were, at least up the 1980s, Spanish-owned firms such as the private companies Compañía Arrendataria del Monopolio de Petróleos (CAMPSA), which monopolized distribution, Compañía Española de Petróleos (CEPSA) and the state-owned company Empresa Nacional Calvo Sotelo. In 1973, only one foreign company—Esso Petróleos Españoles—appeared in the ranking. However, the sector was completely transformed in the democratic age

Table 5.3 Industry distribution of the turnover of the 100 largest corporations in Italy and Spain

	1950		1973		1988		2002	
	Italy	Spain	Italy	Spain	Italy	Spain	Italy	Spain
Brick, pottery, glass and cement	1.08	0	0.3	1.37	0	0.83	2.4	0.24
Chemicals and pharmaceuticals	9.81	5.12	9.34	6.76	8.47	4.85	2.22	0.85
Computer and related activities	0	0	1.21	0.71	3.51	1.58	1.44	0.67
Construction	0	1.22	2.03	7.07	2.47	6.69	1.5	7.03
Electrical and instrument engineering	1.31	1.06	5.15	4.6	4.03	2.55	1.65	1.66
Electricity, gas and water supply	36.73	22.00	7.68	6.20	5.46	13.87	15.35	13.2
Food, drink and tobacco	2.91	5.42	5.27	7.23	4.1	4.96	4.76	0.94
Hotels and restaurants	0	0	0	0.75	0	1.19	0	1.35
Mechanical engineering and metals	16.73	6.55	10.19	10.03	9.27	4.71	6.59	2.21
Mining and extraction	1.47	1.54	0	0.38	0	0.4	0	0.25
Other business activities	0	0	0	0.34	1.75	1.44	0.53	0
Other manufacturing activities	0.34	0.08	0	0	0	0	0.77	0
Other	0	0	0	2.51	0	0	0.63	3.2
Petroleum	5.49	8.03	21.46	17.79	15.06	9.92	14.27	15.95
Post and telecommunications	0.27	5.09	3.53	2.86	7.54	5.18	9.54	17.44
Publishing, printing and reproduction	0.96	0.69	1	3.36	1.77	1.24	1.89	0.28
Real estate activities	0	0.89	0	0	0	0	0	0
Recreational, cultural and sporting activities	0	0	0.8	0	2.74	0	1.7	0
Rubber and plastics	2.51	0	6.72	0	0.81	1.63	2.36	0.56
Shipbuilding	4.23	8.32	0.83	3.84	0.97	0.44	0.53	0.47
Textiles and clothing	4.83	1.54	3.09	0.06	1.42	0	1.25	0.42
Transport	0	26.93	1.39	6.46	2.26	4.72	2.4	3.53
Transportation equipment	11.33	4.6	13.19	8.93	16.82	19.32	20.24	9.46
Wholesale and retail trade	0	0	6.83	8.66	9	14	9.02	20.26

Source: Appendix Tables 1a, 2a, 3a, 4a, 5a, 6a, 7a, 8a.

(Santamaría 1988). A national champion that swallowed up most of the previously private and state-owned companies was created: Repsol. Repsol, founded as a legacy company of the state-owned holding in the energy sector Instituto Nacional de Hidrocarburos, was privatized in the late 1980s and the early 1990s. Also at an international level Repsol became a real giant (Guillén 2005), generating 75% of the total turnover of the largest companies in the Spanish oil sector in 2002. Meanwhile, foreign companies gained a large presence in this sector. The most prominent examples are BP Oil España, Total España and Elf Aquitaine (currently Total), which at the beginning of the 1990s became the major shareholders of the previously private-owned company CEPSA.

The transportation equipment industry was also important to Spanish big business, and maintained its position throughout the second half of the century, even though its main protagonists changed significantly. During the 1950s and part of the 1960s, even though some "minor" companies were active, the sector was basically a duopoly. On one side was SEAT, based on a collaboration between the state-owned holding INI, several Spanish banks and the Italian car producer FIAT, which was founded by the INI in 1950, and on the other side was FASA-Renault, a joint-venture between Spanish and French partners (Sánchez Sánchez 2004). During the 1970s, the number of foreign companies in this sector increased. US giants such as Ford and General Motors were also allowed to operate in Spain (Catalan 2007; Fernández de Sevilla 2011). Foreign presence in car production increased until the acquisition of SEAT by Volkswagen in the mid-1980s basically confirmed the new dominance of the multinationals in this sector in Spain. The automotive industry was almost completely dominated by domestically owned big business until the 1960s, but was totally foreign owned by 2003 (Binda and Colli 2011).

Among Spain's 100 largest corporations, the number, and even more so the turnover, of mechanics and metallurgy companies declined slightly, particularly after the 1970s. The two national champions in metallurgy, the state-owned company Empresa Nacional Siderúrgica (ENSIDESA) and the privately owned company Altos Hornos de Vizcaya had to deal with a severe crisis during the second half of the 1970s and the first part of the 1980s. Despite a process of restructuring of the sector, they were unable to recover fully from this crisis in the face of competition from smaller private firms (e.g., Aristraín). Both of them came under a state-owned holding appositely created in the metallurgic sector—Corporación Siderúrgica Integral (CSI)—and later on passed into the hands of the European giant Arcelor, now Arcelor-Mittal. Things went no better for the big mechanical companies: only one Spanish-owned company remained in the 2002 ranking, namely, Corporación Gestamp. The changing context and the turmoil of the 1970s deeply affected also other big business sectors, such as shipbuilding (Houpt and Ortiz-Villajos 1998; Carreras, Tafunell and Torres 2000, 222–224), which never completely recovered. As in Italy, the importance of

Spain's chemical companies significantly decreased, in terms of both their number and their performance (Puig Raposo 2003). This was due in part to the poor performance of the largest Spanish companies, Cros and Explosivos Río Tinto, from the second half of the 1970s.

Nevertheless, as in Italy during the second half of the twentieth century, new opportunities presented themselves both during the Spanish economic miracle of the 1960s and, later on, from the 1980s onward. After the Plan de Estabilización was enacted in 1959, some sectors were able to improve their performance due to the increasing wealth of the population and the modernization of the country. Among those that prospered were the construction sector, food, the electrical equipment and appliances industry, as well as the hotel and tourism sectors, which benefitted from the increased number of tourists in Spain. However, although tourism remained a positive activity for some large corporations in the long term, the importance of the food and appliances sectors significantly decreased during the last quarter of the century. The construction sector with its private companies such as Dragados y Construcciones, Agromán, Entrecanales y Tavora, Huarte y Compañía, Fomento de Obras y Construcciones and Cubiertas y Tejados experienced impressive growth in the Spanish economic booms, during the 1960s and, later on, during the 1980s and 1990s. The growth of the constructions sector was accompanied also by the growth of a satellite sector; real estate companies were consistently present in the rankings throughout the period under consideration. Following waves of mergers and acquisitions very large companies emerged particularly during the last decades of the century, but big business in the construction sector is currently facing a severe crisis (Torres Villanueva 2011).

More recently, two other industries that have experienced large-scale growth and are currently very important in the big business panorama in Spain are the telecommunications sector and the wholesale and retail trade sector. The former benefitted from the emergence of new technologies, the consolidation of a national champion and new multinational in this field, Telefónica (Calvo 2011), and from the entry of new foreign companies. As a result, this sector grew particularly during the 1990s, and it is currently very important in Spain, in particular in terms of the size of its turnover.

The wholesale and retail trade sector was completely absent in the middle of the autarkic period, but by 1973, it had already grown remarkably in at least two areas: private department stores and supermarkets—such as El Corte Inglés, Galerías Preciados and Simago—and commercial subsidiaries of foreign multinationals—such as Comercial Pegaso, Iberenka, Finanzauto, Grupo Comercial Laminados, Bayer Hispania Comercial and Finanzauto y Servicios. Both in 1988 and in 2002, this sector dominated the list of 100 largest companies, with both national private companies and foreign multinationals featuring. An interpretation of this trend, and in particular that governing the Spanish-owned companies, takes into account the fact that they were able grow more considerably during the 1970s crisis in comparison to other sectors, because they earned in cash and did not need to rely on loans during those though years. However, the history of distribution in Spain is quite complicated, with several large companies changing hands many times, very often also changing the nationality of their main shareholder (Toboso Sánchez 2002; Castro Balaguer 2010).

5.4 FROM INDUSTRY TO SERVICES? A COMPARISON BETWEEN ITALY AND SPAIN

It is not possible to make a direct comparison of the industry distribution of the largest companies in Italy and Spain with that of other nations, since the main investigations dealing with this topic have made detailed studies of the weight of each manufacturing sector, but have almost completely neglected utilities and services within the whole big business panorama.

Nevertheless, it is interesting to directly compare the industry distribution of corporate assets (in 1950) and turnover (in 1973, 1988 and 2002) in these two countries (Table 5.3) and to observe the expansion of the services sector during the 1950–2002 period.

By making a direct comparison of the industry-based distribution of the assets and turnover of their major companies, it can be shown that Italy and Spain were broadly similar throughout this period, even allowing for some exceptions. First of all, it is clear that in the postwar period, the weight of electricity companies was much greater in Italy than in Spain. In this latter country, a more significant role was played by the railway, sea and urban transport sectors, whereas during the same period in Italy, these were much less important in terms of their size. Secondly, Italy in 1950 was more specialized in sectors with a higher added value and scientific content, such as chemicals, mechanics and car production, whereas Spain had not been able yet to create large competitive corporations in these industries. The distribution of the so-called traditional sectors was quite similar in these two nations, although the food and drink sector dominated in Spain versus the textile industry in Italy. Finally, the post and telecommunications sectors were much more important in Spain, where Compañía Telefónica Nacional de España was working on a significant development plan during the first years of Franco's regime, partly to carry out the reconstruction of the national network and, later on, in response to the strong and unfulfilled market demand and to extend the urban network in the most densely populated areas (Torres Villanueva 2003).

At the end of the golden age, in contrast to the previous benchmark year, the information on the 1973 population allows us to stress a strong similarity that appears also in the 1988 population. In both cases, the prevailing sector based on turnover was petroleum in 1973 and the production of transportation equipment in 1988. In 1973, the largest sectors in both nations were followed by the mechanical and metallurgy industries as well as the transportation equipment, chemicals and wholesale and retail trade sectors. The main difference between the two nations concerned the stronger weight of the construction, shipbuilding, cement and transport sectors in the Spanish population all but shipbuilding confirmed in the 1988 ranking. The Italian turnover, meanwhile, was predominantly based on chemicals and petroleum in 1973 and 1988, while between these two benchmark years the contribution of the electricity, rubber and tires and transportation equipment sectors diminished.

Also, in the new millennium, the industrial distribution of the turnover generated by the major companies was broadly similar in these two nations, in particular with regard to electrical equipment, petroleum, electricity and transport. However, there was a difference in where big business in these two economies excelled. Italian strengths in 2002 rested more in cement, food, mechanics, publishing, recreational activities, rubber and transportation equipment, whereas Spanish big business was stronger in particular in construction, post and telecommunications and the wholesale and retail trade.

In looking at the industry distribution of the 100 largest corporations, the rise and decline of macro-sectors and economic activities in these two nations can be observed, with clear similarities and differences in the changing power balance among the primary, secondary and tertiary sectors throughout a period of more than fifty years (Table 5.4).

In 1950, the role of the primary sector among the largest corporations in both countries was already very small. The main differences between these two nations lies in the role of the manufacturing sectors, which dominated Italian big business but not Spain's, because of the decisive role still played in this latter country by the large railway companies as well as the electricity firms, which were strong also in Italy. Looking at the 1973 information, after the decades of economic growth and the golden age, the predominant role of the manufacturing sector in influencing the activities of the large corporations emerges. Surprisingly, Spain overtook Italy, with 80% of its large corporations in 1973 devoted to manufacturing activities versus the 77% of Italy's. However, from this point onward, manufacturing started to decline in both countries. In the 1988 populations, the percentage of industrial companies had decreased to 68% and 51%, respectively, in Italy and Spain, and

Table 5.4 Industry distribution of the 100 largest nonfinancial companies in Italy and Spain

	1950		1973		1988		2002	
	Italy	Spain	Italy	Spain	Italy	Spain	Italy	Spain
Primary sector	2	2	0	0	0	1	0	0
Secondary sector	61	41	77	80	68	51	61	41
Tertiary sector	37	57	23	20	32	48	39	59

Source: Appendix Tables 1a, 2a, 3a, 4a, 5a, 6a, 7a, 8a.

in 2002, it had dropped to 61% and 41%, respectively. Curiously, after the impressive growth of the manufacturing sector during the 1950s and 1960s, the percentage of nonmanufacturing companies among the 100 largest in these countries in 2002 was not too different from that of 1950. However, the identity of these firms is very different. Although in 1950 the tertiary sector was mainly made up of the railway and electricity industries, in particular in Spain, the services companies of 2002 were mainly wholesale and retail trade firms as well as telecommunications companies, construction firms and enterprises devoted to tourism or recreational activities.

When looking at the sector-based distribution of the 100 largest corporations during the second half of the twentieth century it is thus possible to claim that in both Italy and Spain, big business, be it local or foreign, grew in those same sectors that characterized the largest corporations of the United States and the most advanced nations. Moreover, as in the rest of the world, the few big companies that were still engaged in primary activities in 1950 largely disappeared during the second half of the century, whereas big business in manufacturing, and particular in the sectors typical of the Second Industrial Revolution, grew during the 1950s and 1960s and reached its peak at the beginning of the 1970s. Manufacturing then started to decline as the importance of new sectors and of the services industry increased from the mid-1970s onward.

However, the points at which Italy and Spain embraced the various technological waves were slightly different.

This was, for instance, the case in the railway sector, which in 1950, was predominant in the Spanish big business panorama but already relatively marginalized in that of Italy, what with the indisputable onward march of the electricity firms.

Spain also seems more successful than Italy when it came to promoting national nonmanufacturing companies during the 1980s and 1990s, by giving up the manufacturing companies that had developed during the Francoist period to foreign owners when they were no longer able to compete with the foreign companies that entered the country following Spain's inclusion in the ECC. The money generated by the sale of local manufacturing companies to foreign investors allowed Spanish big business to focus on the restructuring of some services sectors mainly through a merger and acquisitions process and to exploit the new technological opportunities, thus fostering large corporations and new multinationals in sectors such as gas and electricity, telecommunications and banking (Binda 2005a; Guillén 2005).

Things went quite differently in Italy, where mainly for political reasons and due to the strength of the trade unions, even the worst-performing manufacturing companies were not sold, closed or significantly restructured. Manufacturing companies thus, even though they lost ground when compared to the 1970s, remained the predominant variety of large corporation in this country still in 2002.

5.5 SUMMARY

As in the rest of the world, technological trends and innovations influenced the composition and the dynamics of the Italian and Spanish big business panoramas.

This chapter has demonstrated that, at first glance, the composition of the population of the largest companies in these two Southern European nations is broadly similar to the industry distribution of the largest corporations in the world's most advanced economies. Nevertheless, some specific dynamics can be identified.

For instance, the significant delay with which Spain industrialized even in comparison to Italy is very apparent when we consider the fact that railway companies formed the largest enterprises in the country and that new large enterprises in the motor vehicle and steel sectors came into being precisely during the 1940s and 1950s, in order to complement or substitute the relatively small companies that had existed in the country up to that point.

In both countries, a process of partial "democratization" of the big business panorama took place. The absolute dominance of the railway companies in Spain and the electricity companies in Italy in the middle of the century was broken down to the benefit of a larger number of industries that are represented in the following benchmark years, such as the mechanical sector as well as the metallurgy, petroleum and transportation equipment industries. This is consistent with what was occurring in the United States and in the most advanced European economies at the same time. We can interpret the increasing importance of nonmanufacturing industries, such as the telecommunications and the wholesale and retail trade sectors, in a similar way.

Nevertheless, within this context, each country has its own specific features and idiosyncrasies. In Spain, for instance, the importance of the construction companies, of the supermarkets and department stores and, to a lesser extent, of the tourist sector, is particularly striking. In Italy, on the other hand, the rubber and tire and the mechanical industries were stronger.

Interestingly, the empirical evidence that has been presented in this chapter does not allow us to claim that a significant shift from manufacturing to services occurred during these years. Indeed, we have argued that the manufacturing sector remained predominant in Italy throughout the second half of the twentieth century, despite the fact that nonmanufacturing industries such as electricity have been both present and important within the population since the first benchmark year. In Spain, on the other hand, nonmanufacturing corporations have dominated during the last few decades with the 1970s benchmark being the only exception, because this is when manufacturing companies had a larger presence within the population. Even though the nature of services changed over time by making the transition from transport to more modern sectors, during the final decades of the twentieth century, nonmanufacturing corporations were clearly not new to Spain.

6   Big-Business Owners and Managers

6.1 CORPORATE OWNERSHIP AND GOVERNANCE AROUND THE WORLD

Understanding the features and the role of the different kinds of enterprise ownership was one of the main aims of several investigations conducted since when big business emerged in the United States.

Adolf Berle and Gardiner Means in the 1930s were among the first to claim that an irreversible fragmentation of ownership and a progressive separation of ownership from control had already occurred within the largest corporations of the United States (Berle and Means 1932; for a debate on Berle and Means see Hannah 2007; Cheffins and Bank 2009). Later on, many studies analyzed the features and ownership structures of the largest companies outside the United States and investigated the diffusion of an eventual "managerial revolution" (e.g., Chandler 1990; Whittington 2007).

In the mid-1990s, Julian Franks and Colin Mayer (1995) effectively summarized the studies conducted up to that point by describing two kinds of control and ownership systems, defined as "insider" and "outsider" systems. The outsider system is basically that described by Berle and Means (1932) in the United States, where ownership is dispersed among many investors external to the company and who in general do not exercise any control. Both the United States and the United Kingdom are currently characterized by this kind of system, where thousands of individual shareholders or institutional investors own a company. In both these nations, no one individual or institutional investor generally owns very large percentages of a firm's capital by his- or herself and thus cannot directly exercise control over a company. As a result, what we find is a separation of the ownership of a company from its control.

However, corporate ownership and governance are quite different in Continental Europe, which can be defined as having an insider system. Compared to the Anglo-Saxon experience, few companies were in fact listed on the stock exchange during the second half of the twentieth century, and even those who were often maintained a strong degree of concentration of their shares. Franks and Mayer in 1995 claimed that in more than 80% of the 170 largest companies listed on the stock exchange in France and Germany, one shareholder held more than 25% of the shares and that in more than 50% of the firms, a single blockholder existed. Later on, Rafael La Porta, Florencio López-de-Silanes and Andrei Shleifer (1999) extended Franks and Mayer's investigations to many other countries in the world, arguing that the results observed in the insider system of Continental Europe were applicable worldwide, whereas those of the Anglo-Saxon outsider system were not.

According to investigations into corporate behavior, this distinction is not irrelevant, and several interpretations have been formulated about the relationship between company ownership and managerial systems on the one hand, and their strategic and organizational behavior on the other (Whittington and Mayer 2000). Chandler, for instance, argued that the predominance of family capitalism, and its preference for dividends compared to investments, was one of the main reasons for the relative economic decline of the United Kingdom (Chandler 1990). Scholars on national institutionalism pointed the finger at corporate ownership and financial systems as being the origin of economic organizational structures that affected the whole economic system. According to Richard Whitley (1994), the decisive elements in an economic system are whether the ownership of a company is private or public, whether it is dispersed or not, and whether volatile financial markets are used in order to increase share capital.

With regard to Europe, Richard Whittington and Michael Mayer in their analysis on big business claimed that at the beginning of the new millennium France, Germany and, to a lesser extent, the United Kingdom were still quite far removed from the American model of dispersed ownership and professional management and that, in particular in France and Germany, family ownership endured in a context of strong diffusion of personal control (Guillén 1994; Whittington and Mayer 2000, 120–121).

In this respect, empirical studies on Italy and Spain during the second half of the century revealed some important differences, but also elements of substantial convergence toward the Continental European system.

6.2 THE OWNERS OF ITALIAN BIG BUSINESS

As has been shown in previous chapters, big business in Italy strong underwent significant changes during the second half of the twentieth century. New sectors and firms emerged, and companies had to adapt not only to the context of a country that experienced a definitive transition to industrialization, a strong economic growth accompanied by a process of social modernization, a severe crisis during the 1970s and a restructuring process but also to new challenges during the 1980s and 1990s.

However, looking at the identity of the shareholders of large Italian corporations during this period, it is evident that all these transformations did not have a decisive impact in changing the identity of their owners (Figure 6.1).

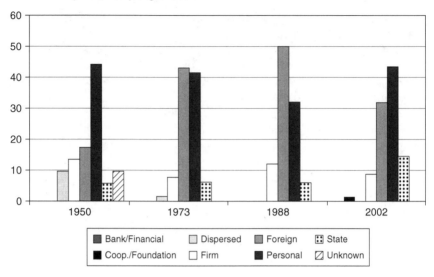

Figure 6.1a Ownership of the largest companies in Italy by number
Source: Appendix Tables 1b, 2b, 3b, 4b.

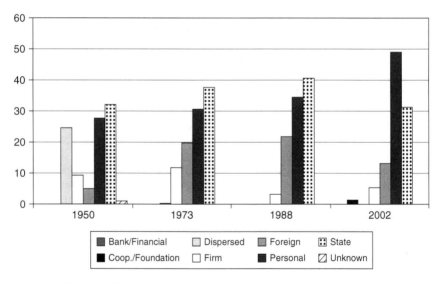

Figure 6.1b Ownership of the largest companies in Italy by turnover
Source: Appendix Tables 1a, 1b, 2a, 2b, 3a, 3b, 4a, 4b.

The information on both the relative number and turnover of one or another kind of owner during this period shows a strong continuity in Italian big business, which has been characterized by three main protagonists throughout the 1950–2002 period: families, the government and subsidiaries of foreign multinational companies, although their relative importance changed slightly over time. The dynamics of the postwar period, the economic miracle, the crisis of the 1970s and the new perspective of the 1980s and 1990s did not diminish the role of the traditional owners of large corporations, while the dispersed ownership model did not spread to any large extent in those years.

In the postwar period, families were the major shareholders of big business in terms of their number and the second-most important owner in terms of assets. Families featured in every industry, from textiles to transportation equipment, chemicals, and so on. Most of the companies in these industries were family-run businesses created well before World War II, whose founders or their heirs still had stable control of the company even though the war had in some cases forced them to leave for a while (Amatori and Brioschi 1997). The 1973 and 1988 populations reflect a relative decline in the number of family-run firms—particularly after the difficult generational transition that many big businesses experienced during the 1970s—but not in their turnover, which continued to represent more than 30% of the total turnover for those benchmark years. The polarization of family-run companies in this framework was relatively pronounced. Very few family-run companies were in fact at the top of the Italian ranking—such as FIAT, Pirelli and Falck—while most were relatively small corporations within the big business population and operated in "traditional" sectors such as food (for instance, Galbani, Industrie Buitoni Perugina and Ferrero), textiles (Gruppo Finanziario Tessile and Marzotto) or publishing (Mondadori and Rizzoli).

New family firms also emerged during the years of the Italian economic miracle as well as in the age of restructuring and effervescence that characterized the country during the 1980s. The financial holding Fininvest, owned by Silvio Berlusconi, and the textiles company Benetton, owned by the Benetton brothers, were for example able to achieve a prominent role in the Italian economy that lasts until the present day.

More than fifty years after the end of World War II, the importance of family-owned business in Italy has not decreased at all. At the beginning of the new millennium, family-run companies maintained a dominant role in terms of both their number and turnover in the big business population. Almost 50% of the total sales of the largest companies in Italy were generated by family firms, who numbered slightly more than 40 out of 100.

The dynamics of European integration could potentially have challenged the predominance of families in Italy. But old habits die hard. At the beginning of the new millennium, family presence was pervasive in several sectors, both traditional and new. Moreover, some families were able to expand their activities thanks to the acquisition of previously state-owned companies during the years of privatization. The Riva family bought the largest steel state-owned company in Italy, Ilva, for a very good price and the Benetton family was able to take advantage of the privatization process by acquiring the Italian network of highways and their associated chain of bars and restaurants:

> If anyone thought, some years ago, that privatization would open a new phase in the history of Italian capitalism, present events will have changed his mind. The conclusion of sixty years of struggle between public and private capitalism in Italy seems to have found only one winner: the family, regardless of whether its name is Agnelli or Brambilla (Segreto 1998, 468. Brambilla is one of the most common surnames in Italy, that is, the representative family small company)

Summarized the Italian business historian Luciano Segreto at the end of the 1990s. The other great entrepreneur of Italian big business was the state, who directly owned many of the very largest corporations in the country during the second half of the twentieth century.

In 1950, state-ownership in big business was minor then family-ownership by number, but was the first in terms of assets. Of the largest companies, 32.6% of the assets came directly from state-owned companies that stood at the very top of the rankings and were active in many sectors (Ministero dell'Industria e del Commercio 1951). The largest of the state-owned holding IRI's firms in this period were in particular electricity companies (SIP, SME), mechanical and shipbuilding firms (Cantieri Riuniti dell'Adriatico, Ansaldo, Alfa Romeo, San Giorgio and Ansaldo San Giorgio) and steel companies (Terni, Ilva and Dalmine). However, the public sector in Italy was not restricted only to IRI. Based on the state-owned company AGIP, in 1953, another state-owned holding was founded and soon flourished: ENI (Colitti 1979; Pozzi 2009).

It is interesting to note how state and privately owned companies interacted very well with each other, in part because, according to the public-sector managers who were administrating them, it was thought that these companies should operate in markets under the same restrictions and be given the same opportunities as private companies. The leader of the IRI's metallurgic subholding Finsider, Oscar Sinigaglia, claimed in 1947 that, because the state had not the knowledge nor the capabilities to manage corporations, the fewer permissions a state-owned company asked the state, the better things went. In his opinion, the IRI's companies should not rely on any favors from the government, and they had to work in the same way as the private companies that competed with them (Osti and Ranieri 1993, 15).

Until the 1980s, the state mantained its position within the national big business panorama in terms of the number and magnitude of state-owned companies, but not in terms of their performance. The "State Entrepreneur" one of the main protagonists of the Italian economic miracle, lost economic efficiency during the following decades by making poor strategic choices. Within a few years, the electricity sector was nationalized, new state-owned economic bodies were founded, and in order to promote some of the underdeveloped areas of the country and, later on, to rescue certain enterprises, the state also entered a number of sectors where state-ownership had no *raison d'être*, such as food or textiles. State-owned companies started to take on "inappropriate burdens" (Pini 2000; Amatori 2012), whose nature was not economic but social, by, for instance, rescuing big private business that employed a large number of workers. The aim to maintain a political consensus and a diffuse system of favoritism accelerated the expansion of the state sector.

The process of privatization that took place during the 1980s and 1990s could have dramatically modified this picture. A big change in the importance of state-owned sectors took place in Italy as well as in the rest of the world during these years. Nevertheless, the effects of these changed dynamics were actually smaller than had been expected. The role of the state as an owner of big business was still important at the beginning of the new millennium. In 2002, by which point the process had largely come to an end, state-owned companies still represented 31.23% of the turnover of the 100 largest companies in the country, despite the fact that the sales value of the Italian process of privatization was one of the highest in the Western World (Privatization Barometer 2005; Barucci and Pierobon 2007). Very important companies such as ENI, Finmeccanica, ENEL, Fincantieri, Alitalia, Poste Italiane, ETI and several others remained, partly or completely, in the hands of the state. The "State Entrepreneur" even though significantly reduced in size, had not vanished.

The state and the families were not the only protagonists of the largest corporations in Italy. Foreign multinationals, whose significance in the country increased up to the 1980s, were also very common as shareholders of the biggest businesses in the country.

Shortly after the end of the war, in 1950, foreign multinationals made up 17.31% of the total population, but represented only 4.96% of its total assets and were concentrated mainly in the oil sector, with some companies in mining, electrical appliances, tires, textiles and mechanics. However, foreign investors later found Italy to provide a good opportunity for investment, in particular in industries that were highly technological and where Italian entrepreneurship was lacking. They could enjoy strong incentives for entry that the Italian government had been providing since the 1950s (Colli 2010), and were interested in basing production in the country due to the opportunities offered by cheap labor and by a domestic market that was becoming both larger and richer in the golden age era. Even though the social instability that characterized the end of the 1960s and the beginning of the 1970s, and a period of terrorism later on, scared some foreign investors (Cingolani 1990), the information gathered on 1973 and 1988 confirms that multinationals in Italy had moved from the periphery to the center of big business.

The major investors in Italy during the golden age were the US multinationals. However, European countries such as the United Kingdom, France,

Germany, the Netherlands, Belgium, Sweden and Switzerland also started to invest heavily in the country. From the 1950s to the 1980s, foreigners invested in particular in the oil sector, but they also had significant interests in others activities such as automotive and mechanical product distribution, the construction of electrical material and equipment, chemicals, mechanics and metallurgy. In some cases, foreign multinationals also entered very traditional Italian sectors were families were facing a serious crisis. This was for instance the case with Barilla, which was sold to the US multinational Grace in 1971 and rebought by the family a few years later, in 1979 (Ori 1973; Gonizzi 2003).

There has been ample literature on the sale of big Italian businesses to large foreign companies during the final decades of the last century, mainly because some very big names were involved (Cingolani 1990; Gallino 2003). However, the phenomenon was not as extensive as has been claimed, at least with regard to the large corporations, in part because big "national" business has traditionally enjoyed substantial political protection. Even though they remained second and third, respectively, by number and turnover among the 100 largest companies in Italy in 2002, foreign multinationals in Italy experienced a slight decline during the 1990s, their number dropping from 50% to 31.88% and their turnover from 21.76% to 13.16% of the total. As in the previous era, the country who established the largest number of large corporations in Italy was the United States, followed by Germany, France and the United Kingdom. Moreover, most of the foreign multinationals in Italy at the beginning of the new millennium operated in the chemical or in the wholesale and retail trade sectors, although their presence in the oil sector also remained significant.

Any shareholders that were not families, the government or foreign investors remained relatively marginal in Italian big business during this period. Corporate ownership by banks and other financial institutions was for instance completely inexistent due to the 1936 bill that forbade the banks to have an active role in industrial companies and that lasted until the 1990s. Companies that belonged to other firms were few and stable during this period. A slight increase in the importance of cooperatives within the big business panorama can also be observed, both in terms of their number and turnover (Zamagni and Felice 2006; Battilani and Zamagni 2010).

The most notably absent element in this picture is dispersed ownership. In addition to the scarce propensity of Italian capitalism to create public companies, it should be added that the few public companies that were included in the populations during this period were sometimes only public on the face of it. Often the relative dispersion of a firm's share capital did not result in an effectively dispersed form of control, and a few—or individual—men were able to exercise control by adopting specific tools which allowed them to do so, even with ridiculously low share percentages (Amatori and Brioschi 1997). Compared to the United Stated, but also to most of the advanced European nations, the number of companies with dispersed ownership has been very low in Italy. Almost all the largest companies in the country had one or more important blockholders during the second half of the previous century and at the beginning of the current one.

The scarce diffusion of public companies was at least in part due to a substantial lack of regulation and transparency for most of the second half of the twentieth century and to the determination on the part of corporate owners to maintain their hold on control. Both of these factors severely limited the use of the stock exchange in the country. During the 1990s, the privatization process and a reform of the stock exchange started to change this situation, furthering the shift of private savings from government securities, whose yields were declining more and more, to industrial shares. Millions of Italians participated in the privatization process, and between 1993 and 2001, 274.563 billion lire entered the stock exchange in terms of both capital increases and new listed companies (Borsa Italiana 2002, 79). But the privatization process was largely unsuccessful in "democratizing" Italian capitalism and creating public companies (Pini 2000, 11; Mucchetti 2003, 32–33). With very few exceptions, privatization was carried out in a context in which both the rules and institutional investors were still very weak. As a result, some of the "privatized companies" remained under the substantial control of the state (Nardozzi 2011), while others were bought at a very good price by a number of large family companies. It has been claimed that Italy went from a system of state monopolies to one of private monopolies, which is perhaps only a slight exaggeration (Pini 2000, 11). At the beginning of the 2000s, established families were using old and new tools to maintain the same power that they had had for decades (Mucchetti 2003).

With regard to the separation between ownership and control and to the entrepreneurial and managerial education in Italy during this period, it is worth noting that a "managerial revolution" did not happen in Italy, even though there was some debate about it as it could be suggested for instance by the fact that the influential book by James Burnham (1941) was translated in Italian in 1946. Families were not simply the owners of the largest companies in the country, but they also almost always wanted to directly control their firms. The founder of the company or his sons, sons-in-law and heirs directly and totally controlled the majority of the previously mentioned companies. Since the postwar period, outsider managers were usually only given important positions in family-run companies if they were trusted persons whom the family had known for a very long time, and in any case, their degree of autonomy was severely limited (Martinoli 1971; Pavan 1976; Rugafiori 1999; Lavista 2004–2005; Pozzi 2012).

The companies that came closest to becoming managerial corporations were the few firms that had a relatively dispersed ownership, for example electricity companies such as Edison (Segreto 2004) or Montecatini in the chemical sector (Amatori and Bezza 1990; Perugini 2009). However, the presence of strong interest groups in these corporations had already made them quite different from truly public companies before World War II. Moreover, the degree of autonomy that managers were permitted in this context was generally low also in these firms (Pavan 1976).

The only enterprises that were able to develop a sort of managerial revolution after the war were the state-owned companies. The period before and partly during the economic miracle could be called a golden age for state managers, whose companies were almost completely free from political interference at least until the mid-1950s (Osti and Ranieri 1993, 69–79). However, managerial teams were seldom educated properly and formally in business administration. Until the early postwar years, only a few initiatives had been undertaken to create institutions where managers could learn the required skills (Sapelli 1994a, 279–280). Moreover, while the state-owned companies were consolidating their position in the country, the autonomy and power of their managers was declining. It was increasingly the politicians who, since the creation of the Ministry of State Shareholdings in 1956, were the ones who took the most important decisions (Rugafiori 1999, 84). As the number of state-owned companies increased and politicians became more and more determinant in defining the aims and strategies of companies, the appointment of state-owned company managers was in most cases merely a perfunctory matter that was decided by the ruling party (Osti and Ranieri 1993; Rugafiori 1999). From the 1970s, managers fared no better in the private sector either, in part because only very few private corporations were not under the direct control of a family.

The education of entrepreneurs and managers in Italy clearly did not result in a more modern system of company administration, and it has to be stressed that the general level of education in the postwar period was quite low. Most of the entrepreneurs and managers during these years had received a predominantly technical-scientific education, and, at the highest levels, were very often engineers (Rinaldi 2003, 372). When it came to training in managerial discipline, an investigation by the Italo-American scholar Robert J. Pavan (1976, 281–288) revealed that in 1970 only a small minority of Italian executives could claim to have been properly prepared, which was due in part to the scarcity of business schools in the country.

In addition to this lack of formal education and training, Italian families seldom asked for the help of foreign consultants in deciding their strategies and structures, since they did not like the presence of strangers within their companies. In contrast to its fortunes in the rest of Europe, even McKinsey found very limited success in Italy (Crucini 2000).

The new dynamics and rules of corporate governance that started to spread in the country during the 1980s demanded change, yet ownership and control structures in Italy remained largely the same (Aganin and Volpin 2005). During the 1990s, Italian families continued to be particularly good at inventing new tools for maintaining their ownership and control over the company, or at reusing use old techniques. One of the most common ways to keep control was the creation of a holding (Colli 2002a; Bianchi, Bianco and Enriques 2001), whereas in other cases, all power lies with a single person. This is for instance the case with one of the main supermarket chains in the country, Esselunga, which is still controlled by its eight-seven-year-old founder

Bernardo Caprotti. Likewise, in 2002, the stylist Giorgio Armani still owned and controlled the fashion emporium that bears his name (Merlo 2011).

With few exceptions, such as Luxottica (Colli 2002a, 56–57), families continued to dominate and to retain control of their enterprises at the beginning of the new millennium, and the separation of ownership from control was still far from becoming the predominant trend among most of the family-owned large Italian companies (Cingolani 1990, 10; Colli 2006a; Amatori and Colli 2000).

6.3 THE OWNERS OF SPANISH BIG BUSINESS

Compared to the Italian experience, the dynamics in the ownership structure of large corporations in Spain were more changeable during the second half of the twentieth century. Some protagonists largely disappeared while others gained a primary role within a few decades (Figure 6.2).

Family companies accounted for more than 50% of the population of the largest companies in Spain in 1950 and represented more than 30% of their total assets. Throughout the next fifty years, however, they experienced a significant decline and only reemerged partially at the beginning of the new century. At the same time foreign corporations, who were almost completely absent in 1950, increased their presence and importance at least up to the 1990s. The state, one of the main protagonists of the big business panorama during the Francoist decades, substantially disappeared during the last decade of the twentieth century. Meanwhile bank ownership, which

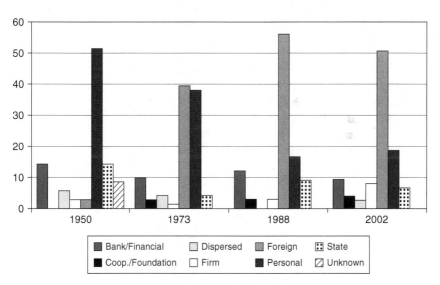

Figure 6.2a Ownership of the largest companies in Spain by number
Source: Appendix Tables 5b, 6b, 7b, 8b.

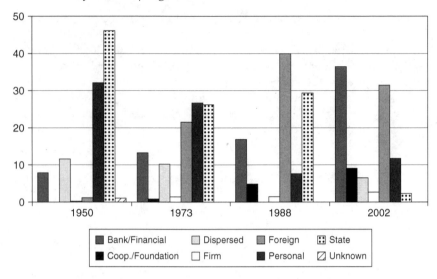

Figure 6.2b Ownership of the largest companies in Spain by turnover
Source: Appendix Tables 5a, 5b, 6a, 6b, 7a, 7b, 8a, 8b.

remained quite important in terms of the number of directly owned corporations, further grew in turnover during the 1980s and 1990s.

As was the case in Italy, public companies largely failed to spread in Spain throughout the considered period. However, there has been both a larger variety of blockholders, because banks could also hold shares in companies, and greater instability over time in relative terms, with no clear predominance of only one or two kinds of shareholders throughout the whole period.

Families, the main protagonists of Italian big business, represented the most common kind of corporate ownership in Spain in 1950 by number, but they were far from having the largest amount of assets in the population. In the middle of the autarkic period, family businesses operated in several industries (Linz and De Miguel 1963) and also owned large banks, through which in some cases they could own and control industrial enterprises (Cabrera and Del Rey 2002, 49; Valdaliso Gago 2004). It is not easy for instance to distinguish between the industrial and banking activities of families like the Ybarras (Díaz Morlán 2002, 2004) or the Urquijos (Tortella Casares and García Ruiz 1999, 211–219; Puig and Torres 2008) in 1950.

During the 1950s and 1960s, the last decade of autarky and, later on, the economic miracle, Spanish families substantially lost ground in terms of both their number and their turnover. Their relative decline was partly due to the increased competition from new and often more efficient foreign rivals. However, many of the problems that family-owned big businesses experienced also originated from the environment in which they had to operate, as it was awash with small and big bureaucratic obstacles and dominated by a pronounced arbitrariness on the part of the government in granting resources, authorizations and permissions. Many firms spent most of their resources and time trying to solve the administrative conundrums crucial to their existence, to avoid strong state intervention from damaging them, to look for ad hoc privileges in links and personal connections with the Francoist authorities and to try to take advantage, in particular during the autarkic era, of the black market (Torres Villanueva 2003, 200).

Despite the difficulties, families did not disappear from the big business scenario during the following decades, and the new opportunities provided by the economic miracle made the growth of new family businesses possible. However, a significant decline of family companies in the big business panorama took place during the 1970s and the 1980s, when their percentage dropped from 38.03% to 16.67% of the total number, and from 26.66% to 7.59% of the total turnover of the largest corporations.

In interpreting the relative decline of family companies during the 1970s and 1980s, two factors have to be taken into account: the uncertainty that entrepreneurs had to face as part of the transition to democracy in the years of the economic crisis and Spain's obligation to eliminate any remaining systems of protection for local firms as part of the new European framework. Because most family companies had been established within a protective environment and often had not developed particularly effective strategies and structures, many fared disastrously when competition became tough, and they very often ended up selling their enterprises to foreign investors (Binda 2005b).

After a very difficult period of transition to democracy and the first serious confrontation with foreign competition, some families were able to gain, or to regain, important positions in the ranking of the largest companies, as is shown by the 2002 population where both the number and the turnover of family companies increased. Still, when compared to the number of foreign multinationals, or to the turnover of financial companies or foreign subsidiaries, their role appears to be relative secondary and certainly not greater than that of other domestic company owners. At the beginning of the new millennium, large family businesses in Spain were concentrated in a few sectors, particularly in construction.

In contrast to the Italian case, families were not the only important private owners of Spanish big business: ownership by the banks was also of great relevance in this nation (Pueyo Sánchez 2006a). In 1950, banks and financial institutions represented 14.29% and 7.87% of the total number and assets of the 100 largest enterprises, respectively. These percentages would be even higher had we included all the companies owned by banks that were in turn owned by families, but these have been considered as family businesses in this study. From the early stages of the industrialization process, in fact, banks acted as universal banks, and they not only financed companies but also actively owned and controlled them. They behaved like holding companies and surrounded themselves with huge and diversified business groups, at first in particular in the mining, transport and electricity sectors (Tortella 1994). Banks were already very powerful in the country before the Civil War, but further increased their wealth during the 1940s and in the years of the dictatorship, when large banks, either as almost completely absent shareholders as directly involved participants, became the main channel through which dispersed family and bank-owned money reached the large corporations.

Banks remained powerful throughout Franco's dictatorship and, despite being hit by a severe crisis at the beginning of the 1980s, also during the democratic period. In 1973 and 1988, fewer banks acted as corporate owners than in 1950, but significantly increased their influence in terms of the turnover coming from these companies. In both these benchmark years, the largest groups were those of the Banco Central, which included important stakes, for instance, in the construction and petroleum sectors; the Banco Español de Crédito (BANESTO), whose companies in the populations belonged to the petroleum, chemical and construction sector; and those of the Banco de Bilbao's and the Banco de Vizcaya, which merged into Banco de Bilbao Vizcaya in 1988.

During the 1980s, the largest banks experienced a severe crisis, owing to the poor performance of their industrial groups, which had in turn been affected by the recession of the 1970s, as well as because of competition from foreign companies that were entering the country (Cuervo García 1988). However, it seems that Spanish banks did not only survive this crisis, but also increased their influence. Within a few years, most of the largest Spanish banks were able to recover thanks to a process of restructuring of the sector involving several mergers and acquisitions. At the beginning of the twenty-first century, they were very active in particular in the ownership and control of the major national firms in the utilities sector (Guillén 2005).

In 2002, banks or financial institutions (including an increasing number of institutional investors and savings banks) (Guillén 2001) controlled 9.33% of the 100 largest companies in Spain and 36.33% of their turnover. This is a strong increase compared to the previous period, as these organizations took advantage of the decline in ownership by foreign multinationals and, even more so, by another very important entrepreneur in Spain, namely the state.

Even though it acted on the conviction that private companies had to be promoted, and that they should be the very core of the Spanish economic system, the Francoist regime fostered one of the most pervasive systems of state ownership in the Western world. In 1950, direct state shareholding was not at its peak, but the government had already taken control of strategically important companies and sectors and had developed some distinctive features that would go on to last for a very long period. The state owned 14.29% of the 100 largest companies, whose assets represented 46.10% of the total assets of the population. The state was the real protagonist of the big business panorama, and its companies belonged to strategic sectors in which it had decided to nationalize private companies (national or foreign) and to establish new state-owned corporations (Comín and Martín Aceña

2003, 35). The number and importance of state-owned companies declined during the 1950s and 1960s in relative terms throughout the whole economy, mainly due to the railway company RENFE losing its position and to the fact that in the same period, the economic growth of the country also allowed big private companies to prosper. Nevertheless, the state as an entrepreneur remained remarkably strong during the 1950s and 1960s and increased its presence even more during the 1970s and the early 1980s: in 1973 and 1988 state-owned turnover represented 26.2% and 29.32%, respectively, of that of the whole population, while the INI represented 3.6% of Spanish GDP in 1973 as well as 14.1% of exports and 5.7% of national employment in 1975. INI, Spain's major industrial conglomerate and one of the twenty largest business groups in Europe, owned a quarter of the top 100 companies in the country (Cabrera and Del Rey 2002, 201).

The system of state-owned enterprises probably reached its maximum extent in Spain around the end of the 1970s and the beginning of the 1980s, when the difficulties associated with the transition to democracy and the economic crisis forced INI to become a major economic policy tool and to rescue several companies across many sectors. At the same time, the limitations of this system and the problems that it had created, ignored or simply failed to resolve in the previous decade came to the forefront. The policies based on rescues and investment lasted until 1983, when INI reached its limit both in terms of the number of companies that belonged to the group as well as in terms of its losses (Martín Aceña and Comín 1991, 523). In that year, INI was largely or fully involved in running sixty-five companies across most sectors, including electricity, metallurgy, mining, defense, shipbuilding, building materials, aluminum, food, electronics and information technology, automobiles, mechanical components, fertilizers, air transport, sea transport, other companies in various activities and regional development (INI Annual Report 1983, 8–9).

The poor results of the public sector were identified as one of the main obstacles to the modernization of Spanish society (López Muñoz 1983, 273), and a search for a "Spanish way" to solve this problem of inefficiency started. A process of privatization and liberalization began in 1984 (González-Páramo 1995; Cuervo García 1997). Several of INI's companies were the first to be privatized, followed by a number of companies belonging to the minor state-owned holding Patrimonio del Estado in 1985 and, later on, by the Instituto Nacional de Hidrocarburos, which had been founded in 1981 in order to coordinate the stakes held by the state in the oil sector.

Compared to the 1988 population, state-owned companies had largely lost their predominant position in 2002, falling from 9.09% to 6.67% of the total population by number and from 29.32% to 2.26% of the total turnover of the population. In contrast to Italy, the state sector almost completely disappeared in Spain after the privatization process and survived in big business only in some specific sectors such as transport (RENFE and Entidad Pública Empresarial Aeropuertos), post and telecommunications

(Sociedad Estatal de Correos y Telégrafos) and public television broadcasting (Televisión Española).

The decline of state-owned companies and family companies greatly benefitted another very important protagonist of the Spanish big business panorama: the subsidiaries of foreign multinationals. In 1950, they were almost completely absent from the picture partly because of the ideologies and policies adopted by Franco's regime. One of the regime's first steps was to introduce legislation that basically forbade free movement of foreign investment, forcing foreign companies to obtain special authorizations and restricting the amounts they could invest. However, it should not be forgotten that in addition to Spain's own autarkic policies, the decision by the international community to isolate the country immediately after World War II also played a part. In 1946, the United Nations morally condemned the Francoist regime.

In this context, many companies were nationalized, passing from foreign ownership to state ownership. The Compañía Telefónica de España, a concession given by the Spanish state to the US company ITT in 1924, was nationalized in the first years of the regime through an expensive revocation of the concession (Álvaro Moya 2010). Naval, a company that was completely dependent on Vickers' technologies and management, was partially nationalized through indemnifications. Iberia, which was German owned, became Spanish without too many difficulties thanks to Spain's good relationship with Hitler's regime. Other foreign enterprises were "naturalized" and moved from foreign to Spanish private ownership, while many were under strong pressure to sell to Spanish entrepreneurs (Carreras 2003, 57–62). However, in many cases, this process of nationalization and naturalization did not bring about a total and definite exit of these foreign shareholders and managers. After all, they were still the most technologically advanced companies in the country and, although the majority of the share capital was in Spanish hands, the know-how, capital and managerial capabilities needed to remain in foreign hands inside these nationalized or naturalized companies (Puig Raposo 2001; Gálvez Muñoz and Comín Comín 2003; Álvaro Moya 2010).

The number and importance of foreign multinationals between 1950 and 1973 grew at an impressive rate. National entrepreneurship had demonstrated to be insufficient to provide the money, the technology and the know-how that the country needed to foster its industrial development all by itself, and foreign multinationals started to come back to Spain from the moment the Plan de Estabilización created a more liberal framework for accepting foreign investment (Tascón Fernández 2003). Restrictions on the import of industrial and consumption goods in a domestic market with strong growth prospects as well as the low cost of labor attracted a great influx of direct foreign investment during the 1960s and 1970s. Foreign companies came especially from the United States, Germany and France, and entered Spain in many different sectors, in particular, manufacturing.

Democratic Spain provided the springboard for a further, impressive increase in the spread of foreign multinationals. In 1988 and 2002, foreign companies, respectively, numbered 56.06% and 50.67% of the 100 largest corporations in Spain and generated 39.94% and 31.43% of their total turnover. Foreign investors were particularly attracted by the opportunities resulting from the economic growth and the European integration of the country (Binda 2005a). At the same time, the government, led by Felipe González, welcomed their entry predominantly for two reasons. The first is that the influx of direct foreign investment was a consequence of the country's inclusion in the EEC, which was something that Spain had keenly desired in order to strengthen its young and potentially still fallible democracy. The second reason relates to the benefits that foreign capital could bring to a still weak economy in aftermath of the energy crisis of the 1970s (Maravall and Pérez Simarro 1985). To this end, the government for instance approved a new law on the liberalization of capital flow to replace the old and relatively restrictive regulations (Camino Blasco and Pradas Poveda 2001). During this period, foreign companies became more successful than several of the Spanish manufacturing companies thanks to the free-market competition policies, or acquired controlling percentages in their share capital. Moreover, multinationals were also able to enter the important services sector.

Finally, other types of owners also entered the Spanish big business panorama during this period, such as cooperatives. These had been completely absent during the first benchmark years and then increased their presence, becoming relatively important in the last few decades (e.g., Medina Albaladejo 2011). It is moreover interesting to observe how, during the Francoist period, very often the ownership of the largest companies was shared among a small partnership of important shareholders. This *escamotage* was probably a way of making different stakeholders coexist effectively in the same company. It was also caused by the asymmetries that characterized the Spanish context in that period (Binda 2008); one could, for instance, see the state and a private firm coexist in equality shareholdings, or find a copartnership between the state and foreign investors or between different foreign investors, or even between the state, banks and foreign investors all at once (for an interesting example in the aluminum industry, see Kipping and Cailluet 2010).

The dispersion of the ownership of large companies seems to have been slightly more widespread in Spain than in Italy, in particular during the final decade of the last century. However, considering the speed with which changes occurred and the scarcity of this kind of company in the population due to the high number of foreign corporations, the results of the current "managerial revolution" in Spain, if it is happening at all, are still uncertain. In this respect, it has to be stressed that dispersed companies were relatively low in number throughout the period under consideration.

In the mid-twentieth century, few public companies existed, and most of them were in the end controlled by banks. They fared no better in 1973, when the number and contribution to turnover of the public companies in Spain marginally decreased and in 1988, dispersed-ownership corporations had substantially disappeared from the population. Democracy and integration into the European economy partly changed this picture. Some public companies do feature in the 2002 benchmark. However, strong continuities with the past remain, and Spanish firms still show highly concentrated ownership structures, even though at the beginning of the new millennium Spanish levels of ownership concentration were the lowest in Europe after those of the United Kingdom (Crespí-Caldera and García-Cestona 2001, 207).

In terms of the coincidence of ownership and control, a "managerial revolution" did not take place in Spain either, where in particular in family-run businesses the coincidence of ownership and control remained strong throughout the period considered, although cases of owners who were prepared to hand over control of their companies did exist. However, the fact that most family-run companies in Spain were linked to banks, which in turn stood at the center of business groups, had made direct personal or family control less diffuse than in the case of Italy. Even though the interest groups and spheres of influence were reasonably consolidated, often more than one center of control existed within a group, although the situation was very different across groups (e.g., Valdaliso Gago 2002). Moreover, ownership and control did not coincide in state-owned companies either. In all these cases, it was possible for the managers to have their own career, to demonstrate their technical and managerial capabilities and to change from one company to another with substantial autonomy (Travesi 1969). However, the fact that the path of career progression in the state-owned companies frequently involved favoritism and nepotism, and that the most important positions were filled by upper-level ministers of the Franco regime once their political career had ended, cannot be ignored (Cabrera and Del Rey 2002).

It must also be stressed that an educated and well-trained managerial class did not emerge during the first phase of Francoism and developed quite slowly in the following decades (Guillén 1994). Until the Civil War, the top management of the largest companies in Spain had almost always been foreign. Later on the Civil War not only caused the managers from abroad to leave, but also meant that the management of important companies that belonged to the Republican party were replaced by groups that strictly conformed to the policies of growth of the large *"empresas nacionales "*(i.e. national enterprises")" (Carreras and Tafunell 1997).

As in Italy, the initial education of Spanish entrepreneurs and managers was predominantly based on science and engineering (Guillén 1994; De Miguel and Linz 1964; INI Annual Report 1950, 11–12). The Marshall Plan did not involve Spain, and "American-style" foreign consultancies and business schools were uncommon at least up to the 1950s. It was thus more difficult for an American-style managerial class to emerge during the first Francoist decades (Kipping and Puig 2003b).

During the 1960s and 1970s, engineers remained very important in determining the direction of both state-owned and private companies. However, new trends emerged when the country opened to outside influences in 1959. An understanding of the complexity of the administration and organization of companies began to spread and the old ways of managing large businesses were questioned (Guillén 1994, 184).

An interest in the economic-administrative side of business was spreading above all in two fundamental areas, which gained an increasing importance during this period. On one hand, management schools were established under the aegis of the Jesuitic Catholic Institutions, which founded ICADE in Madrid and ESADE in Barcelona (Puig Raposo and Fernández Pérez 2003, 2008), or of the Opus Dei, which was strongly committed to the formation of intellectual elites with a sound bureaucratic-managerial education through its private colleges, its university in Pamplona and its business schools such as IESE in Barcelona (Moya 1975; Casanova 1983). On the other hand, since the 1950s, an increasing number of foreign consultants started to come to the country (Kipping and Puig 2003b).

6.4 SUMMARY

In the light of the investigations into the ownership structures and governance systems around the world, this chapter has focused on the corporate ownership of the largest businesses in Italy and Spain.

Consistent with the results of the analysis conducted in the other European countries, the largest corporations were not characterized by a dispersed ownership in Italy and Spain, either. As Richard Whittington and Michael Mayer saw in France and Germany, it is also possible to assert that in these Southern European nations, the Anglo-Saxon model of public companies combined with a very important stock exchange was not imitated to any significant extent at all. Despite the fact that the stock exchange became better regulated and that its role increased over the period considered in this work, the empirical evidence gathered on the large enterprises in Italy and Spain allows us to argue that the ownership and control of big businesses remained in the hands of a few important blockholders in most cases.

Even though their relative importance changed over time, it is possible to identify at least three major shareholders, which the large Italian and Spanish corporations had in common.

First of all, there were the families. Dynasties that created these countries' first industrial enterprises as well as families with a more recent tradition of entrepreneurship, and that started to grow during the economic miracles, represented a solid core of big corporations in both nations. Second, the strength of the state as an entrepreneur was at a similar level; as in both Italy and Spain, governments created holdings of major companies across several different sectors. Third, in those sectors in which local companies were weak or nonexistent, foreign multinationals took over important companies in both countries, although different trends governed their behavior during the various historical periods. The one area where Italy and Spain differed was in that of bank-led ownership of major corporations; in Italy, banks could not own significant industrial shares, whereas in Spain, they represented one of the most important blockholders throughout the second half of the twentieth century.

Within this context, the companies that could at least in theory host a "managerial revolution" in these nations included a very small number of public companies and family firms of which the owners accepted the increasing power of non-family members as executives, the state-owned corporations, the foreign multinationals that hired local managers and, in Spain only, the bank-controlled firms. However, several case studies have demonstrated that Italy and Spain remained relatively hostile to managers at least until quite recently.

Part III
Strategy and Structure

More than fifty years after the publication of *Strategy and Structure* by Alfred Chandler (1962), the debate on the hypothetical convergence of the behavior of the large corporations in the richest industrial powers of the world continues to this day, and has been further extended with the addition of new empirical data and information.

The academic debate during the last few decades has seen two opposite views: that of the "universalists" versus the "contextualists" scholars (Whittington and Mayer 2000, chap. 2).

Universalists have identified the strategies and structures adopted by the large corporations in the United States at the end of the nineteenth century and in the early twentieth century as the most efficient way to foster large successful corporations in the Second Industrial Revolution sectors, namely those industries where big business emerged (Chandler 1962, 1977, 1990). According to this interpretation, the technological opportunities potentially provided by this industrial revolution could be fully exploited basically thanks only to the adoption of a product-related diversification strategy and a multidivisional organizational structure. For this reason, in order to survive in a competitive environment, during the second half of the twentieth century, large corporations in advanced economies were drawn to the model of growth followed by the large US corporations despite there being differences in national contexts and institutional frameworks (Scott 1970; Channon 1973; Rumelt 1974; Dyas and Thanheiser 1976).

Contextualists, on the other hand, have claimed that it is impossible to hypothesize on the emergence of the same entrepreneurial behavior in nations characterized by different contexts and institutional peculiarities. The different backgrounds and institutional and cultural frameworks of nations all over the world would make the adoption of the same managerial response and corporate behavior impossible, despite common technological imperatives and the presumed economic efficiency of one kind of big business strategy or organizational form over another (e.g. Hofstede 1980, 1991; Guillén 1994, 2001; Whitley 1994, 1999; Whitley and Kristensen 1996; Hollingsworth and Boyer 1997; Djelic 1998).

The broader purpose of this part of the investigation is thus to check whether the strategies, structures and managerial practices that originated in the largest companies in the United States and quickly spread to Western Europe from the immediate postwar period onward have been—partly or entirely—adopted in two of the industrial latecomer nations in the Mediterranean.

Moreover, the aim of Part III is not only to verify the predictions for the worldwide spreading of the diversification strategy and of the multidivisional structure in Italy and Spain, but also to analyze the diffusion of alternative strategies and structures in these countries and to add evidence of the adoption of another kind of strategy, the internationalization of business activity.

Short business case studies explain what has occurred in both countries in terms of the adoption of one or another kind of strategy and structure, and how this has changed over time.

7 The Product Diversification Strategy
Between Single Activity Companies and Business Groups

7.1 STRATEGIC TRANSFORMATIONS IN THE UNITED STATES AND EUROPE

The present chapter is devoted to a study of the dynamics of the strategic choices made by large corporations in Italy and Spain as well as to an the investigation of their reactions to the different opportunities and limitations resulting from the changing context from the end of the wars up to the beginning of the new millennium.

The kind of strategy that has so far been most extensively studied is the product diversification strategy. According to Alfred Chandler (1962), the largest companies in the United States began to adopt a product strategy of related diversification already as early as the first half of the twentieth century, in order to re-invest the surplus coming from the scale economies of their core activities and to exploit potential synergies in the production and distribution of their core product by moving into new business areas. Related diversification turned out to be a winning choice for US companies. By venturing into new business areas, in fact, they could spread the risk, find a "way out" in sectors where competition was increasingly fierce and whose markets were saturating and continue their expansion without impediment.

With such advantages, following the US example and adopting a strategy of product related diversification could have been a good choice for large European companies and could have helped them compete with their US rivals. However, the widespread adoption of the product related diversification strategy in the United States involved at least two prerequisites. The first was the achievement of a "critical amount" of resources and competences that allowed companies to enter new sectors with both the necessary funds as well as the technical and market knowledge required to maintain not only their core business, but also to develop in new business areas. Secondly, there needed to be sufficient market demand for the new products. It was thus fundamental that the country was developed or at least in the process of developing, and that companies, or individual customers, were interested and able to buy an increasing number and wider range of intermediate and final goods.

The existence of these prerequisites in the postwar era was not obvious in all nations. European countries were in most cases industrial latecomers with a small and/or poor domestic market. Very often, they had not yet been able to establish very large corporations, and two world wars fought within a relatively short time had destroyed their infrastructure and impoverished their population. Scholars who dealt with corporate strategies in the largest European nations in 1950 found there to be a low level of product diversification compared to that in the United States. Most of the largest corporations in Europe were concentrating on a single or a dominant product (Scott 1970; Channon 1973; Rumelt 1974; Dyas and Thanheiser 1976). The product diversification strategy became increasingly widespread during the second half of the century, although there were differences in how this trend occurred in the Old and New Continents.

Big business in the United States, pushed by a slowdown in demand and by increasing competition from European and Japanese firms during the 1960s, decided to look for new investment and growth opportunities in business areas that had no connection to their core activity and in which they thus had no knowledge or competence (Jacobi 1985). They left the path described in *Strategy and Structure* (Chandler 1962) and started to adopt a strategy of unrelated diversification, a trend that reached its peak in the country around the 1970s. During the 1980s, following waves of disinvestment based on industrial and/or financial perspectives, big corporations in the United States began to refocus on their own core business or on a small number of related activities (Chandler 1994; Markides 1995). During the same period, things went partly differently in Europe. From the 1950s, both related and unrelated diversification strategies spread despite the potential obstacles to adoption. France had a particular financial equilibrium, a unique kind of capitalism and a technical culture that should not have favored the diffusion of the diversification strategy. German industry, sustained by the banks and with a strong technical orientation, should not have accepted the conglomerate model. However, neither the cultural nor institutional peculiarities path dependence prevented the large corporations of these countries from adopting strategies of related or unrelated diversification. At the end of the century, big business in the largest European nations was largely diversified. Of the 100 largest corporations in France, 51.5% and 13.6% were related business and unrelated business companies, respectively, in 1993. In the same year, related diversifiers made up 47.6% and 61.2% of the 100 largest corporations in Germany and the United Kingdom, respectively, while the unrelated diversifiers accounted for 31.7% and 23.9% (Channon 1973; Scott 1970; Dyas and Thanheiser 1976; Whittington and Mayer 2000). As Richard Whittington and Michael Mayer pointed out, "in the 1990s Europe [was] more diversified than ever before" (Whittington and Mayer 2000, 145).

Between 1950 and the beginning of the new millennium, Italy and Spain developed economically and became modern countries. During this time, the sector-based distribution of their large corporations partly changed, as did the identity of their owners, particularly in Spain. This chapter aims to analyze the trends governing the strategies of big business in Italy and Spain as part of this changing context, and to understand if the strategy of related diversification, which became the most common in the most advanced European nations, also spread in these countries or if alternative corporate behaviors predominated.

7.2 THE STRATEGIC TRANSFORMATION OF BIG BUSINESS IN ITALY

The product strategies of the largest Italian companies in the mid-twentieth century were not substantially different from those of other European nations during the same period (Figure 7.1). Looking at the distribution of the 100 largest companies in 1950, there was no clearly dominant product strategy in Italy, even though focused companies slightly outnumbered the diversifiers. Single and dominant activity firms in fact represented 60% of the whole population, belonged to several sectors and were owned by different types of shareholders. At the same time, however, diversification was not an unfamiliar strategy to the majority of large Italian corporations. During the first part of the century, some of the largest corporations had, for instance, already pursued a strategy of diversification through vertical integration, with the main aim of guaranteeing a proper supply of raw materials and energy, to extend their outlets or to internalize high transaction costs.

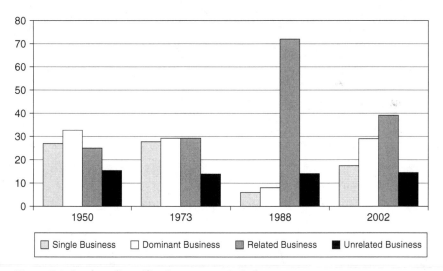

Figure 7.1 Product diversification strategy in Italy
Source: Appendix Tables 1b, 2b, 3b, 4b.

Several metallurgic companies bought mines, mechanical firms extended their activities into the large-scale retail trade and food companies engaged in the production of paper for packaging (Toninelli 2003, 231).

In the immediate postwar period, the harsh conditions facing some companies provided new reasons to diversify. During the difficult second half of the 1940s, some of the largest corporations started to use the capabilities they had so far developed in their core business area to engage in new activities. This was, for example, the case in the aeronautical industry (Box 7.1).

Box 7.1   Need-Driven Diversification in the Postwar Period: New Strategies in the Aeronautical Sector

The decline of demand in the aeronautical sector, as well as the fact that Italian companies were prohibited from continuing their activities in this area until 1947, plunged this sector into crisis at the end of World War II. It forced firms that had so far operated in this sector, such as Costruzioni Aeronautiche Giovanni Agusta and Piaggio, to diversify into the production of motorbikes.

For the family-run Costruzioni Aeronautiche Giovanni Agusta, entering the motorbikes industry during the second half of the 1940s was a decisive moment. After returning to an undeveloped prewar project idea, within a few years the company was able to develop a very successful model, called MV. The turnover generated by the sales of the MV was high enough to allow the company to survive and maintain its center for technical research until, at the beginning of the 1950s, Agusta could resume its aeronautical production. The conclusion of an agreement for the production of Bell's US helicopters was the first step toward a definitive return of the company to its traditional core activity in aeronautics: 9 successful new prototypes were developed during the second half of the 1950s. The diversification into motorbikes remained a long-lasting feature of the company, although Agusta decided to refocus mainly on helicopter production and concentrated most of its research efforts in this area while motorbikes were relegated to a secondary position.

For Piaggio, a family company that produced aeronautic and railway equipment, the postwar diversification into motorbikes represented a first step toward the birth of a new company. Piaggio entered the automotive industry in 1945, promoting the development of a cheap and efficient mean of transport and, three years later, built the first prototypes of the scooter Vespa. The success of this product was tremendous, and by 1959, more than 2 million scooters had been sold. However, the new strategy greatly divided opinion among the members of the family that owned the company. The brothers who were managing Piaggio split it into two separate enterprises, each one led by one of the two brothers. When restrictions on production in the aeronautics industry ended, Armando Piaggio took charge of railway and aeronautical equipment, while Enrico Piaggio continued and consolidated the scooter manufacturing. Twenty years later, the Vespa, which was once a fallback option in the postwar period, had become one of the symbols of the Italian *Dolce Vita*. It generated 50% of the turnover of the company and was exported and produced under license all over the world. Enrico Piaggio's firm continued its growth by diversifying into other models during the 1960s and 1970s, such as the Ciao and the Boxer, and became big enough to buy another big Italian motorcycle manufacturer, Gilera, in 1969.

Sources: Pavan (1976); Fanfani (1994); Rapini (2007); www.agustawestland.com; and www.piaggiogroup.com.

The number of unrelated business companies was relatively low in 1950. However, in spite of this, unrelated business firms represented more than half of the assets of the largest Italian enterprises. The conglomerate model had become an important growth tool for the main companies in particular during the interwar period, when business groups grew thanks to their ability to position themselves in sectors that were highly protected or regulated by the state (Amatori 1997a). Due to their generally poor economic results as well as the problems associated with postwar recovery and the new political climate of the 1940s and 1950s, some of these business groups disappeared immediately after the war. However, some private business groups still appeared in the 1950 population and were placed at the very top of the ranking. This was the case, for instance, with the car producer FIAT, which operated several dozen companies in the mechanical, electricity, electromechanical, railway, publishing and other sectors after World War II (Annibaldi and Berta 1999; Castronovo 1999). There was also the electricity company SADE (Segreto 1998) and the chemical companies Montecatini (Amatori and Bezza 1990) and SNIA Viscosa (SNIA Viscosa Annual Report 1950). Last but not least, the state-owned holding IRI acted through a diversified business group as the largest entrepreneur in the country.

It seems that the Italian economic miracle did not affect the product diversification strategies of the largest corporations in the country to any great extent. Despite an investigation conducted in the early 1970s suggesting that the strategies adopted by large corporations in Italy were converging toward those in the United States (Pavan 1976), the information on the 100 largest businesses in the country shows that diversification did not spread to any significant extent between 1950 and 1973 and that the situation in the 1970s was not very different from that in the immediate postwar years. In contrast to the United Kingdom, Germany and France, in fact, the majority of Italian big businesses decided to maintain a strategy of single or dominant activity and not to enter new business areas. Single business companies grew to almost 30% of the population in Italy, whereas they represented 20%, 27% and 6% of the top 100 companies in France, Germany and the United Kingdom respectively (Whittington and Mayer 2000). Dominant activity companies decreased in number very slightly, and their proportion of the total big business panorama was broadly comparable to that in France and Britain, although their number greatly exceeded that in Germany (Whittington and Mayer 2000).

The strategy of related diversification did not significantly spread during this period; more than 38% of the largest corporations were related diversifiers in France, Germany and the United Kingdom in the early 1970s, whereas in Italy, they made up less than 30% of the population. However, even though relatively few companies adopted a related diversification strategy, some of those that did were among the most successful corporations in the country during the economic miracle, including the publishing firm Arnoldo Mondadori (Arnoldo Mondadori Annual Report 1973) and the food company Ferrero (Box 7.2).

Despite the relatively small number of related diversifiers at the end of the golden age, Italy was far from being a country of very specialized large companies. The number of unrelated diversifiers was in fact very similar to that in other European nations (Whittington and Mayer 2000), and the turnover

---

Box 7.2 A Golden "Sweet Age": Ferrero's Growth and Diversification during the Economic Miracle

Born in 1942 as a small confectioner's laboratory in Alba, Ferrero is one of the Italian companies that grew and diversified most quickly and successfully during the golden age.

Its founder, Pietro Ferrero, was forced by the fragile state of the Italian market and the scarce availability of ingredients during the war to invent a new sweet product based on a cheap and very common raw material in that area: the hazelnut. The first hazelnut cream, called Pasta Gianduja, was commercialized in 1946. It became incredibly successful very quickly, mainly due to its low price in comparison with chocolate. The idea of "democratizing" the confectionery sector by producing good-quality but affordable products was destined to succeed in poor, postwar Italy and even more so in the following decades, when the economic miracle increased the size of the potential market and provided strong incentives for a diversification of company production. As a first step toward diversification, Ferrero started to produce new varieties of goods based on a mixture of chocolate and hazelnut at the beginning of the 1950s.

During the 1960s, the company increased both its level of vertical integration, in particular in hazelnut-based products, and of horizontal diversification. Ferrero quickly understood the new needs and opportunities offered by a bigger and wealthier market, and it decided not only to significantly increase its variety of sweet products (the introduction of the Nutella cream and the Pocket Coffee chocolate was especially important in this sense) but also to start the production of mint candies (Tic Tac), baked goods (Kinder Brioss) and beverages (Estathé). Developing a child-oriented business area was a winning choice considering that a real baby boom was occurring in Italy as well as in the whole of Europe and that the increasing purchasing power of families made them pay more attention to their children's nutrition. The good reputation of its brands allowed Ferrero to continue its related diversification over time and contributed to its growth, making it one of the largest companies in Italy.

Sources: Ferrero (1967); Pavan (1976); Direzione Affari Generali Ferrero (1996); Ferrero Annual Report, various years; and www.ferrero.com.

generated by the largest business groups was impressive. Almost 56% of the total sales of the 100 largest corporations in the country in 1973 came from a conglomerate or a business group. Old, unrelated diversifiers persisted, such as IRI (Amatori 1997a) and Montedison, the latter of which resulted from a merger between the two conglomerates Montecatini and Edison (e.g., Lepore Dubois and Sonzogno 1990). "New" companies also decided to pursue an unrelated diversification strategy during this period, such as for instance the state-owned company ENI (Pavan 1976, 120; Briatico 2004) and the family business Italcementi. The latter had been successful in the cement sector during the golden age and then decided to enter several different industries when competition increased and profits coming from its core activity started to decline (Cingolani 1990, 182; Coltorti 1990, 83; Zamagni 2006a).

The energy crisis of the 1970s and the new dynamics that characterized the Western economies during the 1980s shook up the distribution of companies' strategies. Both single and dominant business enterprises remarkably decreased in importance in the Italian population, and they seemed doomed to decline to the same extent as those in the most advanced European economies during the previous decades. In 1988, the number of related diversifiers in Italy had grown to the levels found among French, German and British companies. Italian corporations seemed to finally be on their way to converge to the model of growth followed by the large US corporations.

However, the predominance of the related diversification strategy was no absolute. In fact, looking at the information on the turnover generated, unrelated diversification confirmed its predominance also in 1988. Almost 70% of the whole turnover of the population came in fact from old and new unrelated diversifiers. New private *condottieri* (commanders) (Amatori 2011), such as Raul Gardini and Silvio Berlusconi, actually created very diversified business groups (Cingolani 1990, 202). Meanwhile, the weight of the state-owned holdings did not diminish. IRI's companies continued to represent about a fifth of the turnover of the whole population, whereas ENI's contribution increased from 11% to 17% between 1973 and 1988 (see Box 7.3).

Box 7.3 The Government and Unrelated Diversification: The Degeneration of IRI and ENI's Strategy

Until the final decade of the twentieth century, the Italian state was one of the country's entrepreneurs most in favor of adopting the strategy of unrelated diversification to manage its companies.

Born as a historical "mishap" (the state had to take over the Italian banks' stakes in large industrial companies that had been badly affected by the 1929 recession), the state-owned holding (IRI) was by necessity a diversified business group since the beginning. However, the level of its diversification and the reasons that pushed it toward this strategy changed over time. In the age of the economic miracle, IRI operated mainly in those industries typical of the Second Industrial Revolution and which were considered as strategic for the growth and development of the country. From the 1960s, however, things started to change. IRI went from being a state-owned holding with predominantly economic aims to representing a "hospital" for enterprises, where social and political aims had become top-priority issues. Entering sectors where it had neither experience nor any real economic *raison d'être* became "normal." For example, during the 1970s, SME, an IRI subholding that used to be an electricity company, became involved in the food sector in order to rescue Motta and Alemagna, two family-owned confectionery companies that produced *panettoni*, one of the typical Italian Christmas cakes. The state *panettoni (panettoni di Stato)* provide an excellent illustration of how much the Italian "State Entrepreneur" had extended its reach into sectors that were not particularly strategic and for which it did not have any defined economic aims.

The state-owned holding ENI, founded in 1953 in the oil sector, was facing similar problems. It too was unable to escape its political commitments and had to diversify its activities into unrelated sectors, usually to rescue companies and safeguard jobs. The process started with diversification into the chemical sector and, later on, with the acquisition of the mechanical company Pignone in 1953 and of the newspaper Il Giorno in 1959. Things further worsened in 1962, when the government forced ENI to rescue the textile company Lanerossi. ENI had gone from being a relatively successful oil company to being one of the tools used by the party in power at the time, the Democrazia Cristiana (Christian Democrats), to generate and maintain political consensus.

Sources: Coltorti (1990, 83); Osti and Ranieri (1993); Amatori (1997b, 2000, 2012); Barca and Trento (1997); Carnevali (2000); (Briatico 2004); AGIP Annual Report, various years; ENI Annual Report, various years; and IRI Annual Report, various years.

Meanwhile, the success of related diversification seems to have been relatively short-lived in Italy. In 2002, the related diversifiers continued to be the most common kind of company and several of the most successful Italian corporations had adopted this kind of strategy. Most of them belonged to sectors typical of the so-called Made in Italy trend, such as Merloni, Luxottica or Giorgio Armani, but there were also some "old" companies that belonged to mature industries, such as steel, who had taken advantage of the opportunities that emerged during the 1980s and 1990s to engage in new related activities. One such company was Riva (Box 7.4).

Box 7.4 Privatization, Diversification and Growth: Riva

The process of refocusing and privatization that characterized the state-owned sector in Italy and other European countries during the final decades of the twentieth century indirectly changed the strategies of some companies and accelerated their growth. A number of private corporations took advantage of the state sell-off to acquire, in some case at a very good price, large national companies and to diversify their activities.

Founded in 1954 by the brothers Emilio and Adriano Riva, Riva began life as a scrap iron trader. Its customers were the steel companies in the Brescia area of Northern Italy.

The company initially expanded by becoming directly involved in the production of steel during the second half of the 1950s and, later on, by acquiring both Italian and foreign companies active in this sector during the 1960s and the 1970s.

However, it was only when a large-scale process of related diversification of the company's production began during the 1980s that Riva was able to achieve a dominant position in its sector. The tactic used by the company in order to grow and diversify, despite the hard times that befell its sector, was to take over former state-owned companies while these were being privatized. In 1988, Riva took the control of the previously state-owned integral cycle steelworks Cornigliano in order to reduce its dependency on scrap iron, and acquired a majority share in the previously state-owned French company ALPA (Aciéries et Laminoirs de Paris). In 1992, the privatization of companies in former Eastern Germany allowed Riva to acquire two steel and iron plants located in the region of Berlin: Brandenburger Elektrostahlwerke and Hennigsdorfer Elektrostahlwerk. Later on, taking advantage of the privatization of Italian state-run steel production, Gruppo Riva bought Ilva Laminati Piani.

By 2002, the group's companies controlled all phases of steel manufacturing, from the production of raw steel (both integral cycle and electric furnace made), to lamination (hot and cold) and the production of covered steel, metal sheets and big pipes for gas and oil pipelines. Its steel production was integrated with other diversified activities that were related to Riva's main business, such as shipbuilding, scrap reclaiming and the production of refractory material drums for lamination.

Thanks to this process of growth and diversification, by 2006, the family-owned Riva had become the leader in its field in Italy, the fifth-largest steel producer in Europe and the tenth largest in the world.

Sources: Amatori and Colli (1999); Colli (2002a); Riva Annual Reports (various years); and www.rivagroup.com.

Despite the relative success of some of the related diversifiers, their number in Italy has diminished, and in 2002, it was clearly lower than the one observed by Whittington and Mayer in the United Kingdom, Germany and France at the end of the previous century (Whittington and Mayer 2000).

Single and dominant business companies very much came to the fore again; almost half of the population pursued a single or dominant business strategy and, despite their turnover being generally lower than that of the diversifiers, this kind of behavior was adopted across several different sectors and ownership types.

Moreover, as in all the previous benchmark years, the largest companies of the country were not related, but unrelated diversifiers. Even though the dismantling of the state-owned business group IRI reduced the weight of the turnover of unrelated business companies, many other business groups survived and new ones were emerging. The Benetton family, for instance, partly sidelined their activities in textiles in order to enter the highways and restaurants sector.

If a partial convergence process toward the model of the related diversified company described by Alfred Chandler thus seems to have taken place during the five decades under consideration, it is clear that a sharp reversal has occurred in the last few years (Binda and Colli 2011). Single and dominant business companies are far from disappearing and unrelated business companies remain important protagonists in Italian big business, although less so than they have been in the past. In fact, it cannot be claimed that one or another kind of strategy of strategic behavior was indisputably predominant among the largest enterprises in Italy at the dawn of the new millennium.

7.3 THE DYNAMICS OF STRATEGIC BEHAVIOR IN SPAIN

Although some similarities do exist, the strategic choices made by large companies in Spain display some interesting peculiarities in comparison to the Italian case (Figure 7.2). As in Italy and in most of the advanced European nations, single and dominant business companies were very well represented in the big business population in 1950. Across sectors and ownership types, many enterprises remained focused completely or mainly on one single product. In some cases, focusing on a single or few businesses was an astute choice, given that the market was small and poor, and that many companies did not have the financial resources nor the knowledge and competences required to engage

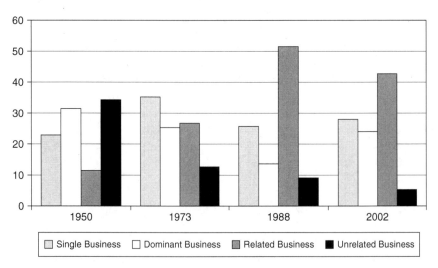

Figure 7.2 Product diversification strategy in Spain
Source: Appendix Tables 5b, 6b, 7b, 8b.

Box 7.5 HYTASA: A Failed Attempt at Diversification in an Autarkic Context

Spain's poverty and insular attitude to foreign trade during the 1940s made the pursuit of a diversification strategy a very difficult task. Several companies in fact failed in their attempt to adopt it, as was the case for example for Hilaturas y Tejidos Andaluces, S.A. (HYTASA). A cotton yarn producer, the company had expanded during the early years of the dictatorship, thanks in part to the political support of the Francoist regime. The agrarian polices at the time provided a very positive framework for the cotton industry, as the regime wished to foster the textile industry in order to completely substitute imports.

In order to grow further, HYTASA started a process of vertical integration and obtained a concession of vast areas of cotton farming from the state. At the same time, the firm began to try to diversify its textile production by moving into the wool sector. Having obtained the necessary permission from the Francoist government, producing wool seemed like it would be an easy and natural step since the company was located in Andalusia and close to Extremadura, two of the Spanish regions where sheep rearing was common and where the raw material needed for wool production was thus readily available.

However, the autarkic regime made this mission much more difficult than it first appeared. Although HYTASA had easy access to raw materials, the company found it was impossible to obtain the foreign currency to import the machinery and the equipment it needed for its new production process. Only during the 1950s, when the availability of foreign currency slightly increased, could the company slowly begin to properly equip the wool section of its factory and diversify its textile production activities.

Sources: Fernández Roca (1996); and Torres Villanueva (2003, 217).

---

in new activities. In other cases, the pursuit of a single or dominant activity was the result of failed attempts at achieving a stronger vertical integration or diversification. The particular conditions of the Spanish economy during the autarkic period had made this impossible, as was the case for the textile company HYTASA (Box 7.5).

Related diversification was a very minor strategy in 1950s Spain, both in terms of the number and the assets of the related diversifiers within the big business population. Only 11% of the largest corporations in Spain had adopted this kind of strategy compared to the more than 25% in France, Germany, the United Kingdom and Italy. The Spanish related diversifiers were generally companies that had decided to adopt a strategy of vertical integration, such as the mining company Española de Minas del Rif and the fishing enterprise Consorcio Nacional Almadrabero. Based on its activities in tuna fishing, the latter moved into conserves and subproducts, and into the transport and distribution of its own products.

Despite the relatively marginal importance of the strategy of related diversification, it is not possible to claim that Spanish large companies were not diversified at all in the middle of the twentieth century. Most of the big businesses in Spain had indeed adopted a strategy of unrelated diversification, and the contribution of unrelated diversifiers to the total assets of the whole population is impressive and comparable only to the Italian case. Out of the ten largest "decision units" of the Spanish population in 1950, seven were very diversified business groups. The most important business group belonged to the public sector; the state-owned holding INI had in fact founded new companies or bought old ones in all the industries that the state considered to be of strategic importance to national development. However, most business groups belonged to private entrepreneurs. A number of individuals or families, such as the Majorcan entrepreneur Juan March, or the Marqués de Comillas Antonio López y López and his heirs (Rodrigo Alharilla 2000), as well as several banks, such as Banco Central (see Box 7.6), Banco de Vizcaya, Banco Hispano Americano-Urquijo and Banco de Bilbao and BANESTO, had by that time already created vast and very diversified business groups (De la Sierra 1951; Muñoz Linares 1955; Muñoz 1969; Aguilera 1998; Pons 1999, 2001; Pueyo Sánchez 2006b).

Box 7.6 Banks and Business Groups: Banco Central in the Mid-Twentieth Century

Established in 1919 by a group of respected Spanish bankers, Banco Central probably represents the most important example of a large bank-based business group during Franco's dictatorship.

Like several other banks in Spain, Banco Central had acted as a universal bank since its inception. Aided by its vast network of contacts and friendships, it directly acquired stakes in a number of large industrial corporations. Even though it initially held relatively few industrial stakes, within a few years the bank bought several companies and began to get actively involved in their management.

When don Ignacio Villalonga Villalba, who was to be the president of the bank for more than thirty years, took office in 1940, the bank's business group was already quite extended. Villalonga started a process of restructuring, separating "good" and "bad" companies and getting rid of the latter. Then, a careful analysis of the sectors where the bank wanted to enter and manage companies was carried out. Once the group had been consolidated, new companies were acquired or directly founded in accordance with a concrete industrial plan.

The level of diversification that this banking group had already achieved by the mid-twentieth century is reflected in the following list, which was drafted by Villalonga in 1947. Banco Central owned and controlled companies in the electricity sector (Saltos del Nansa, Eléctricas Leonesas, and important stakes in Saltos del Sil and Hidroeléctrica del Chorro); the coal industry (active participation in MSP, and a councilor was placed at the Sociedad Hullera Española); iron metallurgy (on the board of Sociedad Nueva Montaña); metallurgy (active participation in Devís, and control of the Catalan company Material para Ferrocarriles y Construcciones); petroleum (control of CEPSA shared with Banco

Hispano Colonial); construction (control of Dragados y Construcciones, an important relationship with the Sociedad Obras y Finanza); the cement industry (an important position at the Sociedad Cementos Cosmos through Saltos del Sil and Elsa, a dominant role at Cementos Zaragoza through Banco de Crédito de Zaragoza and an important position through representation on the board of the Sociedad Financiera y Minera); tobacco (a block of shares in Tabacalera. S.A.); shipbuilding (on the board of Compañía Trasatlántica, control of Compañía Naviera Española shared with Banco Español de Crédito, block of shares in Sociedad Española de Construcción Naval with representation on its board); railways (control of FFCC de Cataluña, important position at Tranvías y Ferrocarriles de Valencia); and the chemical industry (important position at Industrias Químicas Canarias, which in turn had superphosphate plants in Bilbao and Tenerife).

Sources: Tortella Casares and García Ruiz (1999); Tortella Casares (2007); and Banco Central Annual Report (various years).

The new context that characterized the golden age affected the strategic decisions made by large corporations in Spain, but did not represent a real watershed with regard to the diffusion of the related diversification strategy. The most evident change observed in the 1973 benchmark is a reduction in the number of unrelated diversifiers in the country, whereas the number of single business companies and related diversifiers increased.

The single business activity model spread among the large corporations in Spain during the 1950s and 1960s, and in the early 1970s, in complete contrast to the rest of Europe (Whittington and Mayer 2000), single business activities represented the most widespread kind of corporate strategy. At the same time, the dominant business strategy declined slightly, while the number of related diversifiers increased in particular in those industries that were affected by a significant growth during the economic miracle. Meliá, a hotelier company that was founded in 1956, was, for instance, able to take advantage of the ever-greater influx of tourists into the country: it also acted as a travel agency, a real estate agent and a laundry service provider (Fomento de la Producción 1973). Nevertheless, large Spanish corporations remained far from the level of diversification achieved in the United States and other European nations. Only 27% of the largest corporations had moved into related industries in Spain, whereas in France, Germany and the United Kingdom, they numbered 43%, 38% and 57%, respectively (Whittington and Mayer 2000).

The increase in the number of single and related business companies partly explains the smaller role played by unrelated diversifiers in the Spanish big business panorama at the beginning of the 1970s. Business groups and conglomerates decreased from 35% to 13% in terms of their number and from 57% to 45% in contribution to the total turnover of the population. Even so, unrelated diversifiers continued to be the largest contributor

to the turnover of the big business population, and the number of conglomerates and business groups remained relatively high in Spain, in particularly
if compared to France and United Kingdom.

The largest business group in Spain at the beginning of the 1970s was,
just as it had been more than twenty years earlier, the state-owned holding
INI. With regard to the private unrelated diversifiers, the majority of the
business groups already observed in the 1950 population had survived, and,
assisted by the impressive growth of the country, by the increasing wealth
of the population and by some Francoist economic policies (Guillén 2001),
relatively new business groups emerged, for instance, around the chemical
company Explosivos Río Tinto, the steel company Altos Hornos de Vizcaya
and the wine firm Rumasa (see Box 7.7; Cabrera and Del Rey 2002, 320).

Box 7.7 Economic Miracles, Managerial Failures: The Sudden Growth and
         Decline of the Rumasa Business Group

The economic miracle allowed several private companies to grow easily and
quickly and to enter new sectors in Spain during the 1960s. However, the
euphoria of this period also pushed some entrepreneurs to bite off more than
they could chew, which is what happened to Ruiz Mateos S.A. (Rumasa).

Established in Jerez de la Frontera in 1961 in the wine industry, Rumasa soon
became a very diversified company, thanks in part to the extensive personal network of connections of its founder, José María Ruiz Mateos. During the 1960s
and the early 1970s, the enterprise bought several firms across a large variety of
sectors by calling on banks that soon came under the control of Rumasa itself.
In 1974, Rumasa was the largest private holding in the country and, while still a
family business, it owned 121 companies in the following industries: 12 banks,
10 financial companies (of which one was an insurance company), 3 in food,
3 in agriculture, 23 in the production and trade of wines, 2 in chemicals, 1 in
textiles, 9 in construction, 27 in real estate, 3 hotels, 2 in advertising and 26
commercial firms.

However, Rumasa's luck started to run out with the onset of the economic
crisis in the 1970s and the change in political regimes. This unfortunate combination of events brought to light structural problems of a group that could
not be managed effectively and that had grown too quickly. All the while, the
political upheaval affected the company's relationship with its important contacts and connections.

The economic results of this colossus worsened, and when in 1983 the
group's companies were performing so badly that the banks were also in danger,
the government decided to expropriate the group. Among many other justifica-
tions, it claimed that the group had abused the credit extended to it by its banks
to benefit the companies that belonged to the group itself. At that time, Rumasa
employed 65,000 workers, included 700 companies and 18 banks and represented 2% of the Spanish GDP. Rumasa was thus dismantled, and its companies
were sold to several private investors.

Sources: Cabrera and Del Rey (2002); and Rumasa Annual Report (various years).

The years of transition to democracy and of integration into the European Economic Community represented a major watershed for the strategic choices made by the largest corporations in Spain. In essence, the number and turnover of single and dominant business companies declined, while a strategy of related diversification became the preferred option for the largest companies in Spain in 1988.

The increasing number and importance of the latter kind of company was due on the one hand to a process of growth or restructuring of some firms in Spain, which were able to take advantage of the new opportunities emerging in a country that had become democratic and increasingly integrated into the European and world economies. Many examples of such behavior can be found across different sectors and ownership types. On the other hand, some companies that were unrelated diversifiers were not able to maintain their old structure and strategy under the new democratic regime, particularly when the rules imposed by the European community brought about the end of government protection and of the trade and investment asymmetries that had benefitted them so far. Some of them disappeared, while other companies managed to adapt to the new context by changing their strategies. In the state owned-sector, meanwhile, a process of restructuring INI started. Repsol came about, for instance, as the result of the reorganization of the state's mainly INI-based activities, in crucial sectors such as petroleum (see Box 7.8).

Box 7.8 From Chaos to Repsol: The New Governmental Strategy in the Oil Sector

The related diversifier Repsol was founded in 1987 as the final stage of a process of reorganization of the state's activities in the oil and gas sector, and was carried out in order to create a "national champion."

The oil industry in Spain had been strictly regulated by the state since 1927, when a state monopoly was established. A private company that was controlled by the main banks of the country (CAMPSA) obtained a concession for exploiting the monopoly and focused on the distribution phase. At the same time, a system of state concessions for the exploration, extraction and refining of oil and for gasoline stations was established, while the state held on to its power to fix prices within this concessions system. The oil companies and refineries, which in many cases belonged to INI, were forced to sell their products to CAMPSA at the volumes and prices predetermined by the state. They also had to buy a part of their crude oil from another INI-owned company, Hispanoil. This created a very inefficient situation, since there was no one company that could develop a sufficient degree of vertical integration, as would have been advisable in this industry. Moreover, the state intervened by using many different and badly coordinated institutions.

The oil shocks during the 1970s made the severe weaknesses of this system abundantly clear, and the end of the monopoly brought about by Spain's integration into the European Economic Community represented a very serious threat for the survival of Spanish companies in this sector. Motivated by such considerations, a restructuring of the oil industry started in the democratic era.

In 1981, a state-owned holding, Instituto Nacional de Hidrocarburos (INH), was created in order to gather all the companies that had had concessions in this sector into a single group devoted exclusively to oil, and consequently to achieve better coordination between them. The next step was the creation of a national champion. Within the INH was thus founded Repsol, a company that integrated the activities of the previous independent firms. Repsol was the first in this sector in Spain to achieve an efficient level of vertical integration and related diversification in oil, gas and oil-related activities.

The economies of scale and scope achieved thanks to this process and to the new strategy adopted by the state in this industry were impressive if compared with its previous performance. Repsol was successfully privatized and became a multinational company and one of the largest corporations worldwide in its sector, despite the history of inefficiency that had characterized past oil activities in Spain.

Sources: Ramón-Laca Cotorruelo (1978); Fanjul (1989); Nueno (1996); Mochón and Rambla (1999, 231–69); Bosch Badía (2008); INH Annual Report (various years); INI Annual Report (various years); and Repsol Annual Report (various years).

New strategies of refocusing affected not only the state-owned sector: many families and bank-led business groups were also downsized during this era, and most of them refocused on few businesses.

Despite the increase, the number of related diversifiers in Spain at the end of the 1980s was smaller than that in Italy, France, Germany or the United Kingdom. In addition to unrelated diversification, dominant and particularly single business strategies continued to be widely adopted by companies. Looking at turnover percentages, unrelated diversifiers still represented almost 30% of the whole population in 1988 even though, in contrast to other benchmark years, no new companies adopted this kind of strategy. The main business groups remained that of the state-owned holding INI, which was at the time in the early stages of the privatization process, and some "old" bank-led business groups, which were also smaller in size, number and value of industrial stakes than in the past.

At the beginning of the new millennium, the situation had not changed to any great extent. Single and dominant business models, in contrast to the largest economies in Europe, continued to be quite important. More than 50% of the companies in the population of 100 largest companies adopted one of these two strategies in 2002. Far from being a strategy typical of small business, focused strategies were adopted also by some of the major Spanish national champions.

In this framework, the main difference with the previous period is that during the 1990s related diversifiers became much more dominant compared to the unrelated diversifiers in terms of the percentage they contributed to the total turnover of the population. Those business groups that had been the main protagonists of the big business panorama in Spain and that in some cases had survived until the 1980s, had almost completely disappeared at the beginning of the new millennium. The state-owned holding INI no longer existed, nor did most of the bank-led business groups. The main unrelated diversifiers in 2002 were a cooperative, Mondragón (Mondragón Annual Report 2002; Guillén 2005), two family groups, Grupo March and Abengoa (Abengoa Annual Report 2002) and a construction company, Fomento de Construcción y Contratas (Fomento de Construcción y Contratas Annual Report 2002). On the other hand, 43% and 58%, respectively, of the number and the turnover of the 100 largest corporations in Spain relied on related diversification, which was clearly predominant in the population and was adopted across many sectors and by many types of owners. In 2002, there were more large diversified corporations in Spain than in Italy, but fewer than in France, Germany or Britain (Whittington and Mayer 2000).

Despite having been dominated by peculiar trends up to the 1980s, the strategies adopted by the largest corporations in Spain were thus not significantly different from those in Italy, notwithstanding the minor role played in Spain by the unrelated diversifiers in 2002. At the beginning of the new millennium, both these Southern European nations were more similar than they had ever been to the major European economies in terms of the strategic choices made by their largest corporations. Nevertheless, some peculiarities persist, especially in terms of the importance of single and dominant business companies.

7.4 SUMMARY

This chapter has analyzed the strategic transformation of the largest corporations in Italy and Spain in the light of the debate among universalist scholars, who argued for a convergence in the product diversification strategy in the most advanced economies, and the contextualist scholars, who stressed the impact of context in making the predominant strategies of corporations different across the world.

The starting point for our analysis was based on investigations by Whittington and Mayer who, at the turn of the twenty-first century, demonstrated that the different ownership structures and managerial cultures that characterized France, Germany and in part the United Kingdom during the second part of the twentieth century did not cause their companies to avoid adopting a strategy of related diversification and thus copying the US example.

The analysis of the big business strategies in Italy and Spain, however, showed an only partial convergence toward the strategic patterns followed by the major firms in the United States and in the most advanced European economies. The strategy of related diversification, that "universal trend" toward which most of the largest companies had converged, started to spread in Italy and in Spain at a comparatively late stage, and did not reach the same degree of diffusion as in other countries. On the other hand, some contextual factors made it possible, or even convenient, for most companies to adopt alternative product strategies, such as the single or dominant business or the unrelated diversification strategy.

From the middle of the twentieth century, the number of companies that decided to focus on a single business, for example, slightly decreased in Italy but not in Spain, and the dominant-business corporations remained very important in both countries, accounting for about one-third of the population in all the benchmark years. Their continued success is at least in part explained by the relatively small size of these two countries and, at least until the process of European integration gathered pace, by the protection that most of them enjoyed within their national borders.

Moreover, the unrelated diversification strategy was particularly important. This strategy was pursued not only by the major state-owned business groups in both nations but also by the most important families and, in Spain, the banks. In the beginning, unrelated diversification was mainly associated with the first stages of the industrialization process of these nations, as part of which only a few companies had enough financial resources to enter the capital-intensive sectors that were typical of the Second Industrial Revolution. Later on, however, unrelated diversification represented a very common enterprise form until the 1970s, and remained a typical strategy in both Italy and Spain throughout the second half of the century.

8   The Geographic Diversification Strategy

The Rise of Italian and Spanish Multinational Companies?

8.1 NOT ONLY PRODUCT DIVERSIFICATION . . .

International activities undertaken by companies in a variety of ways have represented an important driver for economic growth since the final decades of the nineteenth century. Knowledge, technologies, products and capital from abroad played a very important role in enabling the industrial takeoff in several latecomer nations. At the same time, the existence of markets and/or a labor force and/or raw materials outside national borders was often crucial for the growth strategies of the large corporations in the most advanced nations (Wilkins 1970 1974; Franko 1976; Jones 2005). Alfred Chandler was well aware that the product diversification strategy was, and still is, only one of the possible ways in which companies are able to grow. The main alternative is to diversify the company's own geographical market, to sell its products abroad, or to set up production plants in other countries.

Many studies since the 1960s have analyzed direct investment from the investor's perspective, stressing the advantages and the risks of this growth strategy, and investigating what determines the localization choices of multinational companies. Contributions to this field include some works of industrial organization (Kindleberger 1969; Caves 1971; Hymer 1976), of the theory of the product life cycle (Vernon 1966) and of internalization (Buckley and Casson 1976, 1988), as well as Dunning's (1979) eclectic paradigm and the extensive critical analysis conducted by Caves (1982), Cantwell (2004) and Jones (2005). More than forty years of investigations into these topics has made it possible to offer a quite complex and articulate picture (Álvaro Moya 2010) which, at the same time, opens a path for new studies.

However, scholars who studied the strategic choices of large corporations from a historical perspective have until relatively recently neglected geographic diversification, and have conducted almost no systematic studies on strategies based on foreign trade and investment. Those that do exist concentrate mainly on the United States (Wilkins 1970, 1974) and, with few exceptions, ignore Europe to a large extent. This has been due in part to the fact that European companies' international activities were, particularly right after World War II, far less extensive and successful than were those of their US counterparts. Nevertheless, starting from the golden age during the 1950s and 1960s, international trade also increased significantly among several European nations, and European multinationals emerged and were able to strengthen their international position. More recently, largely thanks to an intensified process of globalization and Europeanization, more late-comer countries have also started to look for a competitive advantage in geographic diversification rather than in alternative strategies (Guillén 2005; Binda and Iversen 2007; Binda 2009a, 2009b; Binda and Colli 2011; Colli, García-Canal and Guillén 2012). The aim of this chapter is to investigate the timescales and dynamics involved in the adoption of these geographic diversification strategies in Italy and Spain from 1950 to 2002.

8.2 TRENDS IN THE ADOPTION OF INTERNATIONALIZATION STRATEGIES AMONG THE LARGE CORPORATIONS IN ITALY

At a general level, the strategy of geographic diversification was not unknown to Italy's firms prior to World War II. Pier Angelo Toninelli (2003) points out that the traditional food industry, for instance, was already actively involved in a process of internationalization during the first part of the twentieth century. Companies such as Bertolli (olive oil and sliced cheese), Perugina (sweets), Buitoni (pasta), Campari (spirits), Gancia (sparkling wines), Ferrarelle (mineral water) and Galbani (cheese) are among the most famous representatives of this category. They initially extended their foreign market share by supplying the communities of Italian emigrants abroad, and then targeted a more expansive market that also included local customers. Nevertheless, it is fair to say that in the mid-twentieth century the largest Italian companies very seldom chose to adopt a strategy of geographic diversification (Figure 8.1).

The percentage of exclusively nationally oriented companies is not surprising considering that both per-capita income and the level of domestic demand was starting to increase in Italy. Future prospects for the domestic market were very good and, conversely, going abroad was difficult for Italian firms, especially in the years that followed World War II. The choice to focus only on the domestic market was a relatively rational one and allowed several corporations to keep on growing thanks to the significant opportunities they could exploit at home. Manufacturing was predominantly oriented toward the domestic market, and only a few of the largest corporations had already opened foreign subsidiaries by the mid-twentieth century. Of the 100 biggest firms in Italy, 65% had decided to focus their production and sales exclusively on the domestic market, and none had adopted a strategy of complete internationalization aggregating more than 90% of their revenues from exports and/or sales generated by foreign branches.

Almost one-fifth of the largest corporations had nevertheless decided to go abroad, focusing only part of their activities within the domestic context. Most of them were relatively big companies or groups, such as IRI, FIAT or

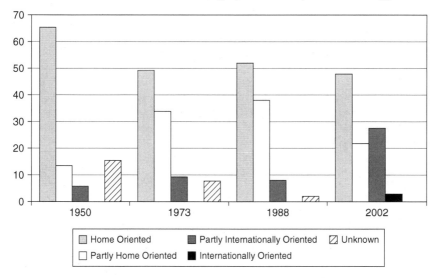

Figure 8.1 The geographic diversification strategy in Italy
Source: Appendix Tables 1b, 2b, 3b, 4b.

AGIP (e.g., Casalino 2004–2005; Pozzi 2009). Their international activities, in the form of exports or sales by foreign subsidiaries, contributed to more than 10% of their total revenues, but less than 50%. They represented 13% of the number, and 43% of the assets, of the whole Italian population in 1950.

At that time, only three companies looked mainly beyond the Italian borders: the chemical company SNIA Viscosa, which owned subsidiaries in Spain, Argentina and in Brazil in addition to being a heavy exporter (SNIA Viscosa Annual Report 1950); the oil firm Mobil (Socony Vacuum Italiana), which had established a subsidiary in Naples during the autarkic period whose exports generated more than 75% of its turnover in 1956 (Pavan 1976, 130); and, last but not least, the rubber company Pirelli (Box 8.1).

Box 8.1 Pirelli, "The Most Multinational among the Largest Italian Enterprises"

Pirelli, a rubber company founded in 1872 in Milan, was one of the largest companies in Italy throughout the twentieth century, and one of the first to start a process of geographic diversification.

Defined by some Italian economic historians as "the most multinational among the largest Italian enterprises" (Castagnoli and Scarpellini 2003, 250), Pirelli had already started to internationalize its activities at the end of the nineteenth century. Relatively low domestic demand in this new sector had encouraged it to do so, as did the important European experiences gained by its founder during the early years of the company.

In 1895, twenty-three years after its foundation, exports already represented more than 30% of Pirelli's production. In 1901, its first foreign subsidiary was created in Spain, followed by the establishment of other commercial subsidiaries in Austria, Argentina, Belgium and France in the same decade. In 1909, furthermore, a trading partnership represented a first foray into the British market before the company established three factories there during the 1910s and 1920s. Internationalization in those years went hand in hand with diversification, and Pirelli moved into the production of several varieties of rubber products, including underground cables, bicycle tires and, later on, automobile tires.

In 1920, the need to coordinate the foreign activities of the corporation pushed it to establish a foreign holding, Compagnie Internationale Pirelli, in Belgium, while its international business was extended to the acquisition of rubber plantations in Java and Malaysia. The corporation was able to maintain and manage its international activities also during the Fascist period, albeit by resorting to underhand practices to an extent. A total of fifty-two factories were opened abroad during the first half of the twentieth century, and after World War II, Pirelli further expanded its process of internationalization. The company's 1950 annual report claimed that it had exported to eighty-three different nations that year. It also included a long list of all its direct foreign investments, which were predominantly concentrated in Europe and Southern America.

Sources: Pavan (1976); Bezza (1987); Bigazzi (1990); Castagnoli and Scarpellini (2003); Polese (2004); Berta and Onida (2011); Pozzi (2012); Pirelli & C. Annual Report (various years); and Pirelli Spa Annual Report (various years).

Particularly from the 1950s onward, Italy became much more open to the international economy. This was mainly thanks to the role played by important politicians with a strong international attitude such as Cesare Merzagora and Ugo La Malfa, who succeeded each other at the Ministry of Foreign Trade between the end of the 1950s and early 1960s. It was principally because of their contribution that Italy decided to become a founding member of the European Economic Community, which was created by the Treaty of Rome in 1957 (Amatori and Colli 1999, 233).

The attitude of relative openness that characterized Italy in the postwar period did not, however, cause a blind acceptance of stronger international competition in the domestic market, nor did it push Italian companies to focus more on the international markets. In fact, a reduction in tariff protection in the domestic market, which they had thus far been able to count on, brought about a palpable fear of failure. Italian businesspeople heavily pressurized the government, which mainly resulted in Italy being able to maintain the highest tariffs in Western Europe in the steel and metal, automobile, electricity equipment and yarn production sectors until the 1960s. In a 1993 interview, Guido Carli, governor of the Bank of Italy from 1960 to 1975, mentioned the "furious telephone calls made by Valletta," the president of the car producer FIAT and one of the most eminent and influential businessmen of the time, "in order to soften as much as possible the constraints of the treaty," and mentioned the "virulent pressures made by Professor Valletta, who was terrified by the idea of a progressive drop of the tariffs" (Carli 1993, 194–95).

In this context, during the golden age, the attitude of the Italian companies toward adopting strategies of stronger geographic diversification changed, but not dramatically. Italian exports had already started to grow during the reconstruction years, and during the 1950s and 1960s, the integration of Italy into the European Economic Community as well as the general drop of tariffs furthered a significant opening of the Italian economy (Zamagni 1990). Italian companies were so actively involved in export that some economists have defined the Italian economic miracle of that period as an "export-led growth" (Zamagni 1990, 465). Even though this interpretation was disputed during the 1970s, and it has been demonstrated that the domestic market was clearly more important than the international one (Zamagni 1990), it is certain that companies in general, and big businesses in particular, increasingly understood the importance of foreign markets. Direct investment abroad also increased during the golden age, but the Italian multinationals remained few in number at least up to the 1960s. The low wages in Italy and the expanding domestic market created a positive environment at home. For most of them, expanding abroad was neither a priority nor a necessity.

Looking at the empirical evidence, the number of large Italian companies that were exclusively devoted to the domestic market in 1973 dropped to less than the half of the 100 biggest firms. The adoption of a strategy of only partial orientation toward the domestic market increased from slightly more than 13% to 34% of the total number of companies within the population between 1950 and 1973. It became the predominant strategy if we consider corporate turnover: a large part of the sales figures achieved by the 100 largest firms in Italy came from companies that only partially focused on the domestic market. Even though they remained a minority, the partially internationally oriented firms increased their significance within the population also during the 1950s and 1960s, almost doubling their presence. One of the companies that effectively pursued a strategy of internationalization during the golden age was Olivetti, the Italian leader in office machinery. Its exports in 1973 represented almost 75% of its turnover, but soon afterward, it experienced a significant decline (Box 8.2).

Box 8.2 The History of Olivetti: An Italian Economic Miracle Abroad

Established in 1908 by Camillo Olivetti to produce typewriters, Olivetti represents an example of rapid growth as part of the pursuit of an internationalization strategy in the Italian postwar period. However, its international success is limited to a specific period, and Olivetti has been described as a "one-season protagonist" among the Italian multinationals.

The company started exporting its products as early as the 1920s and began to directly invest in Spain and Argentina. However, it was mainly from the postwar period onward that, under the leadership of the founder's son Adriano

Olivetti, the firm experienced a period of major growth and international expansion. The adoption of a new production system made significant advances in terms of efficiency possible. The company also started to diversify into the production of the first mechanical calculators and developed one of the most highly innovative electronics division in the world. By the middle of the 1950s, exports already represented more than 50% of Olivetti's turnover. At the same time, new subsidiaries were opened in several Latin American countries, as well as in the United Kingdom, Denmark, Sweden, the Netherlands, Greece and Finland. In 1968, the number of employees abroad greatly exceeded the number in Italy.

A particularly important piece in the puzzle of Olivetti's international growth was the United States. Olivetti Corporation of America was founded in 1950 and since the beginning, it was deeply committed to product quality and innovation in particular in the calculator sector, where the only real competitor was Remington Rand. In 1958, 20% of foreign production was carried out in the United States. However, its troubles started after 1959, when Olivetti decided to acquire a big and prestigious American company in typewriters (Underwood). They had probably underestimated the cost of this venture, and the amount of money that Olivetti had to invest in the modernization of its new American factory greatly impacted on the Italian head office.

When Adriano Olivetti suddenly died, the situation of the company was dire. In 1964, its new owners decided to abandon its pioneering electronics division and sold it to General Electric. It represented the beginning of the decline of the firm, whose poor performance in Italy and abroad was further exacerbated by the 1970s oil crisis.

Sources: Caizzi (1962); Soria (1979); Barbiellini Amidei, Goldstein and Spadoni (2011); and Berta and Onida (2011).

Few things changed with respect to the levels of internationalization during the 1970s and early 1980s. The trend toward the adoption of an increasingly global attitude seems to have stopped at the end of the economic miracle. This was due to important changes in the overall economic scenario. The slowdown of domestic demand during the recession of the 1970s encouraged companies to become more committed to their export activities. At the same time, however, the international economic climate was not favorable and most companies lacked the money to invest abroad. The recovery and restructuring of big companies during the 1980s was at the source of a new wave of international activity, both in terms of exports and of foreign direct investment, particularly during the second part of the decade. The empirical evidence gathered on the largest companies, however, shows that a relative stagnation took place between 1973 and 1988. The number of companies that were exclusively devoted to the domestic market increased by 3 percentage points, the firms that only partially oriented their activities toward home increased only slightly (from 34% to 38%), while the number of partially internationally oriented corporations actually dropped.

Completely internationally oriented companies, which generated more than 90% of their revenue from foreign activities, did not exist in Italy among the 100 largest corporations at least up to the end of the 1990s. It was only with the advent of new technological opportunities provided by the revolution that took place in the electronics, information science and telecommunications sectors, and with the increased processes of globalization and European integration, that the national and international context could start to transform the strategies adopted by companies in Italy to any great extent. Nevertheless, some important continuities remain identifiable, even in the 2002 benchmark.

During the 1990s, a number of companies that were completely oriented toward the international markets emerged, such as the eyeglasses producer Luxottica and the semiconductor company STMicroelectronics. Moreover, partially internationally orientated companies started to spread to a remarkable extent as well. The percentage of companies that generated more than half of their revenue from their international activities, well exemplified by Benetton (Box 8.3), grew from 8% to 27% of the total population. In 2002, these companies' sales represented almost one-third of the total sales of the population. The increasing adoption of a more international strategy took place at the disadvantage of that category of companies that already had an international activity—the only partly home oriented firms. Those companies that had so far been exclusively focused on the domestic market did not significantly lose ground due to the increased trend toward globalization. The number of companies that were only partially oriented toward the domestic market dropped from 38% to 22% between 1988 and 2002, whereas their contribution to the total turnover of the population decreased dramatically, from 75% to 27%. On the other hand, the geographic strategy of orientation toward only the domestic market remained also in 2002 the most commonly adopted one, accounting for in excess of 48% of the largest companies in the country. Moreover, despite the increased process of globalization and Europeanization that took place during the 1990s and at the beginning of the new millennium, in 2002, those companies that were exclusively focused on the domestic market once again became the most important contributors to the total turnover of the population, accumulating 41% of its total sales.

Box 8.3 Benetton, "All the Colors of the World"

Established in 1965 as a small business that produced sweaters in several bright colors, during the final decade of the twentieth century, Benetton became one of the most important companies in Italy and probably epitomized the Italian multinationals of that period. Its first overseas store was opened in 1968, which was soon followed by several others. During the 1970s, Benetton's diversification into several apparel lines and the production of a large variety of items was accompanied by a rapid process of increased internationalization. By 1978, more than 200 stores existed throughout Europe, and the group already exported 60% of its merchandise. In the early 1980s, Benetton opened one shop a day on average, including one in New York in 1980 and one in Tokyo in 1982.

In those years, the company's manufacturing plants were based in Italy, France and Scotland, while a holding company, The Benetton International Holding was created in Luxembourg in 1985 in order to manage the group's international activities. Even though the Benetton family retained firm control of the group, its capital also became increasingly internationalized, with listings on the Milan and, later on, on the Frankfurt and New York stock exchanges. By the mid-1980s, Benetton already had a presence in about sixty countries with 3,200 shops. "Benetton, all the colors of the world" claimed a famous advertising campaign in 1984.

The company's process of internationalization continued during the 1990s. Its production system, meanwhile, underwent an important change by going from an internationalization based on a widespread and exclusive distribution-only system to a mix of international production and outsourcing from local suppliers.

In 2002, the company's annual report claimed that 68.9% of its turnover came from Europe, 9.6% from Asia, 12.6% from America, and 8.9% from other areas. Currently the Benetton Group has a presence in 120 countries around the world.

Sources: Favero (2005); Tattara and Crestanello (2008); Berta and Onida (2011); and Benetton Annual Report (various years).

Even though the new economic trends could have provided new export and foreign investment opportunities, it seems that several of Italy's companies did not take the chance to adopt a geographic diversification strategy to any great extent. This statement is supported by recent analysis that shows the lackluster performance especially of large corporations in becoming multinational firms (Berta and Onida 2011). However, many of the corporations that had already started on a path of internationalization increased their overseas activities during the last decade of the twentieth century and adopted more extreme geographic diversification strategies. The main change that took place during this period thus does not concern the number of internationalized companies in Italy, but the intensity with which the companies that had decided to pursue a geographic diversification strategy did so.

8.3 THE INTERNALIZATION OF SPANISH BIG BUSINESS

The trend followed by the largest corporations in Spain in the adoption of the strategy of geographical diversification was partly different from that in Italy. Due to Franco's autarkic policies the country remained politically and economically isolated at least until international pressures caused by the cold war, on one hand, and the need to import material and immaterial goods necessary for industrialization, on the other, encouraged it to redevelop a relationship with the United States. From the 1950s onward, Spain thus became increasingly integrated. Nevertheless, even though it had already signed an agreement of preferential trade with the European Economic Community in 1970 and had become more open to international capital and products inside its borders since about the early 1960s, the country remained excluded from the EEC until the Francoist dictatorship came to an end. Only in 1986, after a long negotiation process, did Spain succeed in becoming a member of the European Economic Community. It was only then that the great national enterprises began to see the effects of a lack of protection effects on the end of foreign competition on the domestic market: serious consequences for their competitiveness both at home and abroad. In spite of this, the main dynamics seen in the adoption of an international strategy in Spain were broadly similar to those in Italy (Figure 8.2).

The strategy of geographic diversification was almost completely avoided by the largest corporations in Spain in the middle of the twentieth century and during the autarkic period, when the large majority chose to focus their activities only on the domestic market. The firms that were exclusively oriented toward the domestic market represent 89% of the 1950 population and 95.2% of its assets. Even though some Spanish industries had had a relatively strong tradition in exports in the past, such as the food and beverages, weapons or publishing sectors (Fernández Moya 2009; Goñi

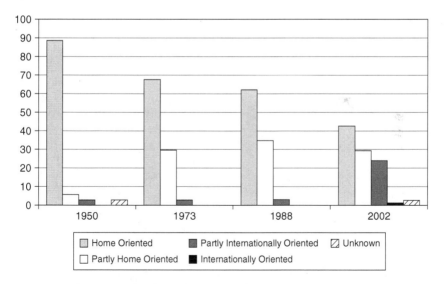

Figure 8.2 The geographic diversification strategy in Spain
Source: Appendix Tables 5b, 6b, 7b, 8b.

Mendizabal 2009), during the 1950s, almost none of the Spanish corporations engaged in export activities or established subsidiaries abroad to any significant extent. The main reason behind the low level of internationalization of Spanish firms is found in the extreme isolation that characterized the Spanish economy at least until the introduction of the Plan de Establización in 1959. The nationalistic economic policies adopted by the Caudillo involved strict controls on currencies and a series of protectionist measures that included tariffs and limits on imports. At first, the Allies responded to this behavior with a trade embargo that lasted until the end of the 1940s. Whereas Italy during the same period had started a process of integration with the major European economies and received financial assistance from the United States through the Marshall Plan, Spain became increasingly closed to the international economy.

The choice not to engage in export to any meaningful extent was thus in effect coherent with Spain's isolation from the European and international economic communities during the first decades of the Francoist dictatorship. There were in any case no strong incentives for companies to export their products. The limited productive capacity of the Spanish corporations could in fact be completely absorbed by the small domestic market of that period, which could not buy foreign products. Even if companies had had the desire and opportunity to export, they produced very few things that could have been exported successfully. Spanish enterprises were very small at this time and were not competitive at an international level, and Spanish direct investments abroad fared no better. During the 1940s and 1950s, only a few companies invested in foreign countries, in particular in projects that were linked to the mining and building industries, such as in Morocco and in some Latin American countries (Guillén 2005, 9).

In the 1950 population, almost no company showed even a limited orientation toward foreign markets, with two major exceptions. The first is the Comillas group, a holding of companies that in many cases were founded with an already strongly international outlook that had seen them engaging in trade in areas extending from the Philippines to Cuba since the end of the nineteenth century and that, even though to a limited extent, meant they maintained their interests and relationships abroad even during the beginning of the Francoist period (Rodrigo Alharilla 2000). In 1950, the tobacco company Tabacos de Filipinas, for instance, had subsidiaries in the Philippines, such as the sugar companies Azucarera de Tarlac and Central Azucarera de Bais, the paper firm Fábrica de Celulosa and Tabacalera Insurance. The other firm that was not just oriented toward the domestic market in 1950s Spain was the paper company Papeleras Reunidas, a relatively large exporter of cigarette paper that had a subsidiary in Portugal (Papeleras Reunidas Annual Report 1950). The only multinational firm based in Spain in 1950 was CHADE (Compañía Hispano-Americana de Electricidad), an electricity company that had been recently nationalized by Perón's government in Argentina (Carreras 2003).

Even though Spain could not take advantage of the opportunities provided by European integration as Italy could, the policies aimed at liberalizing trade that came into effect from the end of the 1950s, as well as the growth of the country and its big business, actually favored an increased internationalization of the largest companies during the 1960s and 1970s. Despite the fact that the majority of Spanish firms remained exclusively oriented toward the domestic market, it is important to note that strategies of geographic diversification became slightly more common, as is reflected by the information included in the 1973 benchmark. However, no significant changes occurred in either 1973 or 1988, when companies were recovering after the severe economic crisis and political transition of the 1970s. The 1988 benchmark may also be too early to observe the effects of Spanish integration into the European Economic Community, which took place in 1986.

The strategy of complete orientation toward the domestic market remained the most commonly adopted one in the 1973 and 1988 populations both in terms of the number of and the turnover generated by the sampled firms. The home-oriented companies constituted 68% of the population in 1973 and 62% in 1988. The characteristics of the market and the competitive edge of the large companies in Spain partly help to explain the low level of internationalization. The substantial market growth at least up to the 1970s was in fact so huge that it not only led the national private and state-owned companies to avoid competing abroad but also provided significant incentives to foreign multinationals to enter the Spanish market.

The strategy that grew most between 1950 and 1973 was that of only partial orientation toward the home market, going from 5% to 30% of the population. A minor increase is detected in 1988, when this figure reached the 35% of the population. The strategy of internationalization was not new in Spain and in some cases survived the worst economic conjunctures in this country's history, in particular for some traditional sectors such as the food and beverages industry, as the history of the wine company González Byass shows (Box 8.4).

Box 8.4 González Byass: A "National Champion" in Exports since the Nineteenth Century

In Spain, companies in traditional sectors were often able to internationalize successfully. One of the most famous examples comes from the wine industry, and in particular the company González Byass, a family firm whose origins date back to 1835 when Manuel María González Ángel became involved in the production and export of Sherry wine. The boom that this industry experienced during those years allowed the company to grow quickly and become successful. In 1885, the company's agent in England, Robert Blake Byass, became a shareholder. The company's export activities spurred on its growth and encouraged it to diversify into brandy varieties, other kinds of spirits and cheaper table wine, the latter of which the company had already started producing during the 1870s, when the international markets of Sherry wine experienced a serious crisis. González

Byass was the leading company in a sector that was crucial to Spanish exports, representing about 19% of the value of the total Spanish exports and 61% of the trade between Spain and the United Kingdom between 1855 and 1869.

Despite a relative decline, the company was able to gain and maintain a leading position in this industry during the first half of the twentieth century. The expansion and internationalization of González Byass continued during the Francoist era. The pace of its growth even increased during the 1960s, when the company started to build big new plants in Spain.

Even though González Byass remained a quite traditional, strictly family-owned and controlled firm and did not open foreign subsidiaries throughout this period, the magnitude of its exports was so large that the company's main brand, Tio Pepe, is one of Spain's most internationally famous brands to this day.

Sources: Fernández Perez (1999); Montañés (2000a, 2000b); Medina Albaladejo (2010); and www.gonzalezbyass.com.

The interest in exporting products and services and in creating subsidiaries abroad grew significantly during this period, and companies made concerted efforts in their annual reports to stress their international activities, if indeed they were engaged in foreign markets. However, both exports and production abroad remained quite limited at least up to the 1990s, in terms of the flow of products and money as well as the number of companies that actually decided to pursue a strategy of significant geographic diversification. In contrast to what happened in Italy, it has to be stressed that foreign multinationals played an important role in achieving an export balance among the largest companies in the country, as can be shown by a case study on the car industry (Box 8.5).

Box 8.5 The Car Industry in Spain: A Birthplace of Multinationals?

As has been shown in previous chapters, foreign multinationals found plenty of opportunity to grow in Spain since the country opened to outside economic investment through the Plan de Estabilización in 1959. They were, of course, attracted by the great domestic market growth potential of a newly industrializing country. In addition, the cheap labor that was available in Spain was very often a good incentive for making the country a key location and an important platform for export aimed at the European markets in particular.

As early as 1973, except for the largest business groups of the country, the most internationalized individual companies belonged to the car production sector that (with the important exception of SEAT) was almost completely made up of multinational companies. Firms like FASA-Renault and Chrysler, Citroën España and Authi (a joint venture between the British Motor Corporation and the Spanish company Nueva Montaña Quijano) were predominantly oriented toward the foreign markets. FASA-Renault, controlled by the French company Renault, had moreover already opened a subsidiary in Portugal.

The situation seen in 1988 is even more telling, since all the companies in the automotive sector were multinationals, which at the same time were only partially home market oriented or even partially internationally oriented. The Spanish subsidiary of General Motors, for instance, ranked sixth among the largest corporations in Spain and was one of its stronger exporters, sending more than 50% of its production abroad. The major national firm in car production, SEAT, largely shifted its strategy toward a more advanced internationalization after being bought by Volkswagen at the beginning of the 1980s.

Maybe even more importantly, it has to be stressed that the presence of foreign multinationals in car manufacturing not only increased Spanish exports in this sector, but also furthered the growth and internationalization of local producers of components for automobiles, as was the case with Grupo Antolín or Gestamp, which developed substantial capabilities in this area and started to internationalize their businesses. They can actually be counted among the main, most successful Spanish multinationals.

Sources: Biggart and Guillén (1999); Guillén (2001); Binda (2005a); Guillen and García-Canal (2010); Colli, Garcia-Canal and Guillén (2012); Chrysler España Annual Report (various years); Citroën Hispania Annual Report (various years); Daimler Chrysler España Holding Annual Report (various years); FASA Annual Report (various years); Fasa Renault Annual Report (various years); Ford Annual Report (various years); General Motors Annual Report (various years); and Mercedes-Benz España Annual Report (various years); Peugeot Talbot España Annual Report (various years); and Seat Annual Report (various years).

The number of companies that were partially internationally oriented did not change to any significant extent until the end of the 1980s, growing from 3% to 4% of the largest corporations between 1950 and 1988. Their contribution to the total turnover of the population, meanwhile, remained relatively insignificant throughout this period. Moreover, none of the largest corporations decided to adopt a strategy of total international orientation.

Things changed dramatically during the last decade of the twentieth century, a period in which Spain continued to grow and converge toward the most advanced economies in the world, and the process of European integration gathered pace. Compared to the previous period, the most obvious change that took place during the 1990s, and that is reflected in 2002 population, is the fact that the majority of the largest companies in Spain abandoned the domestic market as the only point of reference. In interpreting this trend, it is useful to simply remember the fact that foreign investing and exporting became more straightforward following Spain's democratization and integration in to the European Economic Community. In other words, going abroad was both easier and necessary for local corporations. The increasing presence of international competition in the domestic market could have caused many problems for several of the largest corporations in the country. As has already been shown, many of the largest companies were sold to foreign multinationals. On the other hand, many of the big companies that survived these changes were concentrated in the nonmanufacturing sectors, which remained under protection for a longer period and thus had a few more years to recover and restructure through a process of mergers and acquisitions. In many cases, they decided to invest in foreign countries in order to further grow and then be able to face the increasing competition within their national borders when a definitive integration with Europe permanently eliminated any kind of protection and regulation of these sectors.

The trend toward internationalization of large companies was visible throughout Europe at this time, and manifested itself in infra-European flows of goods and capital (Fligstein and Merand 2002; Binda and Iversen 2007; Wilson et al. 2007). Spain was involved in direct investment and export both within Europe and, at certain points predominantly, in Latin America (Durán Herrera 1996, 1997a, 1997b, 2005). The result of this process of internationalization is evident in the 2002 population, when the number of exclusively home oriented companies decreased from 62% to 43% of the whole population, and their contribution to the total turnover dropped from 55% to 20%. The experience of the construction sector, and in particular of the company Dragados y Construcciones, represents a good example of increasing growth and internationalization of an industry that could not remain unaffected by the changing dynamics in domestic and foreign demand in the long term (Box 8.6).

Box 8.6 Between National Booms and Foreign Markets: The Dynamics of Internationalization of the Construction Company Dragados y Construcciones

Dragados y Construcciones, currently part of Actividades de Construcción y Servicios (ACS) group, was established in 1941 thanks to a contribution from one of the most important banks of the country, Banco Central, which for several years remained its largest shareholder.

The company started its business by getting involved with the building and maintenance of harbors and hydraulic works and soon afterward diversified into building-related activities all over Spain, becoming the largest company in this sector during the 1960s.

Following the Plan de Estabilización, the company was able to grow mainly thanks to a boom in the national economy, as the industrialization and modernization process provided a continuous demand for new buildings and infrastructures. It could then also start to draw up plans for international expansion based both on the geographical and/or cultural proximity and on the profitable opportunities offered by certain countries, such as Portugal, Northern Africa and Latin America. The company became the largest Spanish exporter during the 1960s and 1970s.

Hit by the economic crisis, the company had to slow down its international activities during the second part of the 1970s. Later on, during the 1980s, the new Spanish economic boom pushed Dragados y Construcciones to focus mainly on the domestic market at least up to the end of the decade.

It was only with the increase of concurrence in the domestic market, the challenges of integration into Europe and the slowdown of domestic demand that Dragados and several other companies in this sector started to renew and increase their activities abroad, together with their diversification strategies, in particular in the early 1990s. Dragados y Construcciones's volume of business abroad then started to grow continuously at least up to the beginning of the 2000s, mainly lead by a significant growth in its Latin American activities.

Sources: Foncillas Casaus (2002); Torres Villaneuva (2009, 2011); ACS Annual Report (various years); Dragados y Construcciones Annual Report (various years); and www.grupoacs.com.

The number of the Spanish companies that were only partially oriented toward the domestic market slightly declined during the last decade of the twentieth century, while one company that was completely internationally oriented emerged, namely, EADS (EADS Annual Report 2002). At the same time, the strategy of partial international orientation underwent a boom, going from 4% to 24% of the number of companies in the population and from 4% to 43% of their combined turnover. The largest companies in the country were attracted to a strategy of geographic diversification for the first time, and real Spanish multinational companies emerged in the final part of the twentieth century (Guillén 2005; Guillén and García-Canal 2010).

In comparing Spain to Italy, it is possible to claim that in both cases, a gradual shift from strategies exclusively oriented toward the domestic markets to those more oriented toward an increasing level of foreign trade and direct investment took place during the second half of the twentieth century. However, the timing with which the largest companies internationalized was markedly different, with Italy being far ahead of Spain during the golden age. It should moreover be stressed that in both these nations, at the beginning of the new millennium, there remained a vast number of companies that were still completely oriented toward the domestic market only and that they were very well represented among the largest corporations in these Southern European countries. Dangers and opportunities shaped the attitude of big businesses toward internationalization and increased their interest over time, but still in 2002, almost half of the largest corporations in both countries remained active exclusively within their national borders.

8.4 SUMMARY

Although during the last few decades lots of research has been produced across the world on US multinationals, the internationalization strategies of large populations of companies in the European economies have until recently been largely neglected, even more so in countries that were not considered to be home to important multinational corporations such as the Southern European firms.

This chapter has been devoted to an investigation into the long-term internationalization trends of the largest corporations in Italy and Spain. Even though the lack of similar investigations in other countries makes it impossible to draw significant conclusions from a comparative perspective with other European countries as was done in the chapter about the strategy of product diversification, some trends and peculiarities can be detected also in terms of the internationalization strategy in these Southern European nations.

At a general level, and not particularly surprisingly, the level of internationalization of the large corporations in Italy and Spain increased during the second half of the twentieth century, both in terms of exports and of foreign direct investments. Some important multinational corporations emerged or became stronger during this period in both nations. At the same time, however, the timing and the extent of the process of internationalization was in part different between the two nations.

Even though Italy's large corporations were very often focused only on the domestic market, some important exporters as well as a few multinationals were notably present in the big business panorama in the mid-twentieth century, whereas the Spanish companies were basically completely oriented toward their domestic markets. This was due to the particular political climate in the country.

During the second half of the century, the attitude of the largest Italian corporations toward internationalization changed, but not dramatically. The orientation toward the domestic market remained important, and most corporations preferred to venture abroad while still maintaining the core of their activities at home. Most of them were thus only partially oriented toward the domestic market, and the percentage of companies that obtained more than 50% of their turnover from their foreign activities exceeded 10% of the population only in the last benchmark year.

The pattern of internationalization in the Spanish economy has been even slower to emerge, in particular during the years of the dictatorship. Even though it is possible to detect an increase in the adoption of internationalized strategies as early as the 1970s, it is only during the 1980s, and in particular during the 1990s, that truly multinational Spanish companies emerged, in particular in some sectors such as energy, telecommunications, construction, and banking. Latin America played an important role in the first years of these companies' expansion, but the importance of Europe is clearly detectable in the most recent years.

Nevertheless, despite a strengthening process of Europeanization and the increased pressures of globalization, even if strategies of internationalization were increasingly adopted by these large Southern European corporations, even at the beginning of the new millennium, in both Italy and Spain, almost the majority of the largest corporations remained oriented toward the domestic market only.

9 The Organizational Form
H-Form versus M-Form

9.1 THE RELEVANCE OF ORGANIZATIONAL CHOICES

In the earliest years of their expansion, the first large corporations in the United States used a functional kind of organizational form, meaning a structure in which tasks are immediately below the chief executive manager and are organized along the line of operating functions in terms of finance, production, marketing and so on. Nevertheless, this organizational form started to be inadequate when companies became increasingly diversified as they exploited economies of scale and scope. The functional structure demonstrated to be insufficient for simultaneously managing a significant variety of products and effectively dividing long term planning strategies from day-to-day management (Chandler 1962).

To meet such needs, during the 1920s, the first examples of a multidivisional structure started to appear. This kind of organizational form consisted of a number of divisions, each of which focused on one single product or one single geographical area and each of which held all the corporate functions but were coordinated by the company's headquarters. The company's headquarters, in turn, employed a variety of staff, as well as was completely devoted to managing the coordination and the strategy development for the whole process. From this point onward, the multidivisional form started to spread and came to dominate the big business panorama of the large corporations in the United States and, from the second half of the twentieth century, in the most advanced European nations (Scott 1970; Channon 1973; Rumelt 1974; Dyas and Thanheiser 1976). The M-form was posited to be able to provide superior performance to those companies that adopted it (e.g., Williamson 1971). In addition, pressures to conform exercised, among others, by management consultants also explain its diffusion, as a part of the extensive existing literature on this topic stresses (Kipping 1999; Kipping and Westerhuis 2012).

However, the predominance of the M-form was disputed starting from the 1970s, and studies were done on its dynamics and performance (e.g., Franko 1974; Armour and Teece 1978; Donaldson 1982; Di Maggio and Powell 1983; Fligstein 1985; Hill 1985; Hoskisson 1987; Freeland 1996;

Hill 1988; Hoskisson, Hill and Kim 1993). Some scholars began to claim that this organizational form was unable to develop the basic competences due to the separation between divisions, and argued that the rigid fragmentation within divisions was unsuitable for the large corporations of the time, when technologies and markets changed too quickly to allow the top management to opt out of every operational activity without running excessive risks (Whittington, Mayer and Curto 1999).

Nevertheless, the outcomes of empirical investigations conducted in the United States and in the largest European nations demonstrate that at the end of the twentieth century, the multidivisional form was still, in spite of its weaknesses, the most commonly adopted organizational form due to its capability to adapt to single national contexts and to new technologies (Whittington and Mayer 2000). Analyses of this topic showed that the M-form assumed quite different features in each national context, and demonstrated that it was able to follow the changes brought about by new technological developments and to adapt to this new situation by evolving into networks of companies characterized by a stronger flexibility compared to the "classical" M-form, the "N-forms" (Bartlett and Ghoshal 1993; Hedlund 1994; Langlois 1995, 2007; Di Maggio 2001). Some of the French or German multidivisionals, which are more similar to groups than to integrated corporations, and the so-called network multidivisionals, which rose to prominence during the second half of the twentieth century, could appear different to the organizational form as studied by Alfred Chandler. But if we carefully observe the way in which these companies coordinate their activities, it is clear that they are largely managed on the basis of the same fundamental principle that characterizes the US multidivisional: the decentralization of the management of different business areas accompanied by the centralization of control and general strategy in the headquarters (Whittington and Mayer 2000).

Even though the multidivisional form was already diffused among the large corporations in the United States immediately after World War II, the "discovery" of this organizational structure in Europe was a relatively late phenomenon. The M-form was basically unknown in France and Germany in 1950, and only 6 out of the 100 largest companies in the United Kingdom were M-forms (Whittington and Mayer 2000). After World War II, US consultancies, managers, and multinationals brought this structure to Europe with them (Djelic 1998; Kipping and Bjarnar 1998), causing it to spread in the Old Continent from the 1950s onward as well. At the end of the period considered by Whittington and Mayer, in 1993, the multidivisional was the most commonly adopted organizational structure in the three most advanced European nations, representing 76%, 70%, and 90% of the populations respectively in France, Germany and the United Kingdom (Whittington and Mayer 2000).

However, the M-form is an organizational structure that is generally adopted by companies when they are diversified and/or internationalized.

This prerequisite, as has been shown in previous chapters, was far from being obvious for the largest corporations in Italy and Spain during the second half of the twentieth century. Moreover, as was ascertained while composing the populations in these countries, big businesses in Italy and Spain very often decided to operate by creating business groups rather than integrated companies. Based on this assumption, this chapter deals with the dynamics of the organizational forms of the largest companies in Italy and Spain and compares them to what happened in the rest of the Western advanced world.

9.2 ORGANIZATION AND ATTEMPTS AT TRANSFORMATION IN ITALY

The organizational form adopted by Italian companies in 1950 was not very different from that adopted in other European nations (Figure 9.1). Most of the largest corporations had also in fact decided to adopt a functional organizational form, or an even simpler structure. This observation is consistent with what the Italian economic historians Giovanni Federico and Pier Angelo Toninelli had found for the previous period; they claimed that in the vast majority of cases the organizational form of Italian companies was very minimalist and almost always mono-functional and that companies were generally managed by a single entrepreneur, who was sometimes helped by a small group of managers that often belonged to the same family (Federico and Toninelli 2003, 327). In 1950, 60% of the largest companies in Italy were functional

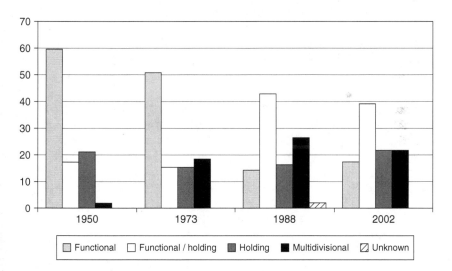

Figure 9.1 Organizational structure in Italy
Source: Appendix Tables 1b, 2b, 3b, 4b.

or mono-functional versus the 56% and 45%, respectively, among French and German companies. Most of the firms in the population simply separated their activity into very simple functions. In other words, they basically separated the "administration" office from the "technical" office. Despite the fact that functional companies were numerous, they were relatively small in size in 1950 and represented only 15% of the population's total assets.

The functional/holding structure was adopted by about one fifth of the companies in the population, very similar to what was seen in France (Whittington and Mayer 2000), and most of the enterprises that belonged to this category in 1950 were firms that pursued focused strategies, single or dominant business, or corporations that had already started to diversify, such as the family-owned cement company Italcementi (Zamagni 2006a; Italcementi Annual Report 1950).

The degree to which the largest corporations in Italy had adopted the H-form in the middle of the twentieth century was similar to that in other countries when we consider their number among the total 100 top corporations. Of the largest Italian companies, 21% had in fact adopted the holding structure versus the 24% and 14%, respectively, in France and Britain. However, the importance of this kind of organizational form was much greater if we look at the relative size of their assets: 49% of the total assets of the population in Italy came from H-forms. They were generally the largest companies in the country, and in 1950 eight out the ten largest decision units in Italy were holdings where a single economic subject controlled, formally or informally, a plurality of subjects. Key industries in this period, such as electricity and chemicals, usually adopted this kind of organizational form (Edison Annual Report 1950; SNIA Annual Report 1950; Amatori and Bezza 1990; Sapelli 1994b; Fortis, Pavese and Quadro Curzio 2003; Federico and Toninelli 2003, 330).

In some cases, the holding form was a direct consequence of the company's process of diversification. However, Italian companies very often also created groups for other reasons. The pyramidal group was, and in some cases still is, a very useful tool for allowing the owners to accrue financial capital without losing control of their companies (e.g., Barca et al. 1997, 160). According to the Italian scholars Fabrizio Barca, Francesca Bertucci, Graziella Capello and Paola Casavola, the adoption of the H-form was in this sense fundamental within the Italian context, in which industrial maturity had not yet been reached. The H-form was crucial because, together with other tools, it allowed companies achieve the necessary degree of separation between the party providing capital and the party that managed the money, which is fundamental for a complete process of industrialization (Barca et al. 1997, 157).

The multidivisional form, finally, was almost completely unknown in Europe immediately after World War II, and in this Italy did not represent an exception. The M-form began to spread in Italy only from the 1960s onward, in a restricted group of companies (Martinoli 1961; Pavan 1976).

However, considering the M-form in a broader sense, in this period, IRI could be considered as a multidivisional, because it had developed some features that, even though with many peculiarities, are quit typical of the M-form. The holding was at the center of a number of financial sectoral subholdings and behaved like a strong headquarters that coordinated the long-term general structure. At the same time, however, it was reluctant to define the strategies of the financial sectoral subholdings and even more so of the single companies, which enjoyed a very clear autonomy. This is what typically happened to the divisions of a multidivisional, and the state steel sector is a very clear example of this attitude (Osti and Ranieri 1993, 115).

The M-form spread throughout Europe after World War II, and in Italy its level of adoption increased but remained relatively low during the golden age. Compared to the 1950 picture, matters in 1973 differed only slightly in terms of the organizational choices made by the largest corporations. The functional form was reducing in importance but it was still the most commonly adopted organizational structure by number, representing 51% of the whole population, versus the 18%, 27% and 8%, respectively, among French, German and British firms (Whittington and Mayer 2000). Although the proportion of the functional/holding and holding companies did not significantly change during this period, a major transformation is found in the increasing number of multidivisionals, which grew from 2% to 18% of the number of the largest corporations. The importance of the H-form declined both in terms of number and turnover. Nevertheless, it remained very common in Italy.

Groups took on many different shapes, and there are many reasons for the continued success of the holding companies (Colli and Vasta 2010). In some cases, the H-form was used to coordinate a corporate growth that occurred very quickly and in a disorderly way through mergers and acquisitions in related or unrelated sectors. But in other cases the holding, as well as the functional/holding, came about for different reasons. During the 1960s and 1970s, a good reason to create a holding was provided, for instance, by domestic economic policies as well as by the need to exploit technical knowledge from abroad. The example of the chemical company SIR (Box 9.1) is typical in this respect.

Box 9.1 Economic Policies and Company Organization: SIR and its Group

The chemical company Società Italiana Resine (SIR) was founded in Milan in 1922 and, during the 1930s, achieved significant growth in the production of phenolic resins. Acquired by the businessman Nino Rovelli in 1948, the company grew substantially during the economic miracle, and in the 1970s it was the third-largest firm in Italy in the chemical sector.

Its growth followed a quite peculiar path. Nino Rovelli expanded the company through the creation of a vast group of firms that were not integrated into the parent company but enjoyed legal autonomy. The construction of a group of formally independent companies was consistent with the aim of maintaining and maximizing the public fiscal and financial privileges resulting from investments in relatively underdeveloped areas in Italy, such as Sardinia and Calabria. Almost every industrial plant that SIR opened in Sardinia had the juridical status of autonomous corporation. Even the US scholar Robert J. Pavan, studying the Italian chemical company RUMIANCA, one of the companies that was affiliated to SIR, had to argue that "the adoption of the multidivisional form can become impossible if the advantages coming from an improved corporate management are put into danger by the fiscal policy of the state" (Pavan 1976, 173). Moreover, in this situation, the holding structure allowed the firm to cooperate more easily and in a more coordinated way with foreign multinationals. Throughout its history, for example, RUMIANCA was involved in a vast number of joint ventures with other Italian as well as foreign partners. With this system, its Italian partners gained access to the foreign knowledge and know-how they needed to enter new advanced sectors, while foreign partners could take advantage of the local partners' knowledge of Italy's financial and fiscal system.

At the end of the 1970s, the company, after growing too rapidly by using this system and having to compete with the state and the privately owned large national firms in this industry, was already in severe crisis. In 1981, it went bankrupt and was bought by the state-owned energy holding ENI.

Sources: Baldi (1976, 191–201); Pavan (1976); Amatori and Colli (1999); Giannetti and Vasta (2003); Zamagni (2006b); and RUMIANCA Annual Report (various years).

In other cases, the adoption of the H-form was the result of the end of a multidivisional experience, which is what happened after the merger between two national champions in chemicals and electricity: Montecatini and Edison (Box 9.2).

Box 9.2 Montedison—From the M-Form Back to the H-Form

Despite a quite troubled history under the Fascist regime and during the recovery years, the Italian chemical company Montecatini during the 1960s was a firm organized in a relatively modern way, with divisions that held clear autonomy in decision making and were given central direction. A few years after the nationalization of the electricity sector, in 1966, the company merged with the largest former private electricity company in Italy, Edison. Edison had started a process of significant diversification into the chemical industry in the postwar years, precisely to be able to manage an eventual nationalization of its core activity.

The merger could have created a giant, a real national champion in the Italian chemical industry. But something went wrong. On one hand, there was a problem of strategy. Both Montecatini and Edison were quite diversified firms. In order to receive tariff and concurrence protection from the state, during the 1930s, Montecatini had rescued companies in several sectors such as lead and marble. After World War II, Montecatini quickly rebuilt its plants, but increased competition and the diversification into obsolete product areas were real impediments to its development in an industry whose modern technology was related to petrochemicals. Edison, at the same time, decided to enter the chemical industry with the expectation that the electricity sector would be nationalized. The company that emerged from the merger, Montedison, received a lot of money through government indemnifications. However, no meaningful rationalization of the activities of the new company occurred, there were many overlaps, and Montedison's focus was simply the sum of the many activities of the two original companies. A very diversified and messy conglomerate had been born. In 1971, Montedison controlled about 400 companies; in addition to the firms belonging to its "core sector," it also owned large stakes in very different areas such as editing, road construction and hotel management.

On the other hand, the multidivisional structure of Montecatini was not adopted by the new company. Prior to the merger Edison had a very centralized organizational form, where all the important issues were decided by the president and his closest collaborators. Following the merger, Edison decided to create an analogous division for every division of Montecatini. A central director in Edison was appointed for each central director in Montecatini. The result was the creation of a group that was bicephalous and one in which power fights were the daily bread.

Sources: Scalfari and Turani (1974); Amatori and Bezza (1990); Lepore Dubois and Sonzogno (1990); Sapelli (1994b); Perugini (2009); and Montedison Annual Report (various years).

The adoption of the M-form did finally become more common also in Italy during this period, but it spread to a lesser extent than in the rest of Europe. Around 1970, multidivisionals accounted for 42%, 40% and 74% of the largest corporations, respectively, in France, Germany and Great Britain. In Italy, they accounted for just 18% in 1973. The major multidivisionals in the early 1970s were the two state-owned holdings, IRI and ENI. As was the case with the H-forms, most of the M-forms were also concentrated at the very top of the ranking. Relatively small companies, such as the family-owned publishing firm Mondadori, were nevertheless present in this category.

The last quarter of the twentieth century saw the organizational forms adopted by big business in Italy become more similar to those in the most advanced European nations than in the past.

As had occurred in France, Germany and the United Kingdom during the 1950s and 1960s, the Italian functional companies significantly decreased in number after the 1973 benchmark, even though both their number and turnover slightly increased again between 1988 and 2002. At the same time, multidivisionals increased within the population between 1973 and 1988, and then experienced a slight decline from the late 1980s up to the turn of the century. The path toward the adoption of the M-form was in many cases long and difficult, as the example of Barilla shows (Box 9.3), but succeeded more easily and quickly in others.

Box 9.3 Family Round-Trip: Changing Ownership and the Transformation
of Barilla's Organizational Form

The spread of the M-form among Italian companies, in particular the family-owned ones, was in some cases the outcome of a long and painful process of restructuring and change in the role of the family.

For instance, during the 1950s, the family-owned pasta manufacturer Barilla, founded in Parma in 1875, began to study a more formal organizational structure that would allow it to better manage its business following a process of increased diversification and internationalization. Following the advice of a French consultant, the company decided to adopt a functional form in 1961. The organization remained unaltered until 1968, at which point the marketing activities in Italy were separated from the marketing activities abroad, and a new section for the planning of production was established.

However, the watershed in the transformation of Barilla's organization took place from the beginning of the 1970s onward, when the company was bought by the US conglomerate Grace and Co. The Americans substantially changed the strategy of the company. The level of diversification increased dramatically through a series of acquisitions and ensured entry into the baked products sector through the creation of the brand Mulino Bianco. A new structure was also needed, and Barilla decided to adopt a multidivisional form, albeit in a peculiar way as its divisions were groups of companies.

When the Barilla family bought the firm back in 1979, they decided not to revert to the old strategies and structures, and kept the company largely as the Americans had shaped it. In 1988, Barilla's activities were based on three divisions, each of which controlled a group of companies that belonged to the holding Barilla: Barilla Alimentare (pasta), Barilla Dolciaria (cookies and bakery products) and Barilla Alimentare Dolciaria (distribution and marketing).

Sources: Ori (1973); Pavan (1976); Mediobanca (1989); Gonizzi (2003); and Barilla Annual Report (various years).

However, at least two important peculiarities continued to characterize the trends governing the organizational structure of Italian companies. The first is the minor role played by the M-form. Despite its relative increase in popularity, the frequency with which this kind of structure was adopted remained far below that in the advanced European nations. Multidivisionals in Italy represented 27% and 22% of the population in 1988 and 2002, respectively, versus the 76%, 70% and 90%, respectively, of the largest firms in France, Germany and the United Kingdom in 1993 (Whittington and Mayer 2000). Secondly, in Italy, the "intermediate" structures, such as the functional/holding and the holding, remained more common than in the other countries. Both in 1988 and in 2002, the majority of big businesses belonged to the "functional/holding" category, and the holding structure in 2002 generated a greater turnover for the whole population than did the multidivisional structure. The relevance of the H-form thus remained high and relatively constant throughout the whole period under consideration.

As in 1973, also in 2002, most of the holdings were at the top of the rankings. They were both "old" national champions and "new entries" that had been able to exploit the new opportunities provided by an effervescent context to enter different sectors and buy several companies during the 1980s. According to the Italian economist Fulvio Coltorti, the crisis of the 1970s brought about a partial dismantling of the previous holdings as well as a process of reorganization of the largest companies in the country (Coltorti 1990, 91–92). However, this process of restructuring did not cause the disappearance of the groups in general and of the pyramidal groups in particular, which continued to strengthen and represent a fundamental tool for the largest companies to raise capital in particular during periods of stock exchange boom without losing control of the company. Old companies such as FIAT, Pirelli and Falck, as well as new ones such as Benetton and Finivest (Box 9.4), displayed this kind of behavior during the 1980s and 1990s (Barca 1997, 161, 179; Mucchetti 2003, 147).

Box 9.4 Diversification, Family, Organization. The Persistent Role Played by the Holding Form in Italy in the Case of Berlusconi's Empire

The organizational form adopted by Fininvest, the financial holding owned by Silvio Berlusconi and his family, aptly reflects the tendency of the main business families of the country to manage enormous business groups through the adoption of holdings that permit them to raise capital from the stock exchange, but at the same time to continue to exert complete control over the whole system.

Fininvest was founded in Milan in 1978 by Silvio Berlusconi in order to bring together all his business interests, which extended from the building industry to the publishing, media and entertainment sectors. Both very successful and dogged by polemics and judicial troubles, in particular since its founder became prime minister in 1994, the holding has been an important protagonist of the Italian economic and political system.

The level of diversification of Fininvest is currently high, and the holding directly owns significant percentages of the share capital of the largest companies of the group: 39% of Mediaset (media), 50% of Mondadori (publishing), 36% of Mediolanum (banking and insurance), 100% of AC Milan (football team) and 100% of Teatro Manzoni (theater) directly belonged to Fininvest at the end of 2010. The holding also controlled foreign subsidiaries in Spain.

Even though the main companies of the group are listed on the Milan stock exchange and have more than 230,000 shareholders, the control of the activities of the holding, and indirectly of its listed companies, is clearly in the hands of its founder and his family. At the end of October 2011, a few days before Silvio Berlusconi resigned as Italian prime minister, he owned 63% of Fininvest through three holdings that are registered in his name (Holding Italiana Prima, Holding Italiana Seconda and Holding Italiana Ottava). The remaining part of the share capital was equally divided among his five children, Marina and Pier Silvio (from Berlusconi's first marriage) and Barbara, Eleonora and Luigi (from his second marriage) through the ownership of other financial companies all named Holding Italiana followed by a number. The two eldest children, who are currently both older than forty, already have key positions in Fininvest and in its listed companies. Marina is the president of Fininvest and of Mondadori, while Pier Silvio is deputy chairman and member of the executive committee of Mediaset.

Sources: Molteni (1998); Fiori (2006); and www.fininvest.it.

9.3 BIG BUSINESS IN SPAIN: THE DYNAMICS OF ORGANIZATIONAL CHANGE

As in Italy, the structures adopted by the largest corporations in Spain in the mid-twentieth century were broadly similar to the predominant organizational forms seen in countries such as the United Kingdom, Germany and France (Figure 9.2). The functional (or mono-functional) companies accounted for almost half of the 100 largest Spanish firms in 1950, while they accounted for 56%, 45% and 60%, respectively, in France, Germany and Italy. Just as in Italy, most of the companies belonging to this category were relatively small and were situated toward the lower end of the ranking. The functional/holding companies were less important in the ranking, representing 17% and 5%, respectively, of the number and the assets of the population. There were for instance several electricity companies, or firms such as the Compañía General de Tabacos de Filipinas, a company that formed part of a larger group controlled by the Marquises of Comillas and

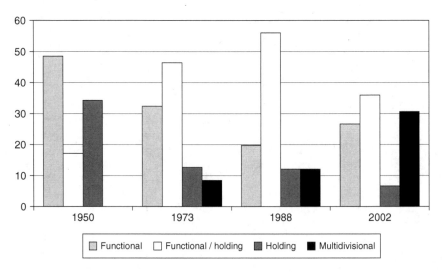

Figure 9.2 Organizational structure in Spain
Source: Appendix Tables 5b, 6b, 7b, 8b.

was involved in the production and retail of tobacco. In 1950, the company was overseen by one director and three vice-directors, under whom a commercial subdirector, an account director and an account responsible operated. Related to its core activity, the company controlled smaller firms both in the Philippines and in Spain.

Whereas the multidivisional form was completely unknown in the country in the middle of the century, the organizational structure that largely dominated in terms of the assets of the population was the holding structure. One-third of the largest companies in Spain were H-forms, compared to 24%, 14% and 21%, respectively, in France, Germany and Italy. In addition, also as in Italy, the very largest companies in the country were holdings. Seven out of ten of the largest companies had adopted this form, whereas the smallest companies rarely did. The holding was also the organizational tool through which the large corporate owners, banks, families and the state controlled their business in a context of even slower industrial development than in Italy. Bringing their activities together in a group of companies not only made it possible for entrepreneurs to gather funds amid a context of capital shortage without risking the loss of their control over the company, but also allowed them to bring together resources from different places into one single "decision-making unit" (Guillén 2001). The existence of business groups in Spain could moreover be considered as an entrepreneurial response to a series of market imperfections, as the case of Naviera Aznar shows (Box 9.5).

Box 9.5 Business Groups and Market Imperfections: The Case of Naviera Aznar

An example of how business groups can solve markets imperfections in a specific context is provided by the shipping company Naviera Aznar. Spanish economy during Franco's dictatorship was characterized by imperfect markets in terms of products, capital and information; by an intense state intervention and regulation of the economy in a very discretionary political context; by the existence of barriers to entry as well as barrier to competition in most of the economics sectors; and finally by a strong protectionism. Within this context, the Aznar group was able not only to enlarge its business in its core activity, but also to repeatedly enter several other sectors. In particular during the 1940s, Naviera Aznar created a group of companies in related and unrelated areas and that were independent from a juridical point of view.

Cross-shareholding, the existence of financial companies within the group and a complicated system of overlapping directorates, together with the sharing of interests with the big business group of the banks Urquijo and Hispano Americano, made it possible for the Aznar family to control many companies and determine their strategy without owning more than 50% of their share capital. Even though an evident and unitary organizational rationality was missing, elements of centralization and coordination were present. For instance, the daily expenditure of the central office was divided among various firms, very often, skilled workers passed from one company to another within the group, and there was a vertical integration among the enterprises within the group.

According to the scholar who studied the history of this company, Jesús María Valdaliso Gago, in Francoist latecomer Spain, this kind of organizational form was indispensable in allowing companies to achieve synergies as well as economies of scale and scope and made it possible for them to establish a good level of vertical integration without the rigidity of a formal integration. In addition to this, cross-shareholdings made it possible for them to find financial resources in a situation where money was otherwise lacking. The involvement of the Urquijo-Hispano Americano bank group also helped the company in this area, as did state assistance.

Sources: Valdaliso Gago (2002, 2004, 2006).

Despite the fact that INI had largely used IRI as a model, the major Spanish state-owned firm was a holding rather than a multidivisional like IRI (Martín Aceña and Comín Comín 1991, 37; INI Annual Report 1950, 11–12).

As mentioned earlier, the multidivisional structure was not an option pursued by the large Spanish companies in the middle of the century. However, in this respect, it is worth remembering that the M-form, at least at the beginning, did not spread in Europe as a "spontaneous transformation." It was mainly "exported" to the Old Continent by the US consultancies, primarily McKinsey, which started to "sell" this organizational form in the postwar period. In Spain, McKinsey did not open any subsidiaries during the Francoist period (Kipping and Puig 2003b). Moreover, the need to adopt a multidivisional organization generally arises when a company starts to diversify its production or geographical market, and as has been shown, most of the large corporations in Spain had not yet achieved a high level of product diversification or internationalization at this stage.

The economic miracle that took place in Spain during the 1960s partly transformed the organizational choices of the large companies in the country, even though big business organization in 1973 was still quite different to that in other advanced nations. The functional structure, even though declining in popularity in comparison to the previous period, continued to play a stronger role in the Spanish population than in the French, German and British populations. This structure was usually adopted across many sectors by relatively "small" big companies that were growing but still had not adopted very sophisticated organizational forms. Roca Radiadores, a company making sanitary wares, provides an example of a functional firm managed by a trusted manager who did not belong to the family that owned it and that was based on the production, marketing and administration functions (Roca Radiadores Annual Report 1973). Another example is Ulgor, a cooperative firm that operated in the appliances sector (Ulgor Annual Report 1973).

The functional/holding structure was the most commonly adopted by the largest corporations in 1973 by both number and turnover. The importance of this structure in Spain was higher than in other European nations, where it accounted for less than 24% in all cases (Whittington and Mayer 2000). It is important to stress that during this period many companies adopted a hybrid structure, adding one division that was partially separated from the original core activity to a basic functional/holding structure. This was for instance the case for General Eléctrica, which had an electro-medicine division (General Eléctrica Annual Report 1973). The spread of the functional/holding structure took place mainly to the detriment of the holding form, which declined between 1950 and 1973. At the same time, the H-form was adopted by half of the ten largest companies in Spain, and almost all of the holdings were located at the very top of the ranking.

In 1973, Spain still represented the bottom of the barrel in terms of the adoption of the multidivisional structure, although it had started to spread. Only 8% of the largest companies had adopted this kind of organizational form while 42%, 40%, 74% and 18% had done so in France, Germany, Great Britain and Italy, respectively. However, the multidivisional was not as minor in importance when looking at the turnover it provided to the whole sample, as it was second only to that generated by the functional/holding structure. Most of the multidivisionals in Spain were subsidiaries of foreign multinationals such as, for instance, Siemens (Siemens Annual Report 1973/4, 6). Only two Spanish-owned companies decided to adopt a multidivisional structure in that year: the state-owned holding INI and the family company Meliá (Box 9.6), which operated in the hotel sector and implemented product divisions in order to manage its strategy of related diversification (Meliá Annual Report 1973).

Box 9.6 Growth, Strategy and Structure: Hoteles Meliá during the Spanish Economic Miracle

Out of the few examples of multidivisionals in Spain during the 1970s, Meliá is perhaps the most interesting one. Taking advantage of the increasing flow of foreign tourists to Spain and of the favorable economic conjuncture of the 1960s, the family-run company Meliá became a diversified and multidivisional company within a relatively short time. Founded in 1956 by José María Meliá Sinisterra and completely managed by the Meliá family, within slightly more than a decade, Meliá became one of the largest companies in the country. This was thanks to a strategy based on related diversification that led it to extend its core activity in the hotel business to related areas such as travel, hotel management, real estate and related services. In addition to this product related diversification, the company also pursued a strategy of geographic diversification. In 1973, the group was made up of Hotel Meliá, which had 17 hotels with 3,500 employees in Spain and 16 hotels abroad; Lavanderías Meliá, which had 2 working establishments and 7 that were under construction; and Viajes Meliá, which operated 124 travel agencies in Spain and 62 travel agencies abroad, and 10 real estate offices.

Structure followed strategy, and Meliá became a M-form. But it was a quite particular M-form, because all the directors of the divisions were members of the family. The 1973 organizational chart of the group is quite explicit: José Meliá Sinisterra was the president, José Meliá Goicoechea was the director of Viajes Meliá, the managing director of Club Meliá and the managing director of J. Meliá, Francisco Meliá was the director of Hoteles Meliá, and of Inmobiliarias Meliá, Rafael Meliá was the general director of Lavanderías Meliá and Luis Enrique Meliá was the director of Electrotécnica Meliá y Friacon.

Sources: Fomento de la Producción (1974); Durán Herrera (1997); and Meliá Annual Report (various years).

It is also important to stress that INI's version of the multidivisional form was quite peculiar. According to the Spanish economist Miguel Boyer (1975, 96), who observed the state-owned holding during that era,

> in contrast to the Italian IRI, which only has a small central staff and is organized in financial companies or sub-holdings, each one of which is in charge of managing an homogeneous sector, INI has a centralized administrative structure, divided into six industries (electricity, oil, mining and metallurgy, mechanical transformation, services and aeronautics, food, chemicals and various) and which employs about a thousand people.

As has been pointed out for the previous benchmark, the limited spread of the multidivisional form during the Francoist era had been brought about both by the low level of diversification reached by most of the largest companies and by the lack of US consultancies in the country. Moreover, the presence of large banking groups could also have hindered the diffusion of the M-form. Cable and Dirrheimer (1983) claimed, for instance, that in Germany, the banks–companies network carried out most of the functions that are generally done by multidivisional companies, since they controlled the performance of the companies and allocated the capital for independent activities.

Things did not significantly change between the second half of the 1970s and the end of the 1980s. The economic crisis that started in 1973 and, later on, the political transition toward democracy and the integration into the European Economic Community made things more difficult and more uncertain for companies. During this period, even though the functional structure continued its decline, the equilibrium of the previous era was not shaken. Functional/holding companies remained largely predominant by both number and turnover in Spain in 1988. The H-form continued to be quite common in terms of the number of firms represented in the population and increased even more in terms of turnover. Meanwhile, the multidivisional companies were very slightly increasing in number, reaching 12% of the population, but their contribution to the total turnover dropped from 26% to 10% in 1988.

Despite the continued importance of the H-form, it has to be stressed that the end of the Francoist period completely changed the rules of the game in terms of protection as well as of policies on foreign trade and investment, and some of the business groups that had grown during the previous period by taking advantage of the asymmetric conditions disappeared or had to change their organizational behavior at the end of the dictatorship, as was the case for the largest companies in the chemical sector (Box 9.7).

Box 9.7 Contacts, Growth and Organizational Structure: The H-Form in the Spanish Chemical Sector

The chemical company Explosivos Río Tinto (ERT) represents one of the most typical examples of a business group that continued to grow in the Francoist era and later on had to restructure within the chemical industry. ERT, established in 1970 as the result of a merger between the chemical company Unión Española de Explosivos and the mining firm Compañía Española de Minas Río Tinto, was a group that in turn orbited around the Banco Urquijo–Hispano Americano group. The merger, which at the beginning aimed to create a company involved in the production of fertilizers, chemical products and explosives as well as in mining in the hope of achieving significant scale and scope economies, represented the first step of a process of extensive diversification in related and unrelated sectors. In a few years, through a series of mergers, acquisitions and joint ventures, ERT became one of the most diversified Spanish companies, operating in fertilizers, explosives, mining, chemical products, plastic products, pharmaceutical products, food, transport, copper, petroleum and real estate. Its annual report in 1973 clearly explains its expansion pattern during that year, mentioning a series of acquisitions, agreements and joint ventures with national private companies and banking groups (such as Banco de Bilbao), as well as with foreign multinationals (such as Gulf, Shell, Hoechst, British Titan Limited and Produits Alimentaires Blanchaud) and state-owned companies (such as Astilleros Españoles). This vast group of controlled and participated companies and of joint ventures was never well integrated into the central company, which behaved as a holding managed by a restricted group of general directors and plant subdirectors without a coherent general organizational plan or project. The main capability that was developed within this group in this period was that of making "agreements" with the state, the banks and the foreign multinationals, which became obsolete a few years later when foreign companies were free to enter Spain and state authorizations were no longer required. The oil crisis made the situation of the already indebted group disastrous, and the company became unable to control such a huge and diversified business group in the following decade, when the political and economic situation changed further.

Sources: Tamames (1992); Bueno Campos (1993); Puig Raposo (2003, 2004); Cros Annual Report (various years); and Explosivos Río Tinto Annual Report (various years).

The largest change in the organizational structure of the big corporations in Spain took place during the 1990s and is reflected in the 2002 population. There remained, however, a substantial degree of continuity with the past (Galán, Sánchez and Zúñiga-Vicente 2005). The Spanish panorama at the beginning of the new millennium was thus more similar to that seen in Italy than to the most advanced European nations, even though the final push toward divisionalization had been more substantial in Spain than in Italy.

The functional structure, which may be the major anomaly of the Spanish population, remained very strongly present in 2002, when it accounted for 27% of the largest corporations. In France, Germany, Great Britain and Italy, functional companies made up, respectively, 2%, 1%, 2% and 19% of the whole population. As in the previous period, the companies belonging to this category were quite small and located toward the lower end of the ranking.

The functional/holding structure, even though it had been declining in popularity since 1988, remained the predominant organizational form by both number and turnover. Of the largest corporations, 36% had adopted this form in Spain compared to the 42%, 9%, 14% and 0%, respectively, in Italy, France, Germany and Britain. These companies varied in size and importance. Big companies that had not significantly changed in the last few decades as well as new firms belonged to this category.

The restructuring process that had taken place in most corporations during the first period of democracy and following integration into the EEC seems to have caused a decline of the H-form. The role of holdings in 2002 was significantly reduced, and Spain became more similar to the other major European nations in this respect. Most of the holdings that operated in the country during this period were subsidiaries of multinationals, but a strong family-based company was also able to survive, namely, Grupo March.

The multidivisional did finally also spread in Spain, going from 12% to 31% and from 10% to 53% of the total number and turnover, respectively, of the large corporations in the population between 1988 and 2002. However, the Spanish experience was still very different from that in the other major European nations: 90% of the largest corporations in the United Kingdom, 70% in Germany and 76% in France were multidivisionals in 1993 (Whittington and Mayer 2000). The most interesting aspect to the spread of this organizational form in Spain is that the M-form started to be adopted also by relatively small companies in the middle and at the bottom of the ranking. However, some of the Spanish "national champions," such as Telefónica (Box 9.8), Repsol and ENDESA, also adopted it. This has been substantially confirmed by an investigation based on different samples looking at the organizational structure of Spanish companies between 1993 and 2003, and that claims both diversification and the M-form spread in Spain, but that the differences between Spain and Europe remained substantial (Sánchez-Bueno, Galán Zazo and Suárez González 2006, 30–31).

Box 9.8 Telefónica: A "Chandlerian" Firm in Spain?

One of the clearest examples of a large Spanish corporation that successfully adopted a multidivisional structure during the 1990s is Telefónica. Founded in 1924 with the American ITT as one of its main shareholders, Compañía Nacional Telefónica de España was nationalized in 1945, when the state took over almost 80% of its shares. During the dictatorship, the company could enjoy a monopoly in its sector as the only telephone operator in the country, and it became one of the largest corporations in Spain.

However, from the 1980s onward, the situation, and the competition that the company faced, changed dramatically. On one hand, integration into the EEC imposed a privatization of the company and a liberalization of its sector, allowing the entrance of national and foreign competitors. On the other hand, a new wave of technologies spread in the telecommunication industry, transforming its dynamics and at the same time providing new business opportunities.

Listed on the main stock exchanges of the world since 1985, Telefónica was privatized between the late 1980s and the early 1990s. The new management team, led by Juan Villalonga, decided to broadly internationalize operations (in particular by investing in Latin America) and to diversify the activities of the company by entering related product areas in the telecommunication, communication, information and entertainment industries. Structure then followed strategy, and during the 1990s, Telefónica became a multidivisional firm by creating a Corporative Center with a top management that coordinated the business activities, and seven divisions: Telefónica de España, Telefónica Móviles, Telefónica Internacional, Telefónica Media, Telefónica Intercontinental, Telefónica Data and Telefónica Interactiva.

The new strategies and structures adopted by Telefónica as part of this framework allowed it to manage both the transition from monopoly to concurrence and the revolution in the communication sector: in 2011, the company was the third largest provider in the world and ranked 78th in the *Fortune Global 500* ranking.

Sources: Nueno (1996); Mochón and Rambla (1999); Calvo (2011); and Telefónica Annual Report (various years).

In comparing the structural transformation of the largest companies in Italy and Spain, it is possible to find a similar path, even though different timings and intensities were at play. In both countries, the functional form dropped in popularity but remained quite widely adopted at the beginning of the new millennium. The functional/holding has been increasingly commonly adopted in the two nations, and it was the most common organizational form in Italy at the beginning of the new millennium, whereas the M-form, which grew more slowly but earlier in the Italian case, grew later but more significantly in Spain during the last decade of the twentieth century. The H-form remained a dominant feature of the Italian and Spanish economies and has continued to be of key importance in Italy, whereas its role has been visibly reduced in Spain.

9.4 SUMMARY

Unsurprisingly, as with the product and geographical market diversification strategies, the organizational forms predominantly adopted by the large corporations in Italy and Spain also partially differed from those predominantly adopted in the United States and in the most advanced European nations.

The organizational form that became the most common throughout Europe and that seemed more efficient for managing diversified companies was the multidivisional structure. According to Whittington and Mayer (2000), at the end of the twentieth century almost all the major corporations in France, Germany and the United Kingdom had adopted the M-form. However, also in this area Italy and Spain did not conform to the general trend.

Even though the multidivisional form was basically unknown in these nations in the middle of the century, it was able to spread to a certain extent during the its second half. If the trend toward the adoption of the M-form was earlier in Italy, it was in Spain that this variety of organizational form had become more widely accepted at the beginning of the new millennium. Nevertheless, its spread was quite slow and, compared to other European countries, less pervasive in both cases. Even during the last decades of the century, only a limited number of the largest corporations had adopted this organizational form in Italy as well in Spain. However, as with the adoption of certain strategies, the unpopularity of the multidivisional form was compensated for by the importance of other organizational structures, which allowed the large corporations in Italy and Spain to gain some advantages.

Although the functional forms became less common in both Italy and Spain and in the most advanced European nations, the persisting importance of the functional/holding and holding forms, in all their varieties, in both Italy and Spain should be stressed. Several reasons lie at the origin of the success of the holding forms. The functional/holding or holding companies came about for instance as a result of the particular fiscal legislation adopted by their countries, because of the way that firms found money in a situation in which financial markets were ineffective or because they were employed as tools to manage the messy process of diversification. Moreover, the holding form is directly connected to the business group strategy that, as was shown in Chapter 7, was very common in both nations.

In any case, here, too, it seems that the pressures pushing companies in other countries toward the convergence of their strategies and organizational structures did not radically change the behavior of the largest corporations in these Southern European nations, given that they maintained most of their idiosyncrasies and remained governed by quite peculiar patterns of strategic and organizational behavior throughout the second half of the twentieth century.

Part IV

Summing Up

The investigation into the historical features of Italian and Spanish capitalism and into the dynamics of big business in each country during the second half of the twentieth century has argued that Italy and Spain shared some characteristics with the most advanced economies in Europe and the United States, but also that the role and behavior of large corporations in these "peripheral" countries remained quite peculiar.

Long-term continuities in the business cultures of these nations combined with new opportunities and constraints in pushing companies to adopt one structure or another, and the relative delay with which Italy and Spain developed a sound process of industrialization greatly affected the circumstances in which firms had to decide on their strategies and structures. Several similarities as well as differences between Italy and Spain, and between Italy and Spain and the rest of the world, can be detected in this framework.

The concluding section of this book interprets the characteristics of capitalism in Italy and Spain as well as the trends that governed the dynamics of big business in each country from a wider comparative perspective.

Chapter 10 focuses on Italy and Spain by investigating the similarities and differences between these two countries and stressing the continuities and discontinuities that characterized big business ownership structures, strategies and organizational forms in each one of these nations over time. While the first part of the chapter underlines how much Italy and Spain have differed from each other, the second part claims that their forms of capitalism have several characteristics in common and that in both cases very similar alternative forms of big business spread; these two nations were similar in the way they developed different kinds of big business from the US-inspired models.

Chapter 11 then explains why were developed these kinds of alternative strategies and structures developed in Italy and Spain. The first part of the explanation will consider the importance of factors that were inherent to company life, such as the industry to which a firm belonged, its ownership structures and its managerial culture, in shaping big business forms. An analysis of the external factors that affected companies' strategic behavior and organizational structures, such as economic policies as well as the Europeanization and the globalization of capital and product markets, then follows.

Finally, the last chapter of the book summarizes the main findings of the research and its contribution to the literature and current debates and provides a general interpretation of the role of big business in these nations and of their dynamics in the long run in the light of what has occurred at a global level.

10 Convergences and Divergences

Does a Southern European Form of Capitalism Exist?

During the twentieth century, Italy and Spain were only similar countries at a superficial level. Although they share a common background made up of a glorious past followed by large-scale decline and a significant industrial delay at the end of the nineteenth century, the empirical evidence gathered on their large corporations shows that several differences can be detected between them in terms of the pattern of industrialization and the development of big business. Several factors, which are deep-rooted, contribute to our understanding of the different environments in which companies developed throughout the twentieth century, and thus of their particular features.

Looking at the political dynamics of these countries, some big differences are evident already at a first glance. Italy was a very young nation when its process of industrialization took off. It is said that the Piedmont statesman Marquis Massimo D'Azeglio, one of the protagonists of the Italian unification process, claimed that "Italy has been made. Now it remains to make Italians" (D'Azeglio 1891, 9). The economy was following its own path. Some Northern Italian areas had already developed successful companies in the First Industrial Revolution industries (e.g., Colli 1999) that centered on the Kingdom of Lombardy–Venetia, to which they belonged, as well as on Switzerland and Germany. The centralized state that was born with the unification of the country was weak. Italian bureaucracy allowed political and economic lobbies to remain strong and influential in the long term (Altan 2000). However, the economic policies pursued around the turn of the century were successful, and despite its industrial delay and political weaknesses, Italy had started its journey as an industrial power and continued it during the twenty-three years of dictatorship. But its main Achilles' heel, its weak central bureaucracy and its politicians looking for consensus and dependent on lobbies, remained a constant feature that definitively shaped the industrial policies of Italian governments throughout the twentieth century (Amatori and Colli 1999).

When industrialization started to spread in Spain, it was a completely different country compared to Italy. It was not a collection of states that at one point unified into one, but was a well established nation-state. Although there were important regional cultural and economic differences (García Ruiz and Manera Erbina 2006), by the turn of the twentieth century, Spain had existed for more than three centuries as a unified state with a central bureaucracy. Moreover, the country had been at the center of a huge empire for a long time. The "empire on which the sun never sets" lasted from the sixteenth to the nineteenth century and provided important business opportunities to Spanish businesspeople. But just as Italy was creating its identity, Spain risked losing its own. The decline of the empire, a succession of wars, and alternating political regimes during the first part of the twentieth century caused a more pronounced delay in the advance of the industrialization process. When the country began catching up, basically from the second half of the century, the economic policies pursued by the government remained strongly influenced by its authoritarian political stance and by its exclusion from the process of European integration until the end of the dictatorship.

These long-term dynamics contribute in part to our understanding of the differences that we see when looking at the sectoral dynamics, at the ownership, at the managerial culture and at the product and geographic diversification strategies, as well at the organizational structures of the large corporations in Italy and Spain during the second half of the twentieth century.

The first clear difference that is apparent when looking at the populations of the largest companies in these two countries is their sectoral distribution during this period. Italy's big business structure was largely based on manufacturing. Industrial sectors were predominant in the middle of the century and maintained their front-row roles over the four benchmark years. Sectors changed over time; the textile industry was of course more important in 1950 than during the following decades, whereas the presence of mechanics and rubber remained constant throughout this period, and chemicals even increased during the 1970s and 1980s but later declined during the 1990s. But manufacturing continued to be the main focus of the largest corporations in the country, and services were confined to relatively few companies that were devoted to utilities, such as communications or electricity, or entertaining and advertising during the most recent period.

Looking at the panorama of big business in Spain, the picture that emerges is quite different. Nonmanufacturing prevailed in the mid-twentieth century as well as at the beginning of the twentieth-first century. Even though big manufacturing corporations were more common that nonmanufacturing ones during the 1970s, the equilibrium was reestablished in the 1980s and services came back as the main focus point in the following decades. As in Italy, corporations changed their focus over time. The main nonmanufacturing companies at the beginning of the 1950s belonged to the transport sector: they were in particular railway companies, but shipping firms were also featured. During the Spanish economic miracle, new nonmanufacturing corporations developed and were able to achieve leading positions in the construction sector and in the hotel and tourism industry. On the eve of the new millennium, the most common kind of service firm among the biggest companies in the country was the commercial company. Supermarkets and distribution activities dominated the panorama, whereas the construction and real estate sectors, connected to a real estate bubble, as well the utilities sector remained important. At the same time, manufacturing remained a common focus of small and medium sized enterprises, but all the major "national champions" in this field have been sold to foreign corporations.

Due to constant fluctuation in what sector dominated, it is difficult to know whether the larger role of services in Spain than in Italy was a structural feature of the Spanish economy, or whether it was related to a series of conjunctures within the Spanish context observed during this period. The extent of the Spanish empire and the connections that the country maintained with Latin America in one sense furthered the trading activities of several companies and helped increase the size of some banks and other financial institutions. However, it should also be mentioned that the predominant role of the railway sector in Spain in the middle of the century is related to a substantial delay in the modernization of the Spanish economy and that the strong distribution sector at the turn of the new millennium was in part dominated by foreign corporations that were able to settle in the country. Beyond these considerations, the fact remains that despite their similar backgrounds several nonmanufacturing sectors developed in different ways in these nations, with large corporations developing in areas such as construction, tourism and distribution in Spain but not in Italy.

Both Italy and Spain experienced an economic miracle and a process of urbanization that brought about the need to built housing and infrastructures. However, whereas in Spain the construction sector was developed by large private and autonomous corporations, in Italy, this sector at its highest levels was dominated by state-owned companies in particular in the infrastructures, with only relatively a few private big businesses emerging (Torres Villanueva 2009). Similar dynamics can be seen in the tourism sector. Even though both countries are endowed with a rich cultural heritage and welcome a large number of tourists each year, which has given rise to other service opportunities at least since the time of their respective economic miracles, the trends that have dominated each of their tourism industries have differed. In Spain, large corporations developed in the hotel sector, which have grown to become big international firms with a significant presence also in Latin America and other parts of the world. In Italy, on the other hand, very few Italian large enterprises emerged in this field. In essence, no one has dominated this sector at an international level, because it is still largely the domain of small and medium sized enterprises (Vila Fradera 1997; Battilani 2011). Spain also created a big multinational department store, El Corte Inglés, that remained independent throughout this period while the leading Italian firm in this field, La Rinascente, changed its ownership over time and for a very long period was owned and controlled by a manufacturing group, FIAT (Amatori 1989; Papadia 2005; Cuartas 2010).

Looking at this issue from an alternative perspective, it could be said that Italy preserved its manufacturing corporations over time, whereas in Spain, most manufacturing sectors were of relatively minor importance or were dominated either by subsidiaries of foreign corporations or former Spanish companies now owned by foreign investors. This happened in manufacturing sectors such as the rubber and mechanical industries, where Italy maintained large corporations, which were less important in Spain. And, even though the Second Industrial Revolution sectors clearly influenced the scenario in both nations, a similar trend is also seen in industries such as the production of automobiles, of which the Spanish national champion was sold to a foreign company.

The different industrial distribution of large corporations is only one of the divergences that are detectable in the populations. The ownership of local big businesses, in particular private businesses, is another clear difference between these nations. Families were the predominant shareholders of the largest private corporations in Italy throughout the considered period, without significant changes in the scale or focus of their activities. The most important banks, on the other hand, with only one major exception (Piluso 2004, 2005), were state owned and have played no role in the ownership and management of corporations since the 1930s. Families have always been strong, and the families that owned the main corporations of the country have been typically very involved in politics, either directly or by lobbying heavily. The continuity in family ownership since the end of the nineteenth century was impressive: the most preeminent families in the country were able to maintain control over their corporations for more than a century. Families are legitimized by the local opinion, in which family businesses are considered as more "human" and good compared to other kinds of private ownership, and the positive values of the family and consequently of family-owned and -run corporations allowed this type of ownership to dominate the panorama for a very long time (Colli 2006b, chap. 4). Weak banks provided the corporate families with further power. Banks were not important at all to the ownership and governance of the large Italian enterprises, and the only bank that played an active role in the big business panorama, Mediobanca, was managed for several decades by a man who believed that families were at the core of the large Italian corporations and should have complete control over them (Amatori and Colli 1999).

In contrast, in Spain the banks were strong and families relatively weak when it came to the ownership and management of the largest corporations. Banks had dominated at least since playing a major role in the railway and electricity boom in the country. After the newly established Francoist government nationalized the railways during the 1940s, their investments were mainly oriented towards large manufacturing and nonmanufacturing corporations. Unlike in Italy, banks privately owned the largest national firms in the country. They maintained their position over the second part of the century, helped in part by the high levels of profitability brought about by strong protection during Franco's regime (Molina and Martín Aceña 2011). Families were important in Spain as well, but if we consider the dynamics of big family businesses in the long run, very few were able to remain under family ownership, and large family-run corporations were far less numerous in Spain than in Italy throughout the twentieth century. The majority of the most preeminent families, who had created large corporations in the nineteenth century or around the turn of the twentieth century, disappeared from the big business panorama at the beginning of the Francoist period. Then, several of the large family businesses created during the dictatorship faced serious problems or even disappeared completely in the new democratic era. With few exceptions, although family-owned businesses were undeniably important among the small and medium-sized enterprises in the country, their role in the Spanish big business panorama was far more controversial and clearly less dominant than in Italy (Binda and Colli 2011). On the other hand, the banks, which were relatively marginal in Italy, were important owners of private big business in Spain (Muñoz 1969; Pons 2001; Pueyo Sánchez 2006a). Their different legislations, which have dictated bank ownership of businesses in the two countries, were at the origin of two different distributions of power.

The different identities of private owners were also probably at the root of a partial difference in the systems of control and in the managerial culture that characterized these nations. Power in companies owned by banks is usually more dispersed than in family firms. The level of centralization is theoretically lower in bank-owned companies than in personal or family-owned corporations, with both managerial power and autonomy being stronger in the former than in the latter. When looking at the history of the largest companies in these nations, it is clear that top managers were also business owners more often in Italy than in Spain. This is due in part to the fact that big family businesses were more numerous in the former country than in the latter, but it is not easy to draw conclusions on the extent of the autonomy of managers in these two contexts, nor should it be taken for granted that it is obvious that in bank-owned companies the level of the managerial autonomy was higher than in family-owned firms.

A number of differences between Italy and Spain can also be seen when looking at managerial formation and education. Whereas in Italy a stronger heterogeneity can be detected, both in terms of the origins and the education of entrepreneurs and managers during the second half of the twentieth century, in Spain, it seems that most managers had an engineering background and that a number of specific and relatively homogeneous groups were predominantly involved in big business. From the end of the 1950s, a number of religious institutions created business schools that remained the most important breeding ground for high-level executives throughout the second half of the twentieth century and that have provided most of the top managers in the country with a common background: IESE, founded in 1958 by Opus Dei and active both in Madrid and Barcelona, and ESADE, founded in 1958 by Jesuits in Barcelona (Guillén 1994; Rugafiori 1999; Cabrera and Del Rey 2002; Castagnoli and Scarpellini 2003; Puig Raposo and Fernández Pérez 2003; Rinaldi 2003).

Looking at the strategic trends of the largest corporations, important differences also emerged between these two Southern European nations. For instance, in Italy, the importance of diversified business groups remained almost constant throughout the period under consideration. Even though the major conglomerates changed their identities and sectors over time, their presence was more or less constant throughout this period, and no cyclicity is evident. On the other hand, business groups and conglomerates in Spain seem to have been a feature of a precise phase in Spanish economic dynamics. Clear protagonists of the economy in the middle of the twentieth century, far more so than in Italy, business groups and conglomerates significantly reduced their presence from the end of the 1970s and currently play a smaller role in Spanish than in Italian big business. The internationalization strategies of the largest corporations also differed, with the Italian corporations more keen to invest abroad and export than Spain's until recently.

Divergent paths were finally followed within these two nations in terms of the organizational forms of the largest corporations. As was the case with strategies, Italy also appears more static and conservative than does Spain in this respect. The holding form with its varieties remained in fact the most commonly adopted organizational form by corporations in Italy, whereas its importance in Spain decreased over time, and the H-form played a relatively marginal role in Spain at the beginning of the new millennium.

10.2 SHARED IDIOSYNCRASIES OF TWO DIFFERENT COUNTRIES

Industries or services, banks or families, managerial education, varieties in strategy and organizational form: these two Southern European nations, at a closer look, are clearly more different than they first appear. But despite all the noteworthy differences, it is possible to identify a common core that linked Italy and Spain and differentiated them from the most advanced European economies.

The first common feature of these two different sisters is without any doubt the role played the state. Even though their political regimes differed, and despite the fact that Spain was much older than Italy as a nation-state, their governments behaved similarly. In both nations, the aim to promote industrialization, foster development and reduce territorial inequalities overlapped with the need to maintain the consensus or to avoid problems within society as much as possible. To this end, large corporations were generally helped and protected by their governments, which in turn were heavily pressured by influential business lobbies of both families and banking sector businesspeople. The Italian and Spanish governments singled out those sectors that were considered as strategically important for the economic growth and development of their country, while looking at the same time for industrial growth, development and social approval. Then they supported some industries and in particular a number of large corporations. Although to differing extents, big private corporations were protected from competition of foreign products on the domestic market, in particular in some sectors. Several firms were rescued by the state even though they belonged to sectors that were in no way of strategic value. Many corporations received direct or indirect financial help from their government, which in the Spanish case even directed private savings to specific targets in an indirect manner. Banks played a key role in this system, since they had to devote a substantial part of their resources to investments that state thought should receive "preferential treatment" (Carreras and Tafunell 2003, 362–363). Another common feature was the direct state ownership of large corporations, the extent of which exceeded state ownership in most other countries across the world. This type of ownership took the form of state-owned holdings. Most of the major industrial companies were state owned, as were in many cases the main utilities. In both nations, the state remained the main entrepreneur by turnover for most of the second half of the twentieth century, with all the consequences that state ownership can bring in terms of political and social aims. Only during the 1990s did things start to change, although in particular in Italy state-owned corporations currently remain the main protagonists of the important economic sectors.

At least two other common features are evident when looking at the owners of big business in Italy and Spain. The first is that dispersed ownership of large corporations did not spread in either of these two countries. Nearly all—and, in some benchmark years, all—the largest firms had at least one blockholder, and the corporate share dispersion that characterized most of the large firms in the Anglo-Saxon context was almost completely lacking in the Italian and Spanish contexts. The idea that the largest corporations could be "public"—namely, owned by thousands of shareholders that delegated the power and management of their corporations to professional executives that were not shareholders of the company—was completely alien to the mentality that was and is characteristic of these Southern European nations.

The second characteristic of corporate ownership that makes Italian and Spanish capitalism similar to each other but different from the most advanced European economies is the extent and importance of foreign-owned corporations to their respective economies (Whittington and Mayer 2000). Basically all of Europe acted as a host economy since the end of World War II. However, the number of subsidiaries of foreign multinationals in these two Mediterranean nations was higher than in the most developed European economies and, in particular in Spain, foreign-owned corporations came to completely dominate several industries. Even though the influx of foreign capital was quite erratic and varied both in quantity and importance, due to the industrial delay or simply because of some industries' failure to develop advanced technologies, foreigner investors remained major players in local capitalism in both nations from the beginning of their respective industrialization processes (Carreras and Tafunell 1997; Colli 2013).

The interaction of private, foreign and public shareholders within joint ventures represents another interesting shared feature of these countries. Even though this phenomenon was more prevalent in Spain than in Italy at least until end of the dictatorship, it has to be stressed that in both nations, many joint ventures were created. In some cases, they involved only national parties, such as joint ventures between private companies, or family businesses and banks, or state-owned companies and private corporations, whether they were bank owned, family owned, or both. But in other cases, they also involved foreign corporations, and it was common to find corporations that involved in essence collaboration between a foreign investor and a state- or a private-owned company, or also between foreign investors, state-owned companies and private-owned corporations. The empirical evidence shows that the connections established through joint ventures between foreign investors and local entrepreneurship represented an important phenomenon both in Italy and Spain during the second half of the twentieth century and that they were in a sense a way of privileged integration between multinationals and the local economic system (Binda 2008).

When it comes to strategic choices, even taking into account differences in the trends that governed the adoption of the unrelated diversification strategy, large corporations in Italy and Spain shared more similarities than differences, which sets these two nations apart from other European economies such as France, Germany and the United Kingdom. In both nations, the total number of companies that were strictly specialized in one single product, or in a dominant business area, was at least as important as the total number of diversified companies, and in some benchmarks years, its importance was even greater. Both in Italy and in Spain, the most commonly adopted strategy by the largest European corporations—related diversification—started to spread at a relatively late stage. It was only from the 1980s that the biggest companies started to diversify into related businesses to any significant extent, and this strategic choice remained less popular in these Mediterranean nations than in the rest of Europe. Despite certain differences, it should also be stressed that the strategy of unrelated diversification was very important in both nations, particularly so in some specific periods and sectors. Moreover, another shared feature in terms of strategy is that in most cases, the strategy of unrelated diversification was not pursued by an individual company that had decided to enter different sectors, as was common, for instance, in the United States, but by a group of corporations more or less formally coordinated by a firm that could own just a small proportion of the shares of the other corporations and use a variety of tools to control them.

Although the timing of the internationalization process of the largest corporations in Italy and Spain was different, it is possible to find many similarities when looking at the internationalization strategies of the big businesses in these nations. It is in fact possible to detect an increase in the international activities of both Italian and Spanish corporations in terms of exports and of foreign direct investment, but in both cases, it is also evident how much the domestic market remained the most important focus for most of the largest corporations.

Common features can finally also be detected in the organizational forms of the major corporations. Even though, as was stressed in the previous paragraph, the adoption of the holding structure followed partially different patterns during the second half of the twentieth century, it can also be said that the H-form played an important role in both nations in comparison to what happened in the United States and in the most advanced European economies. In all their varieties, the holding and the functional/holding forms were the most common organizational forms among the large corporations in Italy and Spain for a very long time, with their biggest companies having been organized as groups for most of their lives. The significance of this is that the holding form in both cases was well suited to local needs, were they cultural, political, social or economic. Another common feature in the organizational forms adopted by the major corporations in both nations is the impressive continuity of the functional form, which declined in importance by only a fraction during this period. This form was very well suited to the strong tendency of some of the largest firms in Italy and Spain to remain focused on a single or dominant business area. It also sets them apart from the largest corporations in the United States and in the most advanced European corporations, where the functional form essentially disappeared. Conversely, what was the most commonly adopted organizational form among the rest of the advanced nations—the multidivisional form—spread only at a later stage in Italy and Spain and was never embraced with much enthusiasm.

When looking at the dynamics of big business in Italy and Spain during the twentieth century, it is clear that in many cases more than individual firms were involved. Large corporations acted in many cases as the centers, or the cores, of complex networks. Networks of people, but also networks of other companies, both from a national and international context, and networks in which economic and political aims came together, and personal and corporate interests overlapped. Usually these networks were not down to historical legacies; capable companies and their entrepreneurs were able to create and manage these networks, making them the most successful way of doing business and generating profit in both the Italian and Spanish contexts for a reasonably long time (Tascón Fernández 2005; Colli and Vasta 2010b). In most cases, these networks took the form of business groups, which were diversified in unrelated sectors and adopted a variety of structures. In both cases, we can identify at least one state-owned business group, which included the largest corporations in the country as well as a large number of smaller companies and which grew immeasurably large over time, alongside a small number of privately controlled business groups that extended their influence over several different products and acted through the inclusion of many companies. There were very few exceptions to this scheme. Business groups represented the most common big business form in both Italy and Spain at least up to the early 1980s. Later on, their importance declined in both countries, although they do remain reasonably important in Italy to this day (Binda 2012).

10.3 COMMON FEATURES OF TWO PERIPHERAL NATIONS: TOWARD A SOUTHERN EUROPEAN CAPITALISM . . . AND BEYOND?

Observed from an international perspective, the Italian and Spanish forms of capitalism and the large corporations that operated within them have been usually considered as exceptions to the model that was supposedly destined to prevail (Whittington and Mayer 2000). However, if we carefully consider the main idiosyncrasies of these two nations, as described in the previous chapter, and compare them with the main features of other economies across the world, it is clear that Italy and Spain were not that original in their pattern of development and in their fostering of large corporations with their particular features.

First of all, it is possible to claim that some features that are characteristic of the Italian and Spanish economies are in fact very common in Southern Europe. Factors such as the determinant role of the state, the importance of foreign capital and know-how, the particular strategies and structures of large corporations in a context where small and medium-sized companies play an important role, and the importance of networks, may be at the core of a variety of capitalism that was common in Southern Europe, even though there were, of course, national variations on the theme.

The Italian and Spanish governments, despite the different nature of their regimes, were in the end not vastly different from those in Portugal, Greece and even Turkey in being in favor of intervening in the economy, supporting and protecting large corporations, creating state-owned companies and shouldering strong pressure from influential lobbies made up either of important local families and/or of banks that in many cases had been among the main participants in the process of industrialization of these nations. Even though large-scale investigations into the characteristics of the economies and the development of large corporations in these nations are in several cases still in progress, there is enough evidence to claim that several of the main pillars of the Italian and Spanish forms of capitalism were not unique at all to Southern Europe.

In terms of the role of the state, it should be mentioned that Portugal, Greece and Turkey, as well as Italy and Spain, grew and developed in a context where the state's intervention in the economy and the protection by the government of local corporations from the competition of foreign companies and products greatly affected the development of a free-market economy.

From the early 1930s, the Portuguese state built up a pervasive system of rules to control economic activity. Even though the circumstances differed slightly, state intervention continued after World War II and the government became an entrepreneur of increasing importance until, as a consequence of the revolution of 1974–1975, the largest companies of the country (and indirectly many others of smaller size) were nationalized. In Portugal, as in Italy and Spain, many of the largest firms of the country also ended up under the control of Ministries, and in 1975, a state-owned holding was founded: Instituto das Participações do Estado. At the same time, the Ministries increased their role in promoting sector-based planning and coordination. However, the Portuguese development strategy of those years, based on big state-owned firms and socialist planning, did not succeed. It was only since the 1980s that the state began to lose its central role in economic life and a process of privatization started (Baklanoff 1986; Corkill 1994; Lains and Ferreira da Silva 2005).

Significant state involvement in the economy in Greece also has its roots in the interwar period, when the government started to devote its efforts to protecting national production from the international markets by developing a strong system of measures and policies that regulated the economy even after World War II. After the fall of military regime of 1967–1974 and democracy returned to the country, the state increased its power over the economy. Whereas private and foreign investors were abandoning the country due to the effects of the oil crisis, the entrepreneurial activities of the Greek state extended into many sectors and corporations. As in other Southern European nations, most public enterprises were not well managed and have often been used as vehicles for implementing broader policy aims that were unrelated to their main economic purposes. Since the 1990s, a new trend toward an increased elimination of state involvement in the economy and the privatization of public enterprises and utilities spread, but even today, the role of the state as an entrepreneur is very important, especially for the largest corporations in the country (Mylonas and Joumar 1999; Patronis and Liargovas 2004).

As with the cases considered previously, Turkish state policies also moved towards more direct intervention and state entrepreneurship in the interwar period. After World War II, many key state-owned businesses were established in order to develop the national economy. State-owned enterprises probably became the main protagonists of the Turkish economy, with the government entering the market as an entrepreneur in the infrastructure-related sectors (such as transportation and energy) as well as manufacturing industries in intermediate goods (such as iron, steel and petroleum). Only from the 1980s did the government start to apply an economic growth model that depended on liberalization, supporting an open market and free movement of goods, and privatizing public enterprises (Önis 1992; Buğra 1994).

All these nations showed quite erratic behavior when it came to attracting and accepting foreign investment, but, although to a different extent in each case, foreign companies played an important role in all of them. In some cases, this was strongly related to the large amounts of capital that the foreign corporations brought into these countries. More importantly, almost in all cases, foreign companies were vital to the local economy because of the knowledge they brought in and the networks they helped create. Even when economic policies acted against the entrance of foreign capital and multinationals played a seemingly minor role, it is possible to detect their presence and contribution to the diffusion of new technologies, know-how, managerial techniques and so on, since the very earliest stage of the industrialization process of these countries.

Foreign corporations have been important in Portugal since the beginning of its industrial growth, by playing a decisive role in determinant sectors, such as infrastructure, where capital supply and entrepreneurial initiative as well as scientific and technological knowledge were lacking (Ferrão 1994; Cardoso de Matos and Ferreira da Silva 2008). Although the Portuguese government had been hostile to foreign direct investment since the early 1930s and international transactions dramatically decreased, during the golden age of the Portuguese economic growth between the late 1950s and 1973, foreign investment was encouraged. Many multinationals entered the country in particular in labor-intensive industries or in industries using local natural resources, although in some cases, these firms also sought to enter a small but protected home market. In these sectors, they brought with them a degree of managerial progress, entrepreneurial competence, capital inflows and technology transfers (Salgado de Matos 1973; Amaral 2003). After a sharp decrease in foreign direct investment during the mid-1970s, the Portuguese government introduced new legislation designed to attract resources from abroad, which were considered to be particularly important for the economy. A new real boom in foreign direct investment took place again in the late 1980s and early 1990s. "Portugal está na moda" (Portugal is in fashion) as the Portuguese government liked to claim, and foreign direct investment gained a new prominence in the larger, export-oriented firms and took on an increasingly hegemonic role in the services sector, while industrial investment experienced a relative decline (Corkill 1999).

Foreign capital played an important role in the development of Greece and Turkey as well, even though in both these countries, both the influx and the impact of foreign direct investment were erratic. In the case of Greece, investment (together with political patronage) originated predominantly from the United Kingdom and France toward the end of the nineteenth century, focusing in particular on the development of railway and communications infrastructure. Foreign expertise and technology continued to enter the country and foreign corporations were established in Greece before World War I, soon becoming among the largest corporations in the country. Foreign capital was also provided in the form of loans that were used to pay for important projects and public works (Dritsas 1993). After World War II, the presence of foreign multinationals also started to increase and the attraction of foreign capital was a goal actively pursued by governments in the years of the Greek economic miracle. Even though a sharp reverse also took place in this nation during the second part of the 1970s, relatively successful policies to attract foreign investment were promoted from the 1980s onward (OECD 1994).

With regard to Turkey, foreign capital also had a large presence at the beginning of the industrialization process, in particular in the services sectors such as banking, transportation, electricity, water and gas, but also played an important role in agriculture and in some infant industries, and remained predominant at least up to World War I. Attempts to reduce dependence on foreign investors were made, but in addition to what was mentioned earlier, investment has flowed into the country since the postwar years. Even though conditions were not favorable for foreign companies during the 1960s and 1970s and Turkey was perceived as a dangerous and unstable country, the nation continued to depend on foreign technologies in some industries in particular. From the end of the 1980s, thanks to similar government incentives as those provided in Greece and Portugal for foreign companies to enter the country, the presence of foreign companies began to rise at increasingly high rates during the 1990s and boomed during the 2000s (Erdilek 2003).

Probably more important than the physical amount of foreign capital that entered these countries is the methods that foreigners chose—or were forced—to adopt and the way in which they affected the behavior and performance of local corporations. In all these Mediterranean countries, even though the extent and timings varied, the creation of joint ventures between local and foreign shareholders was quite common during some periods in particular, when a country needed foreign capital and knowledge on one hand, but did not want foreign corporations to become more powerful than the local ones on the other. The result was that local companies exploited foreign technologies and experiences to survive and grow. Joint ventures were historically intensively used together with other kinds of alliances by the largest Portuguese corporations, such as the CUF economic group, which used its alliances with foreign multinationals as a way of furthering technological innovation and of gaining access to foreign markets (Corkill 1999). The history of the largest Greek corporations is also full of examples of international joint ventures, as was the case with the metal company Viohalco, which from the 1960s onward founded various subsidiaries in cables, steel and aluminum, with minority shareholders such as Siemens and Phelps Dodge (Viohalco 2012). The story of the current largest company in Turkey, the conglomerate Koç, is relatively similar; since the 1950s, it has been a successful producer of automobiles, tractors, lightbulbs, refrigerators and washing machines, among other goods, mostly through joint ventures and licensing agreements with foreign firms that allowed it to reach an adequate level of know-how (Koç 2012).

The large corporations in Italy and Spain shared another feature with the rest of Southern European: the existence and economic importance of large and diversified business groups. As in Italy and Spain, in fact, in contrast to what happened in the United States and in the most advanced European nations, no large numbers of companies that were diversified into related activities and adopted a multidivisional form emerged in Portugal, or in Greece or Turkey. In all these nations, the local private big business panorama was made up of two kinds of actors: relatively "small" large corporations focused on one or a few products and quite simply organized on the one side and big and very diversified business groups that included most of the largest corporations of each nation on the other side.

In Portugal, during the 1960s, the business structure was still made up partly by tens of thousands of micro, family-owned small and medium-sized corporations and partly by seven highly diversified business groups. During the 1970s, new business groups spread within the country (Martins 1973; Santos 1977). The bulk of these groups consisted of the founding firm, the family holding, a bank and an insurance company. Alongside organizational aspects, unrelated diversification was accompanied by the dissemination of formally separated joint-stock companies, as a tool to increase the attraction of savings. At the beginning of the 1970s, the largest business group in Portugal was a family-owned one, namely, CUF. It included more than 100 firms and held more than 10% of the total capital of all existing corporations in the country (Ferreira da Silva).

Business groups played a very important role in Greece and Turkey as well. Banking business groups were among the most important founders of large joint-stock corporations in Greece at the turn of the twentieth century and, at the turn of the twenty-first century, most of the biggest corporations in the country still belonged to a business group. Families were often the main owners and controllers of these groups, as was the case with the Latsis. Yannis Latsis started as a deckhand and eventually worked his way up to ship's captain in the merchant marine. He bought his first cargo vessel in 1938 and owned a fleet of ships by the 1960s. In the late 1960s, he diversified his business to include oil, construction and building (among other things; Lewis 2003).

Diversified business groups have represented a main pillar of the Turkish economy since the beginning of its industrialization process and can be divided into two categories. The first includes the groups founded between the 1920s and the 1950s, which diversified into unrelated areas relatively early, whereas the second category consists of group that were mostly founded in the 1950s but started to significantly diversify their activities from the 1980s onward. In Turkey, most business groups also belonged to families, such as the Koç group, and, in this case, equity holdings such as a pyramidal and/or networks of intercorporate shareholding structures were used to control the group. Companies that belong to a business group still accounted for 57.10% of the total number of employees of the fifty largest employers in the country in 2005 (Colpan 2010).

Within this framework, a final similarity can be found in the strong role that private lobbies belonging to national business groups or to foreign companies continued to play in influencing weak political parties and/or dictatorial regimes in these latecomer countries. Despite the different levels of industrialization achieved by these nations during the past century and the partially heterogeneous political dynamics that characterized Southern Europe, in all these contexts a number of strong private foreign investor groups existed, who continuously attempted—and often succeeded—to shape industrial policies to their advantage (Sapelli 1996). The connection between weak states, strong lobbies, and a restricted number of important players within these nations— such as state-owned corporations, big and very diversified business groups, subsidiaries of foreign multinationals—seems to have been a constant feature of the Southern European economies in the long term, and certainly for most of the second half of the twentieth century.

According to this interpretation, Italy and Spain could be considered as economies that shared several features with other Southern European nations. They could perhaps also be seen as the most developed nations in the European periphery, the most successful countries representative of a particular variety of capitalism: the Southern European form of capitalism. The main features needed to identify this Southern European capitalism could be considered as the dominant role of the state both as an entrepreneur and as a very active agent in the economy; the ambiguous but ultimately important role of foreign investors and companies; and the pervasiveness of not only small and medium-sized corporations but also of a few very big and diversified business groups and networks.

However, things are not that straightforward, since several of these features could be said to exist in most of the industrial latecomer countries across the world. Although the acceptance and importance of foreign direct investment as well as the strength of lobbies in influencing the policy makers varied widely, it can be claimed that the role of the state was overwhelming in most countries across the world, as was the role of business groups. Without distinctive differences between countries and continents, as long as studies remain focused on this organizational form, it seems that the number of nations that are—and historically were—dominated by a number of big business groups is increasing every day. Even though they take on a variety of shapes, it is possible to claim that business groups are today the main protagonists behind the growth of emerging countries worldwide, as they were in Italy and Spain during the nineteenth and twentieth century. Business groups characterized the main big business model in Asia, at first in Japan and Korea, and later on in India and China but also in Taiwan, Thailand and Singapore. However, business groups have represented an important power also in South America (for instance in Argentina, Brazil, Chile and Mexico), as well as in several other latecomer countries throughout the world, such as Israel, Russia and South Africa (Colpan, Hikino and Lincoln 2010). The concentration of power in the hands of few firms that entered several unrelated sectors seems to have been normal all over the world during the last century. Within this framework, families in several cases maintained their control, banks were usually quite proactive in creating business groups or operating within them as the "glue" that held things together, and the state also created business groups.

The performance of business groups cannot be easily generalized on a global scale. The impact of several aspects of their identity and behavior could make them look like paragons in some contexts and like parasites in other ones (Kannah and Yafeh 2005). But despite their heterogeneity one thing seems to be certain: although the diffusion of related diversification and the multidivisional form was limited to a relatively small number of countries—the United States and the most advanced European nations—the business group form played an important part in the industrial growth and development of several late-comer nations, including Japan and Southern Europe, and is currently characteristic of the economic boom of emerging nations in Asia, Latin America and Africa. A comparison of the performance of these two models clearly merits further research efforts in the future. However, the new empirical evidence gathered on Italy and Spain, as well as the increasing number of studies on strategies and organizational forms conducted from a historical perspective throughout the world, have already contributed to say that, if a common pattern of development among the large corporations across the world existed during the twentieth century, it was, probably, the business group form rather than the multidivisional. In this sense, when viewed from a global perspective, the Italian and Spanish examples, which have appeared in this book as exceptions to the general model, seem to follow the rules dominating big business behavior rather than forming the exception.

11 At the Root of an Alternative Model
An Interpretation of Big Business' Diversity in Italy and Spain

11.1 THE DECISION MAKERS: POSSIBLE EXPLANATIONS FOR CONCENTRATED FORMS OF CAPITALISM

When reviewing the features and dynamics of the largest corporations in Italy and Spain, some signs of convergence emerge within the framework of the Western world. However, throughout the twentieth century, big business in these Southern European nations presented significant peculiarities also when compared to the most advanced European countries and, even more so, to the United States. As was shown in the previous chapter, these two nations were similar in "being different" in terms of their ownership structures, product and geographical market strategies and organizational forms.

Focusing on ownership structures, two features of big business in Italy and Spain are particularly striking. The first one is the weakness—or almost complete absence—of public companies in the long term. The second is the identity of the main blockholders of the large corporations, which essentially included the state, foreign investors, families (in particular in Italy) and banks (in particular in Spain).

As has been mentioned in the first section, both the Italian and Spanish forms of capitalism have been "concentrated" during the twentieth century, with only a few parties controlling the main corporations in these economies. Not surprisingly, looking at the ownership structures of these companies, we cannot see a "democratic" structure at least until relatively recently. All corporations basically had one owner or a very restricted coalition of owners. This was an obvious choice for the vast majority of small corporations, which may simply not have needed to involve more parties in order to acquire resources such as capital or technology. Nevertheless, the largest firms, which in particular in the Anglo-Saxon world would usually decide to go public at an early stage mainly with the aim of achieving the amount of funding required for the capital-intensive sectors in which they operated, also remained strongly concentrated in the hands of few shareholders in Italy and Spain.

This outcome was help at least by two facts. The first one is that neither the Italian nor the Spanish "normal" people were able to accumulate large amounts of resources for most of the twentieth century. Until recently, when families had money to spare the general attitude has been to save it, and traditionally people put their savings under their mattresses rather than in a bank account or in the capital market. When they wanted to invest large sums of money, the priority usually was to buy a house. Another form of investment was to start an owned-activity or a small company. Even when private investors decided to go to the stock exchange, government securities were in general preferred since they were supposed to be safer and presented high yields (Amatori and Brioschi 1997). Buying shares in big corporations was not common among Italian and Spanish citizens. It was perceived as very risky, because the stock exchange was barely regulated, the rights of minority shareholders not protected and the transparency and disclosure of information by companies very low.

Consob (Commissione Nazionale per le Società e la Borsa), the public authority responsible for regulating the Italian securities market, was created in 1974 but saw its role and autonomy increase only during the 1980s. Actors such as institutional investors and investment companies did not exist in Italy until the 1980s, whereas corporate governance codes that protected minority shareholders were enacted in the country only at the end of the 1990s, following the introduction of new legislation governing the Italian financial markets (the so-called Draghi Law). Things were similar in Spain, where the securities market was reformed so as to have stronger discipline in 1988 thanks to the Spanish Securities Market Act, which established the independent regulatory authority CNMV (Comisión Nacional del Mercado de Valores), set up a framework for the regulation of trading practices, tender offers and insider trading and required listed companies to comply with more detailed information disclosure and transparency regulations.

Even though in both countries a general lack of resources and an unwillingness to invest in industrial shares was accompanied by a substantial lack of rules, it is interesting to note that even when financial resources increased and new rules made it safer for private citizens to invest in the stock exchange, very few real public companies emerged. The process of privatization of the former state-owned giants, which in most cases was explicitly directed toward the "small people" and was aimed, among other things, to provide the opportunity to create public companies, is symptomatic of the difficulty in spreading the ownership of the large corporations in these nations. In fact, in very few cases privatized corporations did not move from one blockholder to another and some families, banks, or savings banks further increased the extent of their ownership of large corporations to the disadvantage of small investors who, although less so than in the past, continued to consider the spheres of the stock exchange as strange and hostile even in the last decade of the previous century.

It thus seems reasonable to think that the lack of dispersed ownership of the large corporations within these two nations was not only due to the lack of rules or to the poorly functioning capital market. It was also, and maybe predominantly, due to cultural reasons. The idea that the person who puts his or her money into an endeavor is also the one who actually has the right to make decisions is quite common in both nations, both for the small and the big corporations, and explains the paradox of countries that are characterized by a multitude of small enterprises and entrepreneurs but that also have a substantial lack of people participation in big business and of dispersed corporate ownership. The main issue in this sense seems not to be the low level of participation of common people in the economic life of the country and in the creation and administration of companies, but rather the culturally rooted sense of control that investors had over the company in which they invested. The owners of large corporations did not want to lose their power by sharing it with thousands of shareholders or withdrawing from management. At the same time, small investors were not attracted to the idea of putting their money in companies that they could neither control nor understand and over which they had basically no influence, so in many cases, they preferred to invest in their own small endeavors or not to invest at all.

The cultural dimensions that made the Italian and Spanish corporations less likely to have a dispersed ownership structure could be still nowadays quite accurately reflected in an analysis of cultural dimensions conducted by the organizational culture scholar Geert Hofstede (1980, 1991, 1997). In his works on national and organizational cultures, he described both Italy and Spain as nations that are culturally significantly different from Anglo-Saxon countries, where pubic companies were common. According to his description of these two countries, it is possible to detect some cultural reasons why the public company became a common form of enterprise in the United States and in other Western nations, but was a less successful tool in Spain and Italy.

According to Hofstede, the power distance, defined as the extent to which the less powerful members of institutions and organizations within a country expect and accept that power is distributed unequally, is quite high in both Italy and Spain, while it is low in the United States, in the United Kingdom and in Germany. The perception that power and privileges are and will not be equally shared among people could therefore have represented an important factor in discouraging people from getting involved in big organizations with other shareholders. The American premise of "liberty and justice for all," on the other hand, could have represented an important background to the social acceptance of public companies and to the willingness of people to invest in them. Another of the cultural features identified by Hofstede that can influence people's attitudes toward the dispersed ownership of corporations is the uncertainty avoidance. Where the uncertainty avoidance is higher, people will be more likely to invest in government securities, or not to invest at all, whereas in a context where uncertainty is more tolerated, it will be easier to invest in corporate shares and to risk money on the stock exchange. Defining the uncertainty avoidance as the extent to which the members of a culture feel threatened by ambiguous or unknown situations and have created beliefs and institutions that try to avoid these, Hofstede detected that both Italy and

Spain are nations whose citizens are very uncomfortable in ambiguous situations, whereas the US society is "uncertainty accepting." This could help to explain why Italian and Spanish people were less willing to enter a world that they perceived to be as unknown and ambiguous as that of the stock exchange, and were not attracted to the idea of buying companies' shares.

Given the fact that public companies represented a fundamental tool for large corporations to raise the money to enter and develop capital-intensive technologies required by the Second Industrial Revolution industries, which is where big business originally developed, the lack of dispersed ownership among the largest corporations in Italy and Spain could have posed a problem from a historical perspective in acquiring the necessary amount of capital to finance such big enterprises. However, big business was able to finance itself also in these nations thanks to the nature and strategies of its main blockholders and the organizational structures they adopted.

As has been mentioned in the discussion of the particular features of the Italian and Spanish big business ownership structures, at least two actors were fundamental owning large corporations: the state and the banks. As suggested in the classical interpretation by Alexander Gerschenkron (1962), both these owners of course had privileged access to capital and represented in this sense a formidable substitution factor for the local entrepreneurial initiative in creating large corporations. But governments and banks were not the only substitution factors in these nations. Foreign corporations also played a decisive role in some of the capital-intensive industries, although their influence was not continuous during the different economic cycles of each country (e.g., Colli 2013). It can thus be claimed that in these latecomer countries, which are well known for the strong presence of their small corporations and therefore also for their significant entrepreneurial vitality, the presence of the state, the banks and the multinationals as the major shareholders of large corporations was probably not a substitution to compensate for the lack of entrepreneurial spirit of their citizens. Rather, their presence could be explained among many reasons by the need to have access to large amounts of capital in a context where public companies were unable to succeed for a number of reasons.

However, we cannot neglect the fact that some private corporations, often family-owned, also participated in the big business panorama of these nations. In many cases, they were descendants of rich nobles or merchant families, especially at the beginning of the century. This was, for instance, the case for the founders of the car producers in Italy, the banks in Spain and the main companies in the electricity sector in both nations. These families and the others who emerged throughout the century often adopted *escamotages* a number of underhand methods to acquire the resources that they needed without losing control over their businesses. One such method, especially common in Italy, was the creation of pyramidal groups that allowed the family to maintain control over the nonlisted holding of the group and raise funds by listing a multitude of companies that referred back to the holding. However, the main method used to increase the size of a company without losing control over it was to create partnerships and coalitions, as well as real joint-ventures, either with other families or with banks, foreign investors and state-owned companies. The cooperation of different participants within the same company, as the empirical evidence showed in Parts II and III, was an effective way for large corporations to grow as well as remain big, even though a real democratization of the ownership assets of large corporations did not occur and public companies were not common in either country during the twentieth century.

11.2 INSIDE THE CORPORATIONS: EXPLAINING BIG BUSINESS BEHAVIOR THROUGH ENDOGENOUS FACTORS

Looking at the characteristics of the largest corporations in Italy and Spain compared to those in the United States and the most advanced European nations, it appears that ownership assets are nevertheless not the main area where they differ. Concentrated ownership structures were quite common also in Germany and France (Whittington and Mayer 2000). The most evident divergence of these Southern European nations from the most developed ones is related to the behavior of their big businesses, and in particular to their strategies and structures.

As was discussed in Chapter 7, the related diversification strategy, which was the most common product strategy in the United States, was not introduced in Italy and Spain until a relatively late stage and failed to gain much popularity. Most of the companies in these countries preferred to remain focused only on one or very few products, while the very largest companies often adopted a strategy of unrelated diversification. Chapter 9 further showed that, while most of the largest corporations of the world were multidivisionals, the M-form was adopted at a late stage and only partially by the big businesses in these Southern European nations. Organizational structures such as the holding or the functional/holding remained the most commonly adopted forms in both nations throughout the twentieth century.

Related diversification and the M-form were almost completely unknown also in the main European economies immediately after World War II. After that, however, a process of strategic and organizational convergence took place, and big businesses in the United Kingdom, Germany and France enthusiastically adopted the US-inspired strategies and structures during the second half of the twentieth century (Whittington and Mayer 2000). Yet, the level of convergence among the large corporations in Italy and Spain remained remarkably low, and important peculiarities in the strategic and organizational behaviors within these two nations remain present until today.

In order to explain the particular behavior displayed by big business in these contexts, at least two groups of factors should be considered. A first part of the explanation could be related to the internal dynamics of corporations, which had a definitive role in shaping their strategies and structures, while a second group of factors that have to be taken into account is related to what happened in the external environment. The next section deals with the endogenous factors, while the impact of the external framework is assessed in the last section of this chapter.

In order to analyze the determinants of the different strategic choices of the large corporations in Italy and Spain, namely, a persistently widespread diffusion of single or dominant business strategies as well as the large importance of unrelated diversification, two factors should not be neglected: the sectors to which the corporations belonged, and their variety of ownership structures. When considering the features that characterized the organizational choices of the corporations, namely, a widespread diffusion of the functional/holding and holding forms, their industrial categorizations and ownership structures are still important. It is also interesting to consider a third factor that may have been important in shaping the organizational behavior of the corporations: their product strategies.

Industry, Strategy and Structure

The large companies that emerged in the United States at the end of the nineteenth century were based on a precise technological constraint: they were companies whose industry categorization allowed them to exploit opportunities resulting from their activities in manufacturing. According to Chandler (1990), it would have been the particular technology that distinguished the capital-intensive sectors, characterized by the continuous and fast productive processes typical of the Second Industrial Revolution, to constitute the first engine that stimulated in the United States the exploitation of scale and scope economies and led to an increase in the adoption of the related diversification strategy, which had to be managed through the multidivisional structure. The large corporations studied by the Harvard group during the 1970s and by Whittington and Mayer during the 1990s in the United Kingdom, Germany and France were also manufacturing companies that had decided to diversify their core business, which very often was based in one of the few capital-intensive sectors typical of the Second Industrial Revolution. Later on, they adopted the M-form. The relationship between the industry categorization of corporations and their strategies and structures seems to have been consistent in these nations. However, things are not as clear-cut when looking at Italy and Spain.

The technological constraints indicated by Chandler may have been different outside of the United States. It is possible that the companies that emerged in the latecomer countries in those sectors typical of big business in fact faced a very different situation to their US counterparts, even though they operated under the same technological constraints, for instance because big rival businesses already existed and had built up a clear advantage over time. In this sense, the adoption of a related diversification strategy and of the M-form would not have been enough to catch up in a context of pronounced delay compared to companies that had adopted this kind of behavior many decades earlier. Thus, the enterprises that developed in the same sectors as the pioneers but at a much later point in time may have thought that other strategies would be better in order to grow and to survive in the face of competition from their firstcomer rivals.

Moreover, while Chandler and the Harvard Studies analyzed only the manufacturing sector during a period when the technologies of the Third Industrial Revolution had not spread completely, we know that a significant proportion of the largest corporations in these nations are not involved in industry but in services, and that new industrial technologies have demanded new strategies and structures since Chandler wrote *Strategy and Structure* at the beginning of the 1960s. When analyzing the industrial distribution of the population, in which companies have been divided into the categories manufacturing (M) and nonmanufacturing (NM), no clear and stable empirical relationships emerge when trying to connect the strategies and structures adopted by the large corporations with their industrial categorization throughout this period.

For the product diversification strategy (Figure 11.1a and 11.1b), some regularity appears when comparing Italy and Spain in the long term. In both nations, in fact, the manufacturing corporations mostly decided to remain focused or a single or dominant business in 1950 and 1973, but had decided to adopt a strategy of related diversification by 1988 and in 2002. Nevertheless, the trend is not as clear when considering the strategies adopted by nonmanufacturing corporations. In Italy, most had decided to adopt a strategy of very restricted diversification, focusing on one or a few products, but in 1988, the majority of the nonmanufacturing corporations were active in related business sectors. In Spain, on the other hand, in 1950, the nonmanufacturing

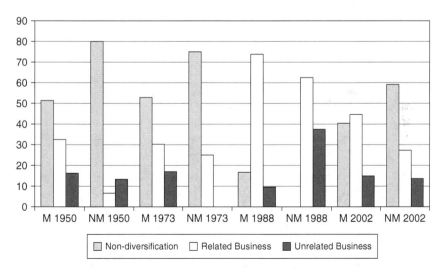

Figure 11.1a Industry and strategy in Italy, 1950–2002
Source: Appendix Tables 1b, 2b, 3b, 4b.

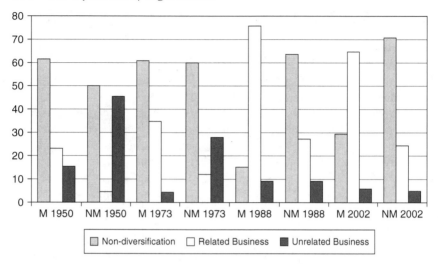

Figure 11.1b Industry and strategy in Spain, 1950–2002
Source: Appendix Tables 5b, 6b, 7b, 8b.

corporations were almost exactly divided into two groups: those that were strictly focused on one area and those that had adopted a strategy of completely unrelated activities. The same phenomenon is observable in 1973 but to a much smaller extent, whereas in 1988 and 2002, most of the nonmanufacturing companies belonged to the nondiversified category.

With regard to the organizational structures (Figures 11.2a and 11.2b), it is also difficult to detect clear and stable trends and relationships. Manu-

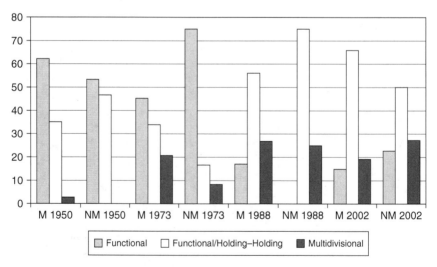

Figure 11.2a Industry and structure in Italy, 1950–2002
Source: Appendix Tables 1b, 2b, 3b, 4b.

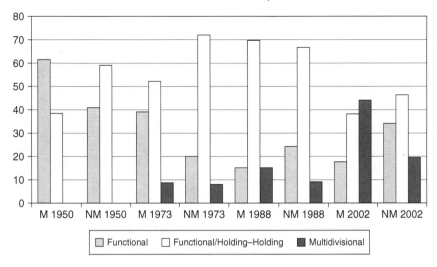

Figure 11.2b Industry and structure in Spain, 1950–2002
Source: Appendix Tables 5b, 6b, 7b, 8b.

facturing corporations in Italy mostly adopted a functional form in the first two benchmark years and a holding form in the latter two, whereas in Spain most of the big firms moved from a functional structure in 1950 to a holding in 1973 and 1988 and finally to a multidivisional structure in 2002. Curiously, in Italy, the nonmanufacturing corporations followed the same pattern as the manufacturing corporations, moving from being predominantly functional in the decades following World War II to mostly being holdings in the last decade of the twentieth century. However, the same trend cannot be detected in the nonmanufacturing corporations in Spain, which remained predominantly organized as holdings throughout the considered period.

Ownership, Strategy and Structure

When considering the influence of ownership structures on the strategic and organizational choices of corporations, it should be remembered that, according to several business interpretations, the ownership of a firm should have an impact on the firm's strategic and organizational choices (Palmer et al. 1987; Fligstein and Brantley 1992; Palmer, Devereaux Jennings and Zhou 1993; Whitley 1994). Families have very often been accused, for instance, of voluntarily limiting the growth, diversification and divisionalization of their own firms for fear of losing control (Chandler 1990). Bank and state ownership have been considered as something that could hinder the process of diversification of a firm, while public companies should have a greater tendency to diversify (Whittington and Mayer 2000). The Italian and Spanish experiences seem to confirm such theories, but only in part (Figures 11.3, 11.4, 11.5 and 11.6).

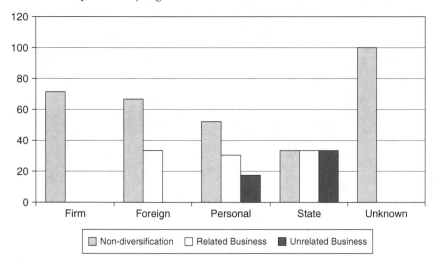

Figure 11.3a Ownership and strategy in Italy, 1950
Source: Appendix Table 1b.

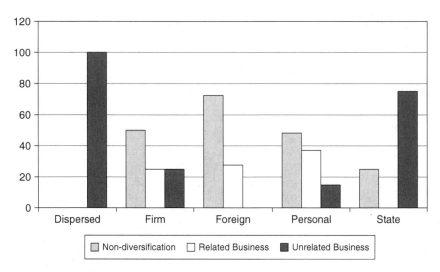

Figure 11.3b Ownership and strategy in Italy, 1973
Source: Appendix Table 2b.

Family firms, in accordance with the main interpretations, were predominantly oriented toward a single or a dominant business activity in both Italy and Spain during the 1950s and 1960s. However, things started to change from the following period onward, and in 1988, most of the family companies were active in related business areas. This trend was confirmed in Spain at the beginning of the new millennium but not in Italy, where a small majority of family companies had returned to being predominantly nondi-

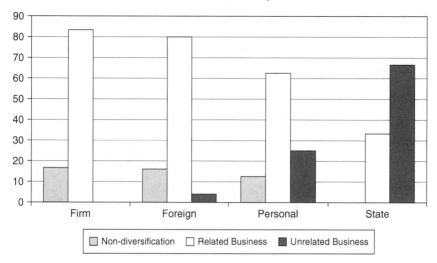

Figure 11.3c Ownership and strategy in Italy, 1988
Source: Appendix Table 3b.

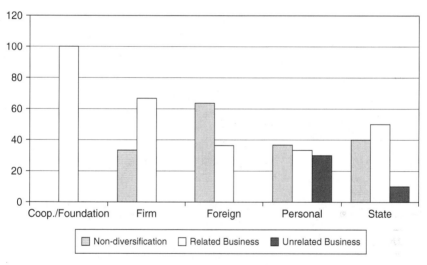

Figure 11.3d Ownership and strategy in Italy, 2002
Source: Appendix Table 4b.

versified. However, there was very little difference in the adoption of the various product strategies in Italy in this last benchmark year, when more or less equal numbers of families adopted strategies of nondiversification, related diversification, and unrelated diversification. In addition, to make things more complicated, in Spain, family businesses had also been very active in the adoption of unrelated business strategies, in particular in the first two benchmark years.

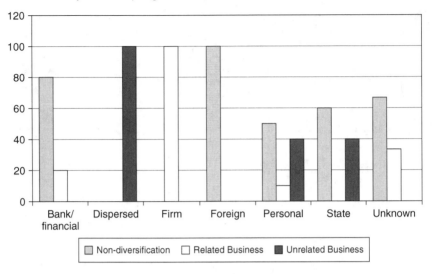

Figure 11.4a Ownership and strategy in Spain, 1950
Source: Appendix Table 5b.

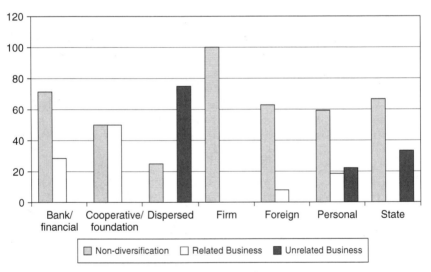

Figure 11.4b Ownership and strategy in Spain, 1973
Source: Appendix Table 6b.

Families were moreover willing to adopt all the varieties of organizational structures, in particular in Italy. Moving from a period when most family businesses adopted a functional or a holding form, the multidivisional became increasingly popular among the Italian business families in 1973. Even though the holding form remained the favorite organizational structure among the family firms in Italy, the M-form was extensively adopted

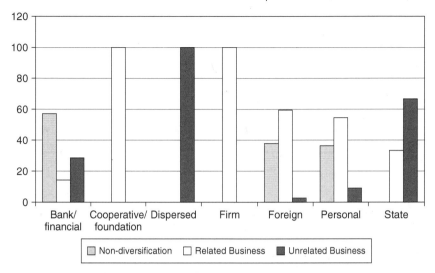

Figure 11.4c Ownership and strategy in Spain, 1988
Source: Appendix Table 7b.

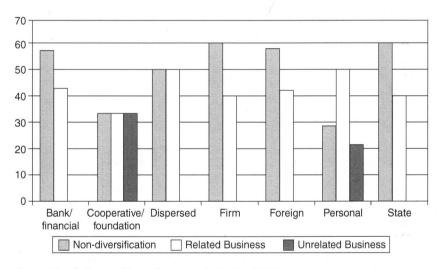

Figure 11.4d Ownership and strategy in Spain, 2002
Source: Appendix Table 8b.

as well. In contrast, the success of the multidivisional form among family companies remained relatively limited throughout the second part of the twentieth century in Spain, where family businesses predominantly adopted holding structures, or functional structures, at least until the last benchmark.

The other major national blockholder, the state, also changed its preferred strategies and structures over time in both nations and basically chose

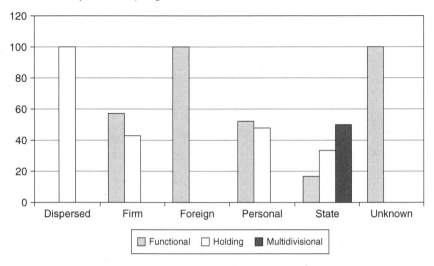

Figure 11.5a Ownership and structure in Italy, 1950
Source: Appendix Table 1b.

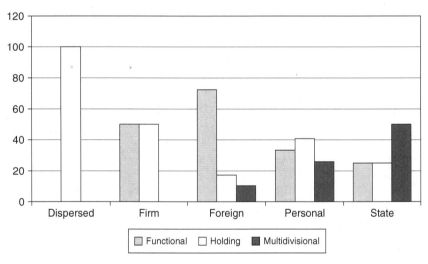

Figure 11.5b Ownership and structure in Italy, 1973
Source: Appendix Table 2b.

the breath of options. The state-owned corporations in Italy in the middle of the century were perfectly divided among nondiversified, related diversified and unrelated diversified corporations, whereas they were unrelated diversified, or not diversified at all in Spain. The adoption of strategies of unrelated diversification by the state-owned companies became prevalent in both nations in particular during the 1970s, but since the 1990s, most of the main state-owned corporations have returned to being related diversifiers in

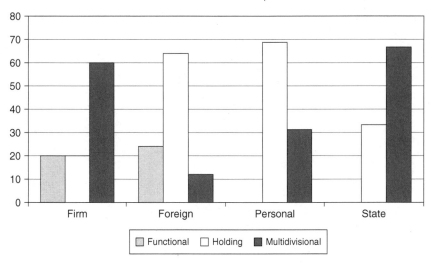

Figure 11.5c Ownership and structure in Italy, 1988
Source: Appendix Table 3b.

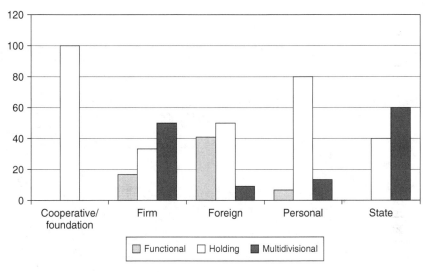

Figure 11.5d Ownership and structure in Italy, 2002
Source: Appendix Table 4b.

Italy and nondiversified companies in Spain. In terms of their organizational structures too, state-owned companies did not always show clear and unambiguous trends. In Italy, they were predominantly multidivisionals or holdings, whereas in Spain the functional form was also quite common among the largest governmental corporations, in particular in 1950 and 1973.

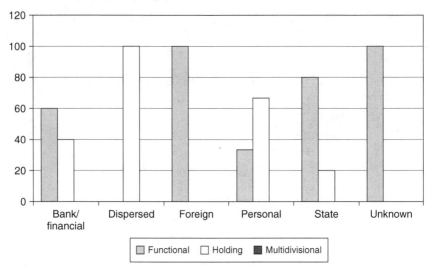

Figure 11.6a Ownership and structure in Spain, 1950
Source: Appendix Table 5b.

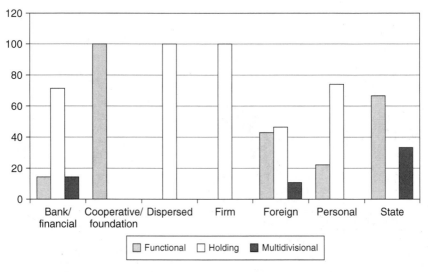

Figure 11.6b Ownership and structure in Spain, 1973
Source: Appendix Table 6b.

Last but not least, foreign corporations adopted a wide variety of strategies and structures too. In Italy, they were predominantly focused on one or a few products in 1950 and 1973, but started to become more and more diversified in the following benchmark year. At the same time, most of the multinationals moved away from the functional structure to functional/ holding and holding structures and, in a few cases, the M-form. Foreign

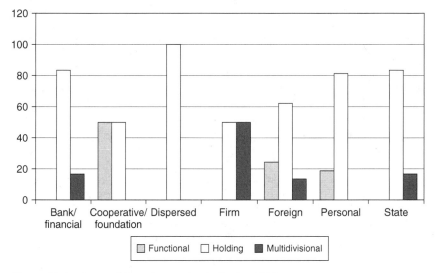

Figure 11.6c Ownership and structure in Spain, 1988
Source: Appendix Table 7b.

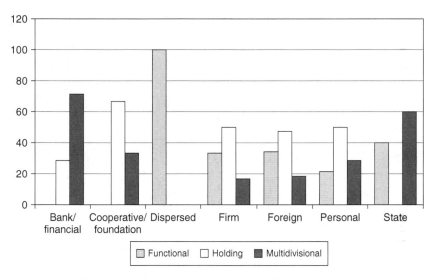

Figure 11.6d Ownership and structure in Spain, 2002
Source: Appendix Table 8b.

companies in Spain, on the other hand, also generally moved from a quite specialized focus toward an increasingly related diversification strategy and usually preferred to adopt a holding structure except for in the first period, when they were predominantly organized by functions. They were not among the most enthusiastic adopters of the M-form, but some multidivisional multinationals have still had a presence in Spain since 1973.

Strategy and Structure

In order to understand the organizational structures of the largest companies, it is also necessary to take their strategies into consideration. In studying the path of growth of the largest successful manufacturing companies in the United States, Alfred Chandler in 1962 claimed that "structure fairly quickly followed strategy" (Chandler 1962, 162). He argued that the multidivisional structure followed a strategy of increasing product related diversification in particular.

However, when considering the strategic choices of big business in Italy and Spain, it has to be stressed that this has not been an absolute rule. In most of the benchmark years, unsurprisingly, it is possible to observe a relatively significant connection between the nondiversified companies and the adoption a functional or functional/holding structure (Figures 11.7 and 11.8).

On the other hand, the most diversified corporations in these nations usually also adopted more sophisticated organizational forms. Nevertheless, at least up to the 1980s, they predominantly adopted a functional/holding or a holding structure, and only in two benchmarks did the multidivisional become the preferred choice of those companies that had adopted a strategy of related diversification in both Italy and Spain. The unrelated diversification strategy followed broadly the same trend: most of the unrelated diversifiers had adopted a functional/holding or a holding structure with the only exception of the 1988 benchmark year. In both Italy and Spain in fact, at the end of the 1980s, the majority of the unrelated diversifiers had adopted a multidivisional structure.

The attempt to interpret the strategies and structures of the largest corporations in Italy and Spain using internal features, such as their sector of

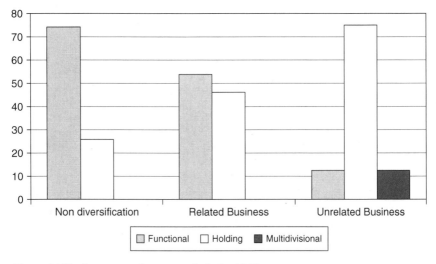

Figure 11.7a Strategy and structure in Italy, 1950
Source: Appendix Table 1b.

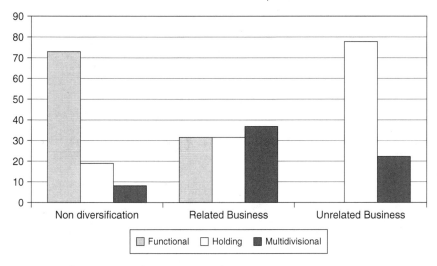

Figure 11.7b Strategy and structure in Italy, 1973
Source: Appendix Table 2b.

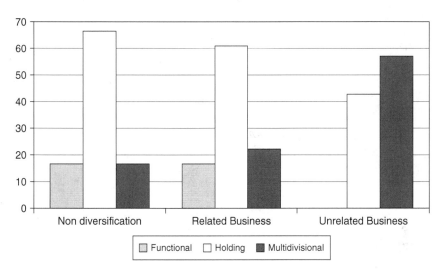

Figure 11.7c Strategy and structure in Italy, 1988
Source: Appendix Table 3b.

activity, ownership and strategy, can thus only be partially successful. In neither of the two countries can the choice of diversification be explained based on technological features: in all the benchmark years a substantial impact of the sectoral categorization of an enterprise on the extension of the variety of its products is not detectable, and the division between manufacturing and nonmanufacturing is not particularly useful for proving the existence of stable relationships. Sectors that should have been characterized by strong

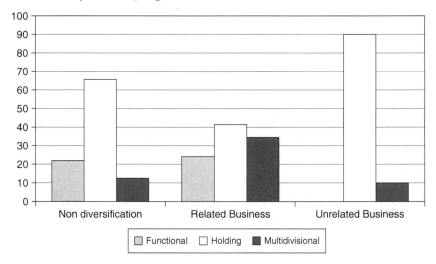

Figure 11.7d Strategy and structure in Italy, 2002
Source: Appendix Table 4b.

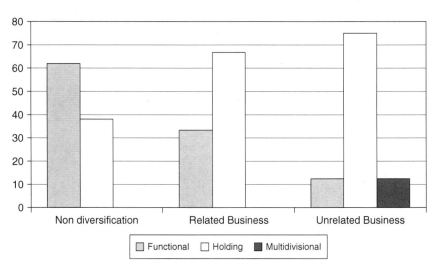

Figure 11.8a Strategy and structure in Spain, 1950
Source: Appendix Table 5b.

diversification strategies remained in various cases single or dominant business oriented. On the other hand, many firms in labor-intensive or services sectors, which would not have found there to be a significant technological advantage in diversifying their production, nonetheless decided to adopt diversification strategies.

Explaining strategies based on ownership is also ineffective in these two Mediterranean countries, where all the types of shareholders have used a

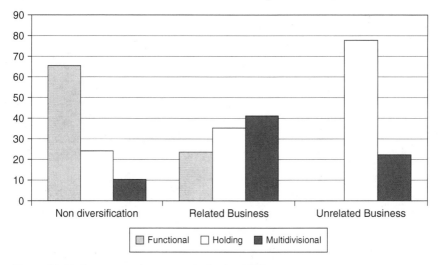

Figure 11.8b Strategy and structure in Spain, 1973
Source: Appendix Table 6b.

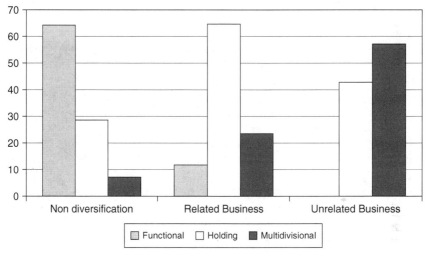

Figure 11.8c Strategy and structure in Spain, 1988
Source: Appendix Table 7b.

wide variety of strategic options. In the database it is possible to observe dispersed ownership firms that, rather than grow through a diversification process as some scholars predicted, decided to pursue a dominant business strategy. On the other hand, families and banks, which are generally considered reluctant to diversify their own entrepreneurial activity, often decided to enter new and very different businesses.

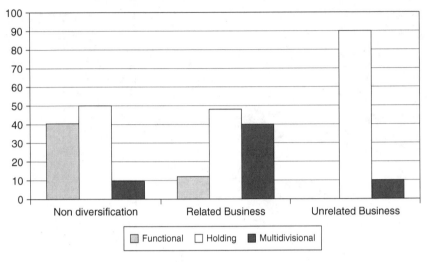

Figure 11.8d Strategy and structure in Spain, 2002
Source: Appendix Table 8b.

And yet, structure in most cases did not follow strategy. Vast groups of enterprises sometimes pursued a single or dominant business strategy and, on the other hand, very diversified firms in some cases had very centralized organizational forms. In this general framework, the holding structure has been adopted across every type of sector and by all owners without any correlation with the firms' product diversification strategies. Against this messy backdrop, the comfortable relationships hypothesized by the Harvard scholars on the relationships between technology and strategy, among ownership, strategy and structure, and between strategy and structure do not fit so well with what really occurred. It is thus necessary to complement the interpretation of the behavior of the large corporations by looking at the external environment in which these corporations grew, and identify new factors and determinants at the root of the entrepreneurial behavior in these countries.

11.3 EXOGENOUS ISSUES: EXPLAINING BIG BUSINESS BEHAVIOR THROUGH THE BUSINESS ENVIRONMENT

The relatively weak relationships that connected the internal features of the corporations in Italy and Spain to their behavior leads us to the analysis of other features that could also have been important in influencing entrepreneurial behavior, and thus in shaping the strategies and structures of enterprises in the Italian and Spanish context. It does make sense that even different owners, or companies belonging to different industries, could decide to adopt the same behavior if incentives were present in their external environment, which were shared by everyone and which pushed them into a particular direction. Ultimately, the goal of any business owner is to ensure that the company survives by adopting strategies and structure that he considers to be useful to this goal in the context in which the corporation operates. The external environment may therefore have been at least as important as the internal one in shaping the particular strategies and structures of the large corporations in Italy and Spain, namely, the persistence of specialized strategies and of the holding form, and the important role played by some very diversified business groups during specific periods.

Looking at the history of big business in Italy and Spain based on the companies in the population, at least three factors appear to have been influential in molding the strategies and structures in these nations throughout the twentieth century, and in particular its second half: the size and dynamism of the domestic market, the state and the political system's behavior and attitude and the international dynamics and pressures in a context of industrial delay.

Even though the numbers are slightly different within these two nations, both Italy and Spain have been characterized by a market that has been relatively small and only partially dynamic during the last century. Before their economic miracles and the urbanization and modernization processes that occurred in these nations during the 1950s and 1960s, respectively, the business environment was quite tough for companies, and even more so for the big ones. The vast majority of the large corporations in Italy and Spain were oriented toward only domestic markets that were relatively small and poor, and whose demand was not big or dynamic enough to allow them to achieve significant economies of scale in their core activities. Some of them, in particular in the Italian case, tried to go abroad, as was discussed in Chapter 8. However, for relatively small companies from a latecomer nation, venturing abroad was too difficult without protection from foreign competition. On the other hand, throughout the first part of the twentieth century, companies who had the necessary amount of resources found it convenient to enter several industries to create conglomerates and business groups, given the fact that achieving relevant scale economies in one sector was almost impossible, but other opportunities were available in several sectors within these two industrializing countries. In the middle of the century, it is therefore not surprising at all that, within this framework, most of the corporations in Italy and Spain were not big companies that had adopted a related diversification strategy, but rather small corporations that were focused on one single product to sell in the small domestic market or very diversified business groups that had entered several activities. The small size of the market thus helps to explain both the strategies of high specialization and of high diversification pursued by big businesses in these nations.

Following their economic miracles, the markets in Italy and Spain became increasingly large. Nevertheless, the protection that companies enjoyed in the domestic market led them to be satisfied, in particular in the Spanish case with a domestic demand that, although increasing, was not that high and discouraged them from trying to become larger or go abroad. Taken in combination with this protection, the domestic market was big enough for most of the large corporations to survive without needing to look for particularly efficient strategies and structures or to go abroad, but not to allow them to become really huge corporations as in the United States or in the bigger and richer European nations.

As has already been stressed, the role of state intervention was decisive when it came to both the lack of diversification and the creation of very diversified holdings in these nations. The protection that governments gave to most companies in fact discouraged them from becoming bigger and diversifying or from adopting new strategies and structures in some industries. But the role of the state was also key in creating and making many very diversified business groups profitable. The largest business groups in Italy and Spain were in fact two state-owned groups, IRI and INI. However, the choice to enter new sectors was also taken by private corporations, who were influenced by state action and policies in many ways.

Fiscal laws and development policies for specific areas, for instance, spurred firms to adopt a strategy of growth only to take advantage of government incentives to invest in the poorer areas of the country or in sectors of "national interest." Companies often expanded without taking into account either their capabilities or the existence of technological opportunities (Pavan 1976; Rinaldi 2003).

In other cases, diversification was a response to the direct entry by state in sectors were private firms operated. Almost in every case, when the Italian and Spanish states intervened in a sector, for instance, through a nationalization, the impact on the enterprises was so great that they noticeably modified their strategies, for example, by diversifying their activities. This was, for instance, what happened in Spain in 1941, when banks started to buy industrial enterprises following indemnifications from the foundation of RENFE through the nationalization of railway firms, of which they were the main shareholders. The same occurred in Italy in 1962, when the nationalization of the electricity suppliers and the foundation of ENEL turned the previously private companies into very diversified companies (Zanetti 1994; Bruno and Segreto 1996; Carreras 2003). Nevertheless, very often similar effects also came about as a result of state actions on a smaller scale (Valdaliso Gago 2004).

The close relationship that most of the largest companies had with the government also meant that moving into unrelated diversification was sometimes not a strategic choice, but a duty. Firms were frequently forced by governments to determine their own strategies and structures, not with the aim of pursuing economic efficiency or maximizing their profits but to pursue political and social outcomes. The rescue of other enterprises in particular was something from which big businesses could not escape and that often forced them to change their strategies and transform themselves into unrelated diversified holdings. This was evident, in particular, in state-owned enterprises, as has been already mentioned. However, private firms often also had to rescue failing enterprises if they wanted to continue receiving state help and protection (e.g., Amatori and Colli 1999, 295).

According to Mauro Guillén (2001), the intervention by and attitude of the state were crucial in providing entrepreneurs with incentives to create diversified holdings in Francoist Spain, based on its economic policies on foreign trade and investment. The economic policies pursued by the state in particular had a strong impact on the rise of business groups whose core skill lay in taking advantage of a number of asymmetric conditions that protected local companies from foreign products and companies, and basically forced multinationals to enter the country only in partnership with a Spanish firm (Binda 2008). Whoever could have good relationships with politicians and representatives of foreign multinationals was able, despite Spain's economic and technological backwardness, to successfully undertake many different activities. The key to success was to combine state-provided advantages (concessions and protection), the national market and its resources (workforce, raw materials) and resources from foreign countries (capital and technologies) to enter different product markets (Guillén 2001). Also in this case, the unrelated business strategy and the holding structure represented good ways of exploiting the opportunities provided by the local environment, which allowed companies to achieve high levels of profitability at least in the medium term. Finally, unrelated diversification has very recently also been indirectly a consequence of the process of privatization of some formerly state-owned companies.

Last but not least, in order to understand the factors that influenced the strategic and structural dynamics of big business in Italy and Spain, it is necessary to remember the increasing international pressure applied during this period on two nations that, even though to a different extent, were industrial latecomers with several still weak corporations. The sudden need to create big corporations that had to be able to compete with the foreign giants probably strengthened the power of those who were already experiencing growth in some sectors, encouraging them to participate in a variety of businesses with the state's support. Business groups could thus have been the entrepreneurial response to a context of increasing pressure on still quite infant economies. Very diversified business groups brought together a multitude of corporations, most of which were joint ventures between the state, the private sector, banks and foreign capital and which operated in many industries. The business group represented probably in this sense a sort of substitution factor in which "togetherness results in strength." The philosophy not of or–or but of and–and made the survival and growth of business groups in latecomers countries and protected environments possible, because it furthered the interests of different parties who for different reasons needed help (foreigners needed help to enter the market, local companies to accumulate funds and technology, etc.), and allowed them to successfully enter several protected and thus profitable sectors.

As has been observed in Parts II and III, as Italy (first) and Spain (later) were integrated into the European Economic Community and the second wave of globalization started to spread, the protection of local companies gradually decreased and the strategies and structures of the large corporations were reshaped in the new—European and global—context. But the inertia was strong. In some cases, firms were able to adapt their behavior well, but several firms were not able to efficiently adapt their strategies and structures, and in some cases, it was only with the involvement of new foreign owners that new strategies and structures, more effective in the new context than the old, were adopted.

12 Conclusion

12.1 BIG BUSINESS AND THE WEALTH OF ITALY AND SPAIN

This journey through the history of an extensive population of the largest corporations in Italy and in Spain over more than fifty years allows us to observe the dynamics of big business in these two nations from a different perspective to previous studies, and helps to shed light onto the current situation in these countries. Thanks to this study of many large corporations and of their transformations over time at a micro level, it has been possible to identify some important protagonists within the Italian and Spanish economies and to investigate a wider, macro panorama that includes the political, economic and social implications of the existence of big business, providing some general insights into the type of capitalism that existed in these countries, and into the behavior of their large corporations.

With regard to the macro level, this book has investigated the role and dynamics of the major corporations in these Southern European nations by checking the currently common opinion that Italy and Spain are and have been basically countries of small corporations and where large corporations were restricted to the government and a few families. Understanding whether this interpretation is well grounded and correct is an important task, because the attitude that governments and people could adopt in the face of the current economic crisis may be greatly influenced by their ideas of whether or not they are able to rely on a model based on big business, on small corporations, or both in varying proportions.

Looking back at the economic history of these two nations, the empirical analysis has shown that the role of big business was not at all marginal in Italy or in Spain throughout the second part of the twentieth century and that during the economic miracles that characterized the 1950s and 1960s, large corporations were important drivers of growth. As has been shown in the fourth chapter, the contribution of the assets and turnover of big business on the GDP in these Southern European nations is definitely comparable to what is seen in the United States, United Kingdom, France, Germany and Japan. Small and medium-sized enterprises have also played a very important role in complementing the activities of large corporations by creating the business community that has been characteristic of the Western economies and in supporting national growth even more in those periods when large corporations faced serious difficulties. The Italian and Spanish experiences in these terms have been characterized by a size of large enterprise that has been on average smaller than in several other nations, but is still similar when it comes to the "weight" of the "unit" of a large corporation in the economy. The Italian and Spanish economic models of growth were based on a large contribution by big business to the national economy, just as in the most advanced Western economies and, as elsewhere, a number of national champions contributed and still contribute to national development.

The main difference when compared to other nations is thus not seen as much in the role of big business, but more in the identity of the large corporations included in the population observed in this work. Differences can be detected from a historical perspective at least at two levels: the first lies in the sectoral distribution, and the second is the ownership and control of the large firms. Based on an analysis of only national and manufacturing activities, several scholars have underestimated the role of big business in these nations. National manufacturing companies probably did contribute less than did those in other nations to the economic development of these countries. However, when we also take the non-manufacturing sectors and the foreign corporations into account, the picture changes and it is possible to claim that big business was important in these nations as well, albeit with partially different sectoral and ownership dynamics.

The sectoral distribution of large corporations in Italy and Spain was partially different from that seen in the most advanced nations, particularly so before their economic miracles, when industries that had become rather marginal in other nations continued to be predominant and other, more modern industries were late to develop. When the sectoral distribution of the largest corporations in these nations definitively converged towards that of other countries, a big difference in the ownership structures of big business became more evident: more foreign multinationals were present in the Italian and Spanish big business panorama. These companies entered Italy and Spain to complement an industrial distribution in which local corporations either did not try or failed to succeed in creating and developing activities in the Second and Third Industrial Revolution sectors. The owners of the domestically owned large corporations were different from those at the helm of public companies in the United States, but not that different from those in other European nations. The state, families and banks were protagonists of the largest corporations also in France and Germany. The main differences in Italy and Spain lie in the extent of direct state ownership of large corporations and the strong support that families and banks companies received in order to remain in charge, thanks in part to the large influence they had over a historically weak political class that struggled to obtain and maintain consensus and looked more at the short than at the long term.

By drawing on the results of the study of the populations of large corporations during the twentieth century, it is thus possible to move away from the interpretation of Italy and Spain as countries of small and medium-sized companies. Big business was important, and in some periods crucial, in these nations. We should also mention the classical interpretation of Italian and Spanish big business as dominated by the state, families and, in Spain, banks. The analysis of large populations of big businesses has allowed us to substantially confirm this view. Nevertheless, other actors were also important and deserve more attention in future analyses, although recent historical studies are increasingly dealing with them. The first of these actors are foreign multinationals, which were real substitution factors when the local initiative failed in developing large corporations in some fields. The second is the network. Big business in these nations was possible and successful thanks to the many relationships that connected governments, families, banks and foreign investors. By moving the network at the center of the investigation, and considering it as a main unit of analysis, the role of the state and of the families does not look as overwhelming. The state and families seem instead to have been pieces, albeit important pieces, of scaffolding that could not have remained standing without the decisive contribution of other actors, such as banks and multinationals, in creating an extensive system of large corporations.

12.2 STRATEGY AND STRUCTURE: WHAT CONVERGENCE?

The empirical investigation into the large corporations of two Southern European nations has also allowed us to contribute to the debate on the strategies and structures of the large corporations across the world and on their hypothetical convergence, a debate that has set both historians and management scholars on fire for several decades.

The large, diversified and multidivisional US corporation represented, for a long time, the main paradigm toward which the advanced world seemed destined to converge. Even though the history and context was different in every country, the rationality in pursuing the "most efficient" strategies and structures was identified by many scholars as the main explanation for the convergence of the forms of behavior of the largest corporations in the more developed Western nations since the golden age. However, the Italian and Spanish experience shows that, even in modern industrialized Western countries, big business can be different and does not follow exactly the same path of development that characterized the US corporations. Diversified and multidivisional companies spread, but at a relatively late stage, and the phenomenon had a less extensive reach in the long term. On the other hand, alternative forms of enterprise, relatively "small" and focused large corporations as well as very big and diversified business groups, led the big business panorama of these nations in the long term.

When considered from the perspective offered by studies on the strategies and structures of the large corporations in the United States and in the most advanced European nations, Italy and Spain probably appear as "divergent" countries, which adopted the strategy of related diversification and the M-form with little enthusiasm during the second part of the twentieth century. However, the alternative strategies that spread in these nations were not unique at all. Specialized large corporations continue to exist all over the world and, according to recent studies, have even increased in number in recent years. Business groups moreover not only characterized the first stages of industrialization in the large majority of countries, but probably also represent the most common and persistent organizational form in many nations nowadays, both in Mediterranean Europe and at a global level.

Does all of this mean that contextualist scholars were absolutely right and that Chandler can be forgotten, at least in Southern Europe? Not at all! Italy and Spain probably represent the middle ground, in which several large corporations adopted alternative strategies and structures in order to grow, but where the Chandlerian "modern enterprise" were also far from being rejected, and the M-form is currently proving increasingly successful among the most profitable companies in these countries. Which option they chose has probably depended on the aims of the corporation and on the environment in which they operated in each historical period. The related diversification and the multidivisional structure spread more extensively when and where companies in a certain sector felt more pressure to look for profits and to operate in a market-driven context, with a low level of state protection and stronger international competition both in the domestic and global arena. In these contexts, the large corporations in Italy and Spain tended to converge more towards the paradigm described by Chandler. On the other hand, the convergence towards the alternative pattern of development of large corporations, that is, the creation of business groups, has been stronger when and where the political and international conditions provided incentives, or made it necessary, for corporations to maintain or increase their profitability not by achieving increased technological or economic efficiency or by lowering their unit costs, but through the exploitation of political connections and advantages provided by the state or of asymmetries that prevented foreign investors from operating freely in the country.

Finally, the empirical evidence on Italy and Spain presented in this book tries to reflect the important transformations that big business has undergone in recent decades, in terms of their industry categorization, the relationship between services and manufacturing and the role of foreign direct investment in the second global economy. The "divergence" in the strategies and structures of the large corporations in Italy and Spain during the second part of the twentieth century should be interpreted by also taking into account the fact that most investigations on strategies and structures from a historical perspective have remained based on Chandler's original definition of big business as observed in the United States shortly after World War II, namely, a national and manufacturing-based big business. Analyzing the largest national manufacturing enterprises in the United States, United Kingdom, Germany and France did make sense in the age of "Strategy and Structure," when most of the large corporations in these nations were domestically owned companies that operated in the Second Industrial Revolution sectors and whose increased efficiency was due to their adoption of a related diversification strategy and of the multidivisional structure.

However, Second Industrial Revolution domestically owned corporations represented only a part of the big business panorama in Italy and Spain as well as in most nations across the world during the second half of the twentieth century, and even more so in the most recent decades. Many large companies belonged to other industrial technological paradigms, and the services sectors also became very important. At the same time, in latecomer countries, large corporations that are nonmanufacturing or typical of the Second Industrial Revolution can be companies that belong to foreign investors, divisions of foreign multinationals that did not adopt a diversification strategy abroad or diversified foreign subsidiaries with a multidivisional structure. This phenomenon may have increased in the second global economy and with the consolidation of the process of European integration. Seen from this perspective, the coexistence of diversified and multidivisional corporations, business groups and relatively small and focused big businesses within the big business panorama of the second half of the twentieth century can be easily understood.

Within this framework, in order to study big business, nonmanufacturing corporations and subsidiaries of foreign multinationals should thus also be included in the research. Both services companies and foreign firms played an important role alongside the national manufacturing enterprises. The most efficient form of behavior for this kinds of large corporation, if it actually exists, still remains largely unexplored.

Appendix

Table 1a The 100 largest nonfinancial firms in Italy, 1950

No.	Company	Sector	Assets (Lire)
1	Edison	Eli	193,801,191,000
2	FIAT	Tre	181,693,416,000
3	Montecatini	Che	137,991,000,000
4	SIP	Eli	98,483,294,000
5	Terni	Mec	78,463,354,000
6	Ilva Alti Forni e Acciaierie d'Italia	Mec	71,935,569,000
7	Cantieri Riuniti dell'Adriatico	Shi	69,416,349,000
8	SADE	Eli	66,058,229,000
9	SME	Eli	64,388,573,000
10	Termoelettrica veneta	Eli	60,975,876,000
11	Ansaldo	Mec	55,670,328,000
12	Finmeccanica	Mec	55,624,375,000
13	Pirelli & C.	Rub	53,048,905,000
14	SRE	Eli	38,558,423,000
15	Società Elettrica Selt Valdarno	Eli	36,977,412,000
16	Eridania Zuccherifici Nazionali	Foo	36,833,472,000
17	Vizzola	Eli	34,951,654,000
18	Esso Standard Italiana	Pet	33,704,762,000
19	CIELI	Eli	33,016,909,000
20	Generale Elettrica Sicilia	Eli	32,738,413,000
21	AGIP	Pet	29,914,496,000
22	SNIA Viscosa	Che	28,281,112,000
23	Finsider	Mec	25,696,508,000
24	Italiana Gas – Italgas	Eli	25,077,520,000
25	Alfa Romeo	Tre	24,902,176,000
26	Orobia	Eli	22,872,684,000

(Continued)

Table 1a (Continued)

No.	Company	Sector	Assets (Lire)
27	Acciaierie e Ferriere Lombarde Falck	Mec	21,221,444,000
28	Nazionale Cogne	Mec	21,138,221,000
29	Shell Italiana	Pet	21,077,300,000
30	CISA – Viscosa	Che	20,521,507,000
31	De Angeli Frua	Tex	20,098,370,000
32	Dalmine	Mec	19,983,603,000
33	G. Marzotto e Figli	Tex	18,502,399,000
34	Unione Esercizi Elettrici (UNES)	Eli	18,324,339,000
35	ANIC	Pet	17,974,394,000
36	Italiana Industria Zuccheri	Foo	17,657,303,000
37	Italcementi	Bri	17,336,747,000
38	Cartiere Burgo	Pub	17,022,404,000
39	San Giorgio Società Anonima Italiana	Shi	16,861,449,000
40	Mobil (Socony Vacuum Italiana)	Pet	16,106,694,000
41	RIV Officine di Villar Perosa	Mec	15,158,162,000
42	Emiliana Esercizi Elettrici	Eli	14,584,662,000
43	Ansaldo San Giorgio	Mec	14,381,157,000
44	Larderello	Eli	14,087,965,000
45	O.M. – Fabbrica Bresciana di Automobili	Tre	14,033,715,000
46	Idroelettrica Sarca – Molveno	Eli	13,521,175,000
47	Linificio Canapificio Nazionale	Tex	13,135,864,000
48	Châtillon	Tex	13,052,215,000
49	Elettrica Sarda	Eli	12,949,107,000
50	Elettrica Bresciana	Eli	12,934,865,000
51	Lancia	Tre	12,873,865,000
52	Franco Tosi	Mec	12,140,557,000
53	Manifatture Cotoniere Meridionali	Tex	12,011,757,000
54	Compagnia Generale Elettricità	Ele	11,999,908,000
55	ACNA	Che	11,929,631,000
56	Lanificio Rossi	Tex	11,536,477,000
57	Officine Elettriche Genovesi	Eli	11,426,690,000
58	Ovesticino	Eli	11,398,094,000
59	Elettrica Campania	Eli	11,150,686,000
60	Società Mineraria Carbonifera Sarda	Min	11,041,402,000
61	Ercole Marelli	Ele	10,426,437,000
62	Agricola Industriale Cellulosa Italiana	Che	10,213,998,000
63	Montevecchio	Min	10,084,602,000
64	Dinamo	Eli	9,625,200,000

65	Cantieri Navali Riuniti	Shi	9,480,778,000
66	Saccarifera Lombarda	Foo	9,476,013,000
67	Cotonificio Vittorio Olcese	Tex	9,390,344,000
68	Magneti Marelli	Ele	9,344,910,000
69	Savigliano	Mec	9,083,916,000
70	Vetrocoke	Bri	8,956,187,000
71	Generale Pugliese Elettricità	Eli	8,909,687,000
72	Piaggio & C.	Tre	8,855,781,000
73	SISMA	Mec	8,837,830,000
74	Idroelettrica Medio Adige	Eli	8,644,773,000
75	Piemonte Centrale Elettricità	Eli	8,581,447,000
76	RUMIANCA	Che	8,499,578,000
77	Officine Galileo	Oma	8,272,974,000
78	Pertusola	Min	8,258,120,000
79	Aquila	Pet	8,236,967,000
80	Idroelettrica Subalpina	Eli	8,130,743,000
81	Mira Lanza	Che	7,930,267,000
82	Innocenti	Tre	7,863,751,000
83	Michelin Italiana	Rub	7,755,786,000
84	Nebiolo	Mec	7,473,900,000
85	Cucirini Cantoni Coats	Tex	6,979,939,000
86	Cantieri del Tirreno	Shi	6,864,072,000
87	Pignone	Mec	6,704,864,000
88	Cotonificio Valle di Susa	Tex	6,592,903,000
89	Distillerie Italiane	Foo	6,561,907,000
90	SIRTI	Pos	6,522,950,000
91	Bombrini Parodi Delfino	Che	6,349,985,000
92	Napoletana d'Illuminazione e Scaldamento	Eli	6,263,939,000
93	Monteponi	Min	6,234,665,000
94	Saffa – Società Fabbriche Fiammiferi ed Affini	Pub	6,184,618,000
95	Idroelettrica Alta Toscana – SIDAT	Eli	6,086,083,000
96	IROM – Industria Raffinazione Olii Minerali	Pet	6,066,695,000
97	Tecnomasio (Tecnomasio Italiano Brown Boveri)	Mec	6,049,231,000
98	Ferrania	Che	5,907,604,000
99	Manifattura Lane Borgosesia	Tex	5,717,739,000
100	Liquigas	Eli	5,537,773,000

Note: Bri = brick, pottery, glass and cement; Che = chemicals and pharmaceuticals; Ele = electronic and instrument equipment; Eli = electricity, gas, and water supply; Foo = food, drink and tobacco; Mec = mechanical engineering and metals; Min = mining; Oma = other manufacturing activities; Pet = petroleum; Pos = post and telecommunications; Pub = printing, paper and publishing; Rub = rubber and plastics; Shi = shipbuilding; Tex = textiles and clothing; Tre = transportation equipment.

Table 1b Main sector, ownership, strategy and structure of large groups in Italy, 1950

Company			Sector	Own.	Div.	Int.	Str.
IRI	Finsider	Terni	Oth	Sta	Ub	Phmo	Md
		Ilva					
		Finsider					
		Dalmine					
	Finmeccanica	Cant. Riuniti Adriatico					
		Finmeccanica					
		Ansaldo					
		Alfa Romeo					
		San Giorgio					
		Ansaldo San Giorgio					
	SIP	Vizzola					
		Piem. Cen. El.					
	SME	UNES					
		El. Campania					
		Gen. Pugl. El.					
	Manifatture Cotoniere Meridionali						
FIAT	RIV Off. Villar Perosa		Tre	Per	Ub	Phmo	Hol
	O.M. – Bresciana Auto						
	Cantieri Navali Riuniti						
	Vetrocoke						
	Ferrania						
Montecatini	Montevecchio		Che	Dis	Ub	Hmo	Hol
	Monteponi						
SADE	Termoelettrica Veneta		Eli	Per	Ub	Hmo	Hol
Edison	CIELI	Off. El. Gen.	Eli	Dis	Rb	Hmo	Hol
	Orobia						
	Emiliana Es. Elettrici						
	Elettrica Bresciana						
	Ovesticino						
	Dinamo						
	SISMA						
	Idr. Medio Adige						
	Idr. Subalpina						
La Centrale	SRE		Eli	Fir	Rb	Hmo	Hol
	Società Elettrica Selt Valdarno						
Snia Viscosa	CISA – Viscosa		Che	Dis	Ub	Pio	Hol
	Agricola Industriale Cellulosa Italiana						
	Cot. Vittorio Olcese						
	Pignone						
AGIP	IROM – Industria Raffinazione		Pet	Sta	Rb	Phmo	Hol
	Olii Minerali						
	ANIC	ACNA					

Bastogi	Gen. Elett. Sicilia El. Sarda Officine Galileo	Eli	Fir	Ub	Hmo	Hol
Pirelli & C.		Rub	Per	Rb	Pio	F/H
Eridania	Saccarifera Lombarda Distillerie Italiane	Foo	Fir	Db	Hmo	Hol
Esso Standard Italiana		Pet	For	Rb	Phmo	F
Falck	Franco Tosi	Mec	Per	Rb	Hmo	F/H
Italgas		Eli	Dis	Db	Hmo	F/H
Gruppo Borletti	Lin. Canap. Nazionale	Mec	Per	Ub	Hmo	Hol
Nazionale Cogne		Mec	Sta	Db	Hmo	F
Shell Italiana		Pet	For	Rb	Hmo	F
De Angeli Frua		Tex	Per	Rb	*	F
G. Marzotto e Figli		Tex	Per	Rb	Hmo	F
Italiana Industria Zuccheri		Foo	Per	Db	Hmo	F
Italcementi		Bri	Per	Db	Hmo	F/H
Cartiere Burgo		Pub	Per	Db	Hmo	F/H
Mobil (Socony Vacuum Italiana)		Pet	For	Rb	Pio	F
Larderello		Eli	Per	Rb	Hmo	F
Idroelettrica Sarca – Molveno		Eli	Fir	Sb	Hmo	F
Châtillon		Tex	Fir	Sb	*	F
Lancia		Tre	Per	Db	Hmo	F
Compagnia Generale Elettricità		Ele	For	Db	Hmo	F
Lanificio Rossi		Tex	Per	Sb	Hmo	F
Società Mineraria Carbonifera Sarda		Min	Per	Sb	Hmo	F
Ercole Marelli		Ele	Per	Rb	Hmo	F/H
Magneti Marelli		Ele	Fir	Rb	Phmo	F
Savigliano		Mec	*	Db	Phmo	F
Piaggio & C.		Tre	Per	Rb	*	F
RUMIANCA		Che	Per	Rb	*	Hol
Società Mineraria e Metallurgica di Pertusola		Min	For	Db	*	F
Aquila		Pet	For	Sb	Hmo	F
Mira Lanza		Che	Per	Db	Hmo	F/H
Innocenti		Tre	Per	Db	Phmo	F/H
Michelin Italiana		Rub	For	Sb	Hmo	F
Nebiolo		Mec	*	Db	*	F
Cucirini Cantoni Coats		Tex	For	Sb	Hmo	F

(*Continued*)

Table 1b (Continued)

Company	Sector	Own.	Div.	Int.	Str.
Cantieri del Tirreno	Shi	*	Db	*	F
Cotonificio Valle di Susa	Tex	Per	Sb	Hmo	F
SIRTI	Pos	Fir	Sb	Hmo	F
Bombrini Parodi Delfino	Che	Per	Ub	*	F
Napoletana d'Illuminazione e Scaldamento	Eli	*	Sb	Hmo	F
Saffa	Pub	Per	Db	Hmo	F
Idroelettrica Alta Toscana – SIDAT	Eli	*	Sb	Hmo	F
Tecnomasio (Tecnomasio Italiano Brown Boveri)	Mec	For	Db	Hmo	F
Manifattura Lane Borgosesia	Tex	Per	Sb	Hmo	F
Liquigas	Eli	Dis	Db	Hmo	F/H

Note: * = unknown; Bri = brick, pottery, glass and cement; Che = chemicals and pharmaceuticals; Db = dominant business; Dis = dispersed; Div = product diversification; Ele = electrical and instrument engineering; Eli = electricity, gas and water supply; F = functional; F/H = functional/holding; Fir = firm; Foo = food, drink and tobacco; For = foreign; Hmo = home market oriented; Hol = holding; Int = internationalization; Md = multidivisional; Mec = mechanical engineering and metals; Min = mining; Oth = other; Own = ownership; Per = personal; Pet = petroleum; Phmo = partly home market oriented; Pio = partly internationally oriented; Pub = printing, paper and publishing; Rb = related business; Rub = rubber and plastics; Sb = single business; Shi = shipbuilding; Sta = state; Str = organizational structure; Tex = textile and clothing; Tre = transportation equipment; Ub = unrelated business.

Table 2a The 100 largest nonfinancial firms in Italy, 1973

No.	Company	Sector	Turnover (Lire)
1	FIAT	Tre	2,370,376,000,000
2	AGIP	Pet	1,670,095,000,000
3	ENEL	Eli	1,403,287,271,376
4	Montedison	Che	1,082,219,000,000
5	Pirelli Spa	Rub	1,500,691,000,000
6	Italsider	Mec	1,082,219,000,000
7	SIP – Italiana Esercizio Telefonico	Pos	842,942,000,000
8	Esso Italiana	Pet	808,210,000,000
9	Shell Italiana	Pet	640,095,000,000
10	Alfa Romeo	Tre	434,790,000,000
11	Standa	Who	403,261,000,000
12	La Rinascente	Who	373,611,000,000
13	ANIC	Che	350,328,000,000
14	BP Italiana	Pet	349,445,000,000
15	Alitalia	Tra	331,934,000,000
16	Total	Pet	311,000,000,000
17	Mobil Oil Italiana	Pet	309,357,000,000
18	SNIA Viscosa	Tex	307,789,000,000
19	SNAM	Eli	304,857,000,000
20	IBM Italia	Com	289,026,000,000
21	Italiana Resine – SIR	Che	277,300,000,000
22	Ing. C. Olivetti & C.	Mec	254,594,000,000
23	Industrie A. Zanussi	Ele	230,845,000,000
24	Montefibre	Tex	207,496,000,000
25	Chevron Oil Italiana	Pet	207,288,000,000
26	Italcantieri	Shi	197,453,000,000
27	Dalmine	Mec	196,223,000,000
28	Italiana Telecomunicazioni Siemens	Ele	193,700,000,000
29	RAI – Radiotelevisione Italiana	Rec	190,985,000,000
30	Acciaierie Ferriere Lombarde Falck	Mec	176,497,000,000
31	Sidercomit	Who	171,377,000,000
32	API – Anonima Petroli Italiana	Pet	158,077,000,000
33	Philips	Ele	150,390,000,000
34	Alimont	Foo	145,835,000,000
35	Autostrade – Concess. Costr. Autost.	Con	141,502,000,000

(*Continued*)

Table 2a (Continued)

No.	Company	Sector	Turnover (Lire)
36	Fina Italiana	Pet	138,415,000,000
37	Italimpianti	Mec	137,722,000,000
38	Galbani	Foo	137,027,000,000
39	Acciaierie di Piombino	Mec	132,975,000,000
40	Gulf Italiana	Pet	127,424,000,000
41	Fabbrica Ital. Magneti Marelli	Ele	125,855,000,000
42	SAIPEM	Eli	125,703,000,000
43	Star – Stabilimento Alimentare	Foo	125,217,000,000
44	Eridania	Foo	124,518,000,000
45	SARAS – Raffinerie Sarde	Pet	120,287,000,000
46	IBP – Industrie Buitoni Perugina	Foo	118,061,000,000
47	Generale Supermercati – G. S.	Who	115,828,000,000
48	RIV – SKF – Officine Villar Perosa	Mec	113,785,000,000
49	SAROM Raffinazione	Pet	113,512,000,000
50	Arnoldo Mondadori Editore	Pub	108,522,000,000
51	Amoco Italia	Pet	106,829,000,000
52	SNAM Progetti	Con	106,326,000,000
53	CEAT	Rub	104,946,000,000
54	Lancia & C.	Tre	104,423,000,000
55	Terni	Mec	102,950,000,000
56	Ford Italiana	Who	102,125,000,000
57	IRE – Ind. Riunite Eurodomestici	Ele	98,761,000,000
58	Italiana Condotte Acqua	Con	98,353,000,000
59	Ferrero & C.	Foo	97,762,000,000
60	Renault Italia	Who	90,385,000,000
61	Nuovo Pignone	Mec	89,289,000,000
62	Motta	Foo	88,275,000,000
63	3M Italia	Che	86,057,000,000
64	Bayer Italia	Che	85,154,000,000
65	Piaggio & C.	Tre	84,213,000,000
66	Aeritalia	Tre	84,072,000,000
67	Carapelli	Foo	83,145,000,000
68	Face Standard	Ele	81,462,000,000
69	Siemens Elettra	Ele	80,926,000,000
70	Italiana Olii e Risi	Foo	79,840,000,000
71	Carlo Erba	Che	79,803,000,000

72	Supermercati Pam	Who	79,216,000,000
73	Cartiere Burgo	Pub	79,062,000,000
74	Gruppo Finanziario Tessile	Tex	78,604,000,000
75	Citroën Italia	Who	77,524,000,000
76	Metalli Preziosi	Mec	77,195,000,000
77	Lanerossi	Tex	77,165,000,000
78	Gruppo Lepetit	Che	75,849,000,000
79	FATME	Ele	75,582,000,000
80	General Motors Italia	Who	75,218,000,000
81	Chrysler Italia	Who	73,296,000,000
82	Compagnia Tecnica Industrie Petroli	Con	72,054,000,000
83	Rizzoli Editore	Pub	71,560,000,000
84	Alemagna	Foo	71,333,000,000
85	Costruzioni Aeronautiche G. Agusta	Tre	70,821,000,000
86	Italcementi	Bri	70,814,000,000
87	Compagnia Singer	Who	69,379,000,000
88	Nazionale Cogne	Mec	69,270,000,000
89	Costruzioni Autostrade Ital. – SCAI	Con	67,689,000,000
90	Ercole Marelli & C.	Ele	66,445,000,000
91	Manifattura Lane G. Marzotto	Tex	65,941,000,000
92	Mira Lanza	Che	64,679,000,000
93	Garrone	Pet	64,618,000,000
94	Colgate-Palmolive	Che	64,444,000,000
95	RUMIANCA	Che	63,331,000,000
96	ASGEN-Ansaldo San Giorgio	Ele	62,990,000,000
97	CIP ZOO	Foo	62,523,000,000
98	Barilla G. e F.lli	Foo	62,474,000,000
99	Honeywell Informationsystems Italia	Ele	62,200,000,000
100	Locatelli	Foo	62,025,000,000

Note: Bri = brick, pottery, glass and cement; Che = chemicals and pharmaceuticals; Com = computer and related activities; Con = construction; Ele = electronic and instrument equipment; Eli = electricity, gas, and water supply; Foo = food, drink and tobacco; Mec = mechanical engineering and metals; Pet = petroleum; Pos = post and telecommunications; Pub = printing, paper and publishing; Rec = recreational, cultural, and sporting activities; Rub = rubber and plastics; Shi = shipbuilding; Tex = textiles and clothing; Tra = transport; Tre = transportation equipment; Who = wholesale and retail trade.

Table 2b Main sector, ownership, strategy and structure of large groups in Italy, 1973

Company			Sector	Own.	Div.	Int.	Str.
IRI	Finsider	Italsider	Oth	Sta	Ub	Phmo	Md
		Dalmine					
		Sidercomit					
		Terni					
	Finmeccanica	Alfa Romeo					
		Italcantieri					
		Italimpianti					
		ASGEN					
	STET	SIP					
		It. Tel. Siemens					
	Alitalia						
	RAI – Radiotelevisione Italiana						
	SME	Alimont					
		Star					
		G.S.					
		Motta					
		Alemagna					
	Autostrade						
	Costr. Autostrade – SCAI						
	Italstat	It. Cond. Acqua					
IFI	FIAT	Magneti Marelli	Tre	Per	Ub	Phmo	Hol
		Lancia & C.					
	La Rinascente						
ENI	AGIP		Pet	Sta	Ub	Phmo	Md
	ANIC						
	SNAM						
	SAIPEM						
	SNAM Progetti						
	Nuovo Pignone						
	SOFID	Lanerossi					
Montedison	Montedison		Che	Fir	Ub	Phmo	Hol
	Standa						
	SNIA Viscosa						
	Montefibre						
	Carlo Erba						
ENEL			Eli	Sta	Rb	Hmo	F
Pirelli Spa			Rub	Per	Rb	Pio	Md
Esso Italiana			Pet	For	Rb	Phmo	Hol
Shell Italiana			Pet	For	Db	Hmo	F
BP Italiana			Pet	For	Db	Phmo	F/H
SIR	SIR		Che	Per	Ub	Phmo	Hol
	RUMIANCA						

Total	Pet	For	Db	Hmo	F
Mobil Oil Italiana	Pet	For	Rb	Phmo	F
IBM Italia	Com	For	Db	Phmo	Md
Ing. C. Olivetti & C.	Mec	Fir	Rb	Pio	F/H
Gruppo Monti Eridania SAROM Raffinazione	Pet	Per	Ub	Hmo	Hol
Philips IRE	Ele	For	Rb	Phmo	Hol
Industrie A. Zanussi	Ele	Per	Rb	Phmo	Md
Chevron Oil Italiana	Pet	For	Db	Hmo	F/H
Acciaierie Ferriere Lombarde Falck	Mec	Per	Rb	Phmo	F/H
API – Anonima Petroli Italiana	Pet	Per	Sb	Hmo	F
Fina Italiana	Pet	For	Db	Hmo	F
Galbani	Foo	Per	Rb	Phmo	F
Acciaierie di Piombino	Mec	Fir	Sb	Hmo	F
Gulf Italiana	Pet	For	Rb	Hmo	F
SARAS – Raffinerie Sarde	Pet	Per	Sb	Hmo	F
IBP – Industrie Buitoni Perugina	Foo	Per	Rb	Phmo	Md
RIV-SKF – Officine Villar Perosa	Mec	For	Db	Hmo	F
Arnoldo Mondadori Editore	Pub	Per	Rb	Phmo	Md
Amoco Italia	Pet	For	Db	Hmo	F
CEAT	Rub	Per	Rb	Phmo	F/H
Ford Italiana	Who	For	Sb	Hmo	F
Ferrero & Co.	Foo	Per	Db	Pio	Md
Renault Italia	Who	For	Sb	Hmo	F
3M Italia	Che	For	Sb	Hmo	F
Bayer Italia	Che	For	Rb	Hmo	F
Piaggio & Co.	Tre	Per	Sb	Phmo	F
Aeritalia	Tre	Fir	Db	Phmo	F
Carapelli	Foo	Per	Sb	*	F
Face Standard	Ele	For	Db	Hmo	F
Siemens Elettra	Ele	For	Rb	Hmo	Md
Ferruzzi Italiana Olii e Risi	Foo	Per	Sb	Pio	Hol
Supermercati Pam	Who	Per	Sb	Hmo	F
Cartiere Burgo	Pub	Per	Db	Hmo	F/H
Gruppo Finanziario Tessile	Tex	Per	Sb	*	F
Citroën Italia	Who	For	Sb	Hmo	F
Metalli Preziosi	Mec	For	Db	Hmo	F
Gruppo Lepetit	Che	For	Db	Pio	Md

(Continued)

224 *Appendix*

Table 2b (Continued)

Company	Sector	Own.	Div.	Int.	Str.
FATME Ericsson	Ele	For	Db	*	F
General Motors Italia	Who	For	Sb	Hmo	F
Chrysler Italia	Who	For	Sb	Hmo	F
Compagnia Tecnica Industrie Petroli	Con	For	Sb	Pio	F
Rizzoli Editore	Pub	Per	Rb	Phmo	F/H
Costruzioni Aeronautiche G. Agusta	Tre	Per	Db	Phmo	F/H
Italmobiliare Italcementi	Bri	Per	Ub	Hmo	Hol
Compagnia Singer	Who	For	Rb	Hmo	F
EGAM Nazionale Cogne	Oth	Sta	Ub	Hmo	Hol
Ercole Marelli & C.	Ele	Per	Rb	Phmo	Md
Manifattura Lane G. Marzotto	Tex	Per	Rb	Phmo	Md
Mira Lanza	Che	Per	Db	Hmo	F/H
Garrone	Pet	Per	Sb	Hmo	F
Colgate-Palmolive	Che	For	Rb	Hmo	F
Liquigas CIP ZOO	Eli	Dis	Ub	Hmo	Hol
Barilla G. e F.lli	Foo	For	Db	*	F
Honeywell Informationsystems Italia	Ele	For	Sb	Hmo	F
Locatelli	Foo	Per	Sb	*	F

Note: * = unknown; Bri = brick, pottery, glass and cement; Che = chemicals and pharmaceuticals; Db = dominant business; Dis = dispersed; Div = product diversification; Ele = electrical and instrument engineering; Eli = electricity, gas and water supply; F = functional; F/H = functional/ holding; Fir = firm; Foo = food, drink and tobacco; For = foreign; Hmo = home market oriented; Hol = holding; Int = internationalization; Md = multidivisional; Mec = mechanical engineering and metals; Min = mining; Oth = other; Own = ownership; Per = personal; Pet = petroleum; Phmo = partly home market oriented; Pio = partly internationally oriented; Pub = printing, paper and publishing; Rb = related business; Rub = rubber and plastics; Sb = single business; Shi = shipbuilding; Sta = state; Str = organizational structure; Tex = textile and clothing; Tre = transportation equipment; Ub = unrelated business.

Table 3a The 100 largest nonfinancial firms in Italy, 1988

No.	Company	Sector	Turnover (Lire)
1	FIAT Auto	Tre	20,263,144,000,000
2	SIP – Italiana Esercizio Telecomunicazioni	Pos	13,374,355,000,000
3	AGIP Petroli	Pet	10,202,444,000,000
4	IBM Italia	Com	6,570,366,000,000
5	SNAM	Eli	6,279,685,000,000
6	AGIP	Pet	5,176,769,000,000
7	Iveco FIAT	Tre	4,770,292,000,000
8	I.P. Italiana Petroli	Pet	4,017,659,000,000
9	Ing. C. Olivetti	Mec	3,827,466,000,000
10	ENICHEM AGIP	Che	3,663,044,000,000
11	Esso Italiana	Pet	3,600,418,000,000
12	Alitalia	Tra	3,524,857,000,000
13	Montedipe	Che	2,881,195,000,000
14	SELM – Società Energia Montedison	Pet	2,755,141,000,000
15	La Rinascente	Who	2,660,616,000,000
16	RAI – Radiotelevisione Italiana	Rec	2,434,343,000,000
17	Standa	Who	2,236,223,000,000
18	Philips	Ele	2,181,388,000,000
19	Publitalia '80 Concessionaria Pubblicità	Oba	1,991,054,000,000
20	Renault	Who	1,934,456,000,000
21	Aeritalia	Tre	1,835,753,000,000
22	Mobil Oil	Pet	1,819,204,000,000
23	Fincantieri – Cantieri Navali Italiani	Shi	1,812,411,000,000
24	FIAT Geotech	Tre	1,799,216,000,000
25	Autostrade – Concessioni e Costruzioni Autostrade	Con	1,687,722,000,000
26	Tamoil Italia	Pet	1,599,040,000,000
27	Fina Italiana	Pet	1,556,239,000,000
28	Barilla G. e F.lli	Foo	1,537,416,000,000
29	API – Anonima Petroli Italiana	Pet	1,534,577,000,000
30	Michelin Italiana	Rub	1,517,149,000,000
31	Industrie Zanussi	Ele	1,472,362,000,000
32	Galbani	Foo	1,444,738,000,000
33	ITALTEL SIT	Ele	1,408,923,000,000
34	Generale Supermercati	Who	1,377,469,000,000

(*Continued*)

Table 3a (Continued)

No.	Company	Sector	Turnover (Lire)
35	Erg Petroli	Pet	1,301,729,000,000
36	Ferrero	Foo	1,296,340,000,000
37	SIPRA – Italiana Pubblicità	Oba	1,285,023,000,000
38	Unil – It	Che	1,258,365,000,000
39	SEVEL – Europea Veicoli Leggeri	Tre	1,236,443,000,000
40	Italimpianti – Italiana Impianti	Mec	1,215,941,000,000
41	SAIPEM	Con	1,211,796,000,000
42	Italiana per il Gas	Eli	1,199,517,000,000
43	Ford Italiana	Who	1,192,924,000,000
44	Benetton	Tex	1,163,759,000,000
45	Teskid	Mec	1,153,757,000,000
46	Peugeot Talbot Automobili Italia	Who	1,134,585,000,000
47	Cartiere Burgo	Pub	1,131,158,000,000
48	RTI – Reti Televisive Italiane	Rec	1,091,853,000,000
49	Arnoldo Mondadori Editore	Pub	1,090,606,000,000
50	ISAB	Pub	1,086,162,000,000
51	SAGIT	Foo	1,071,231,000,000
52	Nuova Samim	Mec	1,062,983,000,000
53	Jacorossi	Pet	1,052,216,000,000
54	Cerealmangimi	Who	1,045,470,000,000
55	FIAT Aviazione	Mec	1,043,980,000,000
56	SNAM Progetti	Con	993,363,000,000
57	Aluminia	Mec	973,504,000,000
58	Ferruzzi Italia	Who	972,231,000,000
59	Bull Hn Information Systems Italia	Ele	960,702,000,000
60	Dalmine	Mec	954,987,000,000
61	Italgrani	Who	940,318,000,000
62	Nuovo Pignone	Mec	933,539,000,000
63	Agrimont	Che	925,210,000,000
64	Siemens	Ele	902,322,000,000
65	Bayer Italia	Che	900,038,000,000
66	Agusta	Tre	883,054,000,000
67	ENICHEM Agricoltura	Che	882,054,000,000
68	Ansaldo Componenti	Mec	867,886,000,000
69	Acciaierie Ferriere Lombarde Falck	Mec	864,297,000,000
70	Procter & Gamble Italia	Che	862,633,000,000

71	Parmalat	Foo	848,285,000,000
72	3M Italia	Che	832,268,000,000
73	RIV – SKF Industrie	Mec	827,825,000,000
74	Manifattura Lane Gaetano Marzotto e Figli	Tex	821,030,000,000
75	Reteitalia	Rec	812,315,000,000
76	Ciba Geigy	Che	809,529,000,000
77	Eridania	Foo	804,449,000,000
78	Canale 5	Rec	793,676,000,000
79	Ansaldo	Mec	777,559,000,000
80	Gruppo Pam	Who	775,819,000,000
81	SARAS – Raffinerie Sarde	Pet	770,551,000,000
82	SIRTI	Pos	764,776,000,000
83	Sidercomit – Siderurgica Commerciale Italiana	Mec	762,218,000,000
84	Kuwait Petroleum Italia	Pet	760,411,000,000
85	Farmitalia Carlo Erba	Che	738,835,000,000
86	Selenia – Industrie Elettroniche Associate	Ele	734,145,000,000
87	Piaggio	Tre	728,685,000,000
88	Italcementi	Con	726,784,000,000
89	Citroën Italia	Who	726,696,000,000
90	Gilardini	Mec	725,164,000,000
91	Montefibre	Che	714,054,000,000
92	Dow Italia	Che	709,305,000,000
93	BMW Italia	Who	709,277,000,000
94	ATI – Aero Trasporti Italiani	Tra	705,309,000,000
95	Oto Melara	Mec	701,613,000,000
96	SNIA Fibre	Che	700,974,000,000
97	Autogrill	Who	691,040,000,000
98	GFT	Tex	684,336,000,000
99	Europa Metalli LMI	Mec	683,671,000,000
100	Star	Foo	675,505,000,000

Note: Che = chemicals and pharmaceuticals; Com = computer and related activities; Con = construction; Ele = electronic and instrument equipment; Eli = electricity, gas, and water supply; Foo = food, drink and tobacco; Mec = mechanical engineering and metals; Oba = other business activities; Pet = petroleum; Pos = post and telecommunications; Pub = printing, paper and publishing; Rec = recreational, cultural, and sporting activities; Rub = rubber and plastics; Shi = shipbuilding; Tex = textiles and clothing; Tra = transport; Tre = transportation equipment; Who = wholesale and retail trade.

Table 3b Main sector, ownership, strategy and structure of large groups in Italy, 1988

Company				Sector	Own.	Div.	Int.	Str.
IRI	STET	SIP		Oth	Sta	Ub	Phmo	Md
		Italtel SIT						
		SIRTI						
		Selenia						
	Finmeccanica Ansaldo	Ansaldo Compon.						
		Aeritalia						
	Finsider	Ilva	Italsider Sidercomit					
			Dalmine					
	SME	Generale Supermercati						
		ALIVAR Autogrill						
		Star						
	Fincantieri – Cantieri Navali Italiani							
	Alitalia	ATI						
	RAI	SIPRA – Italiana Pubblicità						
	Autostrade							
	Italimpianti – Italiana Impianti							
ENI	AGIP	AGIP Pet. Jacorossi		Pet	Sta	Ub	Phmo	Md
		I.P. Italiana Petroli						
		ENICHEM AGIP						
	SNAM	Italiana per il Gas						
	SAIPEM							
	Nuova Samim							
	SNAMprogetti							
	Nuovo Pignone							
	ENICHEM Agricoltura							
IFI	FIAT Auto			Tre	Per	Ub	Phmo	Hol
	FIAT Geotech							
	Teskid							
	Iveco FIAT							
	FIAT Aviazione							
	La Rinascente							
	Galbani							
	Gilardini							
	SNIA BPD	SNIA Fibre						
Ferruzzi	Ferruzzi Italia			Oma	Per	Ub	Phmo	Hol
	Farmitalia Carlo Erba							
	Montedison	Mondedipe						
		Montefibre	Agrimont					
		SELM						
	Eridania							
Fininvest	Standa			Oth	Per	Ub	Hmo	Hol
	Publitalia '80							
	RTI							
	Reteitalia							
	Canale 5							

IBM Italia	Com	For	Rb	Phmo Md
Ing. C. Olivetti	Ele	For	Rb	Pio Md
Esso Italiana	Pet	For	Rb	Hmo F/H
Philips	Ele	For	Rb	Phmo F/H
Renault	Tre	For	Rb	Hmo F/H
Mobil Oil	Pet	For	Rb	Hmo F
Tamoil Italiana	Pet	For	Rb	Hmo F/H
Fina Italiana	Pet	For	Rb	Hmo F
Barilla G. e F.lli	Foo	Per	Rb	Phmo Md
API – Anonima Petroli Italiana	Pet	Per	Rb	Hmo F/H
Michelin Italiana	Rub	For	Db	Hmo F/H
Industrie Zanussi	Ele	For	Rb	Hmo Hol
Erg Petroli	Pet	Per	Rb	Hmo F/H
Ferrero	Foo	Per	Rb	Pio Md
Unil – It SAGIT	Oma	For	Ub	Hmo Md
SEVEL – Europea Veicoli Leggeri	Tre	Fir	Sb	* *
Ford Italiana	Tre	For	Sb	Hmo F/H
Benetton	Tex	Per	Rb	Pio Hol
Peugeot Talbot Automobili Italia	Who	For	Sb	Hmo F
Cartiere Burgo	Pub	Fir	Rb	Phmo F/H
Arnoldo Mondadori Editore	Pub	Fir	Rb	Phmo Md
ISAB	Pet	Fir	Rb	Phmo Md
Cerealmangimi	Who	For	Rb	Hmo F/H
EFIM Aluminia	Mec	Sta	Rb	Phmo Hol
Agusta				
Fin. Breda Oto Melara				
Bull Hn Information Systems Italia	Ele	For	Rb	Phmo F/H
Italgrani	Who	Per	Rb	Hmo F/H
Siemens	Ele	For	Rb	Phmo F
Bayer Italia	Che	For	Rb	Hmo F/H
Acciaierie Ferriere Lombarde Falck	Mec	Per	Rb	Phmo Md
Procter & Gamble Italia	Che	For	Rb	Hmo F/H
Parmalat	Foo	Per	Rb	Hmo Hol
3M Italia	Che	For	Rb	Phmo F/H
RIV – SKF Industrie	Mec	For	Db	Phmo F/H
Manifattura Lane Gaetano Marzotto e Figli	Tex	Per	Ub	Phmo Md
Ciba Geigy	Che	For	Rb	Hmo F/H
Gruppo Pam	Who	Per	Rb	Hmo F/H
SARAS – Raffinerie Sarde	Pet	Per	Rb	Hmo F/H
Kuwait Petroleum Italia	Pet	For	Rb	Hmo F
Piaggio	Tre	Fir	Rb	Phmo Md

(*Continued*)

Table 3b (Continued)

Company		Sector	Own.	Div.	Int.	Str.
Italmobiliare	Italcementi	Bri	Per	Ub	Hmo	Hol
Citroën Italia		Who	For	Rb	Phmo	F/H
Dow Italia		Che	For	Rb	Hmo	F/H
Bmw Italia		Che	For	Rb	Hmo	F
GFT		Tex	Per	Db	Pio	Md
Europa Metalli LMI		Mec	Fir	Rb	Hmo	F

Note: * = unknown; Bri = brick, pottery, glass and cement; Che = chemicals and pharmaceuticals; Db = dominant business; Dis = dispersed; Div = product diversification; Ele = electrical and instrument engineering; Eli = electricity, gas and water supply; F = functional; F/H = functional/holding; Fir = firm; Foo = food, drink and tobacco; For = foreign; Hmo = home market oriented; Hol = holding; Int = internationalization; Md = multidivisional; Mec = mechanical engineering and metals; Min = mining; Oth = other; Own = ownership; Per = personal; Pet = petroleum; Phmo = partly home market oriented; Pio = partly internationally oriented; Pub = printing, paper and publishing; Rb = related business; Rub = rubber and plastics; Sb = single business; Shi = shipbuilding; Sta = state; Str = organizational structure; Tex = textile and clothing; Tre = transportation equipment; Ub = unrelated business.

Table 4a The 100 largest nonfinancial firms in Italy, 2002

No.	Company	Sector	Turnover (Euro)
1	FIAT	Tre	50,815,000,000
2	ENI	Pet	30,555,676,000
3	ENEL Distribuzione	Eli	17,015,889,000
4	Telecom Italia	Pos	16,830,416,000
5	FIAT Auto	Tre	16,459,008,000
6	Edison	Eli	12,174,000,000
7	TIM – Telecom Italia Mobile	Pos	10,665,000,000
8	Finmeccanica	Mec	7,752,080,000
9	Poste Italiane	Pos	7,712,098,000
10	Parmalat Finanziaria	Foo	7,590,014,000
11	ENEL Produzione	Eli	7,044,591,000
12	Esso Italiana	Pet	6,846,346,000
13	Pirelli & C.	Rub	6,733,227,000
14	Gestore Rete di Trasmissione Nazionale	Eli	6,136,850,000
15	ENEL Trade	Eli	5,898,046,000
16	La Rinascente	Who	5,443,564,000
17	Ferrovie dello Stato	Tra	5,084,552,000
18	Riva Acciaio	Mec	4,912,416,000
19	Alitalia – Linee Aeree Italiane	Tra	4,736,748,000
20	Polimeri Europa	Che	4,516,000,000
21	Autogerma	Who	4,427,982,000
22	IBM Italia	Com	4,455,648,000
23	Iveco	Tre	4,356,275,000
24	Italcementi – Fabbriche Riunite Cemento	Bri	4,261,663,000
25	Daimlerchrysler Italia Holding	Who	3,853,033,000
26	Wind Telecomunicazioni	Pos	3,793,758,000
27	Supermarkets Italiani	Who	3,727,419,000
28	Autogrill	Foo	3,356,307,000
29	Kuwait Petroleum Italia	Pet	3,293,054,000
30	Italgas	Eli	3,280,000,000
31	Erg Petroli	Pet	3,219,695,000
32	Ilva	Mec	3,204,123,000
33	SAIPEM	Pet	3,149,000,000
34	Luxottica Group	Oma	3,132,201,000
35	SARAS – Raffinerie Sarde	Pet	3,079,977,000

(*Continued*)

Table 4a (Continued)

No.	Company	Sector	Turnover (Euro)
36	RAI – Radiotelevisione Italiana	Rec	2,764,300,000
37	COFIDE – Compagnia Finanziaria De Benedetti	Oth	2,581,957,000
38	Nuovo Pignone Holding	Mec	2,569,974,000
39	Ford Italia	Who	2,556,809,000
40	Merloni Elettrodomestici	Ele	2,480,225,000
41	Impregilo	Con	2,408,752,000
42	ENEL Energia	Eli	2,391,166,000
43	Autostrade	Con	2,321,616,000
44	ETINERA	Who	2,311,853,000
45	Italgas Più	Eli	2,304,565,000
46	Mediaset	Rec	2,261,200,000
47	Opel Italia	Who	2,260,414,000
48	Shell Italia	Pet	2,225,403,000
49	Gruppo Pam	Who	2,170,143,000
50	HDP – Holding di Partecipazioni Industriali	Pub	2,155,600,000
51	Publitalia '80 – Concessionaria Pubblicità	Oba	2,147,100,000
52	SATA	Tre	2,083,477,000
53	Total Fina Elf Italia	Pet	2,073,029,000
54	GIM – Generale Industrie Metallurgiche	Mec	2,054,940,000
55	Tamoil Italia	Pet	2,053,976,000
56	Fincantieri – Cantieri Navali Italiani	Shi	2,040,910,000
57	Benetton Group	Tex	1,991,823,000
58	Seat Pagine Gialle	Pub	1,990,974,000
59	SMAFIN	Who	1,971,917,000
60	ENEL – Gruppo ENEL	Eli	1,937,977,000
61	RTI – Reti Televisive Italiane	Rec	1,923,814,000
62	De Agostini	Pub	1,901,793,000
63	SEVEL – Societa Europea Veicoli Leggeri	Tre	1,875,572,000
64	Comifar	Who	1,866,856,000
65	API – Anonima Petroli Italiana	Pet	1,857,551,000
66	Barilla Alimentare	Foo	1,838,142,000
67	Marzotto	Tex	1,801,738,000

68	BMW Italia	Who	1,782,653,000
69	Nestlé Italiana	Foo	1,755,524,000
70	SNAM Rete Gas	Eli	1,747,000,000
71	ABB	Mec	1,743,262,000
72	Marcegaglia	Mec	1,694,817,000
73	P. Ferrero & Co.	Foo	1,691,846,000
74	A. Menarini Industrie Farmaceutiche Riunite	Che	1,678,877,000
75	Veronesi Finanziaria	Foo	1,675,158,000
76	Cartiere Burgo	Pub	1,674,481,000
77	Lucchini	Mec	1,669,764,000
78	STmicroelectronics	Ele	1,626,630,000
79	Peugeot Automobili Italia	Who	1,612,388,000
80	Cremonini	Foo	1,570,870,000
81	FIAT – GM PowerTrain Italia	Tre	1,568,905,000
82	ENEL Power	Eli	1,544,078,000
83	Glaxosmithkline	Che	1,541,340,000
84	Teskid	Tre	1,539,337,000
85	FIAT Avio	Tre	1,534,113,000
86	Buzzi Unicem	Bri	1,478,677,000
87	Michelin Italiana	Rub	1,471,048,000
88	Gruppo Coin	Who	1,446,579,000
89	Coop Adriatica	Who	1,438,434,000
90	Pirelli Pneumatici	Rub	1,435,324,000
91	Hewlett Packard Italiana	Com	1,424,662,000
92	SNAM Progetti	Con	1,422,284,000
93	Electrolux Zanussi	Ele	1,400,814,000
94	Thyssenkrupp Acciai Speciali Terni	Mec	1,326,015,000
95	Artsana	Che	1,323,250,000
96	Giorgio Armani	Tex	1,300,894,000
97	Case New Holland Italia	Tre	1,276,126,000
98	ACEA	Eli	1,272,575,000
99	Alenia Aeronautica	Tre	1,261,752,000
100	Ericsson	Ele	1,255,303,000

Note: Bri = brick, pottery, glass and cement; Che = chemicals and pharmaceuticals; Com = computer and related activities; Con = construction; Ele = electronic and instrument equipment; Eli = electricity, gas, and water supply; Foo = food, drink and tobacco; Mec = mechanical engineering and metals; Oba = other business activities; Oma = other manufacturing activities; Oth = Other; Pet = petroleum; Pos = post and telecommunications; Pub = printing, paper and publishing; Rec = recreational, cultural, and sporting activities; Rub = rubber and plastics; Shi = shipbuilding; Tex = textiles and clothing; Tra = transport; Tre = transportation equipment; Who = wholesale and retail trade.

Table 4b Main sector, ownership, strategy and structure of large groups in Italy, 2002

Company			Sector	Own.	Div.	Int.	Str.
IFI	IFIL	La Rinascente SMAFIN	Tre	Per	Ub	Pio	Hol
	FIAT	FIAT Auto Iveco SATA Teksid FIAT Avio Case New Holland It.					
ENI	ENI SAIPEM Italgas Polimeri Europa SNAM	Italgas Più SNAM Rete Gas SNAM Progetti	Pet	Sta	Rb	Phmo	Md
ENEL	ENEL Distribuzione ENEL Produzione Gest. Rete Trasm. Naz. ENEL Trade Wind Telecomunicazioni ENEL – Energia ENEL – Gruppo ENEL ENEL Power		Eli	Sta	Rb	Hmo	Md
Olivetti	Telecom Pir. & C.	Tel. It. Seat TIM Pir. Spa Pirelli Pn.	Oth	Per	Ub	Pio	Hol
Edison			Eli	Fir	Rb	Phmo	Md
Finmeccanica	Alenia Aeronautica		Mec	Sta	Rb	Phmo	Md
Riva Acciaio	Ilva		Mec	Per	Rb	Phmo	F/H
Poste Italiane			Pos	Sta	Ub	Hmo	Md
Edizione Holding		Autogrill Autostrade Benetton Group	Tex	Per	Ub	Pio	Hol
Parmalat Finanziaria			Foo	Per	Ub	Pio	Hol
Esso Italiana			Pet	For	Rb	Phmo	F
Fininvest	Mediaset	Mediaset Publitalia '80 RTI	Rec	Per	Ub	Phmo	Hol
Ferrovie dello Stato			Tra	Sta	Rb	Hmo	F/H
Alitalia			Tra	Sta	Sb	Hmo	F/H
IBM Italia	IBM Italia		Com	For	Rb	Phmo	F
Autogerma			Who	For	Sb	Hmo	F

Italmobiliare	Italcementi	Bri	Per	Ub	Pio	Hol
Daimlerchrysler Italia Holding		Who	For	Sb	Hmo	F/H
Erg	Erg Petroli	Pet	Per	Db	Hmo	Md
Supermarkets Italiani		Who	Per	Rb	Hmo	F
Kuwait Petroleum Italia		Pet	For	Db	Hmo	F/H
Luxottica Group		Oma	Per	Rb	Io	Hol
SARAS – Raffinerie Sarde		Pet	Per	Rb	Hmo	F/H
RAI – Radiotelevisione Italiana		Rec	Sta	Db	Hmo	Md
COFIDE – Compagnia Fnanziaria De Benedetti		Oth	Per	Ub	Phmo	Hol
Nuovo Pignone Holding		Mec	For	Rb	Hmo	F/H
Ford Italia		Who	For	Sb	Hmo	F/H
Fineldo	Merloni Elettrodomestici	Ele	Per	Rb	Pio	Md
ETI	ETINERA	Foo	Sta	Db	Hmo	F/H
Barilla	Barilla Alimentare	Foo	Per	Rb	Pio	F/H
Impregilo		Con	Fir	Db	Phmo	F/H
Opel Italia		Who	For	Sb	Hmo	F
Shell Italia		Pet	For	Rb	Hmo	F/H
GECOS Fin.	Gruppo Pam	Who	Per	Sb	Hmo	F
HDP – Holding di Participazioni Industriali		Pub	Fir	Rb	Phmo	Md
Total Fina Elf Italia		Pet	For	Db	Hmo	F
GIM – Generale Industrie Metallurgiche		Mec	Per	Db	Pio	F/H
Tamoil Italia		Pet	For	Db	Hmo	F/H
Fincantieri – Cantieri Navali Italiani		Shi	Sta	Rb	Pio	Hol
De Agostini		Pub	Per	Ub	Pio	F/H
SEVEL		Tre	Fir	Sb	Pio	F
Comifar		Who	For	Sb	Hmo	Hol
API – Anonima Petroli Italiana		Pet	Per	Db	Hmo	F/H
Marzotto – Manifattura Lane Gaetano Marzotto & Figli		Tex	Per	Db	Pio	Md
BMW Italia		Who	For	Sb	Hmo	F/H
Nestlé Italiana		Foo	For	Rb	Hmo	F
ABB		Mec	For	Rb	Hmo	Md
MARFIN	Marcegaglia	Mec	Per	Ub	Phmo	F/H
P. Ferrero & Co.		Foo	Per	Rb	Pio	F/H
A. Menarini Industrie Farmaceutiche Riunite		Che	Per	Db	Pio	F/H
Veronesi Finanziaria		Foo	Per	Db	Hmo	Hol
Cartiere Burgo		Pub	Per	Db	Pio	F/H
Lucchini		Mec	Per	Sb	Pio	Hol

(*Continued*)

Table 4b (Continued)

Company	Sector	Own.	Div.	Int.	Str.
STMicroelectronics	Ele	Fir	Rb	Io	Md
Peugeot Automobili Italia	Who	For	Sb	Hmo	F
Cremonini	Foo	Per	Rb	Phmo	Md
FIAT – GM Powertrain Italia	Tre	Fir	Sb	Pio	F/H
Glaxosmithkline	Che	For	Db	Hmo	F/H
FIMEDI Buzzi Unicem	Bri	Per	Db	Pio	F/H
Michelin Italiana	Rub	For	Db	Hmo	F
Gruppo Coin	Who	Per	Db	Phmo	F/H
Coop Coop Adriatica	Who	Coo	Rb	Hmo	Hol
Hewlett Packard Italiana	Com	For	Rb	Hmo	Md
Electrolux Zanussi	Ele	For	Rb	Hmo	F
Thyssenkrupp Acciai Speciali Terni	Mec	For	Db	Phmo	F/H
Artsana	Che	Per	Rb	Phmo	Hol
Giorgio Armani	Tex	Per	Rb	Pio	Hol
ACEA	Eli	Sta	Rb	Hmo	Md
Ericsson	Ele	For	Db	Hmo	F/H

Note: * = unknown; Bri = brick, pottery, glass and cement; Che = chemicals and pharmaceuticals; Db = dominant business; Dis = dispersed; Div = product diversification; Ele = electrical and instrument engineering; Eli = electricity, gas and water supply; F = functional; F/H = functional/ holding; Fir = firm; Foo = food, drink and tobacco; For = foreign; Hmo = home market oriented; Hol = holding; Int = internationalization; Md = multidivisional; Mec = mechanical engineering and metals; Min = mining; Oth = other; Own = ownership; Per = personal; Pet = petroleum; Phmo = partly home market oriented; Pio = partly internationally oriented; Pub = printing, paper and publishing; Rb = related business; Rub = rubber and plastics; Sb = single business; Shi = shipbuilding; Sta = state; Str = organizational structure; Tex = textile and clothing; Tre = transportation equipment; Ub = unrelated business.

Table 5a The 100 largest nonfinancial firms in Spain, 1950

No.	Company	Sector	Assets (Pesetas)
1	RENFE	Tra	13,878,237,522
2	Telefónica	Pos	3,098,673,131
3	Bazán	Shi	2,387,264,106
4	CAMPSA	Pet	2,148,673,660
5	Iberduero	Eli	1,764,341,105
6	Calvo Sotelo	Pet	1,699,709,942
7	Naval	Shi	1,270,259,651
8	Hidrola	Eli	1,255,238,805
9	Elcano	Shi	1,165,070,445
10	Altos Hornos de Vizcaya	Mec	1,136,943,373
11	ENSIDESA	Mec	1,000,110,078
12	Tabacalera	Foo	917,995,684
13	Sevillana de Electricidad	Eli	817,168,491
14	Unión Española de Explosivos	Che	786,722,899
15	Electra de Viesgo	Eli	780,026,875
16	CHADE	Eli	696,734,868
17	Unión Eléctrica Madrileña	Eli	687,404,802
18	CEPSA	Pet	667,970,061
19	General Azucarera	Foo	645,297,218
20	ENHER	Eli	638,586,364
21	Cros	Che	621,629,611
22	Trasmediterránea	Tra	608,028,083
23	SEAT	Tre	600,050,222
24	Fenosa	Eli	595,940,887
25	Naviera Aznar	Tra	595,217,566
26	ENASA	Tre	558,150,024
27	SNIACE	Tex	555,762,521
28	Minero Siderúrgica de Ponferrada	Min	530,487,589
29	La Maquinista	Tre	528,567,182
30	ENDESA	Eli	497,302,269
31	Compañía Metropolitano de Madrid	Tre	484,921,614
32	General de Tabacos de Filipinas	Foo	483,199,442
33	Hidroeléctrica del Chorro	Eli	474,538,504
34	Unión Química del Norte de España	Che	472,991,368
35	Gallega de Electricidad	Eli	445,185,200

(*Continued*)

Table 5a (Continued)

No.	Company	Sector	Assets (Pesetas)
36	Mengemor	Eli	432,674,319
37	Tranvías de Barcelona	Tra	420,543,147
38	Eléctricas Reunidas de Zaragoza	Eli	412,377,161
39	Metalúrgica Duro Felguera	Mec	410,834,175
40	Material y Construcciones	Mec	398,549,350
41	Energía Eléctrica de Cataluña	Eli	380,158,320
42	Petróleos de Escombreras	Pet	369,153,029
43	Hidroeléctrica del Cantábrico	Eli	350,201,443
44	Ebro Compañía de Azúcares y Alcoholes	Foo	349,762,455
45	S.dad Esp. Constr. Electro-Mecánicas	Ele	349,398,971
46	Saltos del Sil	Eli	349,046,242
47	S.dad Esp. Constr. "Babcock & Wilcox"	Mec	344,072,842
48	Saltos del Alberche	Eli	342,909,613
49	General de Aguas de Barcelona	Eli	333,876,516
50	Compañía Auxiliar de Ferrocarriles	Tre	329,415,037
51	S.dad Prod. de Fuerzas Motrices	Eli	311,089,836
52	Dragados y Construcciones	Con	306,363,061
53	Saltos del Nansa	Eli	302,515,196
54	Hidrocivil	Con	297,706,922
55	Standard Eléctrica	Ele	296,197,046
56	Unión Eléctrica de Cataluña	Eli	294,727,480
57	SEFANITRO	Che	291,502,921
58	Compañía Industrias Agrícolas	Foo	288,303,167
59	Compañía Trasatlántica	Tra	281,800,631
60	La Papelera Española	Pub	279,767,281
61	Eléctricas Leonesas	Eli	279,435,120
62	Compañía de Luz y Fuerza de Levante	Eli	252,490,479
63	Energía e Industrias Aragonesas	Che	247,229,086
64	FEFASA	Tex	244,640,611
65	Euskalduna	Shi	244,540,036
66	Compañía de Riegos de Levante	Eli	208,453,288
67	Compañía Mercantil Anónima "Iberia"	Tra	207,503,480
68	Compañía Española de Minas del Rif	Min	206,649,919
69	Industrial Asturiana "Santa Bárbara"	Mec	204,247,270
70	Compañía Eléctrica del Langreo	Eli	202,948,252
71	Compañía Anónima Española del Azoe	Che	202,718,387

72	Sociedad Hullera Española	Min	197,545,679
73	Sociedad Industrial Castellana	Foo	192,137,549
74	Compañía Electra Madrid	Eli	187,243,196
75	Compañía Anónima Basconia	Mec	182,350,388
76	Sociedad Ibérica del Nitrógeno	Che	182,038,467
77	Marconi Española	Ele	166,686,852
78	Empresa "Torres Quevedo"	Eli	166,570,262
79	Construcciones Aeronáuticas	Tre	166,124,781
80	S.dad Española de Carburos Metálicos	Che	159,927,067
81	Sociedad Anónima "Echevarría"	Mec	156,203,247
82	Boetticher y Navarro	Mec	155,464,908
83	Sdad. Gral. Inmobiliaria de España	Rea	153,528,022
84	La Unión Resinera Española	Che	151,310,179
85	F.C. Metropolitano de Barcelona	Tre	149,080,816
86	Pesquerías Españolas de Bacalao	Foo	148,115,335
87	Papeleras Reunidas	Pub	142,973,076
88	Fomento de Obras y Construcciones	Con	140,795,358
89	Hilaturas y Tejidos Andaluces	Tex	139,972,608
90	"El Águila"	Foo	139,940,845
91	Compañía General de Inversiones	Rea	139,085,925
92	C.ía de los Ferrocarriles Vascongados	Tra	133,198,380
93	Consorcio Nacional Almadrabero	Foo	132,886,632
94	Española de Electricidad y Gas Lebón	Eli	132,728,095
95	General de Ferrocarriles Catalanes	Tre	130,210,054
96	Urbanizadora Española	Rea	130,133,971
97	Aviación y Comercio	Tra	123,416,337
98	Hidroelétrica Moncabril	Eli	122,115,452
99	Inmobiliaria Alcázar	Rea	120,856,944
100	Compañía Barcelonesa de Electricidad	Eli	117,131,423

Note: Che = chemicals and pharmaceuticals; Con = construction; Ele = electronic and instrument equipment; Eli = electricity, gas, and water supply; Foo = food, drink and tobacco; Mec = mechanical engineering and metals; Min = mining; Pet = petroleum; Pos = post and telecommunications; Pub = printing, paper and publishing; Rea = real estate activities; Shi = shipbuilding; Tex = textiles and clothing; Tra = transport; Tre = transportation equipment.

Table 5b Main sector, ownership, strategy and structure of large groups in Spain, 1950

Company		Sector	Own.	Div.	Int.	Str.
Renfe		Tra	Sta	Sb	Hmo	F
INI	Bazán	Oth	Sta	Ub	Hmo	Hol
	Calvo Sotelo					
	Elcano					
	ENSIDESA					
	ENHER					
	SEAT					
	ENASA					
	ENDESA					
	Petr. de Escombreras					
	FEFASA					
	Iberia					
	Marconi Española					
	Torres Quevedo					
	CASA					
	Boetticher y Navarro					
Banco Central	Naval	Ban	Dis	Ub	Hmo	Hol
	CEPSA					
	General Azucarera					
	Ponferrada					
	MACOSA					
	Saltos del Sil					
	Dragados y Construcciones					
	Saltos del Nansa					
	Eléctricas Leonesas					
	Gral. Inmob. de España					
	C.ía G.ral de Inversiones					
	Ferrocarriles Catalanes					
Banco de Vizcaya	Iberduero	Ban	Per	Ub	Hmo	Hol
	Sevillana de Electricidad					
	Electra de Viesgo					
	SNIACE					
	Metropolitano de Madrid					
	Mengemor					
Hispano Americano Urquijo	Unión Esp. de Explosivos	Ban	Per	Ub	Hmo	Hol
	En. Ind. Riegos de Levante					
	Arag.					
	Un. El. Saltos Alberche					
	Madril.					
	Duro El. del Langreo					

	Felguera						
	S.dad Ibérica del Nitrógeno						
	La Maquinista						
	Hidroeléctrica del Cantábrico						
	C.ía Auxiliar de Ferrocarriles						
Telefónica Nacional de España			Pos	Sta	Db	Hmo	F
Banco de Bilbao	AHV	Basconia	Ban	Per	Ub	Hmo	Hol
	Esp. de Cons. Electro-Mecánicas						
	SEFANITRO						
	Papelera Española						
	Ferrocarriles Vascongados						
CAMPSA			Pet	Ban	Db	Hmo	F
BANESTO	G. Aguas	Lebón	Ban	Dis	Ub	Hmo	Hol
	Bar.						
	Tranvías de Barcelona						
	Ebro						
	Santa Bárbara						
	Carburos Metálicos						
	El Águila						
	Hidroelétrica Moncabril						
Juan March	Compañía Trasmediterránea		Oth	Per	Ub	Hmo	Hol
	Barc. Traction	Barcelonesa de Electricidad					
		Energía Eléctrica de Cataluña					
		Fuerzas Motrices					
		Rie. Fue. Ebro	Un. El. Catal.				
	Inmobiliaria Alcázar						
Hidrola	Luz y Fuerza de Levante		Eli	Ban	Rb	Hmo	F/H
	Compañía Electra Madrid						
Banco Pastor	Fenosa		Ban	Per	Ub	Hmo	Hol
	Gallega de Electricidad						
	Pesquerías Españolas de Bacalao						
Comillas	Tabacos de Filipinas		Oth	Per	Ub	Phmo	Hol
	Compañía Trasatlántica						
	Sociedad Hullera Española						
Tabacalera			Foo	Sta	Ub	Hmo	F
Naviera Aznar	Euskalduna		Tra	Per	Ub	Hmo	Hol
CHADE			Eli	For	Db	Pio	F

(*Continued*)

Table 5b (Continued)

Company		Sector	Own.	Div.	Int.	Str.
Banco Santander	Hidroeléctrica del Chorro La Unión Resinera Española	Ban	Per	Ub	Hmo	Hol
Cros		Che	Per	Db	Hmo	F/H
Unión Química del Norte de España		Che	Per	Db	Hmo	Hol
Eléctricas Reunidas de Zaragoza		Eli	Ban	Db	Hmo	F/H
S.dad Esp. de Construcciones "Babcock & Wilcox"		Mec	Ban	Rb	Hmo	F
Hidrocivil		Con	Per	Sb	Hmo	F
Standard Eléctrica		Ele	*	Db	Hmo	F
Compañía Industrias Agrícolas		Foo	Per	Sb	Hmo	F/H
Española de Minas del Rif		Min	*	Rb	*	F
Española del Azoe		Che	Per	Db	Hmo	F
Sociedad Industrial Castellana		Foo	Ban	Sb	Hmo	F
Sociedad Anónima "Echevarría"		Mec	Per	Rb	Hmo	F
F.C. Metropolitano de Barcelona		Tre	Sta	Sb	Hmo	F
Papeleras Reunidas		Pub	Per	Db	Phmo	F/H
Fomento de Obras y Construcciones		Con	Per	Db	Hmo	F
Hilaturas y Tejidos Andaluces		Tex	Per	Db	Hmo	F
Consorcio Nacional Almadrabero		Foo	Fir	Rb	Hmo	F/H
Urbanizadora Española		Rea	*	Sb	Hmo	F
Aviación y Comercio		Tra	Per	Sb	Hmo	F

Note: * = unknown; Ban = bank/financial; Bri = brick, pottery, glass and cement; Che = chemicals and pharmaceuticals; Db = dominant business; Dis = dispersed; Div = product diversification; Ele = electrical and instrument engineering; Eli = electricity, gas and water supply; F = functional; F/H = functional/holding; Fir = firm; Foo = food, drink and tobacco; For = foreign; Hmo = home market oriented; Hol = holding; Int = internationalization; Md = multidivisional; Mec = mechanical engineering and metals; Min = mining; Oth = other; Own = ownership; Per = personal; Pet = petroleum; Phmo = partly home market oriented; Pio = partly internationally oriented; Pub = printing, paper and publishing; Rb = related business; Rea = real estate activities; Rub = rubber and plastics; Sb = single business; Shi = shipbuilding; Sta = state; Str = organizational structure; Tex = textile and clothing; Tre = transportation equipment; Ub = unrelated business.

Table 6a The 100 largest nonfinancial firms in Spain, 1973

No.	Company	Sector	Turnover (Pesetas)
1	CAMPSA	Pet	107,153,000,000
2	ENSIDESA	Mec	50,169,000,000
3	SEAT	Tre	47,313,000,000
4	Unión Explosivos Río Tinto	Che	40,604,000,000
5	Compañía Telefónica	Pos	35,506,000,000
6	CEPSA	Pet	34,229,000,000
7	Altos Hornos de Vizcaya	Mec	34,099,000,000
8	Dragados y Construcciones	Con	33,378,000,000
9	Astilleros Españoles	Shi	30,936,000,000
10	Iberia	Tra	30,312,000,000
11	RENFE	Tra	28,665,000,000
12	El Corte Inglés	Who	24,435,000,000
13	FASA-Renault	Tra	21,073,000,000
14	REPESA	Pet	20,355,000,000
15	Standard Eléctrica	Ele	19,853,000,000
16	Iberduero	Eli	19,720,000,000
17	Tabacalera	Oth	19,126,000,000
18	ENASA	Tre	17,935,000,000
19	Comercial Pegaso	Who	17,960,000,000
20	Chrysler España	Tre	17,479,000,000
21	Butano	Pet	17,476,000,000
22	Hidroeléctrica Española	Eli	15,897,000,000
23	Cros	Che	15,403,000,000
24	Agromán	Con	14,702,000,000
25	E.N. Calvo Sotelo	Pet	13,973,000,000
26	Nestlé	Foo	13,150,000,000
27	Entrecanales y Tavora	Con	12,900,000,000
28	Petronor	Pet	12,610,000,000
29	Rumasa	Foo	12,190,000,000
30	Galerías Preciados	Who	12,067,000,000
31	INI	Oth	12,011,000,000
32	E.N. Bazán	Shi	12,010,000,000
33	SAFE Michelin	Rub	11,471,000,000
34	Huarte y Compañía	Con	10,975,000,000
35	FECSA	Eli	10,577,000,000

(Continued)

Table 6a (Continued)

No.	Company	Sector	Turnover (Pesetas)
36	Iberenka	Who	10,400,000,000
37	Ebro Cia Azucares y Alco.	Foo	10,400,000,000
38	Cía Sevillana de Electricidad	Eli	10,083,000,000
39	Motor Ibérica	Tre	9,824,000,000
40	Finanzauto	Who	8,742,000,000
41	IBM	Com	8,750,000,000
42	Unión Eléctrica	Eli	8,126,000,000
43	Fomento de Obras y Construcciones	Con	8,112,000,000
44	Petroliber	Pet	8,072,000,000
45	Productos Pirelli	Rub	7,958,000,000
46	SECEM	Mec	7,841,000,000
47	Citroën España	Tre	7,753,000,000
48	La Seda de Barcelona	Tex	7,662,000,000
49	Cubiertas y Tejados	Con	7,535,000,000
50	C.ía Industrial y de Abastecimientos	Foo	7,500,000,000
51	C.ía Industrias Agrícolas	Foo	7,500,000,000
52	Simago	Who	7,429,000,000
53	Río Tinto Patiño	Mec	7,405,000,000
54	Grupo Comercial Laminados	Who	7,300,000,000
55	Bayer Hispania Comercial	Who	7,153,000,000
56	Firestone Hispania	Rub	7,092,000,000
57	Hoechst Ibérica	Che	7,000,000,000
58	Finanzauto y Servicios	Who	6,810,000,000
59	FEMSA	Ele	6,738,000,000
60	Esso Petróleos Españoles	Pet	6,674,000,000
61	Basf Española	Che	6,200,000,000
62	Asland	Bri	6,040,000,000
63	Roca Radiadores	Bri	5,946,000,000
64	Siemens	Ele	5,846,000,000
65	Sandersa Industrial	Foo	5,617,000,000
66	Babcock Wilcox	Mec	5,514,000,000
67	E.N. del Aluminio	Mec	4,284,000,000
68	Dow Unquinesa	Che	5,276,000,000
69	Echevarría	Mec	5,250,000,000
70	Philips Ibérica	Ele	5,241,000,000
71	José María Aristraín	Mec	5,230,000,000

72	Authi	Tre	5,190,000,000
73	La Papelera Española	Pub	5,164,000,000
74	MEVOSA	Tre	5,160,000,000
75	General Eléctrica Española	Ele	5,127,000,000
76	General Azucarera España	Foo	5,115,000,000
77	Shell	Who	5,100,000,000
78	Ulgor	Ele	5,062,000,000
79	E.N. de Celulosa	Pub	5,031,000,000
80	Uralita	Bri	5,000,000,000
81	Unión Agraria Coop. Reus	Foo	4,950,000,000
82	AEG Ibérica Electricidad	Ele	4,918,000,000
83	SNIACE	Che	4,903,000,000
84	Sarrió	Pub	4,900,000,000
85	Piensos Hens	Foo	4,836,000,000
86	Centrales Lecheras Españolas	Foo	4,800,000,000
87	ENHER	Eli	4,757,000,000
88	HUNOSA	Min	4,757,000,000
89	Meliá	Hot	4,750,000,000
90	Nut Export	Foo	4,706,000,000
91	Coca Cola de España	Foo	4,700,000,000
92	Astano	Shi	4,667,000,000
93	Aluminio de Galicia	Mec	4,570,000,000
94	Fenosa	Eli	4,525,000,000
95	Wagons-Lits Cook	Hot	4,486,000,000
96	Ciba Geigy	Che	4,468,000,000
97	E.N. Electricidad	Eli	4,234,000,000
98	González Byass	Foo	4,218,000,000
99	Victor Sagi Publicidad	Oba	4,200,000,000
100	Orbaiceta	Ele	4,200,000,000

Note: Bri = brick, pottery, glass, and cement; Che = chemicals and pharmaceuticals; Com = computer and related activities; Con = construction; Ele = electronic and instrument equipment; Eli = electricity, gas, and water supply; Foo = food, drink and tobacco; Hot = hotels and restaurants; Mec = mechanical engineering and metals; Min = mining; Oba = other business activities; Oth = other; Pet = petroleum; Pos = post and telecommunications; Pub = printing, paper and publishing; Rub = rubber and plastics; Shi = shipbuilding; Tex = textiles and clothing; Tra = transport; Tre = transportation equipment; Who = wholesale and retail trade.

Table 6b Main sector, ownership, strategy and structure of large groups in Spain, 1973

Company			Sector	Own.	Div.	Int.	Str.
INI	ENSIDESA		Oth	Sta	Ub	Phmo	Md
	Compañía Telefónica						
	Astilleros Españoles						
	Iberia						
	REPESA						
	Tabacalera						
	ENASA	Com.					
		Pegaso					
	E.N. Calvo Sotelo						
	INI						
	E.N. Bazán						
	E.N. del Aluminio						
	E.N. de Celulosa						
	ENHER						
	HUNOSA						
	Astano						
	E.N. Electricidad						
CAMPSA			Pet	Ban	Rb	Hmo	F/H
Banco Central	CEPSA		Ban	Dis	Ub	Phmo	Hol
	Dragados y						
	Construcciones						
	General Azucarera						
Hispano Americano – Urquijo	Firestone		Ban	Per	Ub	Phmo	Hol
	Hispania						
	Unión	SECEM					
	Expl.	Río Tinto					
	Río Tinto	Patiño					
SEAT			Tre	For	Rb	Hmo	F/H
BANESTO	Esso Petróleos		Ban	Dis	Ub	Phmo	Hol
	Españoles						
	Cros						
	Agromán						
	Asland						
Banco de Bilbao	Altos Hornos		Ban	Per	Ub	Hmo	Hol
	de Vizcaya						
	La Papelera Española						
Banco de Vizcaya	Iberduero		Ban	Per	Ub	Hmo	Hol
	Sevillana de						
	Electricidad						
RENFE			Tra	Sta	Sb	Hmo	F
El Corte Inglés			Who	Per	Rb	Hmo	F/H
FASA-Renault			Tre	For	Rb	Phmo	F/H

Standard Eléctrica		Ele	For	Db	Hmo	F
Chrysler España		Tre	For	Rb	Phmo	Hol
Butano		Pet	Fir	Sb	Hmo	F/H
Hidrola		Eli	Ban	Rb	Hmo	F/H
Grupo March	FECSA Uralita	Oth	Per	Ub	Hmo	Hol
Finanzauto	Finanzauto y Servicios	Who	Per	Sb	Hmo	F/H
Nestlé		Foo	For	Db	Hmo	F
Entrecanales y Tavora		Con	Per	Sb	Hmo	F
Petronor		Pet	Ban	Sb	Phmo	F
Rumasa		Foo	Per	Ub	Phmo	Hol
Galerías Preciados		Who	Per	Sb	Hmo	F/H
SAFE Michelin		Rub	Fpr	Sb	Phmo	F
La Seda de Barcelona	Iberenka	Tex	For	Db	Pio	F/H
Huarte y Compañía		Con	Per	Sb	Hmo	F
Ebro C.ía Azucares y Alco.		Foo	Dis	Sb	Hmo	F/H
Motor Ibérica		Tre	Ban	Db	Hmo	F/H
IBM		Who	For	Rb	Hmo	Md
Unión Eléctrica		Eli	Ban	Rb	Hmo	F/H
Fomento de Obras y Construcciones		Con	Per	Db	Hmo	F/H
Petroliber		Pet	Sta	Sb	Phmo	F
Productos Pirelli		Rub	For	Rb	Hmo	Md
Citroën España		Tre	For	Rb	Phmo	F/H
Cubiertas y Tejados		Con	Per	Sb	Hmo	F/H
C.ía Industrial y de Abastecimientos		Foo	For	Db	Hmo	F
C.ía Industrias Agrícolas		Foo	Per	Db	Hmo	F/H
SIMAGO		Who	For	Sb	Hmo	F/H
Grupo Comercial Laminados		Who	Per	Db	Hmo	F/H
Bayer Hispania Comercial		Who	For	Sb	Hmo	F/H
Hoechst Ibérica		Che	For	Rb	Hmo	F
FEMSA		Ele	Per	Rb	Phmo	F/H
Basf Española		Che	For	Db	Hmo	F
Roca Radiadores		Bri	Per	Rb	Hmo	F
Siemens		Ele	For	Rb	Hmo	Md
Sandersa Industrial		Foo	For	Sb	Hmo	F/H
Babcock Wilcox		Mec	Ban	Rb	Phmo	Md
Dow Unquinesa		Che	For	Db	Hmo	F
Echevarría		Mec	Per	Sb	Hmo	F

(*Continued*)

Table 6b (Continued)

Company		Sector	Own.	Div.	Int.	Str.
Philips Ibérica		Who	For	Sb	Hmo	F/H
José María Aristraín		Mec	Per	Rb	Phmo	F/H
Authi		Tre	For	Db	Phmo	F/H
MEVOSA		Tre	For	Rb	Hmo	F/H
General Eléctrica Española		Ele	For	Rb	Hmo	F/H
Shell		Who	For	Sb	Hmo	F
Ulgor		Ele	Coo	Db	Phmo	F
Unión Agraria Coop. Reus		Foo	Coo	Rb	Hmo	F
AEG Ibérica Electricidad		Ele	For	Db	Hmo	F/H
SNIACE		Che	Ban	Db	Hmo	F/H
Sarrió		Pub	Per	Sb	Phmo	F/H
Piensos Hens		Foo	Per	Sb	Hmo	F
Centrales Lecheras Españolas		Foo	Per	Sb	Hmo	F/H
Meliá		Hot	Per	Rb	Phmo	Md
Nut Export		Foo	Per	Sb	Phmo	F/H
Coca Cola de España		Foo	For	Sb	Hmo	F
Aluminio de Galicia		Mec	For	Rb	Hmo	F
Banco Pastor	Fenosa	Ban	Per	Ub	Hmo	Hol
Wagons-Lits Cook		Hot	For	Db	Hmo	F
Ciba Geigy		Che	For	Db	Hmo	F
González Byass		Foo	Per	Sb	Phmo	F/H
Victor Sagi Publicidad		Oba	Per	Db	Hmo	F
Orbaiceta		Ele	Per	Db	Phmo	F/H

Note: Ban = bank/financial; Bri = brick, pottery, glass and cement; Che = chemicals and plastics; Con = construction; Coo = cooperative/foundation; Db = dominant business; Dis = dispersed; Div = product diversification; Ele = electrical and instrument engineering; Eli = electricity, gas and water supply; F = functional; F/H = functional/holding; Fir = firm; Foo = food, drink and tobacco; For = foreign; Hmo = home market oriented; Hol = holding; Hot = hotels and restaurants; Int = internationalization; Md = multidivisional; Mec = mechanical engineering and metals; Oba = other business activities; Oth = other; Own = ownership; Per = personal; Pet = petroleum; Phmo = partly home market oriented; Pio = partly internationally oriented; Pub = printing, paper and publishing; Rb = related business; Rub = rubber and plastics; Sb = single business; Sta = state; Str = organizational structure; Tex = textile and clothing; Tre = transportation equipment; Ub = unrelated business; Who = wholesale and retail trade.

Table 7a The 100 largest nonfinancial firms in Spain, 1988

No.	Company	Sector	Turnover (Pesetas)
1	Telefónica de España	Pos	612,536,000,000
2	El Corte Inglés	Who	475,282,000,000
3	SEAT	Tre	404,130,000,000
4	FASA-Renault	Tre	382,225,000,000
5	Repsol Petróleo	Pet	374,740,000,000
6	General Motors España	Tre	359,461,000,000
7	Iberia	Tra	334,736,000,000
8	E.N. de Electricidad	Eli	295,852,000,000
9	Ford España	Tre	290,586,000,000
10	Hidroeléctrica Española	Eli	257,080,000,000
11	Tabacalera	Foo	256,073,000,000
12	Española de Petróleos	Pet	251,589,000,000
13	Iberduero	Eli	245,273,000,000
14	Hipermercados Pryca	Who	212,556,000,000
15	Unión Eléctrica Fenosa	Eli	202,732,000,000
16	Sevillana de Electricidad	Eli	189,152,000,000
17	Citroën Hispania	Tre	187,696,000,000
18	IBM España	Com	187,090,000,000
19	Peugeot Talbot España	Tre	176,534,000,000
20	RENFE	Tra	159,678,000,000
21	Dragados y Costrucciones	Con	156,275,000,000
22	E.N. Siderúrgica	Mec	153,321,000,000
23	Fuerzas Eléctricas de Cataluña	Eli	152,580,000,000
24	Auxiliar de Distribucción	Who	147,330,000,000
25	Neumáticos Nichelin	Rub	137,000,000,000
26	CAMPSA	Pet	135,370,000,000
27	Nissan Motor Ibérica	Tre	133,955,000,000
28	Alcampo	Who	121,500,000,000
29	Repsol Química	Che	120,860,000,000
30	ERCROS	Che	119,730,000,000
31	E.N. de Autocamiones	Tre	116,281,000,000
32	Repsol Butano	Pet	112,251,000,000
33	Petróleos del Norte	Pet	106,195,000,000
34	Fomento de Obras y Construcciones	Con	101,212,000,000
35	Mercedes Benz España	Tre	100,835,000,000

(*Continued*)

Table 7a (Continued)

No.	Company	Sector	Turnover (Pesetas)
36	Altos Hornos de Vizcaya	Mec	100,766,000,000
37	Nestlé	Foo	98,319,000,000
38	Cubiertas y Mzov	Con	97,070,000,000
39	Alcatel Standard Eléctrica	Ele	95,931,000,000
40	Galerías Preciados	Who	95,600,000,000
41	Entrecanales y Tavora	Con	91,000,000,000
42	Repsol Exploración	Pet	89,992,000,000
43	E.N. Hidroeléctrica Ribagorzana	Eli	86,998,000,000
44	Ferrovial	Con	86,200,000,000
45	Dow Chemical Ibérica	Che	83,648,000,000
46	Agromán Empresa Constructora	Con	83,375,000,000
47	Mercadona	Who	81,000,000,000
48	FESA Fertilizantes Españoles	Che	80,208,000,000
49	Hoteles Mallorquines Asociados	Hot	80,000,000,000
50	Industria Española del Aluminio	Mec	78,350,000,000
51	Construcciones Aeronáuticas	Tre	77,152,000,000
52	Hoechst Ibérica	Che	77,055,000,000
53	Acerinox	Mec	76,660,000,000
54	CIRSA	Oba	75,900,000,000
55	Hasa	Con	75,000,000,000
56	Industrial y Abastecimientos	Foo	72,500,000,000
57	FIAT Auto España	Who	71,690,000,000
58	Hidroeléctrica del Cantábrico	Eli	66,134,000,000
59	E.N. del Gas	Eli	64,561,000,000
60	Fernando Roque Transp. Internac.	Tra	64,400,000,000
61	Mercados en Origen	Who	62,795,000,000
62	Torras Papel	Pub	62,779,000,000
63	Petróleos del Mediterráneo	Pet	61,490,000,000
64	Viajes Meliá	Hot	60,921,000,000
65	Philips Ibérica	Ele	58,800,000,000
66	Acenor	Mec	58,650,000,000
67	Río Tinto Minera	Min	57,534,000,000
68	Renault Vehículos Industriales	Tre	57,301,000,000
69	Ebro C.ía Azucares y Alcoholes	Foo	56,400,000,000
70	Fábrica Española de Magnetos	Ele	55,974,000,000
71	Firestone Hispania	Rub	55,448,000,000

72	Simago	Who	55,430,000,000
73	Bayer Hispania Comercial	Who	55,000,000,000
74	Danone	Foo	54,900,000,000
75	Huarte	Con	54,293,000,000
76	E.N. Bazán	Shi	52,565,000,000
77	Media Europe España	Oba	52,500,000,000
78	Basf Española	Che	51,536,000,000
79	Hipercor	Who	50,986,000,000
80	Siemens	Ele	50,278,000,000
81	Roca Radiadores	Bri	49,860,000,000
82	Cristalería Española	Bri	48,662,000,000
83	NANTA	Foo	48,579,000,000
84	Sesostris	Who	48,000,000,000
85	Eroski	Who	47,522,000,000
86	Aluminio Español	Mec	47,300,000,000
87	Construcciones y Contratas	Con	47,251,000,000
88	E.N. del Uranio	Min	47,957,000,000
89	Alfa Romeo Española	Who	44,650,000,000
90	Makro Autoservicio Mayorista	Who	44,442,000,000
91	Finanzauto	Who	43,588,000,000
92	E.N. de Celulosa	Pub	43,413,000,000
93	Shell España	Pet	42,473,000,000
94	José María Aristraín	Mec	42,248,000,000
95	Publintegral	Oba	41,812,000,000
96	Eléctricas Reunidas de Zaragoza	Eli	41,175,000,000
97	Sony España	Ele	40,845,000,000
98	Henkel Ibérica	Che	40,700,000,000
99	Sarrió	Pub	40,010,000,000
100	Hidroeléctrica de Cataluña	Eli	39,788,000,000

Note: Bri = brick, pottery, glass and cement; Che = chemicals and pharmaceuticals; Com = computer and related activities; Con = construction; Ele = electronic and instrument equipment; Eli = electricity, gas, and water supply; Foo = food, drink and tobacco; Hot = hotels and restaurants; Mec = mechanical engineering and metals; Oba = other business activities; Pet = petroleum; Pos = post and telecommunications; Pub = printing, paper and publishing; Rub = rubber and plastics; Shi = shipbuilding; Tex = textiles and clothing; Tra = transport; Tre = transportation equipment; Who = wholesale and retail trade

Table 7b Main sector, ownership, strategy and structure of large groups in Spain, 1988

Company			Sector	Own.	Div.	Int.	Str.
INI	Iberia		Oth	Sta	Ub	Phmo	Hol
	E.N. de	Ribagorz.					
	Electricidad	Reun. Zar.					
	E.N. Siderúrgica						
	E.N. de Autocamiones						
	Industria Española						
	del Aluminio						
	Construcciones						
	Aeronáuticas						
	E.N. Bazán						
	Aluminio Español						
	E.N. del Uranio						
	E.N. de Celulosa						
INH	Repsol	Rep. Pet.	Pet	Sta	Rb	Hmo	Hol
		Rep. Qui.					
		Rep. But.					
		Rep. Expl.					
	CAMPSA						
	Petróleos del Norte						
	E.N. del Gas						
Banco Central	Española de Petróleos		Ban	Dis	Ub	Phmo	Md
	Dragados y Costrucciones						
Banco Bilbao	Hidroel.	Hidr. Cat.	Ban	Ban	Ub	Hmo	F/H
Vizcaya	Española						
	Iberduero						
	Altos Hornos de Vizcaya						
Telefónica de España			Pos	Sta	Db	Hmo	F/H
El Corte Inglés	Hipercor		Who	Coo	Rb	Hmo	F/H
Española de Automóviles Turismo			Tre	For	Rb	Phmo	F/H
FASA-Renault	Renault Vehículos		Tre	For	Rb	Phmo	F/H
	Industriales						
General Motors España			Tre	For	Db	Pio	F
Ford España			Tre	For	Db	Phmo	F
Tabacalera			Foo	Sta	Ub	Hmo	Md
Hipermercados Pryca			Who	For	Rb	Hmo	Md
Unión Eléctrica Fenosa			Eli	Ban	Rb	Hmo	F/H
Sevillana de Electricidad			Eli	Ban	Rb	Hmo	F/H
Citroën Hispania			Tre	For	Rb	Phmo	F/H
IBM España			Who	For	Rb	Phmo	F/H
Peugeot Talbot España			Tre	For	Rb	Phmo	F/H

RENFE			Tra	Sta	Sb	Hmo	F/H
Grupo March	Fuerzas Eléctricas de Cataluña Simago		Oth	Per	Ub	Hmo	Hol
Auxiliar de Distribucción			Who	For	Sb	Hmo	F/H
Neumáticos Michelin			Rub	For	Db	Phmo	F
Nissan Motor Ibérica			Tre	For	Rb	Phmo	F/H
Alcampo			Who	For	Sb	Hmo	F
Torras	ERCROS	Fert. Esp. Río Tinto Min.	Oth	For	Ub	Phmo	Hol
	Ebro C.ía Azucares y Alcoholes						
FOC	Construcciones y Contratas		Con	Per	Rb	Hmo	Hol
Mercedes Benz España			Tre	For	Rb	Phmo	F/H
Nestlé			Foo	For	Rb	Hmo	F/H
Ferrovial	Cubiertas y Mzov		Con	Per	Rb	Hmo	Hol
Alcatel Standard Eléctrica			Ele	For	Db	Hmo	Md
Galerías Preciados			Who	For	Sb	Hmo	F
Entrecanales y Tavora			Con	Per	Rb	Hmo	F
Dow Chemical Ibérica			Che	For	Rb	Phmo	F/H
BANESTO	Agromán Acerinox Petr. del Mediterráneo		Con	Dis	Ub	Hmo	Hol
Mercadona			Who	Per	Sb	Hmo	F
Hoteles Mallorquines Asociados			Hot	Per	Db	Hmo	F/H
Hoechst Ibérica			Che	For	Rb	Hmo	F/H
CIRSA			Oba	Per	Rb	Hmo	F/H
Hasa	Huarte		Con	Fir	Rb	Phmo	F/H
Industrial y Abastecimientos			Foo	For	Rb	Phmo	F/H
FIAT Auto Es.	Alfa Romeo Española		Who	For	Sb	Hmo	F/H
Hidroeléctrica del Cantábrico			Eli	Ban	Db	Hmo	F/H
Fernando Roque Transp. Internac.			Tra	For	Db	Hmo	F/H
Mercados en Origen			Who	Sta	Sb	Hmo	F/H
Viajes Meliá			Hot	Per	Rb	Phmo	Hol
Philips Ibérica			Ele	For	Rb	Hmo	F/H
Acenor			Mec	Ban	Rb	Phmo	F/H
Fábrica Española de Magnetos			Ele	For	Rb	Pio	F

(*Continued*)

Table 7b (Continued)

Company	Sector	Own.	Div.	Int.	Str.
Firestone Hispania	Rub	For	Sb	Phmo	F/H
Bayer Hispania Comercial	Who	For	Db	Hmo	F/H
Danone	Foo	For	Rb	Hmo	F/H
Media Europe España	Oba	For	Sb	Hmo	F
Basf Española	Che	For	Rb	Hmo	F/H
Siemens	Ele	For	Rb	Phmo	Md
Roca Radiadores	Bri	Per	Rb	Phmo	F/H
Cristalería Española	Bri	For	Rb	Phmo	Md
NANTA	Foo	For	Rb	Hmo	Hol
Sesostris	Who	For	Sb	Hmo	F
Eroski	Who	Coo	Rb	Hmo	F
Makro Autoservicio Mayorista	Who	For	Sb	Hmo	F/H
Finanzauto	Who	Per	Db	Hmo	F/H
Shell España	Pet	For	Rb	Hmo	Md
José María Aristraín	Mec	Per	Rb	Phmo	F/H
Publintegral	Oba	Per	Sb	Hmo	F
Sony España	Ele	For	Rb	Hmo	F
Henkel Ibérica	Che	For	Rb	Hmo	F/H
Sarrió	Sta	Fir	Rb	Phmo	Md

Note: * = unknown; Ban = bank/financial; Bri = brick, pottery, glass, and cement; Che = chemicals and pharmaceuticals; Con = construction; Coo = cooperative/foundation; Db = dominant business; Dis = dispersed; Div = product diversification; Ele = electrical and instrument engineering; Eli = electricity, gas and water supply; F = functional; F/H = functional/holding; Foo = food, drink and tobacco; For = foreign; Hmo = home market oriented; Hol = holding; Hot = hotels and restaurants; Int = internationalization; Md = multidivisional; Mec = mechanical engineering and metals; Oba = other business activities; Oth = other; Own = ownership; Per = personal; Pet = petroleum; Phmo = partly home market oriented; Pio = partly internationally oriented; Pos = post and telecommunications; Rb = related business; Rub = rubber and plastics; Sb = single business; Str = organizational structure; Tra = transport; Tre = transportation equipment; Ub = unrelated business; Who = wholesale and retail trade.

Table 8a The 100 largest nonfinancial firms in Spain, 2002

No.	Company	Sector	Turnover (Euro)
1	Repsol – YPF	Pet	35,555,000,000
2	Telefónica	Pos	28,411,000,000
3	ENDESA	Eli	16,739,000,000
4	El Corte Inglés	Who	12,587,000,000
5	Iberdrola	Eli	9,594,330,000
6	Comp. Española de Petróleos	Pet	9,348,390,000
7	Mondragón	Oth	9,232,000,000
8	Telefónica Móviles España	Pos	9,139,830,000
9	Telefónica Internacional España	Pos	6,954,110,000
10	Centros Comerciales Carrefour	Who	6,439,340,000
11	Unión Fenosa	Eli	5,831,240,000
12	SEAT	Tre	5,616,320,000
13	Fomento de Construcción y Contratas	Con	5,497,160,000
14	Mercadona	Who	5,377,560,000
15	General Motors Holding España	Tre	5,351,000,000
16	Gas Natural SDG	Eli	5,267,900,000
17	Grupo Ferrovial	Con	5,040,220,000
18	Renault España	Tre	4,875,600,000
19	Volkswagen Audi España	Who	4,522,630,000
20	Ford España	Tre	4,477,850,000
21	ACS Actividades de Constr. y Serv.	Con	4,420,190,000
22	Iberia	Tra	4,407,800,000
23	Acciona	Con	3,414,730,000
24	AUNA Operadores de Telecomunic.	Pos	3,242,000,000
25	BP Oil España	Pet	3,060,060,000
26	Comp. de Distribución Int. Logista	Tra	2,986,380,000
27	CEPSA Estaciones de Servicio	Who	2,961,800,000
28	Vodafone España	Pos	2,931,870,000
29	Daimlerchrysler España	Tre	2,812,520,000
30	Distribuidora Internaci. Aliment.	Who	2,804,640,000
31	Petróleos del Norte	Pet	2,801,250,000
32	Hipercor	Who	2,676,510,000
33	Renault España Comercial	Who	2,622,060,000
34	Alcampo	Who	2,610,900,000
35	Automóviles Citroën España	Who	2,427,380,000

(Continued)

Table 8a (Continued)

No.	Company	Sector	Turnover (Euro)
36	Siemens	Ele	2,413,690,000
37	Volkswagen Navarra	Tre	2,284,050,000
38	Peugeot España	Tre	2,254,180,000
39	Corporación Gestamp	Mec	2,198,000,000
40	Coop. Farmacéutica Española	Who	2,118,240,000
41	Aceralia Grupo Arcelor	Mec	2,087,080,000
42	Ahold Supermercados	Who	2,009,200,000
43	Michelin España Portugal	Rub	1,825,370,000
44	ENAGAS	Eli	1,807,860,000
45	Amadeus Global Travel Distrib.	Hot	1,782,680,000
46	ACS Proyectos, Obras y Construc.	Con	1,676,210,000
47	RENFE	Tra	1,680,570,000
48	Soc. Estatal Correos y Telégrafos	Pos	1,656,440,000
49	Repsol Química	Che	1,604,840,000
50	Grupo Eroski	Who	1,586,790,000
51	Entidad Pública Emp. Aeropuertos	Tra	1,561,910,000
52	Caprabo	Who	1,560,890,000
53	Izar Construcciones Navales	Shi	1,536,840,000
54	Abengoa	Ele	1,521,930,000
55	Iveco Pegaso	Tre	1,521,180,000
56	Nissan Motor Ibérica	Tre	1,502,860,000
57	Globalia Corporación Empresarial	Hot	1,486,200,000
58	Shell España	Who	1,442,660,000
59	Hidroeléctrica del Cantábrico	Eli	1,440,000,000
60	Industria de Diseño Textil	Tex	1,365,500,000
61	Sony España	Ele	1,354,730,000
62	ENDESA Energía	Eli	1,323,210,000
63	Nestlé España	Foo	1,294,080,000
64	Acerinox	Mec	1,197,880,000
65	Dow Chemical Ibérica	Che	1,169,060,000
66	Hewlett Packard Española	Com	1,163,010,000
67	Altadis	Oth	1,158,080,000
68	Viajes El Corte Inglés	Hot	1,134,060,000
69	Makro Autoservicio Mayorista	Who	1,084,820,000
70	Corporación Admira Media	Pos	1,076,200,000
71	Obrascón Huarte Laín	Con	1,073,930,000

72	BMW Ibérica	Who	1,050,990,000
73	Total España	Pet	1,011,500,000
74	IBM	Com	1,005,780,000
75	Reguladora de Compras del Medit.	Who	981,420,000
76	Danone	Foo	972,920,000
77	AGIP España	Who	947,520,000
78	Lidl Supermercados	Who	946,330,000
79	Aceralia Redondos Comercial	Who	938,760,000
80	Zara España	Who	933,360,000
81	Safa Galenica	Who	918,830,000
82	Nissan Motor España	Who	911,560,000
83	Televisión Española	Rec	911,420,000
84	Bsh Electrodomésticos España	Ele	893,720,000
85	Vallehermoso	Con	882,825,000
86	FIAT Auto España	Who	869,680,000
87	Corporación Sidenor	Mec	865,080,000
88	Sagane	Eli	847,220,000
89	Constructora San José	Con	822,020,000
90	Atlantic Copper	Min	816,420,000
91	Grupo El Árbol Distribuc. y Sup.	Who	814,820,000
92	EADS Construcciones Aeronáuticas	Mec	813,250,000
93	Supermercados Sabeco	Who	811,060,000
94	Spanair	Tra	809,540,000
95	Philips Ibérica	Ele	808,110,000
96	Samsung Electronics Iberia	Ele	799,620,000
97	Heineken España	Who	798,160,000
98	Cobega	Foo	790,000,000
99	Roca Corporación Empresarial	Bri	785,430,000
100	Telefónica Data España	Pos	769,760,000

Note: Bri = brick, pottery, glass and cement; Che = chemicals and pharmaceuticals; Com = computer and related activities; Con = construction; Ele = electronic and instrument equipment; Eli = electricity, gas, and water supply; Foo = food, drink and tobacco; Hot = hotels and restaurants; Mec = mechanical engineering and metals; Oth = other; Pet = petroleum; Pos = post and telecommunications; Pub = printing, paper and publishing; Rec = recreational, cultural, and sporting activities; Rub = rubber and plastics; Shi = shipbuilding; Tex = textiles and clothing; Tra = transport; Tre = transportation equipment; Who = wholesale and retail trade.

Table 8b Main sector, ownership, strategy and structure of large groups in Spain, 2002

Company			Sector	Own.	Div.	Int.	Str.
Telefónica	Telefónica Móviles España Telefónica Internacional España Corporación Admira Media Telefónica Data España		Pos	Ban	Rb	Pio	Md
Repsol-YPF	Petróleos del Norte Repsol Química		Pet	Ban	Rb	Pio	Md
ENDESA	ENDESA Energía		Eli	Dis	Rb	Phmo	Md
El Corte Inglés	Hipercor Viajes El Corte Inglés		Who	Coo	Rb	Phmo	F/H
Volkswagen	SEAT Volkswagen Navarra	Volks. Audi Esp.	Tre	For	Rb	Pio	Hol
CEPSA	CEPSA Est. de Servicio		Pet	For	Db	Phmo	Md
Mondragón	Grupo Eroski		Oth	Coo	Ub	Phmo	Md
Iberdrola			Eli	Ban	Rb	Phmo	Md
Carrefour	Distribuidora Internaci. Aliment.		Who	For	Rb	Hmo	Hol
Gas Natural SDG	ENAGAS Sagane		Eli	Ban	Db	Hmo	F/H
Renault	Renault España Renault España Comercial		Tre	For	Rb	Pio	F/H
March – Alba	ACS Act. Const. Serv.	ACS Pro, Obr Con.	Con	Per	Ub	Phmo	Hol
Unión Fenosa			Eli	Ban	Db	Phmo	Md
Fomento de Construcción y Contratas			Con	Per	Ub	Phmo	Md
Mercadona			Who	Per	Sb	Hmo	F/H
General Motors Holding España			Tre	For	Sb	Pio	F
Grupo Ferrovial			Con	Per	Rb	Phmo	F/H
Peugeot Citroën	Automóviles Citroën España Peugeot España		Tre	For	Rb	Pio	F/H
Ford España			Tre	For	Sb	Pio	F/H
Iberia			Tra	Ban	Db	Phmo	F/H
Altadis	Logista		Foo	Ban	Rb	Pio	Md
Auchan	Alcampo Supermercados Sabeco		Who	For	Rb	Hmo	F/H

Acciona		Con	Per	Rb	Phmo	F
AUNA Operadores de Telecomunicación		Pos	Fir	Db	Hmo	F
BP Oil España		Pet	For	Sb	Hmo	F/H
Arcelor	Aceralia Aceralia Redondos Comercial	Mec	Dis	Rb	Pio	Md
Vodafone España		Pos	For	Sb	Hmo	F
Daimlerchrysler España		Tre	For	Rb	Phmo	F/H
Nissan	Nissan Motor Ibérica Nissan Motor España	Tre	For	Rb	Pio	F/H
Siemens		Ele	For	Rb	Hmo	Md
FIAT	Iveco Pegaso FIAT Auto España	Tre	For	Rb	Phmo	F/H
INDITEX	Zara España	Tex	Per	Rb	Pio	F/H
Corporación Gestamp		Mec	Per	Rb	Phmo	Md
Coop. Farmacéutica Española		Who	Coo	Sb	Hmo	Hol
Ahold Supermercados		Who	For	Sb	Hmo	F/H
Michelin España Portugal		Rub	For	Db	Pio	F/H
Amadeus Global Travel Distr.		Pos	Fir	Rb	Phmo	F/H
RENFE		Tra	Sta	Sb	Hmo	F
Soc. Estatal Correos y Telégrafos		Pos	Sta	Sb	Hmo	F
Entidad Pública Emp. Aeropuertos		Tra	Sta	Rb	Phmo	Md
Caprabo		Who	Per	Sb	Hmo	F
Izar Construcciones Navales		Shi	Sta	Rb	Pio	Md
Abengoa		Ele	Per	Ub	Phmo	Md
Globalia Corporación Empresarial		Hot	Per	Rb	Phmo	Hol
Shell España		Who	For	Db	Hmo	F/H
Hidroeléctrica del Cantábrico		Eli	For	Db	Hmo	F
Sony España		Ele	For	Db	Pio	F
Nestlé España		Foo	For	Rb	Hmo	Md
Acerinox		Mec	For	Sb	Pio	F/H
Dow Chemical Ibérica		Che	For	Db	Phmo	F
Hewlett Packard Española		Com	For	Rb	Hmo	Md
Makro Autoservicio Mayorista		Who	For	Sb	Hmo	F/H
Obrascón Huarte Laín		Con	Per	Db	Hmo	F/H
BMW Ibérica		Who	For	Sb	Hmo	F
Total España		Pet	For	Rb	Hmo	F/H
International Business Machines		Com	For	Rb	Phmo	Md

(Continued)

Table 8b (Continued)

Company	Sector	Own.	Div.	Int.	Str.
Reguladora de Compras del Mediterráneo	Who	Fir	Sb	*	F
Danone	Foo	For	Db	Phmo	F
AGIP España	Who	For	Sb	Hmo	F
Lidl Supermercados	Who	For	Sb	Hmo	F
Safa Galenica	Who	For	Sb	Hmo	F/H
Televisión Española	Rec	Sta	Db	Hmo	Md
Bsh Electrodomésticos España	Ele	For	Rb	Pio	F
Vallehermoso	Con	Fir	Db	Hmo	F/H
Corporación Sidenor	Mec	Fir	Db	*	F/H
Constructora San José	Con	Per	Db	Hmo	F/H
Atlantic Copper	Min	For	Db	Pio	F
Grupo El Árbol Distribuc. y Sup.	Who	For	Sb	Hmo	F/H
EADS Construcciones Aeronáuticas	Mec	Fir	Rb	Io	Md
Spanair	Tra	For	Sb	Phmo	F
Philips Ibérica	Ele	For	Rb	Hmo	Md
Samsung Electronics Iberia	Ele	For	Rb	Pio	Md
Heineken España	Who	For	Sb	Hmo	F
Cobega	Foo	Per	Rb	Hmo	F
Roca Corporación Empresarial	Bri	Per	Rb	Phmo	Md

Note: * = unknown; Ban = bank-financial; Bri = brick, pottery, glass and cement; Com = computer and related activity; Con = construction; Coo = cooperative/foundation; Db = dominant business; Dis = dispersed; Div = product diversification; Ele = electrical and instrument engineering; Eli = electricity, gas and water supply; F = functional; F/H = functional/holding; Fir = firm; Foo = food, drink and tobacco; For = foreign; Hmo = home market oriented; Hol = holding; Hot = hotels and restaurants; Int = internationalization; Md = multidivisional; Mec = mechanical engineering and metals; Min = mining; Own = ownership; Per = personal; Pet = petroleum; Phmo = partly home market oriented; Pio = partly internationally oriented; Pos = post and telecommunications; Rb = related business; Rec = recreational, cultural, and sporting activities; Rub = rubber and plastics; Sb = single business; Sta = state; Str = organizational structure; Tex = textile and clothing; Tra = transport; Tre = transportation equipment; Ub = unrelated business; and Who = wholesale and retail trade.

References

Accornero, Aris. *La Parabola del Sindacato*. Bologna: Il Mulino, 1992.

Affinito, Massimiliano, Marcello De Cecco, and Angelo Dringoli. *Le Privatizzazioni dell'Industria Manifatturiera Italiana*. Rome: Donzelli, 2000.

Aganin, Alexander, and Paolo Volpin. "The History of Corporate Ownership in Italy." In *A History of Corporate Governance around the World: Family Business Groups to Professional Managers*, edited by Randall K. Morck, 325–365. Chicago: University of Chicago Press, 2005.

Aguilera, Ruth. "Directorship Interlocks in Comparative Perspective: The Case of Spain." *European Sociological Review* 14, no. 4 (1998): 319–342.

Albert, Michel. *Capitalisme Contre Capitalisme*. Paris: Seuil, 1991.

Alford, Bernard W. "Chandlerism: the New Orthodoxy of US and European Corporate Development." *Journal of European Economic History* 23, no. 3 (1994): 631–643.

Altan, Carlo Tullio. *La Nostra Italia. Clientelismo, Trasformismo e Ribellismo dall'Unità al 2000*. Milan: Egea, 2000.

Álvaro Moya, Adoración. "Inversión Directa Extranjera y Formación de Capacidades Organizativas Locales. Un Análisis del Impacto de Estados Unidos en la Empresa Española (1918–1975)." PhD diss., Complutense University of Madrid, 2010.

Amaral, Luciano. "How a Country Catches Up: Explaining Economic Growth in Portugal in the Post-War Period (1950s to 1973)." PhD diss., European University Institute, Florence, 2003.

Amatori, Franco. *Proprietà e Direzione. La Rinascente 1917–1969*. Milan: Franco Angeli, 1989.

———. "The Tormented Development of Large Industrial Enterprise between the Government and Families: Italy." In *Ownership and Governance: The Case of Italian Enterprises and Public Administration*, edited by Giuseppe Airoldi, Franco Amatori and Giorgio Invernizzi, 243–255. Milan: Egea, 1995.

———. *Impresa e Mercato. Lancia 1906–1969*. Bologna: Il Mulino, 1996.

———. "Growth via Politics. Business Groups Italian-Style." In *Business Groups in International and Historical Perspective*, edited by Takao Shiba and Masahiro Shimotani, 109–134. Oxford, UK: Oxford University Press, 1997a.

———. "Italy: The Tormented Rise of Organizational Capabilities between Government and Families." In *Big Business and the Wealth of Nations*, edited by Alfred D. Chandler, Franco Amatori and Takashi Hikino, 246–276. Cambridge, MA: Cambridge University Press, 1997b.

———. "European Business: New Strategies, Old Structures." *Foreign Policy* (Summer 1999): 78–89.

———. "Beyond State and Market: Italy's Futile Search for a Third Way." In *The Rise and Fall of State Owned Enterprise in the Western World*, edited by Pier Angelo Toninelli, 128–156. New York and Cambridge: Cambridge University Press, 2000.

———. "Big and Small Business in Italy's Industrial History." *Rivista di Storia Economica* 2 (2008): 207–224.

———. "Entrepreneurial Typologies in the History of Industrial Italy: Reconsiderations." *Business History Review* 85 (2011): 151–180.

Amatori, Franco, ed. *Storia dell'IRI. Volume 2. Il Miracolo Economico e i Suoi Limiti: il Ruolo dell'IRI (1949–1968)*. Rome-Bari: Laterza, 2012.

Amatori, Franco, and Bruno Bezza, eds. *Montecatini 1888–1966. Capitoli di Storia di una Grande Impresa*. Bologna: Il Mulino, 1990.

Amatori, Franco, and Giorgio Bigatti. "Business History in Italy at the Turn of the Century." In *Business History around the World*, edited by Franco Amatori and Geoffrey Jones, 215–231. Cambridge, MA: Cambridge University Press, 2003.

Amatori, Franco, Duccio Bigazzi, Renato Giannetti, and Luciano Segreto, eds. *Storia d'Italia Einaudi, Annale 15. L'Industria*. Turin, Italy: Einaudi, 1999.

Amatori, Franco, and Francesco Brioschi. "Le Grandi Imprese Private: Famiglie e Coalizioni." In *Storia del Capitalismo Italiano*, edited by Fabrizio Barca, 118–154. Rome: Donzelli, 1997.

Amatori, Franco, and Andrea Colli. *Impresa e Industria in Italia dall'Unità a oggi*. Venice: Marsilio, 1999.

———. "Corporate Governance: the Italian Story." Working paper, December 2000. Accessed November 24, 2012. ftp://ns1.ystp.ac.ir/YSTP/1/1/ROOT/DATA/PDF/unclassified/CGITALY.PDF.

———. *Business History: Complexity and Comparisons*. New York: Routledge, 2011.

Amatori, Franco, and Geoffrey Jones, eds. *Business History around the World*. Cambridge, MA: Cambridge University Press, 2003.

Amsden Alice H. *Asia's Next Giant: South Korea and Late Industrialization*. Oxford, UK: Oxford University Press, 1989.

Annibaldi, Cesare, and Giuseppe Berta, eds. *Grande Impresa e Sviluppo Italiano. Studi per i Cento Anni della FIAT*. Bologna: Il Mulino, 1999.

Antolín, Francesca. "Iniciativa Privada y Política Pública de la Industria Eléctrica en España." *Revista de Historia Económica* 2, no. 17 (1999): 411–445.

Ariño Ortiz, Gaspar, ed. *Privatizaciones y Liberalizaciones en España: Balance y Resultados*. Granada: Editorial Comares, 2004.

Armour, Henry O., and David J. Teece. "Organizational Structure and Economic Performance: A test of the Multidivisional Hypothesis. *The Bell Journal of Economics* 9, no. 1 (1978): 106–122.

Associazione Disiano Preite. *Rapporto sulla Società Aperta. 100 Tesi per la Riforma del Governo Societario in Italia*. Bologna: Il Mulino, 1997.

Avagliano, Lucio. *Alessandro Rossi e le Origini dell'Italia Industriale*. Napoli, Italy: Libreria Scientifica Editrice, 1970.

Bagnasco, Arnaldo. *Tre Italie. La Problematica Territoriale dello Sviluppo Italiano*. Bologna, Italy: Il Mulino, 1977.

Bairati, Piero. *Valletta*. Turin, Italy: UTET, 1983.

Baklanoff, Eric N. "The State and Economy in Portugal: Perspectives on Corporatism, Revolution, and Incipient Privatization." In *State Shrinking: A Comparative Inquiry into Privatization, Office for Public Sector Studies*, edited by William P. Glade, 257–281. Austin, TX: Ilas, 1986.

Balcet, Giovanni. *L'Economia Italiana. Evoluzione, Problemi e Paradossi*. Milan: Feltrinelli, 1997.

Balconi, Margherita. *La Siderurgia Italiana 1945–1990. Tra Controllo Pubblico e Incentivi del Mercato*. Bologna: Il Mulino, Bologna, 1991.

Baldi, Gianni. *I Potenti del Sistema*. Milan: Mondadori, 1976.

Ballestero, Alfonso. *Juan Antonio Suanzes. 1891–1977. La Política Industrial de la Posguerra*. Madrid: Lid, 1993.

Balloni, Valeriano. *Origini, Sviluppo e Maturità dell'Industria degli Elettrodomestici.* Bologna: Il Mulino, 1978.

Barbero, María Inés. "Business History in Latin America. Issues and Debates." In *Business History around the World,* edited by Franco Amatori and Geoffrey Jones, 317–336. Cambridge, MA: Cambridge University Press, 2003.

Barbiellini Amidei, Federico, Andrea Goldstein, and Marcella Spadoni. "Old and New Italian Multinational Firms. European Acquisitions in the United States: Re-examining Olivetti-Underwood Fifty Years Later." Economic History Working Papers, Banca d'Italia, Rome, 2011.

Barca, Fabrizio, ed. *Storia del Capitalismo Italiano dal Dopoguerra ad Oggi.* Rome: Donzelli, 1997.

Barca, Fabrizio, and Marco Becht, eds. *The Control of Corporate Europe.* Oxford, UK: Oxford University Press, 2001.

Barca, Fabrizio, Francesca Bertucci, Graziella Capello, and Paola Casavola. "La Trasformazione Proprietaria di FIAT, Pirelli e Falck dal 1947 ad oggi." In *Storia del Capitalismo Italiano dal Dopoguerra ad Oggi,* edited by Fabrizio Barca, 155–185. Rome: Donzelli, 1997.

Barca, Fabrizio, and Stefano Trento. "La Parabola delle Partecipazioni Statali: Una Missione Tradita." In *Storia del Capitalismo Italiano dal Dopoguerra ad Oggi,* edited by Fabrizio Barca, 185–236 Rome: Donzelli, 1997.

Barciela López, Carlos, ed. *Autarquía y Mercado Negro. El Fracaso Económico del Primer Franquismo, 1939–1959.* Barcelona: Crítica, 2003.

Barciela López, Carlos, and Antonio Di Vittorio, eds. *Las Industrias Agroalimentarias en Italia y España durante los Siglos XIX y XX.* Alicante, Spain: Publicaciones de la Universidad de Alicante, 2003.

Bartlett, Christopher A., and Sumantra Ghoshal. "Beyond the M-form: Toward a Managerial Theory of the Firm." *Strategic Management Journal* 14 (1993): 23–46.

Barucci, Emilio, and Federico Pierobon. *Le Privatizzazioni in Italia.* Rome: Carocci, 2007.

———. *Stato e Mercato nella Seconda Repubblica. Dalle Privatizzazioni alla Crisi Finanziaria.* Bologna: Il Mulino, 2010.

Battilani, Patrizia, ed. "Storia del Turismo: Le Imprese." In *Annale 8.* Milan: Franco Angeli, 2011.

Battilani, Patrizia, and Vera Zamagni. "Co-operatives (1951–2001)." In *Forms of Enterprises in 20th Century Italy. Boundaries, Structures, and Strategies,* edited by Andrea Colli, and Michelangelo Vasta, 273–293. Cheltenham, UK: Edward Elgar, 2010.

Battilossi, Stefano. "Accumulazione e Finanza. Per una Storia degli Investitori Istituzionali in Italia (1945–1990)." *Annali di Storia dell'Impresa* 8 (1992): 183–259.

Becattini, Giacomo, ed. *Mercato e Forze Locali: il Distretto Industriale.* Bologna: Il Mulino, 1987.

Becattini, Giacomo. *Modelli Locali di Sviluppo.* Bologna: Il Mulino, 1989.

———. *Distretti Industriali e Made in Italy. Le Basi Socioculturali del Nostro Sviluppo Economico.* Turin, Italy: Bollati Boringhieri, 1998.

———. *Il Distretto Industriale.* Turin: Rosenberg & Sellier, 2000.

Bel, Germà, and Antón Costas. "La Privatización y Sus Motivaciones en España: De Instrumento a Política." *Revista de Historia Industrial* 19–20 (2001): 105–132.

Bellandi, Marco. "'Terza Italia' e 'Distretti Industriali' Italiani dopo la Seconda Guerra Mondiale." In *Storia d'Italia, Annali, no. 15. L'industria,* edited by Franco Amatori, Duccio Bigazzi, Renato Giannetti and Luciano Segreto, 843–891. Turin, Italy: Einaudi, 1999.

Belvedere Paola, Alberto Manzini, Stefano Mechelli, Niccolò Moreschini, Nicoletta Mincato, Ferruccio Papi Rossi, Nicola Squillace, and Claudio Tatozzi, eds. *Le Offerte Pubbliche d'Acquisto.* Milan: Il Sole 24 Ore, 2000.

Berle, Adolf A., and Gardiner C. Means. *The Modern Corporation and Private Property*. New York: Macmillan, 1932.

Berta, Giuseppe. *Le Idee al Potere. Adriano Olivetti e il Progetto Comunitario tra Fabbrica e Territorio sullo Sfondo della Società Italiana del "Miracolo Economico."* Milan: Edizioni di Comunità, 1980.

———. *Mirafiori*. Bologna: Il Mulino, 1998.

———. *Metamorfosi. L'Industria Italiana tra Declino e Trasformazione*. Milan: Egea, 2004.

———. "Un Manifesto per la Grande Impresa." *Il Mulino* 6 (2006): 1022–1032.

Berta, Giuseppe, ed. *La Questione Settentrionale. Economia e Società in Trasformazione*. Milan: Feltrinelli, 2007.

Berta, Giuseppe, and Fabrizio Onida. "Old and New Italian Multinational Firms." Economic History Working Papers 15, Banca d'Italia, Rome, 2011.

Bezza, Bruno. "L'Attività Multinazionale della Pirelli (1883–1914)." *Società e Storia* 10, no. 35 (1987): 53–80.

Bianchi, Marcello, Magda Bianco, and Luca Enriques. "Pyramidal Groups and the Separation between Ownership and Control in Italy." In *The Control of Corporate Europe*, edited by Fabrizio Barca and Marco Becht, 145–187. Oxford, UK: Oxford University Press, 2001.

Biggart, Nicole W., and Mauro F. Guillén. "Developing Difference: Social Organization and the Rise of the Auto Industries of South Korea, Taiwan, Spain, and Argentina." *American Sociological Review* 64 (1999): 722–747.

Binda, Veronica. "Entre el Estado y las Multinacionales: La Empresa Industrial Española en los Años de la Integración a la CEE." *Revista de Historia Industrial—Economía y Empresa* 28 (2005a): 117–154.

———. "L'Accidentato Percorso della Grande Impresa Spagnola tra Stato e Multinazionali, 1975–2000." *Imprese e Storia* 31 (2005b): 79–111.

———. "National Business Systems and Foreign Multinationals. The Changing Connections among State, Entrepreneurs and Foreign Investors in Italy and Spain during the Second Half of the XXth Century." Paper presented at the Business History Conference, Sacramento, April 10–12, 2008.

———. "Grandes Empresas Salen Fuera de Casa: La Experiencia Española e Italiana en el Largo Plazo." *Información Comercial Española – Revista de Economía* 849 (2009a): 9–26.

———. "La Internacionalización de las Grandes Empresas en Dos Naciones Mediterráneas. Italia y España, 1950–2002." *Revista de Historia Industrial—Economía y Empresa* 40 (2009b): 95–124.

———. "Spagna." In *Privatizzazioni e Competitività delle Imprese*, edited by Giangiacomo Nardozzi, 135–160. Genoa: Fondazione Ansaldo Editore, 2011.

———. "Strategy and Structure in Large Italian and Spanish Firms, 1950–2002." *Business History Review* 86 (2012): 503–525.

Binda, Veronica, and Andrea Colli. "Changing Big Business in Italy and Spain, 1973–2003: Strategic Responses to a New Context." *Business History* 63, no. 1 (2011): 14–39.

———. "Changing Big Business in Italy and Spain, 1973–2003: Strategic Responses to a New Context." In *Mapping the European Corporations. Strategy, Structure, Ownership and Performance*, edited by Andrea Colli, Abe de Jong, and Martin Jes Iversen, 14–39. London: Routledge, 2012.

Binda, Veronica, and Martin J. Iversen. "Towards a 'Managerial Revolution' in European Business? The Transformation of Danish and Spanish Big Business, 1973–2003." *Business History* 49, no. 4 (2007): 506–530.

Boix Domenech, Rafael, and Vittorio Galletto. "Identificación de Sistemas Locales de Trabajo y Distritos Industriales en España." Dirección General de Política de la Pequeña y Mediana Empresa, MITYC, Madrid, 2004.

Bolchini, Pietro, Emilio Colombo, Adolfo Battaglia, and Franco Viezzoli. *La Nazionalizzazione dell'Energia Elettrica: L'Esperienza Italiana e di Altri Paesi Europei. Atti del Convegno Internazionale di Studi del 9–10 Novembre 1988 per il 25° Anniversario dell'Istituzione dell'ENEL*. Rome-Bari: Laterza, 1989.

Bolchini, Pietro. "Piccole e Grandi Industrie, Liberismo e Protezionismo." In *Storia Economica d'Italia*, vol. 3, *Industrie, Mercati, Istituzioni, no. 1, Le Strutture dell'Economia*, edited by Pierluigi Ciocca, and Gianni Toniolo, 348–426. Rome-Bari: Laterza, 2002.

Bonelli, Franco. *Lo Sviluppo di una Grande Impresa in Italia. La Terni dal 1884 al 1962*. Turin: Einaudi, 1975.

———. "Il Capitalismo Italiano. Linee Generali d'Interpretazione." In *Storia d'Italia Einaudi, Annale 1. Dal Feudalesimo al Capitalismo*, edited by Ruggiero Romano and Corrado Vivanti, 1193–1255. Turin: Einaudi, 1978.

Bortolotti, Bernardo, and Mara Faccio. "Reluctant Privatization." *Fondazione Eni Enrico Mattei*, no. 30 (2004).

Bosch Badía, María Teresa. "Repsol: De Empresa Pública a Multinacional del Petróleo." *Información Comercial Española* 842 (2008): 217–234.

Botti, Alfonso. "La Spagna di Aznar." *Il Mulino* 395 (2000): 399–407.

Boyer, Miguel. "La Empresa Pública en la Estrategia Industrial Española: El INI." In *Información Comercial Española* 500, 1975.

Briatico, Franco. *Ascesa e Declino del Capitale Pubblico in Italia. Vicende e Protagonisti*. Bologna: Il Mulino, 2004.

Brioschi, Francesco, Luigi Buzzacchi, and Massimo G. Colombo. *Gruppi d'Imprese e Mercato Finanziario. La Struttura di Potere nell'Industria Italiana*. Rome: Carocci, 1990.

Brusco Sebastiano, and Sergio Paba. "Per una Storia dei Distretti Industriali Italiani dal Primo Dopoguerra agli Anni Novanta." In *Storia del Capitalismo Italiano*, edited by Fabrizio Barca, 265–334. Rome: Donzelli, 1997.

Bruno, Giovanni, and Luciano Segreto. "Finanza e Industria in Italia." In *Storia dell'Italia Repubblicana, Vol. 3*, 497–694 Turin: Einaudi, 1996.

Buckley, Peter, and Mark Casson. *The Future of the Multinational Enterprise*. London: Homes & Meier, 1976.

———. "Analyzing Foreign Market Entry Strategies: Extending the Internalization Approach." *Journal of International Business Studies* 29, no. 3 (1988): 539–562.

Bueno Campos, Eduardo. *Dirección Estrategica de la Empresa: Metodologia, Técnicas y Casos*. Madrid: Piramide, 1993.

Buğra, Ayşe. *State and Business in Modern Turkey: A Comparative Study*. New York: State University of New York Press, 1994.

Burnham, James. *The Managerial Revolution*. New York: John Day & Co., 1941.

Cable, John, and Manfred J. Dirrheimer. "Hierarchies and Markets: An Empirical Test of the Multidivisional Hypotesis in West Germany." *International Journal of Industrial Organization* 1 (1983): 43–62.

Cabrera, Mercedes, and Fernando Del Rey. *El Poder de los Empresarios. Política y Economía en la España Contemporánea (1975–2000)*. Madrid: Taurus, 2002.

Cafagna, Luciano. *Dualismo e Sviluppo nella Storia d'Italia*. Venice: Marsilio, 1989.

Caizzi, Bruno. *Gli Olivetti*. Turin: Utet, 1962.

Calvo, Ángel. *Historia de Telefónica: 1924–1975*. Barcelona: Fundación Telefónica/Ariel, 2011.

Camino Blasco, David, and José Ignacio Pradas Poveda. "Los Procesos de Integración Económica Regional y la Política de Promoción de Inversión Extranjera Directa. Una Aproximación al Caso Español." *Información Comercial Española* 794 (2001):163–195.

Cantwell, John, ed. *Globalization and the Location of Firms*. Cheltelham, UK: Edward Elgar, 2004.

Caracciolo, Alberto, ed. *La Formazione dell'Italia Industriale: Discussioni e Ricerche.* Rome-Bari, Laterza, 1969.

Cardoso de Matos, Ana, and Álvaro Ferreira da Silva. "Foreign Capital and Problems of Agency: The Companhias Reunidas de Gás e Electricidade in Lisbon (1890–1920)." *Transportes, Servicios y Telecomunicaciones* 14 (2008): 142–161.

Carli, Guido. *Cinquant'Anni di Vita Italiana.* Milan: CDE, 1993.

Carli, Maria Rosaria. "Il Commercio e gli Investimenti Diretti Esteri. Permanenze e Cambiamenti nella Struttura degli Scambi Mediterranei." In *Rapporto sulle Economie del Mediterraneo*, edited by Paolo Malanima, 93–117. Bologna: Il Mulino, 2008.

Carnevali, Francesca. "State Enterprise and Italy's 'Economic Miracle': The Ente Nazionale Idrocarburi, 1945–1962." *Enterprise and Society* 1, no. 1 (2000): 249–278.

————. *Europe's Advantage. Banks and Small Firms in Britain, France, Germany, and Italy since 1918.* Oxford, UK: Oxford University Press, 2005.

Carreras, Albert. "La Industrialización Española en el Marco de la Historia Económica Europea: Ritmos y Carácteres Comparados." In *España, Economía*, edited by José Luis García Delgado, 79–115. Madrid: Espasa Calpe, 1993.

————. "La Gran Empresa Durante el Primer Franquísmo: Un Momento Fundamental en la Historia del Capitalismo Español." In *Los Empresarios de Franco. Política y Economía en España, 1936–1957*, edited by Glicerio Sánchez Recio, and Julio Tascón Fernández, 47–65. Barcelona: Crítica, 2003.

————. "Industria." In *Estadísticas Históricas de España. Siglos XIX-XX*, 2nd ed., edited by Albert Carreras, and Xavier Tafunell, 357–454. Madrid: Fundación BBVA, 2005.

Carreras, Albert, and Xavier Tafunell. "National Enterprise. Spanish Big Manufacturing Firms (1917–1990), between State and Market." Economic Working Paper Universitat Pompeu Fabra 93, Barcelona, 1994.

————. "Spain: Big Manufacturing Firms between State and Market, 1917–1990." In *Big Business and the Wealth of Nations*, edited by Alfred D. Chandler, Franco Amatori, and Takashi Hikino, 277–304. Cambridge, MA: Cambridge University Press, 1997.

————. *Historia Económica de la España Contemporánea.* Barcelona, Crítica, 2003.

Carreras, Albert, and Xavier Tafunell, eds. *Estadísticas Históricas de España. Siglos XIX-XX*, Bilbao: Fundación BBVA, 2005.

Carreras, Albert, Xavier Tafunell, and Eugenio Torres Villanueva, "The Rise and Decline of Spanish State-Owned Firms." In *The Rise and Fall of State-Owned Enterprise in the Western World*, edited by Pier Angelo Toninelli, 208–236. Cambridge, MA: Cambridge University Press, 2000.

Carreras, Albert, Leandro Prados de la Escosura, and Joan Rosés. "Renta e Riqueza." In *Estadísticas Históricas de España. Siglos XIX-XX*, edited by Albert Carreras and Xavier Tafunell. Bilbao: Fundación BBVA, 2005.

Carreras, Albert and Emanuele Felice. "L'Industria Italiana dal 1911 al 1938: Ricostruzione della Serie del Valore Aggiunto e Interpretazioni." *Rivista di Storia Economica* 3 (2010): 285–334.

Carreras, Albert, Xavier Tafunell, and Eugenio Torres Villanueva. "Business History in Spain." In *Business History around the World*, edited by Franco Amatori and Geoffrey Jones, 232–254. Cambridge, MA: Cambridge University Press, 2003.

Casalino, Chiara. "La FIAT e l'Internazionalizzazione. Dalla Presidenza di Vittorio Valletta alla Riorganizzazione (1946–1972)." *Annali di Storia dell'Impresa* 15–16 (2004–2005): 455–485.

Casanova, José V. "The Opus Dei Ethic and the Modernization of Spain." PhD diss., New School for Social Research, University of Michigan, Ann Arbor, 1983.

Cassis, Youssef. *Big Business: The European Experience in the Twentieth Century.* Oxford, UK: Oxford University Press, 1997.

————. "Big Business." In *The Oxford Handbook of Business History*, edited by Geoffrey Jones and Jonathan Zeitlin, 171–193. New York: Oxford University Press, 2008.

Castagnoli, Adriana, and Emanuela Scarpellini. *Storia degli Imprenditori Italiani.* Turin: Einaudi, 2003.

Castro Balaguer, Rafael. "Génesis y Transformación de un Modelo de Inversión Internacional: El Capital Francés en la España del Siglo XX." PhD diss., Complutense University of Madrid, 2010.

Castronovo, Valerio. *L'Industria Cotoniera in Piemonte nel Secolo XIX.* Turin: Ilte, 1965.

————. *L'Industria Italiana dall'Ottocento ad oggi.* Milan: Mondadori, 1980.

Castronovo, Valerio, ed. *Storia dell'Industria Elettrica in Italia.* Rome-Bari: Laterza, 1994.

————. *FIAT. Storia di un'Impresa 1899–1999.* Milan: Rizzoli, 1999.

Castronovo, Valerio, ed. *Storia dell'IRI. Volume 1. L'IRI dalle Origini al Dopoguerra (1933–1948).* Rome-Bari: Laterza, 2011.

Catalan, Jordi. "La Reconstrucción Franquista y la Experiencia de la Europa Occidental, 1934–1959." In *Autarquía y Mercado Negro. El Fracaso Económico del Primer Franquismo, 1939–1959*, edited by Carlos Barciela López, 123–168. Barcelona: Crítica, 2003.

————. "The First Crisis of SEAT: The Veto to General Motors and the Purchase of AUTHI by British Leyland (1972–1976)." *Investigaciones de Historia Económica* 9 (2007): 141–172.

Catalan, Jordi, José Antonio Miranda Encarnación, and Ramón Ramón Muñoz, eds. *Distritos y Clusters en la Europa del Sur.* Madrid: Lid, 2011.

Cavazzuti, Filippo. *Privatizzazioni, Imprenditori e Mercati.* Bologna: Il Mulino, 1996.

Caves, Richard E. "Industrial Corporations: The Industrial Economics of Foreign Investment." *Economica* 38 (1971): 1–27.

————. *Multinational Enterprise and Economic Analysis.* Cambridge, MA: Cambridge University Press, 1982.

Chandler, Alfred D. *Strategy and Structure: Chapters in the History of the American Industrial Enterprise.* Cambridge, MA: MIT Press, 1962.

————. *The Visible Hand. The Managerial Revolution in American Business.* Cambridge, MA: The Belknap Press of Harvard University Press, 1977.

————. *Scale and Scope. The Dynamics of Industrial Capitalism*, Cambridge, MA: The Belknap Press of Harvard University Press, 1990.

————. "The Competitive Performance of U.S. Industrial Enterprises since Second World War: Strategic and Structural Change" *Business History Review* 68 (1994): 1–72.

Chandler Alfred D., Franco Amatori, and Takashi Hikino, eds. *Big Business and the Wealth of Nations.* Cambridge, MA: Cambridge University Press, 1997.

Chandler, Alfred D., and Takashi Hikino. "The Large Industrial Enterprise and the Dynamics of Modern Economic Growth." In *Big Business and the Wealth of Nations*, edited by Alfred D. Chandler, Franco Amatori, and Takashi Hikino, 24–57. Cambridge, MA: Cambridge University Press, 1997.

Channon, Derek F. *The Strategy and Structure of British Enterprise.* London: Macmillan Press, 1973.

Cheffins, Brian, and Steven Bank. "Is Berle and Means Really a Myth?" *Business History Review* 83 (2009): 443–474.

Cianci, Ernesto. *Nascita dello Stato Imprenditore in Italia.* Milan: Mursia, 1977.

Cingolani, Stefano. *Le Grandi Famiglie del Capitalismo Italiano.* Rome-Bari: Laterza, 1990.

Ciocca, Pierluigi, and Gianni Toniolo, editors. *Storia Economica d'Italia—III. Industrie, Mercati, Istituzioni.* Rome-Bari: Laterza, 2003.

Cipolla, Carlo M. *Before the Industrial Revolution: European Society and Economy, 1000–1700*. 3rd ed. London: Routledge, 1993.

Ciuffetti, Augusto. *Casa e Lavoro. Dal Paternalismo Aziendale alle Comunità Globali: Villaggi e Quartieri Operai in Italia tra Otto e Novecento*. Perugia, Italy: CRACE, 2004.

Clark, Gordon L., and Won Bae Kim. *Asian NIEs and the Global Economy: Industrial Restructuring and Corporate Strategy in the 1990s*. Baltimore and London: The Johns Hopkins University Press, 1995.

Clifton, Judith, Francisco Comín Comín, and Daniel Díaz Fuentes. *Privatisation in the European Union. Public Enterprises and Integration*. Dordrecht, the Netherlands: Kluwer Academic Publishers, 2003.

Cohen, Jon, and Giovanni Federico. *Lo Sviluppo Economico Italiano, 1820–1960*. Bologna: Il Mulino, 2001.

Colajanni, Napoleone, ed. *L'Economia Italiana dal Dopoguerra ad Oggi*. Milan: Sperling & Kupfer, 1990.

Colajanni, Napoleone. *Storia della Banca in Italia*. Rome: Newton Compton, 1995.

Colitti, Marcello. *Energia e Sviluppo in Italia*. Bari, Italy: De Donato, 1979.

———. *ENI. Cronache dall'Interno di un'Azienda*. Milan: Egea, 2008.

Colli, Andrea. *Legami di Ferro*. Catanzaro: Meridiana, 1999.

———. *Il Quarto Capitalismo. Un Profilo Italiano*. Venice: Marsilio, 2002a.

———. *I Volti di Proteo. Storia della Piccola Impresa in Italia nel Novecento*. Turin: Bollati Boringhieri, 2002b.

———. *The History of Family Business, 1850–2000*. Cambridge: Cambridge University Press, 2002c.

———. *Corporate Governance e Assetti Proprietari. Genesi, Dinamiche e Comparazioni Internazionali*. Venice: Marsilio, 2006a.

———. *Capitalismo Famigliare*. Bologna: Il Mulino, 2006b.

———. "Foreign Enterprises (1913–1973)." In *Forms of Enterprises in 20th Century Italy. Boundaries, Structures and Strategies*, edited by Andrea Colli, and Michelangelo Vasta, 87–111. Cheltenham, UK: Edward Elgar, 2010.

———. "Host Country Attractiveness and Economic Development: Multinationals in Italy during the Twentieth Century." *Business History Review*, forthcoming 2013.

Colli, Andrea, Paloma Fernández Pérez, and Mary B. Rose. "National Determinants of Family Firm Development? Family Firms in Britain, Spain, and Italy in the Nineteenth and Twentieth Centuries." *Enterprise & Society* 4 (2003): 28–64.

Colli, Andrea, Esteban García-Canal, and Mauro F. Guillén. "Family Character and International Entrepreneurship: A Historical Comparison of Italian and Spanish 'New Multinationals.'" *Business History* 55/1 (2013): 119–138.

Colli, Andrea, and Michelangelo Vasta, eds. *Forms of Enterprises in 20th Century Italy. Boundaries, Structures, and Strategies*. Cheltenham, UK: Edward Elgar, 2010a.

Colli, Andrea, and Michelangelo Vasta. "I Grandi Gruppi nel Capitalismo Italiano del Novecento." In *Grandi Gruppi e Informazione Finanziaria nel Novecento. Vol. 5 Tra Imprese e Istituzioni 100 anni di Assonime*, edited by Fulvio Coltorti, 111–178. Rome-Bari: Assonime, 2010b.

Colpan, Asli M.. "Business Groups in Turkey." In *The Oxford Handbook of Business Group*, edited by Asli M. Colpan, Takashi Hikino, and James R. Lincoln, 486–525. Oxford, UK, and New York: Oxford University Press, 2010.

Colpan, Asli M., Takashi Hikino, and James R. Lincoln, eds. *The Oxford Handbook of Business Groups*. Oxford, UK, and New York: Oxford University Press: 2010.

Coltorti, Fulvio. "Le Fasi dello Sviluppo Industriale Italiano e l'Intreccio tra Settore Privato e Impresa Pubblica." In *La Politica Industriale in Italia dal '45 a Oggi*, edited by Mario Baldassarri, 65. Rome: SIPI, 1990.

Comín Comín, Francisco, and Pablo Martín Aceña. "La Política Autárquica y el INI." In *Los Empresarios de Franco. Política y Economía en España, 1936–1957*, edited by Glicerio Sánchez Recio, and Julio Tascón Fernández, 23–46. Barcelona: Crítica, 2003.

Comín Comín, Francisco. "Los Mitos y los Milagros de Suanzes: La Empresa Privada y el INI Durante la Autarquía." *Revista de Historia Industrial* 18 (2000): 221–245.

Conte, Leandro, and Giandomenico Piluso. "Financing the Largest Manufacturing Firms: Ownership, Equity, and Debt, 1936–2001." In *Forms of Enterprises in 20th Century Italy. Boundaries, Structures, and Strategies*, edited by Andrea Colli and Michelangelo Vasta, 132–159. Cheltenham, UK: Edward Elgar, 2010.

Conti, Ettore. *Dal Taccuino di un Borghese*. Bologna: Il Mulino, 1946.

Corkill, David. "Privatization in Portugal." In *Privatization in Western Europe. Pressures, Problems, and Paradoxes*, edited by Vincent Wright, 215–227. London: Pinter, 1994.

———. *The Development of the Portuguese Economy. A Case of Europeanization*. London and New York: Routledge, 1999.

Cotula, Franco, ed. *La Politica Monetaria in Italia*. Bologna: Il Mulino, 1989.

Crespí-Cladera Rafael, and Miguel A. García-Cestona. "Ownership and Control of Spanish Listed Firms." In *The Control of Corporate Europe*, edited by Fabrizio Barca and Marco Becht, 207–227. Oxford, UK: Oxford University Press, 2001.

Crucini, Cristina. "The Development and Professionalization of the Italian Consultancy Market after WWII." *Business and Economic History* 28, no. 2 (1999): 7–18.

———. "The Evolution of the Italian Management Consultancy Market." Discussion Paper in Economics and Management, 7/413, The University of Reading, Reading, UK, 2000.

Cuartas, Javier. *Biografía de El Corte Inglés*. Barcelona: Dictext, 2010.

Cuervo García, Álvaro. *La Crisis Bancaria en España 1977–1985. Causas, Sistemas de Tratamiento y Coste*. Barcelona: Ariel, 1988.

———. *La Privatización de la Empresa Pública*. Madrid: Encuentro, 1997.

Davies, Stephen, Catherine Matraves, David Petts, and Lars-Hendrik Röller. *The Corporate Structure of UK and German Manufacturing Firms: Changes in Response to the SEM*. London: Angolo-German Foundation, 1999.

D'Azeglio, Massimo Taparelli. *Massimo Taparelli D'Azeglio: I Miei Ricordi*. Firenze: Barbera, 1891.

De Biase, Luca, and Marco Borsa. *Capitani di Sventura. Agnelli, De Benedetti, Romiti, Ferruzzi, Gardini, Pirelli: Perché Rischiano di Farci Perdere la Sfida degli Anni '90*. Milan: Mondadori, 1992.

De la Sierra, Fermín. "La Situación Monopolística de la Banca Privada en España." *Revista de Economía Política* 3, no. 1/2 (1951): 57–93.

———. *La Concentración Económica en las Industrias Básicas Españolas*. Madrid: Instituto de Estudios Políticos, 1953.

Del Buttero, Anna. *Il Capitale Estero nell'Industria Italiana*. Rome: Ministero per la Costituente, 1946.

De Miguel, Amando, and Juan José Linz. "Nivel de Estudios del Empresario Español." *Arbor* 57 219 (1964): 33–63.

De Nardis, Sergio, ed. *Le Privatizzazioni Italiane*. Bologna: Il Mulino, 2000.

De Pablo Torrente, Joaquín. "El Proteccionismo que Adormece." *Dinero* 44 (1983): 66–71.

———. "Manos libres." *Actualidad Económica* 1483 (1986): 29–30.

Díaz Morlán, Pablo. *Los Ybarra: Una Dinastía de Empresarios (1801–2001)*. Madrid: Marcial Pons, 2002.

———. "La Importancia de Llamarse Ybarra. Los Nuevos Negocios Desde Arriba y Otros Beneficios Capitalistas." *Información Comercial Española* 812 (2004): 153–162.

Di Maggio, Paul J., and Walter W. Powell. "The Iron Cage Revisited: Institutional Isomorphism and Collective Rationality in Organizational Fields." *American Sociological Review* 48 (1983): 147–160.

Di Maggio, Paul, ed. *The Twenty-First-Century Firm: Changing Economic Organiza-tion in International Perspective*. Princeton, NJ: Princeton University Press, 2001.

Di Pietro, Antonio, and Giovanni Valentini. *Intervista su Tangentopoli*. Rome-Bari: Laterza, 2001.

Direzione Affari Generali Ferrero. *Ferrero 1946 – 1996: l'Industria Attraverso Mezzo Secolo di Storia e Costumi*. Turin: 1996.

Di Vittorio, Antonio, ed. *An Economic History of Europe: From Expansion to Development*. London: Routledge, 2006.

Djelic, Marie-Laure. *Exporting the American Model. The Postwar Transformation of European Business*. Oxford, UK: Oxford University Press, 1998.

Donaldson, Lex. (1982). "Divisionalization and Size: A Theoretical and Empirical Critique." *Organization Studies* 3, no. 4 (1982): 321–337.

Dore, Ronald. *Stock Market Capitalism, Welfare Capitalism: Japan and Germany versus the Anglo-Saxons*. Oxford, UK: Oxford University Press, 2000.

Dritsas, Margarita. "Foreign Capital and Greek Development in a Historical Per-spective." Uppsala Papers in Economic History, no. 10, Uppsala University, Uppsala, Sweden, 1993.

Drucker, Peter. *The Concept of the Corporation*. London: John Day, 1946.

Dunning, John H. "Explaining Changing Patterns of International Production: In Defence of the Eclectic Theory." *Oxford Bulletin of Economics and Statistics* 41 (1979): 269–295.

Durán Herrera, Juan José, ed. *Multinacionales Españolas I. Algunos Casos Rel-evantes*. Madrid: Piramide, 1996.

———. *Multinacionales Españolas en Iberoamérica: Valor Estratétigico*. Madrid: Piramide, 1997a.

———. *Multinacionales españolas II. Nuevas Experiencias de Internacionalización*. Madrid: Piramide, 1997b.

———. *La Empresa Multinacional Española. Estrategias y Ventajas Competitivas*. Madrid: Minerva, 2005.

Dyas, Gareth P. "Strategy and Structure of French Enterprise." PhD diss., Harvard Business School, Cambridge, Massachusetts, 1972.

Dyas, Gareth P., and Heinz T. Thanheiser. *The Emerging European Enterprise*. London: Macmillan Press, 1976.

Eichengreen, Barry. *The European Economy since 1945*. Princeton, NJ: Princeton University Press, 2007.

Erdilek, Asim. "A Comparative Analysis of Inward and Outward FDI in Turkey." *Transnational Corporations* 12, no. 3 (2003): 79–106.

Faini, Riccardo. "Fu Vero Declino? L'Italia degli Anni Novanta." *Il Mulino* 6 (2003): 1072–1083.

Fanfani, Tommaso. *Una Leggenda verso il Futuro: I Centodieci Anni di Storia della Piaggio*. Pisa: Pacini, 1994.

Fanjul, Óscar. "La Empresa Pública en el Sector de Hidrocarburos." *Papeles de Economìa Española* 38 (1989): 322–339.

Fauri, Francesca. *L'Integrazione Economica Europea, 1947–2006*. Bologna: Il Mulino, 2006.

Favero, Giovanni. *Benetton. I Colori del Successo*. Milan: Egea, 2005.

Federico, Giovanni, and Pier Angelo Toninelli. "Le Strategie delle Imprese dall'Unità al 1973." In *L'Impresa Italiana nel Novecento*, edited by Renato Giannetti and Michelangelo Vasta, 299–370. Bologna: Il Mulino, 2003a.

Federico, Giovanni. "La Struttura Industriale (1911–1996)." In *L'Impresa Italiana nel Novecento*, edited by Renato Giannetti and Michelangelo Vasta, 41–88. Bologna: Il Mulino, 2003b.

Federico, Giovanni, and Nikolaus Wolf. "Comparative Advantages in Italy: A Long-Run Perspective." Economic History Working Papers 9, Banca d'Italia, Rome, 2011.

Fenoaltea, Stefano. *L'Economia Italiana dall'Unità alla Grande Guerra*. Rome-Bari: Laterza, 2003.

Fernández de Sevilla, Tomás. "Responses to a Crisis: FASA-Renault in Spain during the 1970s." Working Papers in Economics from Universitat de Barcelona 261, 2011.

Fernández Moya, María. "Editoriales Españolas en América Latina. Un Proceso de Internacionalización Secular." *Información Comercial Española* 849 (2009): 65–77.

Fernández Pérez, Paloma. "Challenging the Loss of an Empire: González & Byass of Jerez." *Business History* 41 (1999): 72–87.

Ferrão, João. "TNC Operations and Host Regional Economies: A Typology for the Portuguese Case." In *Transnational Corporations and Europen Regional Restructuring*, edited by Peter Dicken and Michel Quevit, 45–60. Utrecht: Netherlands Geographical Studies, 1994.

Ferreira da Silva, Álvaro. "Foreign Investment and Multinationals in Portugal (1926–1974)." In *European Economic and Business Development. National Historical Perspectives and European Osmosis 19th-20th Centuries*, edited by Margarita Dritsas, Chris Kobrak, and Gerasimos Notaras, XX–XX. New York: Berghan Books.

Fernández Roca, Francisco Javier. "HYTASA. Fundación y Desarrollo de una Empresa Textil en el Marco de la Política Económica del Primer Franquísmo (1937–1949)" Fundación Empresa Pública, Documento de Trabajo 9604.

Ferrero. *Ferrero la Più grande Industria Dolciaria del MEC*. Turin: Aeda, 1967.

Filippi, Enrico. "Le 200 Maggiori Società Industriali Italiane." *L'Impresa* 1 (1970): 16.

Fiori, Giuseppe. *Il Venditore: Storia di Silvio Berlusconi e della Fininvest*. Milan: Garzanti, 2006.

Fligstein, Neil. "The Spread of Multidivisional Form among Large Firms." *American Sociological Review* 50 (1985): 377–391.

———. *The Transformation of Corporate Control*. Cambridge, MA: The President and Fellows of Harvard College, 1990.

Fligstein, Neil, and Peter Brantley. "Bank Control, Owner Control, or Organizational Dynamics: Who Controls the Large Modern Corporation?" *American Journal of Sociology* 98 (1992): 280–307.

Fligstein, Neil, and Frederic Merand. "Globalization or Europeanization? Evidence of the European Economy since 1980." *Acta Sociologica* 45 (2002): 7–22.

Foncillas Casaus, Santiago. "La Política de Internacionalización en la Estrategia Empresarial del Grupo Dragados." *Información Comercial Española* 799 (2002): 133–138.

Fornengo, Graziella, and Francesco Silva, eds. *Strategie di Crescita dei Grandi Gruppi Italiani (1976-1985)*. Milan: Franco Angeli, 1993.

Fortis, Marco, Claudio Pavese, and Alberto Quadro Curzio, eds. *Il Gruppo Edison: 1883–2003*. Bologna: Il Mulino, 2003.

Franko, Lawrence. *The European Multinationals*. New York: Harper and Row, 1976.

———. "The Move towards a Multidivisional Structure in European Organizations." *Administrative Science Quarterly* 19 (1974): 493–506.

Franks, Julian R., and Colin Mayer. "Ownership and Control." In *Trends in Business Organization: Do Participation and Cooperation Increase Competitiveness?*, edited by Horst Siebert, 171–200. Tübingen, Germany: Mohr, 1995.

Freeland, Robert F. "The Myth of the M-form? Governance, Consent and Organizational Change." *American Journal of Sociology* 102 (1996): 483–526.

Freeman, Christopher, and Francisco Louçã. *As Times Goes By: From the Industrial Revolution to the Information Revolution*. Oxford, UK: Oxford University Press, 2001.

Friedman, Walter A. "Business History, Post-Chandler." In *The New Ways of History*, edited by Gelina Harlaftis, Nikos Karapidakis, Kostas Sbonias, and Vaios Vaiopolous, 146–165. London and New York: Tauris Academic Studies, 2010.

Fruin, Mark. *The Japanese Enterprise System. Competitive Strategies and Coopera-tive Structures.* Oxford, UK: Clarendon Press, 1992.

Fuà Giorgio, and Carlo Zacchia, eds. *Industrializzazione Senza Fratture.* Il Mulino: Bologna, 1983.

Fusi, Juan Pablo, and Jordi Palafox. *España: 1808–1996. El Desafío de la Moderni-dad.* Madrid: Espasa Calpe, 1997.

Galambos, Louis. *L'Impresa nell'America Moderna. Alla Ricerca di una Nuova Sintesi.* Bologna: Il Mulino, 2000.

Galán, José I., María J. Sánchez-Bueno, and José Ángel Zúñiga-Vicente. "Strategic and Organizational Evolution of Spanish Firms: Towards a Holding Network Form?" *British Journal of Management* 16 (2005): 279–292.

Galán, José I., and María J. Sánchez-Bueno. "The Continuing Validity of the Strategy-Structure Nexus: New Findings, 1993–2003." *Strategic Management Journal* 30 (2009a): 1234–1243.

Galán, José I., and María J. Sánchez-Bueno, "Strategy and Structure in Context: Universalism versus Institutional Effects." *Organization Studies* 30 (2009b): 609–619.

Galimberti, Fabrizio, and Luca Paolazzi. *Il Volo del Calabrone. Breve Storia dell'Economia Italiana nel Novecento.* Florence: Le Monnier, 1998.

Gallino, Luciano. *La Scomparsa dell'Italia Industriale.* Turin, Italy: Einaudi, 2003.

Gálvez Muñoz, Lina, and Francisco Comín Comín. "Multinacionales, Atraso Tec-nológico y Marco Institucional. Las Nacionalizaciones de Empresas Extranjeras Durante la Autarquía Franquista." *Cuadernos de Economía y Dirección de la Empresa* 17 (2003): 139–179.

Gámir Casares, Luis. *Las Privatizaciones en España.* Madrid: Ediciones Pirámide, 1999.

García Abadillo, Casimiro, and Luis F. Fidalgo. *La Rebelión de Los Albertos.* Madrid: Temas de Hoy, 1989.

García Ruiz, José Luis, and Carles Manera Erbina. *Historia Empresarial de España. Un Enfoque Regional en Profundidad.* Madrid: LID, 2006.

García Ruiz, José Luis, ed. *Revista de la Historia de la Economía y de la Empresa 1: Instituciones Financieras en España.* Bilbao: BBVA—Archivo Histórico, 2007.

Garmendia Ibáñez, Jesús. *La Economía Española en la Unión Europea 1986–2002.* Gipuzcoa, Spain: Euskal Herriko Unibersitateko Argitalpen Zerbitzua, 2004.

Gerschenkron, Alexander. *Economic Backwardness in Historical Perspective. A Book of Essays.* Cambridge, MA: The Belknap Press of Harvard University Press, 1962.

Giannetti, Renato, and Michelangelo Vasta, eds. *L'Impresa Italiana nel Novecento.* Bologna: Il Mulino, 2003.

Giannetti, Renato, and Michelangelo Vasta. "Big Business (1913–2001)." *In Forms of Enterprises in 20th Century Italy. Boundaries, Structures, and Strategies,* edited by Andrea Colli, and Michelangelo Vasta, 25–51. Cheltenham, UK: Edward Elgar, 2010.

Giner, José Miguel, and María Jesús Santa María. "Territorial Systems of Small Firms in Spain: An Analysis of Productive and Organizational Characteristics in Industrial Districts." *Entrepreneurship and Regional Development* 14 (2002): 211–228.

Goldstein, Andrea. "Privatization in Italy, 1993–2003: Goals, Institutions, Outcomes, and Outstanding Issues." In *Privatization Experiences in the European Union,* edited by Marco Köthenbürger, Hans-Werner Sinn, and John Whalley, 225–264. Cambridge, MA: MIT Press, 2006.

Gómez Mendoza, Antonio, ed. *De Mitos y Milagros. El Instituto Nacional de Autar-quía (1941–1963).* Barcelona: Publicacions i Edicions UB, 2000.

Goñi Mendizabal, Igor. "La Internacionalización de la Industria Armera Vasca, 1876–1970. El Distrito Industrial de Eibar y Sus Empresas." *Información Com-ercial Española* 849 (2009): 79–96.

Gonizzi, Giancarlo, ed. *Barilla: Centoventicinque Anni di Pubblicità e Comunicazione*. Parma, Italy: Barilla, 2003.

González Páramo, José Manuel. "Privatización y Eficiencia: ¿Es Irrelevante la Titularidad?" *Economistas* 63 (1995): 32–43.

González Postilla, Manuel, and José María Garmendia Urdangarín. "Corrupción y Mercado Negro: Nuevas Formas de Acumulación Capitalista." In *Los Empresarios de Franco. Política y Economía en España, 1936–1957*, edited by Glicerio Sánchez Recio and Julio Tascón Fernández, 237–260. Barcelona: Crítica, 2003.

Graziani, Augusto. *Lo Sviluppo dell'Economia Italiana. Dalla Ricostruzione alla Moneta Europea*. Turin, Italy: Bollati Boringhieri, 1998.

Gualerni, Gualberto. *Industria e Fascismo: Per una Interpretazione dello Sviluppo Economico Italiano tra le Due Guerre*. Milan: Vita e Pensiero, 1976.

Guillén, Mauro F. *Models of Management. Work, Authority, and Organization in a Comparative Perspective*. Chicago: University of Chicago Press, 1994.

———. "Business Groups in Emerging Economies: A Resource-Based View." *Academy of Management Journal* 43, no. 3 (2000): 362–380.

———. *The Limits of Convergence. Globalization and Organizational Change in Argentina, South Korea, and Spain*. Princeton, NJ: Princeton University Press, 2001.

———. *The Rise of Spanish Multinationals: European Business in the Global Economy*. New York: Cambridge University Press, 2005.

Guillén, Mauro F., and Esteban García-Canal. *The New Multinationals: Spanish Firms in a Global Context*. Cambridge: Cambridge University Press, 2010.

Guirao, Fernando. *Spain and the Reconstruction of Western Europe, 1945–1957*. New York: St. Martins Press, in association with St. Antony's College, Oxford, UK, 1998.

Haggard, Stephan. *Pathways from the Periphery. The Politics of Growth in the Newly Industrializing Countries*. Ithaca, NY: Cornell University Press, 1990.

Hannah, Leslie. *Delusions of a Durable Dominance or the Invisibile Hand Strikes Back*. London: London School of Economics, 1995.

———. "The American Miracle, 1875–1950, and After: A View in the European Mirror." *Business and Economic History* 24 (1995): 197–220.

———. "The 'Divorce' of Ownership from Control from 1900 Onwards: Re-calibrating Imagined Global Trends." *Business History* 49 (2007): 404–438.

Harrison, Bennett. "The Return of the Big Firms." *Social Policy* (Summer 1990): 7–18.

———. "The Myth of Small Firms as the Predominant Job Generators." *Economic Development Quarterly* February (1994): 3–18.

Hedlund, Gunnar. "A Model of Knowledge Management and the N-Form Corporation." *Strategic Management Journal* 15 (1994): 73–90.

Hill, Charles W. L. "Oliver Williamson and the M-Form Firm: A Critical Review." *Journal of Economic Issues* 19, no. 3 (1985): 731–751.

———. "Internal Capital Market Controls and Financial Performance in Multidivisional Firms." *Journal of Industrial Economics* 37, no. 1 (1988): 67–83.

Hofstede, Geert. *Culture's Consequence*. Newbury Park, CA: Sage, 1980.

———. *Cultures and Organizations*. London: McGraw-Hill, 1991.

Hofstede, Geert, Gert Jan Hofstede, and Michael Minkov. *Cultures and Organizations: Software of the Mind: Intercultural Cooperation and Its Importance for Survival*. New York: McGraw-Hill, 1997.

Hollingsworth, Rogers, and Robert Boyer, eds. *Contemporary Capitalism: The Embeddedness of Institutions*. Cambridge, MA: Cambridge University Press, 1997.

Hoskisson, Robert E. "Multidivisional Structure and Performance: The Diversification Strategy Contingency." *Academy of Management Journal* 30 (1987): 625–644.

Hoskisson, Robert E., Charles W. L. Hill, and Hicheon Kim. "The Multidivisional Structure: Organizational Fossil or Source of Value?" *Journal of Management* 19 (1993): 269–298.

Houpt, Stefan, and José María Ortiz-Villajos, eds. *Astilleros Españoles 1872–1998. La Construcción Naval en España*. Madrid: Lid, 1998.

Hymer, Stephen. *The International Operations of the Firm*. Cambridge, MA: MIT Press, 1976.

Ito, Takatoshi. *The Japanese Economy*. Cambridge, MA: MIT Press, 1992.

Jacobi, Neil H. "The Conglomerate Corporation." In *The Coming of Managerial Capitalism: A Casebook on the History of American Economic Institutions*, edited by Alfred D. Chandler, and Richard S. Tedlow, 740–755. Homewood, IL: R.D. Irwin, 1985.

John, Richard R. "Elaborations, Revisions, Dissents: Alfred D. Chandler Jr.'s The Visible Hand after Twenty Years." *Business History Review* 71, no. 2 (1997): 151–200.

John, Richard R., ed. *Ruling Passions: Political Economy in Nineteenth Century America*. University Park: The Pennsylvania State University Press, 2006.

Jones, Geoffrey. *Multinationals and Global Capitalism: From the Nineteenth to the Twenty-first Century*. Oxford, UK: Oxford University Press, 2005.

Jones, Geoffrey, and Jonathan Zeitlin, eds. *The Oxford Handbook of Business History*. Oxford, UK, and New York: Oxford University Press, 2008.

Kannah, Tarun, and Yishay Yafeh. "Business Groups in Emerging Markets: Paragons or Parasites?" ECGI – Finance Working Paper 95, European Corporate Governance Institute, Brussells, 2005.

Kindleberger, Charles. *American Business Abroad*. London: New Haven, 1969.

Kipping, Matthias. "American Management Consulting Companies in Western Europe, 1920 to 1990: Products, Reputation and Relationships." *Business History Review* 73, no. 2 (1999): 190–220.

Kipping, Matthias, and Ove Bjarnar, eds. *The Americanization of European Business: The Marshall Plan and the Transfer of U.S. Management*. London and New York: Routledge, 1998.

Kipping, Matthias, and Ludovic Cailluet. "Ménage à Trois: Alcan in Spain, 1950s to 1980s." *Cahiers d'Histoire de l'Aluminium* 44–45 (2010): 78–105.

Kipping, Matthias, and Núria Puig Raposo. "De la Teoría a la Práctica: Las Consultoras y la Organización de Empresas en Perspectiva Histórica." In *Historia Empresarial. Pasado, Presente y Retos de Futuro*, edited by Carmen Erro, 101–131. Barcelona: Ariel, 2003a.

———. "Entre Influencias Internacionales y Tradiciones Nacionales: Las Consultoras de Empresa en la España del Siglo XX." *Cuadernos de Economía y Dirección de la Empresa* 17 (2003b): 105–137.

Kipping, Matthias, and Gerarda Westerhuis. "Strategy, Ideology, and Structure: The Political Processes of Introducing the M-form in two Banks." In *History and Strategy (Advances in Strategic Management 29)*, edited by Steven J. Kahl, Brian S. Silverman, and Michael A. Cusumano, 187–237. City: Emerald Group Publishing Limited, 2012.

Koç Group. "1926 until Today." Accessed July 31, 2012. http://www.koc.com.tr/en-us/Corporate/History/Pages/1926_until_Today.aspx.Viohalco. "Company Profile." Accessed July 31, 2012. http://www.viohalco.gr/eng/company_profile.html.

Kogut, Bruce. "National Organizing Principles of Work and the Erstwhile Dominance of the American Multinational Corporation." *Industrial and Corporate Change* 1 (1992): 285–323.

Lai, Chi-Kong. "Chinese Business History: Its Development, Present Situation and Future Direction." In *Business History around the World*, edited by Franco Amatori, and Geoffrey Jones, 298–316. Cambridge, MA: Cambridge University Press, 2003.

Lains, Pedro, and Álvaro Ferreira da Silva, eds. *História Económica de Portugal 1700–2000, vol. 3*. Lisbon: ICS, 2005.

Langlois, Richard, and Paul Robertson. *Firms, Markets, and Economic Change: A Dynamic Theory of Business Institutions*. London: Routledge, 1995.

Langlois, Richard. "The Vanishing Hand: The Changing Dynamics of Industrial Capitalism." *Industrial and Corporate Change* 12 (2003): 351–385.
———. *The Dynamics of Industrial Capitalism: Schumpeter, Chandler, and the New Economy*. Oxford, UK: Oxford University Press, 2007.
La Porta, Rafael, Florencio López-de-Silanes, and Andrei Shleifer. "Corporate Ownership around the World." *Journal of Finance* 54, no. 2 (1999): 471–517.
Lavista, Fabio. "Diffondere la Cultura Manageriale. Trasformazioni Tecnologiche e Organizzative nell'Industria Meccanica Italiana tra la Fine della Seconda Guerra Mondiale e il Boom Economico." *Annali di Storia dell'Impresa* 15–16 (2004–2005): 531–552.
Lazonick, William H.. *Business Organization and the Myth of the Market Economy*. New York: Cambridge University Press, 1991.
Lepore Dubois, Gian Franco, and Claudio Sonzogno. *L'Impero della Chimica*. Rome: Newton Compton, 1990.
Lewis, Paul. "John S. Latsis, 92, Billionaire Who Built Empire in Shipping." *New York Times*, April 18, 2003.
Linz, Juan José, and Amando De Miguel. "Fundadores, Herederos, y Directores en las Empresas Españolas." *Revista Internacional de Sociología* 20, no. 81 (1963): 5–38.
López Muñoz, Ángel. "El Debate sobre la Empresa Pública". *Anuario El País* 1983.
Louçã, Francisco, and Sandro Mendonça. "Steady Change: The 200 Largest US Manufacturing Firms Throughout the Twentieth Century." *Industrial & Corporate Change* 11, no. 4 (2002): 817–845.
Luzzatto, Gino. *L'Economia Italiana dal 1861 al 1894*. Turin: Einaudi, 1980.
Macchiati, Alfredo. "Breve Storia delle Privatizzazioni in Italia: 1992–1999. Ovvero: Si Poteva far Meglio?" *Il Mulino* 3 (1999): 447–470.
Malefakis, Edward. "La Economía Española y la Guerra Civil" In *La Economía Española en el Siglo XX. Una Perspectiva Histórica*, edited by Jordi Nadal, Albert Carreras, and Carles Sudrià, 150–163. Barcelona: Ariel, 1987.
Malerba, Franco, and Luigi Orsenigo. "The Dynamics and Evolution of Industries." *Industrial and Corporate Change* 5, no. 1 (1996): 51–87.
Maravall, Fernando, and Ramón Pérez Simarro. *Estudios de Economía Española. Estructura y Resultados de las Grandes Empresas Industriales*. Madrid: MINER, Secretaría General Tecnica, 1985.
Markides, Constantinos. *Diversification, Refocusing, and Economic Performance*. Cambridge, MA: MIT Press, 1995.
Maroto Acín, Juan Antonio. "La Situación Empresarial en España, 1982–1989." *Cuadernos de Información Económica* 44–45 (1990): 1–23.
Martín Aceña, Pablo, and Francisco Comín Comín. *INI, 50 Años de Industrialización en España*. Madrid: Espasa Calpe, 1991.
Martín Aceña, Pablo, *El Servicio de Estudios del Banco de España, 1930–2000*. Madrid: Banco de España, 2000.
Martinelli, Alberto, and Antonio M. Chiesi. *La Società Italiana*. Rome-Bari: Laterza, 2002.
Martinoli, Gino. *Il Dirigente oggi: Un Mestiere difficile*. Milan: Etas Kompass, 1971.
Martins, Maria Belmira. *Sociedades e Grupos em Portugal*. Lisbon: Seara Nova, 1973.
McCraw, Thomas K., ed. *America versus Japan*. Boston: Harvard Business School Press, 1986.
———. *The Essential Alfred Chandler. Essays Towards a Historical Theory of Big Business*. Boston: Harvard Business School Press, 1988.
McKenna, Christopher D. "The American Challenge: McKinsey & Company's Role in the Transfer of Decentralization to Europe. 1957–1975." *Academy of Management Best Paper Proceedings* (1997): 226–231.
Medina Albaladejo, Francisco José. "External Competitiveness of Spanish Canned Fruit and Vegetable Businesses during the Second Half of the Twentieth Century." *Business History* 52/3 (2010): 417–434.

————. "Cooperativismo y Sector Vitivinícola en España, 1940–2009." PhD diss., Murcia University, Murcia, Spain, 2011.

Merlo, Elisabetta, "Italian Fashion Business: Achievements and Challenges (1970s–2000s)." *Business History* 53 (2011): 344–362.

Miranda Encarnación, José Antonio. "El Fracaso de la Industrialización Autárquica." In *Autarquía y Mercado Negro. El Fracaso Económico del Primer Franquismo, 1939–1959*, edited by Carlos Barciela López, 95–121. Barcelona: Crítica, 2003.

Mochón, Francisco, and Alfredo Rambla. *La Creación de Valor y las Grandes Empresas Españolas*. Barcelona: Ariel, 1999.

Molina, José Luis, and Pablo Martín Aceña, eds. *The Spanish Financial System. Growth and Development since 1900*. Madrid: Alianza, 2011.

Molinero, Carme, and Pere Ysas. "Las Condiciones de Vida y Laborales Durante el Primer Franquismo. La Subsistencia ¿Un Problema Político?," 2003. http://www.unizer.es/eveez/cache/molinero.pdf.

Molteni, Mario. *Il Gruppo Fininvest: Imprenditorialità, Crescita, Riassetto*. Turin: Isedi, 1998.

Montañés, Enrique. *La Empresa Exportadora del Jerez. Historia Económica de González Byass, 1835–1885*. Cádiz, Spain: Universidad de Cádiz, 2000a.

————. "El Vino de Jerez en el Sector Exterior Español, 1838–1885." *Revista de Historia Industrial* 17 (2000b): 113–123.

Mori, Giorgio. *Il Capitalismo Industriale in Italia*. Rome: Editori Riuniti, 1977.

Morikawa, Hidemasa. *Zaibatsu: The Rise and Fall of Family Enterprise Groups in Japan*. Tokyo: University of Tokyo Press, 1992.

Morikawa, Hidemasa, ed. *A History of Top Management in Japan: Managerial Enterprises and Family Enterprises*. Oxford, UK: Oxford University Press, 2001.

Moya, Carlos. *El Poder Económico en Espana, (1939–1970). Un Análisis Sociológico*. Madrid: Túcar, 1975.

Mucchetti, Massimo. *Licenziare i Padroni?* Milan: Feltrinelli, 2003.

Muñoz, Juan. *El Poder de la Banca en España*. Madrid: ZYX, 1969.

Muñoz, Juan, Santiago Roldán, and Ángel Serrano. *La Internacionalización del Capital en España 1959–1977*. Madrid: Cuadernos para el Dialogo, 1978.

Muñoz Linares, Carlos. "El Pliopolio en Algunos Sectores del Sistema Económico Español." *Revista de Economía Política* 7, no. 1 (1955): 3–66.

Mylonas, Paul, and Isabelle Joumar. "Greek Public Enterprises: Challenges for Reform." Economics Department Working Papers 214, OECD Papers, eco/wkp(99)6, Organisation for Economic Co-operation and Development, Paris.

Nadal, Jordi. *El Fracaso de la Revolución Industrial en España, 1814–1913*. Barcelona: Ariel, 1975.

Nadal, Jordi, Albert Carreras, and Xoán Carmona Badía. *Pautas Regionales de la Industrialización Española, Siglos XIX y XX*. Ariel: Barcelona, 1990.

Nardozzi, Giangiacomo, ed. *Privatizzazioni e Competitività delle Imprese*. Genoa: Fondazione Ansaldo Editore, 2011.

Navas, José Antonio and Fernando Nadal. *El Secreto de Torre Picasso: La Verdadera Historia de la Batalla Koplowitz-Albertos*. Barcelona: Planeta, 1990.

Nicolau, Roser. "Población, Salud y Actividad." In *Estadísticas Históricas de España. Siglos XIX-XX*, edited by Albert Carreras and Xavier Tafunell, 77–154. Bilbao, Spain: Fundación BBVA, 2005.

Nitti, Francesco Saverio. *Il Capitale Straniero in Italia*. Naples: Tipografia Federico San Giovanni, 1915.

Nohria, Nitin, Davis Dyer, and Frederick Dalzell. *Changing Fortunes. Remaking the Industrial Corporation*. New York: John Wiley & Sons, 2002.

Nueno, Pedro. *Las 49 Empresas con Más Futuro*. Barcelona: Gestión, 1996.

Önis, Ziya. "Redemocratization and Economic Liberation in Turkey: The Limits of State Economy." *Studies in Comparative International Development* 27 (1992): 3–23.

Ori, Angiolo Silvio. *Dove va l'Industria Alimentare Italiana? Anatomia di una Crisi.* Modena: STEM Mucchi, 1973.

Osti, Gian Lupo, and Ruggero Ranieri. *L'Industria di Stato dall'Ascesa al Degrado.* Bologna: Il Mulino, 1993.

Pagano Marco, Fabio Panetta, and Luigi Zingales. "The Stock Market as a Source of Capital: Some Lessons from Initial Public Offerings in Italy." *European Economic Review* 40 (1996): 1057–1069.

Palmer, Donald, Roger Friedland, P. Devereaux Jennings, and Melanie Powers. "The Economics and Politics of Structure: The Multidivisional Form and the Large U.S. Corporation." *Administrative Science Quarterly* 32 (1987): 25–48.

Palmer, Donald, P. Devereaux Jennings, and Zueguang Zhou, "Late Adoption of the Multidivisional Form by Large U.S. Corporations: Institutional, Political and Economic Accounts." *Administrative Science Quarterly* 38 (1993): 100–131.

Papadia, Elena. *La Rinascente.* Bologna: Il Mulino, 2005.

Patronis, Vassilis, and Panagiotis Liargovas. "Economic Policy in Greece, 1974–2000: Nationalization, State's Intervention or Market Forces?" *Enterprises et Histoire* 37 (2004): 120–134.

Pavan, Robert J. *Strutture e Strategie delle Imprese Italiane.* Bologna: Il Mulino, 1976.

Pellegrini, Guido. "Lo Sviluppo Strutturale dell'Economia Italiana dal Dopoguerra al Nuovo Secolo." In *Storia economica d'Italia*, vol. 3.1, edited by Pierluigi Ciocca and Gianni Toniolo 195–224. Rome-Bari: Laterza, 2003.

Pérez, Sofía A. *Banking on Privilege: The Politics of Spanish Financial Reform.* Ithaca, NY: Cornell University Press, 1997.

Pérez Díaz, Víctor. *Spain at the Crossroads. Civil Society, Politics, and the Rule of Law.* Cambridge, MA: Harvard University Press, 1999.

Pérez García, Encarna, and Miguel Ángel Nieto Solís. *Los Complices de Mario Conde. La Verdad sobre Banesto, su Presidente y la Corporación Industrial.* Madrid: Temas de Hoy, 1993.

Perrini, Francesco. *Le Nuove Quotazioni alla Borsa Italiana. Evidenze Empiriche delle PMI.* Milan: Egea, 1999.

Perugini, Mario. "Grande Impresa e Italia Autarchica. La Montecatini 1929–1943." PhD diss., Bocconi University, Milan, 2009.

Perugini, Mario, and Valentina Romei. "Small Firms and Local Production Systems." In *Forms of Enterprises in 20th Century Italy. Boundaries, Structures, and Strategies,* edited by Andrea Colli and Michelangelo Vasta, 161–184. Cheltenham: Edward Elgar, 2010.

Piluso, Giandomenico. *Il Banchiere Dimezzato. Finanza e Impresa in Italia.* Venice: Marsilio, 2004.

———. *Mediobanca. Tra Regole e Mercato.* Milan: Egea, 2005.

Pini, Massimo. *I Giorni dell'IRI—Storie e Misfatti da Beneduce a Prodi.* Milan: Mondadori, 2000.

Piol, Elserino. *Il Sogno di un'Impresa.* Milan: Il Sole 24 Ore, 2004.

Piore, Michael J., and Charles F. Sabel. *The Second Industrial Divide: Possibilities for Prosperity.* New York: Basic Books, 1984.

Pirani, Mario. "Tre Appuntamenti Mancati dell'Industria Italiana." *Il Mulino* 6 (1991): 1045–1051.

Pizzorni, Geoffrey J., ed. *L'Industria Chimica Italiana nel Novecento.* Milan: Angeli, 2006.

Polese, Francesca. *Alla Ricerca di un'Industria Nuova. Il Viaggio all'Estero del Giovane Pirelli e le Origini di una Grande Impresa (1870–1877).* Venice: Marsilio, 2004.

Pons, Maria Ángeles. "Capture or Agreement? Why Spanish Banking Was Regulated under the Franco Regime (1939–1975)." *Financial History Review* 6 (1999): 25–46.

———. "Banca e Industria en España, 1939–1985: La Influencia de la Banca Universal en el Crecimiento Económico." *Revista de Historia Industrial* 19–20 (2001).

Porter, Michael E. *The Competitive Advantage of Nations.* London: Macmillan, 1990.

Pozzi, Daniele. *Dai Gatti Selvaggi al Cane a Sei Zampe. Tecnologia, Conoscenza e Organizzazione nell'AGIP e nell'Eni di Enrico Mattei.* Venice: Marsilio, 2009.

———. *Una Sfida al Capitalismo: Giuseppe E. Luraghi.* Venice: Marsilio, 2012.

Prados de la Escosura, Leandro, and Vera Zamagni. *El Desarrollo Económico en la Europa del Sur: España e Italia en Perspectiva Histórica.* Madrid: Alianza, 1992.

Pueyo Sánchez, Javier. *El Comportamiento de la Gran Banca en España (1921–1974).* Estudios de Historia Económica, Banco de España, no. 48, Madrid, 2006a.

———. "Relaciones Interempresariales y Consejeros Comunes en la Banca Española del Siglo XX." *Investigaciones de Historia Económica* 6 (2006b): 137–168.

Puig Raposo, Núria. "La Nacionalización de la Industria Farmacéutica en España: El Caso de las Empresas Alemanas, 1914–1975." Documento de Trabajo, Fundación Empresa Pública, Madrid, 2001.

———. *Bayer, Cepsa, Repsol, Puig, Schering y La Seda. Constructores de la Química Española.* Madrid: Lid, 2003.

———. "Redes Empresariales de Oportunidad en la España del siglo XX: El Caso de la Industria Químico-Farmacéutica." *Información Comercial Española—Historia Empresarial* 812 (2004): 179–188.

Puig Raposo, Núria, and Adoración Álvaro Moya, "¿Misión Imposible? La Expropiación de las Empresas Alemanas en España, 1945–1975." *Investigaciones de Historia Económica* 7 (2007): 101–130.

Puig Raposo, Núria, and Paloma Fernández Pérez. "The Education of Spanish Entreperenurs and Managers: Madrid and Barcelona Business Schools, 1950–1975." *Paedagogica Histórica* 39, no. 5 (2003): 651–672.

———. "La Gran Empresa Familiar Española en el Siglo XX: Claves de Su Profesionalización." *Revista de Historia de la Economía y de la Empresa. Historia Empresarial Española* 2 (2008): 93–122.

Ramella, Franco. *Terra e Telai. Sistemi di Parentela e Manifattura nel Biellese dell'Ottocento.* Turin: Einaudi, 1984.

Ramón-Laca Cotorruelo, Jesús J. "El Monopolio de Petróleos y la Industria Española del Petréleo." *Hacienda Pública Española* 53 (1978): 133–171.

Rapini, Andrea. *La Nazionalizzazione a Due Ruote: Genesi e Decollo di uno Scooter Italiano.* Bologna: Il Mulino, 2007.

Rinaldi, Alberto. "Imprenditori e Manager (1913–1972)." In *L'Impresa Italiana nel Novecento,* edited by Renato Giannetti and Michelangelo Vasta, 371–417. Bologna: Il Mulino: 2003.

Rodrigo Alharilla, Martín. *Los Marqueses de Comillas, 1817–1925. Antonio y Claudio López.* Madrid: Lid, 2000.

———. *La Familia Gil. Empresarios Catalanes en la Europa del Siglo XIX.* Barcelona: Fundación Gas Natural, 2010.

Román, Manuel. *Los Límites del Crecimiento Económico en España, 1959–1967.* Madrid: Ayuso, 1972.

Romano, Roberto. "Il Cotonificio Cantoni dalle Origini al 1900." *Studi Storici* 16 (1975): 461–494.

Romeo, Rosario. *Risorgimento e Capitalismo.* Rome-Bari: Laterza, 1959.

———. *Breve Storia della Grande Industria in Italia.* Milan: Mondadori, 1988.

Rossi, Nicola, Andrea Sorgato, and Gianni Toniolo. "I Conti Economici Italiani: Una Ricostruzione Statistica, 1890–1990." *Rivista di Storia Economica* 10, no. 1 (1993): 1–47.

Roy, William G. *Socializing Capital. The Rise of the Large Industrial Corporation in America.* Princeton, NJ: Princeton University Press, 1997.

Rugafiori, Paride. *Imprenditori e Manager nella Storia d'Italia.* Rome-Bari: Laterza, 1999.

Rumelt, Richard P. *Strategy, Structure and Economic Performance.*Cambridge, MA: Harvard University Press, 1974.

Sabel, Charles F., and Jonathan Zeitlin. *World of Possibilities.* New York and Cambridge: Cambridge University Press, 1997.

Salgado de Matos, Luís. *Investimentos Estrangeiros em Portugal.* Lisbon: Seara Nova, 1973.

Salvati, Michele. *Occasioni Mancate. Economia e Politica in Italia dagli Anni Sessanta ad Oggi.* Rome-Bari: Laterza 2000.

Sánchez-Bueno, María J., José I. Galán Zazo, and Isabel Suárez González. "Evolución de la Estrategia y la Estructura de la Gran Empresa Española: Análisis Comparado con la Evidencia Europea." *Universia Business Review* 11 (2006): 22–35.

Sánchez Recio, Glicerio. "El Franquismo como Red de Intereses." In *Los Empresarios de Franco. Política y Economía en España, 1936–1957,* edited by Glicerio Sánchez Recio and Julio Tascón Fernández 13–22. Barcelona: Crítica, 2003.

Sánchez Sánchez, Esther M. "La Implantación Industrial de Renault en España: Los Origines de FASA-Renault, 1950–1970." *Revista de Historia Económica* 1, no. 22 (2004): 147–175.

San Román, Elena, and Carles Sudrià. "Synthetic Fuels in Spain, 1942–66: The Failure of Franco's Autarkic Dream." *Business History* 45, no. 4 (2003): 73–88.

Santamaría, Javier. *El Petróleo en España del Monopolio a la Libertad.* Madrid: Espasa Calpe, 1988.

Santos, Américo dos. "Desenvolvimento Monopolista em Portugal (Fase 1968–73): Estructuras Fundamentais." *Análise Social* 49 (1977): 69–95.

Sapelli, Giulio. *Organizzazione, Lavoro e Innovazione Industriale nell'Italia tra le Due Guerre.* Turin, Italy: Rosenberg & Sellier, 1978.

———. "L'Organizzazione del Lavoro all'Alfa Romeo, 1930–1951. Contraddizioni e Superamento del 'Modello Svizzero'" *Storia in Lombardia* 2 (1987): 316–332

———. *Economia, Tecnologia e Direzione d'Impresa in Italia.* Turin, Italy: Einaudi, 1994a.

———. "La Edison di Giorgio Valerio." In *Storia dell'Industria Elettrica in Italia. Dal Dopoguerra alla Nazionalizzazione 1945–1962,* edited by Valerio Castronovo, 521–546. Rome-Bari: Laterza, 1994b.

———. *L'Europa del Sud dopo il 1945. Tradizione e Modernità in Portogallo, Spagna, Italia, Grecia e Turchia.* Soveria Mannelli, Italy: Rubbettino Editore, 1996.

Sarti, Roland. *Fascismo e Grande Industria: 1919–1940.* Milan: Moizzi, 1977.

Scalfari, Eugenio, and Giuseppe Turani. *Razza Padrona. Storia della Borghesia di Stato.* Milan: Feltrinelli, 1974.

Scalfari, Eugenio. *Guido Carli: Intervista sul Capitalismo Italiano.* Turin, Italy: Bollati Boringhieri, 2008.

Scarpellini, Emanuela. *Comprare all'Americana. Le Origini della Rivoluzione Commerciale in Italia, 1945–1971.* Bologna: Il Mulino, 2001.

Schröter, Harm, ed. *The European Enterprise. Historical Investigation into a Future Species,* Berlin: Springer, 2007.

Schumacher, Ernest F. *Small is Beautiful. Economics as if People Mattered.* London: Blond and Briggs, 1973.

Scott, Bruce R.. *Stages of Corporate Development.* Boston: Harvard Graduate School of Business Administration, 1970.

Scranton, Philip. *Endless Novelty: Specialty Production and American Industrialization, 1865–1925.* Princeton, NJ: Princeton University Press, 1997.

Segreto, Luciano. "Italian Capitalism between the Private and Public Sectors, 1933–1993." *Business and Economic History* 27, no. 2 (1998): 649–661.

———. *Giacinto Motta: Un Ingegnere alla Testa del Capitalismo Industriale Italiano.* Rome-Bari: Laterza, 2004.

Sereni, Emilio. *Il Capitalismo nelle Campagne (1860–1900)*. Turin, Italy: Einaudi, 1947.

Servan-Schreiber, Jean-Jacques. *Le Défi Américain*. Paris: Denoël, 1967.

Shleifer, Andrei, and Robert W. Vishny. "Large Shareholders and Corporate Control." *Journal of Political Economy* 94 (1996): 461–488.

Shutt, John, and Richard Whittington. "Fragmentation Strategies and the Rise of Small Units: Cases from the North West." *Regional Studies*, 21 (1987): 13–23.

Siciliano, Giovanni. *Cento Anni di Borsa in Italia*. Bologna: Il Mulino, 2001.

Sierra Álvarez, José. *El Obrero Soñado. Ensayo sobre el Paternalismo Industrial (Asturias, 1860–1917)*. Madrid: Siglo Ventiuno de España, 1990.

Siniscalco, Domenico, Bernardo Bortolotti, Marcella Fantini, and Serena Vitalini. *Privatizzazioni Difficili*. Bologna: Il Mulino, 1999.

Soria, Luciano. *Un'Occasione Perduta. La Divisione Elettronica dell'Olivetti nei Primi Anni del Centrosinistra*. Turin: Einaudi, 1979.

Soto Carmona, Álvaro. "Ruptura y Continuidades en las Relaciones Laborales del Primer Franquismo, 1938–1958." In *Autarquía y Mercado Negro. El Fracaso Económico del Primer Franquismo*, edited by Carlos Barciela López, 217–246. Barcelona: Crítica, 2003.

Supple, Barry. "Scale and Scope: Alfred Chandler and the Dynamics of Industrial Capitalism. Review of *Scale and Scope: The Dynamics of Industrial Capitalism* by Alfred D. Chandler." *The Economic History Review* 44 (1991): 500–514.

Tafunell, Xavier. "Empresa y Bolsa." In *Estadísticas Históricas de España. Siglos XIX-XX*, edited by Albert Carreras, and Xavier Tafunell, 707–834. Bilbao, Spain: Fundación BBVA, 2005.

Tamames, Ramón. *Estructura Económica de España*. Madrid: Alianza, 1992.

Tascón Fernández, Julio. "Las Inversiones Extranjeras en España Durante el Franquísmo: Para un Estado de la Cuestión" *Pasado y Memoria* 1 (2002): 5–35.

———. "Capital Internacional antes de la "Internacionalización del Capital" en España, 1936–1959." In *Los Empresarios de Franco. Política y Economía en España, 1936–1957*, edited by Glicerio Sánchez Recio and Julio Tascón Fernández, 281–306. Barcelona: Crítica, 2003.

———. *Redes de Empresas en España. Una Perspectiva Teórica, Histórica y Global*. Madrid: Lid, 2005.

Tattara Giuseppe, and Paolo Crestanello. "Towards a Global Network. Competition and Restructuring of the Benetton." MPRA Paper, University Library of Munich, 2008.

Teece, David J. "The Dynamics of Industrial Capitalism: Perspective on Scale and Scope." *Journal of Economic Literature* 31 (1993): 199–225.

Thanheiser, Heinz T. "The Strategy and Structure of German Enterprise." Phd diss., Harvard Business School, Cambridge, MA, 1972.

Toboso Sánchez, Pilar. "Grandes Almacenes y Almacenes Populares en España. Una Visión Histórica." Documento de Trabajo 2, Fundación SEPI, 2002.

Toninelli, Pier Angelo. *Industria, Impresa e Stato. Tre Saggi sullo Sviluppo Economico Italiano*. Trieste, Italy: Università di Trieste, 2003.

Toninelli, Pier Angelo, and Michelangelo Vasta, "State-Owned Enterprises (1936–1983)." In *Forms of Enterprises in 20th Century Italy. Boundaries, Structures, and Strategies*, edited by Andrea Colli and Michelangelo Vasta, 52–86. Cheltenham, UK: Edward Elgar, 2010.

Toniolo, Gianni. *L'Economia dell'Italia Fascista*. Rome-Bari: Laterza, 1980.

Toniolo, Gianni, and Vincenzo Visco, eds. *Il Declino Economico dell'Italia. Cause e Rimedi*. Milan: Bruno Mondadori, 2004.

Torres Villanueva, Eugenio, ed. *Los 100 Empresarios Españoles del Siglo XX*. Madrid: Lid, 2000.

Torres Villanueva, Eugenio. "La Empresa en la Autarquía, 1939–1959. Iniciativa Pública versus Inciativa Privada." In *Autarquía y Mercado Negro. El Fracaso*

Económico del Primer Franquísmo, 1939–1959, edited by Carlos Barciela López, 169–216. Barcelona: Crítica, 2003.

———. "Comportamientos Empresariales en una Economía Intervenida: España, 1936–1957." In *Los Empresarios de Franco. Política y Economía en España, 1936–1957*, edited by Glicerio Sánchez Recio and Julio Tascón Fernández, 198–224. Barcelona: Crítica, 2003.

———. "Las Grandes Empresas Constructoras Españolas. Crecimiento e Internacionalización en la Segunda Mitad del Siglo XX." *Información Comercial Española* 849 (2009): 113–127.

———. *Origen, Crecimiento e Internacionalización de las Grandes Empresas Españolas de la Construcción (1900–2008)*. Bogotá: Universidad de los Andes, 2011.

Tortella Casares, Gabriel. *El Desarrollo de la España Contemporánea. Historia Económica de los Siglos XIX y XX*. Madrid: Alianza, 1994.

Tortella Casares, Gabriel, and José Luis García Ruiz. *Una Historia de los Bancos Central e Hispano Américano. Un Siglo de Gran Banca en España*. Unpublished manuscript, 1999.

Tortella Casares, Gabriel. "El Triunfo del Centralismo: Breve Historia del Banco Central, 1920–1991." *Revista de la Historia de la Economía y de la Empresa* 1 (2007): 213–249.

Travesi, Andrés. *La Empresa Española*. Madrid: Asociación para el Progreso de la Dirección, 1969.

Trigo Portela, Joaquín. *Veinte Años de Privatizaciones en España*. Madrid: Instituto de Estudios Económicos, 2004.

Tripathi, Dwijendra. *The Oxford History of Indian Business*. New Delhi: Oxford University Press, 2004.

Turani, Giuseppe. *I Sogni del Grande Nord*. Bologna: Il Mulino, 1996.

Turone, Sergio. *Storia del Sindacato in Italia*. Rome-Bari: Laterza, 1992.

Valdaliso Gago, Jesús María. "Grupos Empresariales, Marco Institucional y Desarrollo Económico en España en el Siglo XX: Los Negocios de la Familia Aznar (c. 1937–c. 1983)." *Revista de Historia Económica* 3, no. 20 (2002): 577–624.

———. "Grupos Empresariales y Relaciones Banca-Industria en España durante el Franquísmo: Una Aproximación Microeconómica." *Información Comercial Española—Historia Empresarial* 812 (2004): 163–177.

———. *La Familia Aznar y Sus Negocios (1830–1983). Cuatro Generaciones de Empresarios en la España Contemporánea*. Madrid: Marcial Pons, 2006.

Vasta, Michelangelo, "The Largest 200 Manufacturing Firms (1913–2001)." In *Evolution of Italian Enterprises in the 20th Century*, edited by Renato Giannetti and Michelangelo Vasta, 87–110. Heidelberg and New York: Physica-Verlag (Springer), 2006.

Vernon, Raymond. "International Investment and International Trade in the Product Cycle." *Quarterly Journal of Economics* 80 (1966): 190–207.

Vernon, Raymond. *Storm over the Multinationals: The Real Issues*. Cambridge, MA: Harvard Univerity Press, 1977.

Vidal Olivares, Javier. *Las Alas de España. Iberia, Lineas Aéreas (1940–2005)*. Valencia, Spain: Publicacions de la Universitat de València, 2008.

Vila Fradera, Jorge. *La Gran Aventura del Turismo en España*. Barcelona: Editur, 1997.

Waddington, Conrad H. *The Ethical Animal*. London: G. Allen & Unwin, 1960.

Wardley, Peter. "The Anatomy of Big Business. Aspects of Corporate Development in the Twentieth Century." *Business History* 33 (1991): 268–296.

Weimer, Jeroen, and Joost C. Pape. "A Taxonomy of Systems of Corporate Governance." *Corporate Governance* 7 (1999): 152–166.

Whitley, Richard. "Dominant Form of Economic Organization in Market Economies." *Organization Studies* 15 (1994): 153–182.

———. *Divergent Capitalisms. The Social Structuring and Change of Business Systems.* Oxford, UK: Oxford University Press, 1999.

Whitley, Richard, and Peer Hull Kristensen. *The Changing European Firm. Limits to Convergence.* London: Routledge, 1996.

Whittington, Richard, ed. *Comparative Perspectives on the "Managerial Revolution."* Special issue. *Business History* 49, no. 4 (2007).

Whittington, Richard, Michael Mayer, and Francesco Curto. "Chandlerism in Postwar Europe: Strategic and Structural Change in France, Germany, and the UK, 1950–1993." *Industrial and Corporate Change* 8, no. 3 (1999): 519–551.

Whittington, Richard, and Michael Mayer. *The European Corporation: Strategy, Structure and Social Science.* Oxford, UK: Oxford University Press, 2000.

Wilkins, Mira. *The Emergence of Multinational Enterprise: American Business Abroad from the Colonial Era to 1914.* Cambridge, MA: Harvard University Press, 1970.

———. *The Maturing of Multinational Enterprise: American Business Abroad from 1914 to 1970.* Cambridge, MA: Harvard University Press, 1974.

Williamson, Oliver E. "The Multidivisional Hypothesis." In *The Corporate Economy: Growth, Competition, and Innovative Potential,* edited by Robin Marris and Adrian Wood, 343–386. London: Macmillan, 1971.

Wilson, John F., Martin Jes Iversen, Harm Schröter, Andrea Colli, Veronica Binda, and Valerie Antcliffe. "Mapping Corporate Europe: Business Responses to Institutional Change, 1957–2007." *European Journal of International Management* 1, no. 3 (2007): 225–238.

Wrigley, Leonard. "Divisional Autonomy and Diversification." PhD diss., Harvard Business School, Cambridge, MA, 1970.

Zamagni, Vera. *Industrializzazione e Squilibri Regionali in Italia.* Il Mulino: Bologna, 1978.

———. *Dalla Periferia al Centro. La Seconda Rinascita Economica dell'Italia (1861–1990).* Bologna: Il Mulino, 1990.

Zamagni, Vera, ed. *Come Perdere la Guerra e Vincere la Pace.* Bologna: Il Mulino, 1997.

Zamagni, Vera. *Italcementi. Dalla Leadership Nazionale all'Internazionalizzazione.* Bologna: Il Mulino, 2006a.

———. "The Rise and Fall of the Italian Chemical Industry, 1950s-1990s." In *The Global Chemical Industry in the Age of the Petrochemical Revolution,* edited by Louis Galambos, Takashi Hikino, and Vera Zamagni, 347–367. Cambridge: Cambridge University Press, 2006b.

Zamagni, Vera, and Emanuele Felice. *Oltre il Secolo: le Trasformazioni del Sistema Cooperativo Legacoop alla Fine del Secondo Millennio.* Bologna: Il Mulino, 2006.

Zanetti, Giovanni. *Gli Sviluppi dell'ENEL: 1963–1990. Storia dell'Industria Elettrica in Italia. Vol. 5.* Rome-Bari: Laterza, 1994.

SOURCES: YEARBOOKS, STATISTICAL SURVEYS AND ANNUAL REPORTS

Yearbooks and Statistical Surveys

Anuario Financiero que Comprende el Historial de Valores Públicos y de Sociedades Anónimas de España, Madrid, various years.

Anuario Oficial de Valores de las Bolsas de Madrid y Barcelona, Madrid: various years.

Associazione fra le Società Italiane per Azioni. *Società Italiane per Azioni: Notizie Statistiche,* Rome: various years.

Associazione Nazionale fra le Società Italiane per Azioni, ed. *Repertorio delle Società Italiane per Azioni,* Rome, various years.

Banco de Bilbao, *Agenda Financiera*. Bilbao: various years.
Bolsa de Barcelona. *Boletín Financiero*. Barcelona: various years.
Bolsa de Madrid. *Anuario Oficial de Valores*. Madrid: various years.
Borsa Italiana. *Fatti e cifre*. Milan: various years.
Credito Italiano. *Guida dell'Azionista*. Milan: various years.
————. *Rapporto sulle Esportazioni Italiane*. Various years.
El Pais. *Anuario*. Madrid: various years.
Equipo Mundo. *Los 90 Ministros de Franco*. Barcelona: Dopesa, 1970.
European Commision's Directorate General for Economic & Financial Affairs. *European Economy—The Statistical Annex*. Various years.
Fomento de la Producción. *Campeones 1973 de la Exportación Española*. Barcelona: 1974.
————. *Las Mayores Empresas Españolas en 1973*. Barcelona: 1974.
————. *Las Mayores Empresas Españolas en 1988*. Barcelona: 1989.
————. *Las Mayores Empresas Españolas en 2002*. Barcelona: 2003.
————. *Las Mayores Exportadoras en . . . .* Various years.
Fortune Global 500 (special issue), *Fortune*, 21 July 2003: 1–42.
Il mondo in cifre. The Economist Newspaper Ltd., various years.
Instituto Nacional de Estadística. *Estadística Industrial 1973*. Madrid, 1975
International Monetary Fund. *International financial statistic yearbook*. Washington, DC: Various years.
Maddison, Angus. *Monitoring the World Economy*. Paris: OECD, 1995.
————. *Historical Statistics for the World Economy: 1–2003 AD*, 2007. http://www.ggdc.net/.
Mediobanca. *Calepino dell'azionista*. Milan: various years.
————. *Indici e Dati Relativi ad Investimenti in Titoli Quotati nelle Borse Italiane*. Milan: various years.
————. *Le Principali Società Italiane 1973*. Milan: 1974.
————. *Le Principali Società Italiane 1988*. Milan: 1989.
————. *Le Principali Società Italiane 2003*. Milan: 2004.
————. *R&S*. Milan: various years.
Mediobanca Ricerche e Studi. *Le Privatizzazioni in Italia dal 1992*. Milan: Commissione Bilancio della Camera dei Deputati, 2001.
Ministerio de Industria y Energía. *Informe Anual sobre la Industria Española*. Madrid: various years.
Ministerio de Industria y Energía. *La Industria Española en . . . .*Madrid: various years.
————. *La Industria Española en el Siglo XX*. Madrid: 1980.
Ministerio de la Gobernación, Dirección General de Correos y Telecomunicación, Oficina de Estudios. *Memoria de los Servicios de Telecomunicación de España Año 1949*.
Ministerio de Industria y Energía. *Las 500 Grandes Empresas Industriales Españolas en 1974*. Madrid: 1975.
Ministerio dell'Industria e del Commercio. *L'Istituto*. Rome: various years.
Ministero per la Costituente, *Rapporto della Commissione Economica presentato all'Assemblea Costituente, II, Industria*, Poligrafico dello Stato, Rome, 1947.
Monotti, Carlo. *I Gruppi Industriali in Italia*. Turin: Valentino, 1975.
Organisation for Economic Co-operation and Development (OECD). *OECD Reviews of Foreign Direct Investment, Greece*. Paris: Head of Publications Service, OECD, 1994.
Organsiation for Economic Co-operation and Development (OECD). *OECD Economic Surveys: Spain*. 2010.
Privatization Barometer. Various years.
Rey, Guido M., ed. *I conti Economici dell'Italia*. Rome-Bari: Laterza, 1991.
"Spain Rocks." *Time*, 163, no. 10 (March 8, 2004): XX–XX.

"The 300 Largest Industrial Companies Outside the U.S." *Fortune*, May 1974: 176–185.

World Bank. "Gross domestic product (2009)." World Development Indicators database, September 27, 2010, World Bank, Washington, DC. Accessed January 1, 2011. http://siteresources.worldbank.org/DATASTATISTICS/Resources/GDP.pdf.

———. *World Development Indicators*. Washington, DC: World Bank, 2007.

www.ine.es

www.istat.it

ANNUAL REPORTS (VARIOUS YEARS)

Abengoa; Acciaierie e Ferriere Lombarde Falck; Acciona, Desarrollo y Gestión de Infraestructuras y Servicios; Acenor; Acerinox; ACS; AENA; AGIP; Alcatel; Allianz Seguros; Altadis; Altos Hornos de Vizcaya; Amadeus; ANIC; Ansaldo; API; Arcelor; Arnoldo Mondadori; Asepeyo; Asland; Assicurazioni Generali; Astilleros Españoles; AUNA; Autogrill; Autostrade; Aviación y Comercio; Azucarera Española; Banca Intesa; Banco Central Madrid; Banco Central; Banco de Bilbao; Banco de Bilbao Vizcaya y Argentaria; Banco de Santander; Banco de Vizcaya; Banco Español de Crédito BANESTO; Banco Exterior de España; Banco Hispano Americano; Banco Ibérico; Banco Popular Español; Banco Popular, Banco Santander Central Hispano; Banco Urquijo; Banco Vitalicio de España, Compañía Anónima de Seguros y Reaseguros y Sociedades Dependientes; BANESTO; Barilla; Basf; Bayer Italia; Bazán; Benetton; Bnp Paribas; BSN Groupe; Bsh Elecrodomésticos España; Burgo—Marchi Paper Solutions; Butano, Buzzi Unicem; CAF, Construcciones y Auxiliar de Ferrocarriles; Caja de Pensiones para la Vejez y de Ahorros de Cataluña y Baleares; Caja Madrid; CAMPSA; Capitalia Gruppo Bancario; Carburos Metálicos; Carrefour; Cartiere Burgo; Caser, Caja de Seguros Reunidos, Compañía de Seguros y Reaseguros; CASA; Catalana de Gas y Electricidad; Catalana Occidente; Central de Inversión y Crédito; CEPSA, Compañía Española de Petróleos; CEPSA; Chrysler España; Citroën Hispania; COFIDE Compagnia Finanziaria De Benedetti; Coin; Compañía Barcelonesa de Electricidad; Compañía de Industrias Agrícolas; Compañía de Industrias Agrícolas; Compañía de Luz y Fuerzas de Levante; Compañía Española de Electricidad y Gas Lebón; Compañía General de Asfaltos y Portland Asland Barcelona; Compañía General de Ferrocarriles Catalanes; Compañía Roca Radiadores; Compañía Sevillana de Electricidad; Compañía Telefónica Nacional de España; Compañía Trasmediterránea; Compañía Valenciana de Cementos Portland; Correos; Cremonini; Cristalería Española; Cubiertas y Mzov, Compañía General de Construcciones; Daimler Chrysler España Holding; Dalmine; Dow Chemical Ibérica; Dragados y Construcciones; EADS CASA; Ebro, Compañía de Azucares y Alcoholes; Edison; El Aguila; El Arbol; Electrometalúrgica del Ebro; Empresa Nacional de Autocamiones; Empresa Nacional del Aluminio; Empresa Nacional Siderúrgica; ENAGAS; ENDESA; ENEL; ENHER, Empresa Nacional Hidroeléctrica del Ribagorzana; ENI; Erg Petroli; Erg; Española del Zinc, Sociedad Anónima Z.I.N.S.A.; ERZ—Eléctricas Reunidas de Zaragoza; Esso Petróleos Españoles; F.C. Metropolitano de Barcelona, (Transversal); FASA-Renault; FECSA; FEMSA, Fábrica Española Magnetos; Ferrero; Ferrovial; Ferrovie dello Stato; FIAT; Finanzauto y Servicios; Finanzauto; Fincantieri; Finmeccanica; Finsider; Firestone Hispania; Fomento de Construcciones y Contratas; Fomento de Obras y Construcciones; Fondiaria—SAI, Società per Azioni; Ford; Fremap, Mutua de Accidentes de Trabajo y Enfermedades Profesionales de la Seguridad Social; Galerías Preciados; Gas Natural; General Motors; GIM Generale Industrie Metallurgiche; Globalia Corporación Empresarial; Gran Metropolitano de Barcelona—Sociedad Anónima; Grandes Almacenes El Siglo—Sociedad Anónima; GRTN, Gestore Rete Trasmissione Nazionale; Grupo Eroski; Grupo Uralita; HDP, Holding di Partecipazioni Industriali; Hidrocantábrico; Hidroeléctrica de Cataluña; Hidroeléctrica Española; Huarte; Iberdrola; Iberduero; Iberia, Lineas Aéreas de España; IBM Italia; IBM España; IFI; IFIL, Finanziaria di Partecipazioni; Ilva Alti Forni e Acciaierie d'Italia; Impregilo; Instituto Nacional de Industria; IROM; Istituto di Ricostruzione Industriale; Italcementi; Italmobiliare; Italsider; Koipe; La Caixa; La Estrella; La Maquinista Terrestre y Marítima; La Papelera Española; La Rinascente; La Seda de Barcelona; La Unión y El Fénix Español; Logista; Luxottica Group; Magneti Marelli; Mapfre; Marzotto; Mediaset; Mediobanca; Mercedes-Benz España; Merloni Elettrodomestici; Michelin; Mondragón; Monte dei Paschi di Siena; Montedison; Motor Ibérica; Nestlé; Nissan Motor Ibérica; Nuovo Pignone, Industrie Meccaniche e Fonderia; Obrascón Huarte Laín; Olivetti; Papeleras Reunidas; Parmalat; Petróleos del Mediterráneo; Petroliber; Petronor, Refinería de Petróleos del Norte; Peugeot Talbot España; Pirelli & C.; Pirelli; Polimeri Europa; Productos Pirelli; Pryca; RAI; RAS; Red Nacional de los Ferrocarriles Españoles; Repsol; RUMIANCA; Sacyr Vallehermoso; Sacyr; Saipem; San José; San Paolo; Sarrió; Seat Pagine Gialle; Sefanitro, Sociedad Espanola de Fabricaciones Nitrogenadas; Siemens; SIP; Sirti; SME; SNAM Rete Gas; SNIA Viscosa; SNIA; Sociedad Anónima Cros Barcelona; Sociedad Española de Automóviles de Turismo, SEAT; Sociedad Española de Carburos Metálicos; Sociedad Española de Construcciones Babcock & Wilcox; Sociedad General de Aguas de Barcelona; Società Edison; Società Italiana Ernesto Breda; Società Italiana per Condotte d'Acqua; Standa; Standard Eléctrica, Una asociada Española de ITT; STET; STMicroelectronics; Tabacalera; Telecom; Telefónica de España; Telefónica Móviles; Toro Assicurazioni; Tranvías de Barcelona, Sociedad Anónima; Trasmediterránea; Ulgor; Unicredito Italiano; Unión Explosivos Río Tinto ERT; Unión Fenosa; Unipol; Vallehermoso; Vidacaixa; Vodafone España; Wind.

Index